VALUES AND
EDUCATIONAL LEADERSHIP

SUNY Series, Educational Leadership
Daniel L. Duke, editor

VALUES AND EDUCATIONAL LEADERSHIP

Edited by
Paul T. Begley

State University of New York Press

Published by
State University of New York Press, Albany

For information, address State University of New York Press
State University Plaza, Albany, New York 12246

Production by Dana Foote
Marketing by Patrick Durocher

Library of Congress Cataloging-in-Publication Data

Values and educational leadership / edited by Paul T. Begley.
p.   cm. — (SUNY series, educational leadership)
Includes bibliographical references and index.
ISBN 0–7914–4291–8 (hc. : alk. paper). — ISBN 0–7914–4292–6 (pbk.
alk. paper)
1. Educational leadership.   2. School management and organization.
3. Values.   I. Begley, Paul Thomas, 1949– .   II. Series: SUNY
series in educational leadership.
LB2806.V25   1999
371.2—dc21   99–26254
CIP

10   9   8   7   6   5   3   2   1

To my mother and father,
whose values shape the individual that I am—
sustaining me and giving meaning to what I do,
in ways knowable and not.
This book is for you.

CONTENTS

FOREWORD

The title of this book and certainly its contents are not as innocuous or uncontentious as, at first glance, they might appear. Initially, the connection between values on the one hand and leadership on the other might seem rather obvious, perhaps even transparent. But this is not necessarily so. Let me illustrate.

Confidently assured of the place of values in the great game of administration, I was once so naive as to ask a very senior Canadian mandarin about the religious habits of a certain famous prime minister with whom he was professionally intimate. The official at once became incensed, and it rapidly became clear that I had committed a gross act of *lèse-majesté*. What right had I to ask about the leader's private beliefs? Private life and public work were as alien to each other as the sacred and the secular—what the PM did on Sunday was no affair of the State, and his beliefs with all their attendant values had no more role in the business of leadership than had the State in the bedrooms of the nation. On the topic of leadership values then it would seem that certain boundaries were not to be crossed. One could probe so far but no further. And anyway, what difference did it make as long as the leader did the job and met the criteria of general satisfaction?

The problem raised here has a contemporary resonance. For example, the sexual peccadilloes of an American president are popularly ruled out as irrelevant to executive performance. Mores and ethos discount morals and ethics. What does count is success. Ends justify means. Power, reinforced by public sentiment or public apathy, pragmatically trumps any appeal to principle.

So, while values and leadership might still seem inseparably intertwined, the linkage itself says nothing about what values and what leadership, and the exploration of the connection may be deliberately inhibited. Against such a "thus far and no further" this text seeks to go further.

An added complexity to the subject matter of this book arises from the problem of the value-fact dichotomy in philosophy and a consequent emphasis upon epistemology as opposed to axiology within the discipline of educational administration. In coarser language, this could be called a concern with know-how rather than know-why, and it has been in vogue over the last decades. Again, the chapters of this book act as a corrective to this trend.

Other discriminations apply to the theme of this work, for example: the administration versus management and the policy making versus policy implementation distinctions familiar to students of administrative theory. Not to mention the common fallacies, peculiarly endemic in educational administration, that "all leaders are (presumptively) honorable" or that (à la Simon) the organization is a bus, and the leader, merely its driver. That is, values are delivered from the "outside."

Complexity is yet more complexified by the subtle pressures of cultural and social impress. One could argue—to take the cases of president and prime minister already cited—that popular wisdom and the conventional orthodoxy are often misguided if not just downright wrong. Consider the fallacy neatly tagged as the Dogma of the Immaculate Perception. This holds, in essence, that the "facts of the matter" can be surgically severed from the attitudes, values, beliefs, sentiments, emotions, character, personality, biology, biography, and physiology of the agents in the matter. To take this position is to argue, paraphrasing Heidegger, that it is possible to just look (or "stare") at things and people, circumstances and situations, encountering all their manifold properties simply as "data of perception." It would also be to regard the leader as some sort of alienlike "observer." From which it ultimately follows that it matters little if at all who is in the leadership role, whether a Stalin or a Pol Pot, a Saddam or a Clinton—as long as, pragmatically, the desired job gets done. And bear in mind Pol Pot and Stalin were, after all, pretty competent—it takes skills to set up and manage gulags and killing fields.

The point I am belaboring here is that the whole actor enters into the administrative chamber. Not just eyes or intellect or technical competence. We bring our hormones and our gods and demons with us to the table, as well as our pride and prejudice, all our fallacies and fallibilities—whether consciously or not. In an important sense, the leader just *is* a historically unique *complex of values*. And this value orientation affects *everything*. Competence is not separable from character in the administrative world. But what is intriguing and curious is that we so often and so stubbornly resist closer examination of this stark truth. And again, this text is in many ways an overcoming of that resistance.

Another leitmotif to these chapters is the tacit acceptance of the Nietzschean aphorism that there are no truths, only interpretations, an acceptance entirely consistent with postmodernism. Yet a word should be added here. Nietzsche's followers include a cohort of French enthusiasts whose intellectual pretensions have disproportionately influenced the North American academy. They have taken us at times to the ultimate limits of nihilism. To drop but one name, Derrida gave us both deconstruction and the doctrine *il n'y a pas que texte:* there is no meaning other than that projected by the interpreter. A doctrine which also paradoxically yields all the phenomena of political correctness (where only one interpretation is permissible) that so inhibit freedom of speech yet form a real-life constraint upon contemporary leadership. Dogmatic meaning on the one hand and meaninglessness on the other contribute to a fractionated society and identity politics. All of these are value-based aspects of modern culture with which leadership in whatever form has to contend and with which themes this book also attempts to come to grips.

But Nietzsche might well have approved at least the overall logic and structure of this text for he himself was neither a nihilist nor a decadent. His version of subjective perspectivalism does not deny Truth but only argues for multiple approaches to the real and the true. In educational administration this is entirely consonant with the influential thinking of Thom Greenfield. The more ways we look at a problem, the more voices we listen to and actually *hear,* the more eyes beyond our own we use to *see with,* the greater the depth of *understanding.* These contributions all serve the end of assisting the serious reader to deepen the understanding of leader-value phenomena.

The chapters assembled in this carefully edited book run the gamut. From philosophy to praxis, from theory to practice, they comprise administration and management, leadership and followership, the abstract and the concrete. They are in the very best sense interdisciplinary. Together they make a notable contribution to reconciling the contemplative and the active and to overcoming the philosophobia that so often plagues our discipline, a blight that turns potential educational leaders into cultural followers and sycophants rather than cultural shapers and formers. Under the skillful and dedicated editorship of Paul Begley, the voices speaking through this book will sophisticate and educate on the topics that they treat.

Decisional leadership demands both competence and character. Another way of putting it is to discriminate the external from the internal. The former consists of context: events and facts, probabilities and possibilities—all of which demand interpretation. The latter is subjective, personal, individual, private, but above all value-laden. It is the genetic site of morals, ethics, and leadership. And the linking factor is the organization that forms the leader's ambit of responsibility. Yes, all this is complex. Yes, it is difficult. Yes, it is contentious. No, it is not beyond our understanding. Nor need we shy away through discretion or take refuge in Wittgensteinian silence. Values are concepts of the desirable that seek their social translation through the art of leadership. Begley and his contributors facilitate that art.

Christopher Hodgkinson
Victoria, British Columbia

Acknowledgments

We are grateful to Priscilla Ross, editor in chief at State University of New York Press, for her patience and support throughout the preparation of this book. Thanks also to our associates at the Centre for the Study of Values and Leadership (OISE/UT), its affiliate the UCEA Center for the Study of Leadership and Ethics (University of Virginia), and the various manuscript reviewers for their support and helpful comments. With their advice we have produced a better book. Finally, a special thank you to Heather Rintoul for her assistance in editing the original version of the manuscript.

Material included in the introduction to part 1 describing the orientations of administrators toward values and portions of the introduction to part 2 describing the place of values in administration were previously published in 1996 in P. Begley. Cognitive Perspectives on Values in Administration: A Quest for Coherence and Relevance, *Educational Administration Quarterly* 32, 3: 403–426. Chapter 8, "Ethical School Leadership: Problems of an Elusive Role," by E. Campbell, was originally published in May 1997 in the *Journal of School Leadership* 7, 3: 287–300 (Lancaster PA: Technomic Publishing). Sections of the introduction to part 3 addressing the place of values within research methodologies are taken from P. Begley, 1996, chapter 17, "Cognitive Perspectives on the Nature and Function of Values in Educational Administration, in the *International Handbook on Educational Leadership and Administration*, ed. K. A. Leithwood, (Boston: Kluwer Academic). A longer version of chapter 12, "Value Preferences, Ethics, and Conflicts in School Administration," by P. Begley, was published in the July 1998 issue of the *Journal of School Leadership* (Lancaster PA: Technomic Publishing). Chapter 14, "A Feminist Perspective of Women Superintendents' Approaches to Moral Dilemmas," by M. Grogan and F. Smith, was originally published in the *Journal for a Just and Caring Education 4*, 2, April 1998.

INTRODUCTION

This book is devoted to the exploration of a topic that, in recent years, has achieved an increasing degree of importance for theorists, researchers, and practitioners working in the field of educational administration. That topic is values: the personal values manifested by individuals, the professional values of administration, and the collective values manifested by groups, societies, and organizations. Such matters are explored comprehensively in this book, perhaps more so than in any other publication of which we are aware. It covers the theory, research, and the practices associated with values and valuation in educational leadership contexts.

While other books have been published in recent years promoting various notions associated with moral leadership, we believe our book is unique. It extends beyond the presentation of "expert opinion," and, because it blends theory and research, it appeals to a broader audience composed of both academics and practitioners. Furthermore, a quick scan of the table of contents will show that this book brings together the collective wisdom of some of the best known and most respected philosophers, theorists, and researchers currently working in the field. It is with considerable pride that the authors present to you, the reader, this compilation of knowledge and debate relating to an important topic.

Values traditionally have been considered an important influence on administrative practices. Chester Barnard's seminal work, *The Functions of the Executive*, proposes a definition of leadership, dating back to 1938, that highlights the moral dimension of leadership as essential to administration. More recent works by Herbert Simon, Christopher Hodgkinson (a contributor), Thomas Greenfield, Donald Willower (a contributor), Kenneth Leithwood (a contributor), Colin Evers, and Gabriele Lakomski (contributors) have reinforced the relevance of values as influences on administration and promoted active debate on the subject. Moreover, values is a topic which typically has been included as a component of core courses in most university programs of study on educational administration. While this alone should be sufficient justification for a book that brings together the thinking of the leading experts in a single manuscript, there is also the added incentive of a recent surge of interest among practitioners in values and ethics as guides to action and supports to reflective practice.

Most of the chapters that make up this book began as papers delivered at the October 1996 Toronto Conference on Values and Educational Leadership. This memorable gathering held in Toronto was an inaugural event sponsored by the newly founded OISE Centre for the Study of Values and Educational Leadership and its University Council for Educational Administration (UCEA) affiliate, the Centre for the Study of Leadership and Ethics, based at the University of Virginia. The conference brought together an impressive international team of expert philosophers, theorists, and researchers in the field of values, ethics, and leadership. This book represents the outcomes of that most productive gathering in the form of updated, expanded, and synthesized versions of the best of those original papers.

This book is organized in three sections of five chapters each. There is an introductory chapter for each section of the book that outlines in some detail the relevant themes and issues to be addressed in that section. To summarize briefly, the first section of the book is devoted to the application of theory and research through reflective educational practice, a process often termed "values praxis." The contributors include several of the most respected international scholars of the educational leadership field: Leithwood, Duke, Foster, Ryan, Bredeson, and Johansson.

The second section of the book is devoted to theoretical and conceptual perspectives. Both traditional debates and several intriguing new perspectives are presented. Three chapters are authored by giants of the field: Willower, Hodgkinson, Evers, and Lakomski. Two chapters are authored by more recently recognized authorities of the field, Allison, Ellett, and Campbell.

The final section of the book reviews the findings of existing values research and reports new findings, some previously unpublished. The contributors are promising young scholars as well as established authorities. The newcomers to the field are Leonard, Grogan, Roche, and Shakotko. Begley and Walker, both midcareer academics, contribute the remaining two chapters. A concluding chapter by Begley provides a template useful for mapping out existing theory and research findings in the values field and speculates on an agenda for future theory building and research in the field.

It is the hope of the authors that this book will satisfy the primary audience for which it was intended: university faculty, graduate students, and experienced educational administrators. We recommend the book with confidence as a text in support of the increasing number of graduate-level courses focused on the topics of values, ethics, and moral leadership. Finally, we are grateful to the editors of SUNY Press who accepted this manuscript for publication and included it as a volume in the SUNY series, Educational Leadership edited by Daniel L. Duke. We are honored to be in such good company.

Paul T. Begley
OISE/UT

Part I

Value Praxis and Ethical Leadership

Practitioner and Organizational Perspectives on Values in Administration

Paul T. Begley

There is a prevailing stereotype of administrative practice that holds that administrators are much inclined toward being focused pragmatically and unreflectively on procedural matters. Although such notions are now largely outdated, they are still commonly articulated, especially in the university community, perhaps perpetuated by those who have lost touch with the field or abetted by traditional organizational theories (e.g., Simon 1965) that emphasize the managerial functions of administration. In today's school leadership situations, competing value orientations manifest themselves within particular educational communities quite readily. Administrators are aware of values issues without any particular need for prior training in philosophy or exposure to the literature on administrative ethics. They have become increasingly sensitive to values issues simply because of the pluralistic societies in which they live and work.

As social and cultural diversity increases, as equity becomes a greater social priority, and as demands for fiscal restraint persist, the circumstances of decision making in educational organizations become more complex and challenging. As demonstrated by the research-findings report by Begley and Roche in chapters 12 and 13 respectively, one significant outcome is an increase in the frequency of value-conflict situations to which administrators must respond. Such value conflicts become particularly apparent when administrator perspectives run across the organizational boundaries that traditionally separated community from school, school from district office, and district office from department or ministry: social thresholds that have become increasingly transparent organizational boundaries in a postmodernist world.

More than ever before, administrators recognize that the values manifested by individuals, groups, and organizations have an impact on what happens in schools, chiefly by influencing the screening of information or definition of alternatives. The more reflective administrators are also conscious of how their own personal values may blind or illuminate the assess-

---

*The sections of this chapter that describe the orientations of administrators toward values are taken from P. T. Begley, 1996, "Cognitive Perspectives on Values in Administration: A Quest for Coherence and Relevance, *Educational Administration Quarterly* 32, 3: 403–426.

ment of situations. As long as the development of consensus on educational purposes among stakeholders, or even the more modest goal of mediating conflicts among competing interest groups, remains a defining goal for those in educational administrator roles, then effective school leadership practices need to be not only contextually differentiated but sensitive to the value orientations of the various educational stakeholders.

These changing educational circumstances imply a number of conceptual as well as operational justifications for studying the nature and function of values in administration. These justifications are summarized here in seven points. The nature and function of values in administration merit study because

- Leadership and administration involve considerable amounts of decision making and problem solving. Such decision making inevitably involves values to the extent that preferred alternatives are selected and others are rejected.
- There has been an overemphasis in administrative theory, research, and training on the technical and rational aspects of leadership and a neglect of the nonrational moral aspects of educational administration.
- Educational leaders increasingly find themselves working in environments where value conflicts are common. Students living in a postmodern world confront the representatives and guardians of a preceding modernist generation within educational organizations. Racial, ethnic, and religious groups increasingly intermingle, and educational stakeholders regularly disagree about what is desirable in policies, procedures, and outcomes.
- There can be an important difference between the values *articulated* by a group or individual and the values to which they are actually committed. In administration, ethics are sometimes employed as a smokescreen to obscure less justifiable motives, sometimes in an attempt to feign objectivity about something that is highly subjective. Similarly, ethical codes can be sufficiently vague that they are vulnerable to interpretation by individuals and groups according to criteria that reflect personal preferences more than socially defensible ends.
- In an increasingly pluralistic or global society, administrators must understand and reflect on their motivations, biases, and actions as leaders. In particular, they must become aware of the possible existence of relatively fixed and unnegotiable core values that may be incompatible with organizational or community values.
- Administrators can be more effective when they understand or are able to interpret the actions of others. In particular, they need to

understand and be able to give reason to the actions of superordinates, peers, subordinates, and students. They must also recognize the sources and causes of value conflicts.
* When called upon to mediate value conflicts, it is useful for administrators to be able to distinguish between personal, professional, organizational, and social values. They must know which values are appropriate to a situation and justifiable by educational leaders who are simultaneously autonomous individuals, agents of society accountable to an established system of educational governance, professionals, and members of the community served by the education system.

Part I focuses specifically on organizational perspectives. This is in contrast to part III where the perspective and valuation processes employed by individuals, teachers, and administrators working within educational organizations are highlighted. The first three chapters, those by Duke (chapter 1), Leithwood (chapter 2), and Johansson and Bredeson (chapter 3), present particular organizational perspectives that clarify and, in some cases, challenge the function of values as influences on administrative practice. The final two chapters by Ryan (chapter 4) and Foster (chapter 5) represent more critical postmodern perspectives of educational organizations.

In chapter 1, Duke offers an approach to thinking systematically about what is desirable in an organization. The central concern is captured in his simple question, "What is a good organization?" It is a question that, as he points out, has attracted relatively little attention. He argues convincingly that such matters should be because of the priority given the ubiquitousness and importance of organizations in our society. As he asserts, we ought to be moved as much by ideals as by concern for inputs and outputs. The chapter's goals are to propose a conception of the good organization and identify some of the issues that need to be addressed in the process of constructing a philosophy of organization.

In chapter 2 Leithwood questions the practical utility of much scholarly inquiry about values in educational administration. He outlines four reasons why the practical utility of scholarship aimed at promoting more ethical administrative practice needs to be challenged. His goal with this chapter is to propose a system of values to guide the work of educational leaders, but one based on the needs of future schools and the processes required to develop those schools. These alternatives include taxonomies of values rooted in moral philosophy (e.g., Hodgkinson 1978) and those emerging from empirical efforts to describe the values of practicing educational leaders (e.g., Walker and Shakotko, chapter 15; Leithwood, Begley, and Cousins 1992). To illustrate what might be required to accomplish this goal, Leithwood argues for an incremental orientation in the process of transforming today's schools and the need to identify some of the more critical values to support such an orientation. He also dicusses several challenges facing those responsible for assisting in the development of current and future school leaders with respect to these values.

Chapter 3 by Johansson and Bredeson exposes what they consider the myth that the policy community has the capacity to govern the learning community and that policy decisions influence the values of educational leaders and the educational process. Using illustrations from the Swedish and American context, the authors advance a reverse position. Their claim is that it is within the educational community that educational values are created and subsequently transferred to the political policy community. The authors argue that the policy community very seldom has the knowledge and information that would allow it to confront and convert the prevailing school culture to the benefits of various reform initiatives being advocated. Successful reforms tend to be those that are formulated by, and out of needs articulated by, the learning community. Furthermore, prevailing educational values are rooted in the particular functional roles of administrators and teachers, and hence the degree of commitment to particular educational activities is governed by the local school culture.

Ryan's "Beyond the Veil" (chapter 4) argues that the increasing complexity of the choice-making process associated with educational organizations has begun to noticeably impede decisive and sure-footed action by administrators. He asserts that in a postmodern world there is more uncertainty than sureness, more ambivalence as opposed to faith. Philosophy and science have played an important part in promoting what Ryan argues is the illusion of an orderly existence. In recent decades, the belief in the possibility of fashioning a universal moral order has dissipated and the veil has lifted on a rather chaotic world. At least two unanswered or open questions relating to values arise: What is, or should be, the purpose of inquiry in the field? How does it, or should it, relate to the moral nature of administration and organization of schools in an increasingly fragmented, ambivalent, and uncertain world? Ryan concludes that inquiry in the field needs to be organized around efforts to help administrators provide the conditions that will allow all individuals and groups in school communities and in the wider community to search out, understand, critique, and create moral forms of life.

In chapter 5 Foster presents a second and final critical perspective on organizational theory and the ethics of administration. He asks, "If administration did not exist, would we have to invent it?" While acknowledging that administration does exist, he suggests that it needs to be re-invented, that it is time to move beyond those models of administration that have dominated the discipline in this century, and that it is time to begin to consider other ways of conceiving the field.

References

Hodgkinson, C. 1978. *Toward a philosophy of administration*. Oxford: Basil Blackwell.

Leithwood, K. A., Begley, P. T., and Cousins, J. B. 1992. *Developing expert leadership for future schools*. London: Falmer Press.

Simon, H. 1965. *Administrative behaviour,* 2nd ed. New York: Free Press.

CHAPTER ONE

Envisioning the Good Organization: Steps toward a Philosophy of Organization*

Daniel L. Duke

It seems we are never satisfied with our organizations. We are forever trying to restructure, reinvent, and re-engineer them. One of the rituals attending changes in organizational leadership is re-organization. If we examine closely these various efforts to improve and transform organizations, we sense that reformers are clearer about what they do not want than about what they do want in an organization.

The present chapter offers an approach to thinking systematically about what we want in an organization. The central concern is captured in the deceptively simple question What is a good organization? It is a question that oddly enough, has attracted relatively little attention, given the ubiquitousness and importance of organizations in our society. Perhaps the question is perceived to come dangerously close to social planning, or possibly it is regarded as irrelevant by those moved less by ideals than by inputs and outputs. Effectiveness and efficiency, for these individuals, may supersede goodness in importance. Alternatively, they may equate goodness with effectiveness and efficiency.

Fuller noted in his lectures on law and morality that there are really two moralities. The morality of duty "starts at the bottom" and "lays down the basic rules without which an ordered society is impossible." It is a morality replete with "thou shalt nots." The morality of aspiration, on the other hand, "starts at the top" and addresses "the morality of the Good Life, of excellence, of the fullest realization of human powers" (Fuller 1969, 5).

Considerable energy has been expended during the past half-century to prevent organizations from "failing to respect the basic requirements of social living" (Fuller 1969, 6). Operating on the basis of a morality of duty, in other words, our leaders, legislators, and judges have tried to pass and enforce laws to constrain organizations. Such a focus can obscure a morality of aspiration and its concern for helping organizations pursue noble ends. Being prevented from acting in harmful ways is not the same as striving to be good. A good organization must embrace both a morality of duty and a morality of aspirations.

---

* The author would like to express his appreciation to Professor Eric Bredo of the University of Virginia for his careful and constructive critique of this chapter.

The chapter's goals are to propose a conception of the good organization and identify some of the issues that need to be addressed in the process of constructing a philosophy of organization around it. The first part distinguishes a philosophy of organization from an organizational philosophy and discusses several reasons why developing a philosophy of organization is worth the effort. Succeeding sections introduce a conception of the good organization and analyze its various aspects. In the process, a series of questions is raised to help in the identification of good organizations.

The Importance of a Philosophy of Organization

The contemporary literature on organizations contains numerous references to the importance of the normative dimension, including a meaningful mission, shared values, and a robust organizational culture. As early as 1978, Ouchi and Price were extolling the benefits of organizational philosophy. "The clarity and the widespread acceptance of an organizational philosophy," they wrote, "most clearly separates the Type Z from the Type A organization" (Ouchi and Price 1993, 68). They went on to note that most large Japanese organizations possessed a philosophy and that many Japanese leaders regarded as vitally important their responsibility to develop, refine, and articulate this philosophy.

There is no disputing the key role that an organizational philosophy can play, but this chapter is concerned primarily with a philosophy of organization. What is the difference? A particular organization may possess a statement of its core beliefs, which can be referred to as an organizational philosophy. It is reasonable to expect such statements to vary in style, content, and even purpose across organizations. Ouchi and Price (1978, 68) suggest, for example, that an organizational philosophy can serve as a "mechanism for integrating an individual into an organization" or a "mechanism for integrating an organization into the society." However, a philosophy of organization is more inclusive and less idiosyncratic. It provides a normative basis for judging the goodness of all organizations. A philosophy of organization offers criteria against which the contents of various organizational philosophies can be evaluated. In addition, a philosophy of organization includes a rationale or set of justificatory statements for these criteria. The focus of the criteria and rationale, of course, need not be "goodness." For instance, a philosophy of organization might address the nature of a just organization or an effective organization. However, the nature of a good organization may be the most valuable focus for a contemporary philosophy of organization. Discussions of justice too often drift into legalistic arguments more representative of a morality of duty than a morality of aspiration, while the issue of organizational effectiveness often is approached as strictly a technical matter divorced from the realm of normative concerns.

A chief reason for basing a philosophy of organization on the pursuit of the good is my belief that contemporary organizations, both private and public, must assume a leadership role in promoting a good society. While many argue that it is the responsibility of individuals to define and work for a good society, they overlook the complexity of today's society and the necessity of collective action. The locus of collective action is, increasingly, the organization. Organizations are pervasive and powerful. Organizational incentives and rewards exert a substantial influence on the beliefs and behavior of individuals. Making headway toward a good society is unlikely to occur without organizational initiative.

Green (1988, 129) supports this view when he disputes the value of a "heroic" perspective on morality. "In a world where being moral means being heroic," he states, "there will not be much morality around." He proceeds to offer an "economic" approach to understanding virtue. The essence of his argument is that virtue is most likely to be found where the costs of virtue and the benefits of evil are slight (Green 1988, 132). To the extent that organizations control a large percentage of social rewards and sanctions, ranging from grades in school to promotions in business, they are in a prime position to influence the nature and allocation of costs and benefits. If positive value can be placed on hard work and punctuality, organizations also can encourage and reward honesty, community service, and other social goods.

A philosophy of organization helps individuals in organizations, or subject to their influence, to evaluate organizations and what they stand for. In thinking about evaluation, Scriven (1967) has noted that it can be of two basic kinds—intrinsic and payoff. The latter is of primary concern here.

Intrinsic evaluation presumes that a blueprint or set of design specifications exists. The act of evaluation involves determining the extent to which the actual conforms to the expected. A good organization, according to the tenets of intrinsic evaluation, is one that matches its specifications. Intrinsic evaluation is perfectly suited to the concerns of those who embrace the idea of organizational design (Galbraith 1977; Peters 1992; Pfeffer 1978). A rational and somewhat linear process, organizational design entails selecting components from a set of structural and process variables, such as role configurations and decision-making patterns.

Over the years, a variety of organization theorists have taken a turn at describing the make-up of a good organization. Current notions of a well-designed organization almost always include, for example, a mission or vision statement for the organization. From the organizational design standpoint, what is crucial is having a mission or vision statement and making steady progress toward achieving it. Typically, no framework is provided for determining whether one mission statement or vision is any better than another. Instead of normative criteria, empirical research is offered as a useful basis for making organizational design choices. Certain configurations of organizational components are presumed to be more effective at achieving particular goals than other arrangements.

Should a good organization represent more than a close match between design specifications and organizational reality? Absent from such an approach is any connection to what the organization actually does. Here is where pay-off evaluation, or evaluation that focuses on what the organization accomplishes and its impact on the context in which the organization exists, makes a contribution. A company that produces highly toxic chemicals may possess all the elements of a good organization from an intrinsic point of view—a clear and shared sense of purpose, an authority structure that permits high levels of worker participation, and open channels of communication across units. In pay-off terms, though, it may not constitute a good organization, since the process of producing chemicals may compromise workers' health and poison the environment. What is needed then is a framework to assist people in arriving at judgments about organizations and organizational philosophies that take into account what organizations intend to and actually do.

Some people, of course, might question whether it is valid to judge an organization to be *good* or *bad*. They could argue that only people are capable of goodness or badness. While there is obvious merit to this position, it ignores the fact that organizations enjoy legal status. Many organizations, over time, become institutions, taking on qualities and symbolic values quite distinct from those intended by their individual members (Selznick 1992, 233–34). In this sense, organizations reflect Durkheim's concept of 'society'—entities greater than the sum of their parts and separable from their individual members (Durkheim 1993, 39–41).

Other reasons support the view that organizations can, and should, be judged in terms of their goodness or badness. First, it is known that groups behave differently from individuals. Gathering together good individuals is no guarantee that they will function in a manner that advances goodness. This is due, in part, to human diversity, the second reason. Consensus regarding what constitutes a good individual does not exist. In fact, democratic societies value each individual's right to develop his or her own concept of 'personal goodness' (Strike, Haller, and Soltis 1988, 97). To the extent that organizations attract people holding different views of the good individual, they constitute arenas for possible disagreement and conflict. In other words, the fact that each individual in an organization possesses a view of goodness is no guarantee that these views will be compatible. Add to human diversity the fact that humans are imperfect, and a third reason exists for differentiating good individuals from good organizations. People may strive to be good, but it is their fate to make mistakes, errors in judgment, and poor choices, all of which is to say that well-intentioned people do not ensure that an organization will be good.

Another reason to think of organizational goodness and individual goodness separately concerns complexity. Organizations are complex entities situated in contexts that are also characterized by complexity. As a result, it may be difficult or impossible for individuals in organizations to comprehend fully the consequences of their actions. Their limited knowledge may lead them to think they are doing good when, in reality, they are promoting evil.

The case to be made, then, is that organizations and individuals are different and, as a result, require different approaches to judging goodness. A good individual is not identical to a good organization. The problems caused by organizations will not necessarily disappear if only good people are selected to staff them. Similarly, the presence of bad people in organizations does not necessarily preclude the achievement of good ends. A prison, for example, may accomplish a much needed public works project.

Whether or not an organization is good, of course, depends on how goodness is defined. This chapter takes the position that organizational goodness is a function of three conditions. The first, or *intentionality* condition, is related to the purposes or intended outcomes of the organization. The second, or *success* condition, concerns the extent to which the organization achieves what it sets out to achieve. The third, or *carefulness* condition, involves efforts to prevent the occurrence of harmful side effects resulting from the achievement of intended outcomes. A good organization, based on these three conditions, is an organization that (1) *intends to accomplish good ends*, (2) *attains a reasonable degree of success in achieving these good ends*, and (3) *exercises care to prevent negative side effects*. Let us examine each of these conditions more closely.

Good Ends—the Intentionality Condition

The notion of intentionality enjoys a longstanding position of importance in Western tradition. Much of Judeo-Christian morality rests on the individual's commitment to do good. Goodness that results from inadvertent action or luck is not valued as highly as goodness that derives from purposeful initiative. In determining whether or not an organization meets the intentionality condition, therefore, it is necessary to discern whether an organization *actually intends* to achieve certain ends deemed to be good. It is possible, for example, for an organization to pretend to serve ends that it has no real intention of achieving. Separating actual ends from espoused ends can be difficult and may require an analysis of various indicators of organizational commitment, such as resource allocation and operational strategies. Most would agree, though, that organizations that purposefully pursue goals other than intended goals are guilty of deception and, as such, unlikely to be judged good.

In order to arrive at a judgment regarding the extent to which an organization actually intends to achieve good ends, we must first be able to identify a good end. This task is not without challenge. Take the goal of organizational survival. Is it a good end? Dewey was adamant that organization is not an end in itself: "It follows that organization is never an end in itself. It is a means of promoting association, or multiplying effective points of contact between persons, directing their intercourse into the modes of greatest fruitfulness" (1950, 160–61).

He went on to argue that "the tendency to treat organization as an end in itself" resulted in theory that diminished individuals and treated them as subordinate to the collectivity. Dewey stopped short of idealizing the individual, however. Instead, he claimed that both the individual and the organization derived meaning through association, by which he meant the interactional process that enables experiences, ideas, emotions, and values to be transmitted and made common (Dewey 1950, 161).

Dewey's position gives rise to a question. If organization facilitates association, and if association is considered to be good, could not a case be made that organizational survival is a good end? In other words, it could be argued that protecting that which enables good ends to be accomplished constitutes a good end in and of itself. Dewey's argument still holds, though, for organizational survival represents a good end only insomuch as organization contributes to the achievement of other good ends.

In order to analyze issues such as the one just discussed, a normative framework is needed. One such framework has been used by Strike, Haller, and Soltis (1988) to examine the ethics of school administration. Drawing on traditional thinking about ethics and morality, they note that two basic positions can be identified. A consequentialist position relies solely on an assessment of consequences or results to determine the goodness of an action or goal. However, a nonconsequentialist position derives judgments of goodness from fidelity to principles or ideals. Actual consequences are subordinate to right intentions. Let us consider how each of these positions might be applied to judging the goodness of organizational goals.

From the perspective of a consequentialist, organizational goals are regarded as good if they actually lead to outcomes that are deemed good. However upon what basis or bases, are determinations of good consequences to be made? Of the various perspectives on consequences found in Western culture, three seem particularly appropriate for a philosophy of organization. The first may be termed a needs-based perspective, in that good consequences are associated with the satisfaction of basic human needs. The second perspective, referred to as a "developmental perspective," regards as good those consequences that relate to the healthy and continuing development of individuals. A social welfare perspective is the third approach. It holds that good consequences are those that contribute to the well-being of society in general, or at least significant portions of society.

That human beings require certain needs to be met in order to survive is beyond question. The satisfaction of needs serves as the foundation for several theories of human motivation (Aldefer 1972; Maslow 1970) and leadership (Burns 1978). However, consensus, regarding the exact nature of these basic needs does not extend much further than biological imperatives such as food and warmth. Whether humans need caring, literacy, self-actualization, or other higher-order phenomena is the subject of considerable debate. So, too, is the matter of who determines what constitutes a human need. Are such decisions the province of scientists, philosophers, the clergy, political bodies, or each individual? Is a need that without which a particular individual cannot survive, or must needs apply to the species in general to be considered legitimate? Is survival the appropriate consequence of satisfying a need, or should the outcome encompass loftier results as well, such as that which enables life to be meaningful?

Despite such challenging questions, it is the author's position that the satisfaction of human needs is an important consequence on which to focus determinations of the goodness of organizational goals. From a consequentialist position, in other words, an organizational goal may be considered good if it contributes to the satisfaction of human needs. The nature of these specific needs is likely, of course, to vary across time and culture. With the possible exceptions of a few basic biological needs, the identification of needs is subject to shifting values and beliefs.

Question 1.1: Do organizational goals contribute to satisfying what are generally regarded at the time to be basic human needs? While the primary focus of needs-based perspectives is existence, developmental perspectives concentrate on growth. For the most part, growth carries with it a positive connotation, as in maturation, cognitive improvement, and moral development. Leading exponents of a developmental perspective include Dewey (1959), Kolhberg (1970), and Piaget (Guber and Voneche 1977). While these theorists regard development as a natural process, it is by no means automatic or purely biological. Various factors can intervene to arrest or interfere with healthy development. Development does not occur in a vacuum, but in a sociocultural context. Healthy development is as much a function of social and cultural factors as of biological factors. Implicit in a developmental perspective is the belief that that which facilitates the appropriate development of the individual is good and that which inhibits the process is bad.

Scholars, of course, debate the exact nature of healthy development. Some concentrate on psycho-social factors (Rich Harris, 1998), while others like Piaget track movement from lower to higher levels of cognitive functioning (Guber and Voneche 1977). Kohlberg (1970) attempted to identify stages of moral development, only to have his views challenged on the grounds that they excluded possible gender differences (Gilligan 1982). Despite differences of opinion among theorists and different developmental foci, it is fair to say that conventional wisdom recognizes that growth in skill, knowledge, understanding, and moral conduct is desirable. It is rare to hear arguments that goodness resides in the perpetuation of a childlike state of naive innocence. The absence of growth typically is considered pathological, a condition necessitating intervention and assistance.

It may be difficult to imagine some organizations affecting the development of individuals. Of course, certain organizations, such as schools, universities, and churches, deal directly with developmental issues. Other organizations, such as those involved in mass media and advertising, have the capacity to influence how people think about development and their images of healthy development. Ultimately, though, all organizations employ individuals whose development may be affected positively or adversely as a result of their work experience. Morally, it would be hard to justify an organization that contributed to the development of those it served at the expense of its employees' growth.

Question 1.2: Do organizational goals contribute to the healthy development of individuals? While a developmental perspective focuses on the individual, a social welfare perspective takes account of the group. The group may be as great as society-in-general, or smaller, such as a community or collection of people sharing similar characteristics or beliefs.

A social welfare perspective acknowledges that all organizations exist in a variety of social contexts. Depending on the focus of concern and the particular paradigm within which the observer is operating, these contexts may be characterized as sociopolitical, socio-economic, or sociocultural. The basic point remains—organizations do not exist in a vacuum. In order to survive, they must adapt to their context, and adaptation typically entails contributing in ways that make it likely the context will continue to exist. An organization that aims to achieve goals that are likely to harm the community within which it is located probably will adversely affect its own chances for survival.

While organizations must be careful not to harm their host environments, they are cautioned by some theorists to avoid identifying too closely with community goals. Adaptation is one thing, integration, another. Drucker, for example, warns that "the modern organization must be in a community but cannot be of it. An organization's members live in a particular place, speak its language, send their children to its schools, vote, pay taxes, and need to feel at home there. Yet the organization cannot submerge itself in the community nor subordinate itself to the community's ends. Its 'culture' has to transcend community" (1992, 98).

As many organizations become global in scope, the issue of adaptation becomes more complex. In order to survive in a global economy, a multinational organization may feel it is necessary to exploit residents of one part of the world. Exploitation can take the form of substandard wages, environmental degradation, or inhumane working conditions. A social welfare perspective is premised on the sanctity of all human beings. A good organizational goal cannot be one that benefits one group at the expense of another. Having said this, it also should be noted that an organizational goal need not benefit all groups in order to be good. As long as achievement of a social welfare goal does not harm one group as it helps another, the goal may be considered good.

According to a social welfare perspective, an organization, be it private or public, has an obligation to support and enhance society. Society does not exist to serve organizations. Rather, organizations exist to serve society. Organizations simply constitute a recognition that the complex tasks needed for social well-being cannot be accomplished by individuals and informal groups alone.

Question 1.3: Do organizational goals contribute to the well-being of society? The preceding three perspectives on organizational goals pertain to the anticipated consequences of organizational initiative. An alternative approach to determining the goodness of organizational goals focuses on the extent to which goals uphold or embody sacred principles or ideals. This nonconsequentialist view honors good intentions while acknowledging that things do not always work out the way they are intended, often for reasons beyond individuals' control.

Confusion sometimes attends efforts to differentiate between principles and ideals. For present purposes, an ideal represents a desired state, one that need exist for no purpose other than its own realization. Principles guide action aimed at realizing ideals. Burns (1978) refers to ideals as "end values" and principles as "model values." It should be noted that these distinctions do not eliminate confusion completely, for one person's ideal may be another person's principle, and vice versa. Democracy, for example, may constitute an ideal and justice a principle that enables the democratic ideal to be achieved. Alternatively, justice may be the ideal and democracy an enabling principle.

Of all the principles and ideals upon which judgments of goodness may be based, those associated with democracy are among the most sacred, at least in much of the West. In the absence of democracy, other principles and ideals, such as those that derive from religious doctrine, may suffer a precarious existence at best. It is the ideal of a democratic society that both the individual and the collectivity enjoy status before the law and that the law exists apart from both.

Democratic principles embrace the notion that the moral behavior of individuals depends on appropriate social support (Selznick 1992, 183). How that social support is organized and implemented is the focus of the democratic process, a process that values direct participation whenever possible and representation whenever direct participation is not possible. Socially negotiated rules govern the development of laws and the resolution of conflicts.

Two principles that lie close to the heart of the democratic ideal are freedom and justice. However, Hunter points out, that these terms may mean something quite different to individuals on opposite ends of the political spectrum: "Where cultural conservatives tend to define freedom economically (as individual economic initiative) and justice socially (as righteous living); progressives tend to define freedom socially (as individual rights) and justice economically (as equity)" (1991, 115). Hunter goes on to suggest that most people, the ones who do not occupy positions on the political extremes, share a common working understanding of democratic principles.

McMahon (1994, 128–65) argues that the key values with regard to democracy in organizations are fairness and welfare maximization. While he acknowledges that democracy has intrinsic value, this value is closely linked to democracy's capacity to promote fair treatment and an equitable distribution of benefits. McMahon believes that the design of democratic organizations ultimately depends on the willingness and ability of managers to be accountable to employees (1994, 13).

Although democracy may not ensure agreement regarding key principles, its unique quality as an ideal is its provision for the reasonable resolution of disagreements. In other words, democracy embodies not only a desired destination for society, but also a way to handle disputes regarding how best to get there. For this reason, the ideal of democracy together with democratic principles such as freedom and justice constitute a worthy foundation for a nonconsequentialist approach to judging the goodness of organization goals.

Question 1.4: Do organizational goals uphold the ideal of democracy and the principles that support and sustain it? The issue that now arises concerns the articulation of two distinct approaches to judging the goodness of organizational goals. Must a choice be made between the nonconsequentialist's regard for universal ideals and principles and the consequentialist's devotion to outcomes? Strike and Soltis contend that the optimal approach involves embedding "a concern for consequences within a framework of non-consequentialist ideals" (1985, 62). The present philosophy of organization is committed to such an approach.

To judge the goodness of an organization, the actual consequences of goal-directed action must be assessed. It has been argued that these consequences should be considered good if they satisfy human needs, contribute to individual development, or enhance social well-being. A qualifier must be added, however. These conditions are necessary but not sufficient alone to warrant a judgment of goodness. A final condition must be met as well. Goal-directed action must uphold the democratic ideal and related principles. For example, an organization may achieve good consequences, such as helping to satisfy basic needs for food and shelter, but its actions may undermine the democratic ideal by seeking to limit competition through unjust means, such as collusion or false advertising.

In certain instances, it is possible that the consequences of goal-directed action may lead to consequences that satisfy one consequentialist position while undermining another. For example, the general welfare may be advanced, but at the expense of individual development. In such cases, the existence of democratic principles as an overarching normative framework provides a basis for examining organizational goals and resolving conflicts among them.

If an organizational goal does not meet the criteria of goodness, must it necessarily be regarded as a bad goal? The position taken in this chapter is that certain goals under particular circumstances may neither serve nor interfere with the achievement of good ends. These goals can be considered neutral goals as far as the quest for good organization is concerned.

Another issue concerns the fact that most organizations undertake multiple goals. How should organizations be judged when some of their goals are good and some are not? A good organization does not consciously seek to accomplish harmful goals, though it may include neutral goals in its plans. Should the goodness of an organization be considered a continuous variable? Goodness is more complex than simply determining the percentage of an organization's goals that are good. Some good goals clearly are more important than other good goals. And what of the good that organizations may achieve without intending to do so?

Organizations neutrally accomplish other things besides what they purposefully seek to accomplish. However, goals represent public statements of organizational priorities. As such, they command attention and deserve scrutiny. It is hard to imagine any credible effort to identify what constitutes a good organization that ignores the organization's formal intentions. There is, after all, nothing wrong with intending to do good. Given the choice of two organizations, one that strives to achieve goals judged to be good and the other that strives to achieve neutral goals or goals that interfere with the achievement of good ends, is there any question which organization would be preferable? As for the argument that organizations accomplish good things that are not intended, the position taken here is that unintended good outcomes are fortuitous, but they do not constitute a sound basis for a philosophy of organization. Furthermore, it is hard to imagine that concern for the goodness of organizational goals would preclude, or inhibit in any way, the achievement of unintended good outcomes.

One additional point must be made. This philosophy of organization is not based exclusively on judgments of organizational goals. If it were, it rightly could be accused of being "hyper-rational" and naive. The goodness of intended goals is only one of three conditions that must be satisfied for an organization to be judged good. The success and carefulness conditions also must be met. It is to the success condition that I now turn.

Good Work—the Success Condition

It is one thing to intend to do good and another thing to do it. The success condition concerns the extent to which organizations achieve their good goals. Of what value, after all, are good intentions if they are more honored in the breach than the observance? Organizations do not exist to try; they exist to succeed. The question is, what constitutes success? Is it necessary fully to achieve every goal in order to be regarded as good? Such a high standard easily could lead organizations to aim low. Setting modest goals may increase the likelihood of goal accomplishment, but are the benefits to individuals and society likely to be as great as making reasonable progress toward ambitious goals? It is laudable, for example, that public schools strive to provide equal educational opportunity for all students, even if some students are not able or willing to take advantage of the opportunity. Similarly, churches should not shy away from promoting righteousness simply because parishioners fail on occasion to conduct themselves morally.

While lofty goals inspire, impossible expectations frustrate people. A major reason why many behavioral interventions have proven effective with dysfunctional patients is the recognition by behaviorists of the value of approximations to a goal. One hundred percent is not a practical criterion for judging success in situations where problems are deep-seated and daunting. It is the position of this philosophy of organization that impossible standards can be counterproductive. For this reason, the success condition holds that good organizations are ones that make "reasonable" progress toward the accomplishment of goals judged to be good. But what is "reasonable" progress? And who is to judge?

These questions depend, to some extent, on the nature of the organizational goal. Consider goals related to the satisfaction of basic human needs. Braybrooke (1987, 39) maintains that who determines what constitutes a need and who evaluates the extent to which the need is being satisfied may vary. The "needy" are in the best position, he claims, to articulate what the concept of "needs" means to them. Observers of the needy, on the other hand, may be better qualified to determine the extent to which needs are being met.

The commitment to democratic principles, on which the present philosophy of organization is based, strongly suggests that those with needs should have a voice in determining both the nature of their needs and the extent to which their needs are being met. Democracy provides mechanisms, as indicated earlier, for resolving disagreements regarding needs. Without such mechanisms it would be possible for those who were more numerous or more powerful to insist on satisfying their needs first or on diminishing the needs of others.

The issue of reasonable progress may be addressed somewhat differently in the case of goals related to individual development or social well-being. In both cases, though, those to whom the goal is directed should have a voice. What constitutes healthy development or social well-being is not a matter solely for experts and organizational leaders. The same can be said of organizational goals that relate to the democratic ideal. Thus it is that, while technical decisions regarding organizational effectiveness and efficiency may be left to experts and leaders, determinations of organizational goodness by nature require a broader base of participation.

Good Management—the Carefulness Condition

Question 2.1: Is reasonable progress being made on goals judged to be good? Question 2.2: Are those affected by organizational actions involved in determining whether or not reasonable progress on goals is being made? Charting an organization's direction may be the province of leadership, but ensuring that the destination is reached without substantial losses is the realm of management. The carefulness condition is an acknowledgment of the potential within any organization to cause harm in the very act of striving to do good. While certain harmful by-products may be impossible to anticipate, it is nonetheless incumbent upon all organizations to be mindful of their efforts, no matter how well intentioned. It is this obligation that serves as the organizational basis for Fuller's morality of duty.

Being mindful entails a variety of actions, ranging from frequent efforts to obtain feedback from clients and customers to quality control mechanisms and error analysis. The feelings of employees also should be solicited on a regular basis. An organization that ignores or exploits its workers in order to achieve its goals hardly can be regarded as a good organization.

In a very real sense, the avoidance of harmful side-effects is a function of adopting good means to achieve good ends. Means may be good in and of themselves, as in the case of democratic decision-making processes or by virtue of the fact that they entail the fewest negative by-products. In order to monitor the goodness of their processes, practices, and procedures, organizations may need to broaden the scope of periodic review to encompass more than the stated, or official, goals.

Scriven (1972) has referred to such review as goal-free evaluation. For example, if the goal of a new elementary school program is to improve reading, a conventional evaluation strategy may be to search for improvements in the reading performance of students. Such a strategy is not necessarily a mindful one, though. If the new program succeeds in raising reading performance by taking time away from mathematics instruction and if, as a consequence, mathematics performance drops, this information might only come to light if educators gathered data on more than students' reading performance. Ultimately, of course, a decision may be made by those involved to trade off lower mathematics performance for higher reading performance, but such a decision cannot be made if the information never comes to light.

Contemporary newspapers are full of examples of questionable organizational actions. Spokespersons for organizations often justify these actions as necessary by-products of competition. It might be relatively easy to be good if an organization existed alone, but most organizations share their circumstances with competitors. Fulfilling the conditions of organizational goodness becomes more challenging in a competitive environment. The key is for competing organizations to maintain a clear commitment to good outcomes and resist the temptation to displace these good intentions with more self-serving ones.

In this chapter, an effort is made to provide a basis for judging the goodness of outcomes. Good outcomes provide a framework for thinking about harmful side effects of organizational action. Thus, a good organization makes a conscientious effort to minimize by-products of goal-directed action that interfere with the satisfaction of basic human needs, the healthy development of individuals, or the well-being of society. Furthermore, a good organization is vigilant regarding actions that might violate democratic principles or undermine the democratic ideal. Such actions may include concealing information, denying employees a voice in organizational affairs and ignoring employees' right to due process.

Conclusion

Question 3.1: Is a conscientious effort made by the organization to monitor its actions in ways that minimize harmful side effects? In a provocative essay in the *Harvard*

Business Review, Drucker (1992) characterizes the contemporary postindustrial world as a "society of organizations." Organizations, he notes, have been able to effect miracles of modernization through their capacity for focusing on the achievement of relatively narrow sets of goals. Drucker sees this strength as a potential weakness, as well. In a world filled with specialized organizations, he asks who will take care of the Common Good? In the past, the Common Good was defined by monarchs. Monarchy gave way to states, but the fall of socialism suggests that the all-powerful state may not be the best definer of the Common Good. Drucker expresses the task that confronts contemporary society thus: "The challenge that faces us now, and especially in the developed, free-market democracies such as the United States, is to make the pluralism of autonomous, knowledge-based organizations redound both to economic performance and to political and social cohesion" (1992, 104). Drucker recognizes what an increasing number of private-sector leaders are acknowledging, and what public-sector leaders long have known—that organizations should embrace a moral mission along with their more mundane targets. In support of this aim, the present chapter argues that a good organization is one that intends to accomplish good ends, makes reasonable progress toward the accomplishment of these ends, and exercises care that, in the process of achieving good ends, it does as little harm as possible.

This chapter goes further to address the nature of good ends, associating them with satisfying basic human needs, promoting healthy development of individuals, providing for the well-being of society, and upholding the ideal of democracy. This effort to define good ends is meant to serve as a starting place for conversation within and among organizations. The author does not presume to speak for others when it comes to determining the precise nature of good organizational goals and outcomes. Daunting as coming to agreement on what constitutes a good end may seem, the challenge is well worth the effort. The road to good organization is not paved with private reflection and conflict avoidance, but public discourse and creative confrontation of differences.

References

Aldefer, C. P. 1972. *Existence, relatedness and growth.* New York: Free Press.

Braybrooke, D. 1987. *Meeting needs.* Princeton: Princeton University Press.

Burns, J. M. 1978. *Leadership.* New York: Harper.

Dewey, J. 1959. *Dewey on Education.* New York: Teachers College Press. 1950.

———. 1950. *Reconstruction in Philosophy.* New York: Mentor Books.

Drucker, P. F. The new society of organizations. *Harvard Business Review,* September-October 1992, 95–104.

Durkheim, E. 1993. *Ethics and the sociology of morals.* Buffalo: Prometheus Books.

Erikson, E. H. 1963. *Childhood and society.* New York: Norton.

Fuller, L. L. 1964. *The morality of law,* rev. ed. New Haven: Yale University Press.

Galbraith, J. R. 1977. *Organization design.* Reading, MA: Addison-Wesley.

Gilligan, C. 1982, *In a different voice.* Cambridge, MA: Harvard University Press.

Green, T. F. 1988.The economy of virtue and the primacy of prudence. *American Journal of Education* 96, February, 2:127–142.

Guber, H. E. and Voneche, J. J. ed. 1977. *The essential Piaget.* New York: Basic Books.

Hunter, J. D. 1991. *Culture wars.* New York: Basic Books.

Kohlberg, L. 1970. Education for justice: A modern statement of the platonic view. In *Moral education.* Cambridge, MA: Harvard University Press.

Maslow, A. H. 1970. *Motivation and personality,* rev. ed. New York: Harper Row.

McMahon, C. 1994. *Authority and democracy.* Princeton: Princeton University Press.

Ouchi, W. G., and Price, R. L. 1993. Hierarchies, clans, and theory z: A new perspective on organization development. *Organizational Dynamics* 21: 62–70.

Peters, T. 1992. *Liberation management.* New York: Fawcett Columbine.

Pfeffer, J. 1978. *Organizational Design.* Arlington Heights, IL: AHNI Publishing Company.

Rich Harris, J. 1998. *The nurture assumption.* New York: New York Free Press.

Scriven, M. 1967. The methodology of evaluation. In *Perspectives of curriculum evaluation,* ed. R. W. Tyler. Chicago: Rand McNally.

———. 1972. Pros and cons about goal free evaluation. *Evaluation Comment* 3:1–4.

Selznick, P. 1992. *The moral commonwealth.* Berkeley: University of California Press.

Strike, K. A., Haller, E. J., and Soltis, J. F. 1988. *The ethics of school administration.* New York: Teachers College Press.

Strike, K. A., and Soltis, J. F. 1985. *The ethics of teaching.* New York: Teachers College Press.

CHAPTER TWO

An Organizational Perspective on Values for Leaders of Future Schools

Kenneth Leithwood

Introduction

"Practical utility" is one of the defining attributes of good scholarship in the field of educational administration. Practical utility may be achieved in many different ways and manifest itself in a multitude of forms. Even with such caveats in mind, however, the practical utility of most of the existing scholarship concerning values in educational administration, is questionable. There are at least four reasons why the practical utility of scholarship aimed at promoting more ethical administrative practice needs to be challenged.

W. Greenfield (1995) has argued that morality is one of five "interrelated role demands" or imperatives for school leaders. Because of this "school administrators have a special responsibility to be deliberately moral in their conduct, that is, to consider the value premises underlying their actions and decisions" (Greenfield 1995, 69). A first reason for challenging the practical utility of much existing scholarship is that, possibly, because of this imperative, virtually all relevant evidence suggests that school administrative practice is already highly ethical. For example, Raun and Leithwood (1993) found that the values entering into the problem solving of senior school district leaders were largely those of pragmatism, participation, and duty. Walker (1995) reported district-level leaders to be actively concerned about their staffs' adherence to such values as caring, fairness, integrity, loyalty, and honesty. And while Begley (1988) found evidence of some school-level leaders basing decisions on personal preferences, more knowledge usually resulted in a shift to "consequences for students" as the overriding value in their decision making. These findings ought not to be surprising since administrative ranks are populated by former teachers and the main source of teachers' professional satisfaction is visible evidence that they have contributed to the intellectual emotional and social well-being of their students (Lortie 1975; Feimen-Nemser and Floden 1986).

A second reason for challenging the practical utility of this line of research is summed up reasonably well by Willower. After asserting that "most educators are principled individuals who want the best for their students," Willower argues: "Caring and altruism are not nearly so problematic as is the ability to make judgements about how to complete the successful implementation of ethically desirable aims" (1996, 359).

There are at least two different inferences to be drawn from this claim. One inference is that a distinction should be drawn between "end" values and "instrumental" values (not a distinction that can be pressed too far) and that the problematic issues for administrators concern instrumental values. No doubt there are such issues. But the second inference, and the one most consistent with my own evidence (Leithwood and Steinbach 1995, chapter 2), is that the truly swampy problems most frequently encountered by school leaders concern the design of effective strategies for realizing values to which they and most other stakeholders in the school adhere (e.g., equity) and to do so in the uncertain, interpersonally intense and resource-constrained environments which characterize today's schools. Solving problems of this sort demands what scholars in the field of expertise refer to as "domain-specific knowledge," knowledge about how to teach children from disadvantaged family backgrounds to read, for example. Scholarly inquiry concerning administrative values is irrelevant to the solving of this type of problem.

Even if school administrators set out to behave in a professionally unethical manner, it is extremely difficult for them to do so for long without being detected. This is the third reason for questioning the practical utility of scholarly inquiry about values in educational administration. Organizations and their administrators occupying largely technical environments (DiMaggio and Powell 1991), such as many private-sector corporations, are judged by their efficiency in accomplishing relatively clear and widely agreed-upon goals such as reasonable profit for shareholders. Such environments nourish a "means justifies the ends" perspective. This, in combination with relatively low levels of public scrutiny, warrants special vigilance concerning ethical practices and interventions designed to assist administrators in making more ethically defensible decisions.

In contrast, organizations, like schools, with sometimes unclear, difficult to assess, and contested goals, occupy institutional environments. Organizations and their administrators in such environments are more likely to be judged by the extent to which they conform to rules and public expectations necessary for their continued support and legitimation (Scott and Meyer 1991). Much of the work of school administrators is highly visible to students, parents, teachers, and members of the nonparent community. Under these conditions there is little incentive to behave unethically; widely shared norms of ethical behavior carry special weight; and the information required to make judgements concerning the ethical practices of administrators is readily accessible to many people.

Finally, those few instances of unethical practice by school administrators that do occur (and they are widely reported in the media, especially in cases of sexual misconduct) seem quite unlikely to be either prevented or re-mediated by most forms of intensive personal therapy, never mind the types of interventions likely to emerge from current scholarship. William Greenfield (1985) has offered sensible reasons why normative aspects of the administrator's job are unlikely to be developed through formal programs, the form such interventions are most likely to take.

If the practical utility of current scholarship in enhancing the ethical defensibility of administrative practice is low, toward what other practical goals might such scholarship aim? This chapter offers no comprehensive answer to this question as worthwhile to pursue as that would be. Rather, this chapter aims to draw attention to only one goal and to illustrate the nature of the work its achievement would entail. This goal is to develop a system of values to guide the work of educational leaders based on the needs of future schools and the processes required to develop those schools. Such a basis for a system of values stands in contrast to most other alternatives currently available. These alternatives include taxonomies of values rooted in moral philosophy (e.g., Hodgkinson 1978) and those emerging from empirical efforts to describe the values of practicing educational leaders (e.g., Walker 1995; Leithwood, Begley, and Cousins 1992).

Robert Starratt's (1991) work in "Building an Ethical School" comes closest to accomplishing the goal I pursue here, although we begin from different premises. To illustrate what might be required to accomplish this goal, remaining sections of this chapter

- argue for an incremental orientation to the process of transforming today's schools and identify some of the more critical values needed to support such an orientation;
- consider the consequences for future school designs of a sample of social, political, and economic forces shaping the evolution of to-day's schools;
- identify school designs that would productively accommodate these forces and the values that would need to underpin school leaders' practices in order to develop and maintain such designs;
- identify several challenges facing those responsible for assisting in the development of current and future school leaders with respect to these values.

An Incremental Orientation to the Design of Future Schools

I take the problem of imagining the design of future schools to include the problem of how they will get to be future schools. Future schools, however much we may wish it, will not spring into existence full blown on, say, January 1, 2000. Rather, they will evolve into something different from, but connected to, today's schools on a broken front, over a very unpredictable time-line, and without any sense of ever completing that evolution. Most likely, as O. L. Davis argues, this evolution will involve a long series of "marginal improvements" (1996, 201).

Such incremental approaches to change are quite inconsistent with current calls for "systemic" change (Epps 1994), "break-the-mold schools" (Cooperman 1994), and radical "restructuring" (Bast and Walberg 1994).

Incremental approaches to change neither spark the imagination of educational reformers nor offer much leverage to policy makers. However, they do avoid the debilitating and, finally, destructive "rhetoric of excess" (Davis 1996) that typically has accompanied previous reform efforts.

As much as we might wish that we are entering a brave new world in which many things (including schools) will somehow behave differently, the prudent bet is that incrementalism will prevail; it will prevail as the most accurate description of how schools will change over the next twenty years just as it is the most accurate description of how they have changed over the past fifty years. This is not bad, explains Davis: "Willingness to seek and to accept marginal change is not acceptance of second- or third-best . . . [it is] not minimal, not superficial, not trivial. . . . Marginal improvements in education are actual, real, practical improvements. . . . Marginal improvements do not deny the nature of the boundaries of their context" (1996, 204).

Justification for incremental approaches to change also can be found in the work of institutional theorists alluded to above. Because schools occupy largely institutional environments, they are rewarded primarily for establishing prevailing views of "correct" structures and procedures and much less for the quality or quantity of their output. Legitimacy depends on the plausibility of these structures and procedures, and establishing and maintaining this legitimacy is a crucial problem. Especially relevant to schools, Meyer and Scott (1983) argue that legitimacy of organizations in institutional environments is negatively affected by the number of different authorities with some type of power over them and by the diversity of their beliefs about how they should function. Any design of future schools that does not reflect aspects of current schools highly valued by such authorities will prove to be politically unacceptable and unlikely to survive.

Given the improbability of nonincremental or revolutionary change, future school designs must be ones that we "can get to from here"; they must be images of organizations whose main features are capable of growing out of the seeds of today's school designs. Acknowledging the authenticity and robustness of practices and organizational features potentially resulting from incremental change processes makes it imperative that we respect the durability of today's schools. Popular perceptions notwithstanding, it also means that we recognize just how remarkably effective schools have been in meeting the ambiguous, slippery, and wildly ambitious expectations of their many masters, in comparison with the effectiveness of almost any other social institution. We would be sadly remiss if we did not systematically build on the hard-won lessons in organizational design available to be learned from schools in their relatively short histories.

Legions of people are unprepared to acknowledge the durability and effectiveness of schools to which I allude. For purposes of this chapter, we will have to agree to disagree; the chapter is premised in no small measure on this positive perspective I hold of schools, without further justification (to be clear, this perspective still admits of endless efforts to improve and in no way denies the existence of some pretty awful schools).

Three sets of values underlie incremental orientations to change and are an important part of the value system of those who would exercise leadership for incremental change:

- *Carefulness and a constructively critical perspective:* this set of values is evident in an incremental approach to change, an orientation that acknowledges the improbability of radical change no matter how much we may wish for it (if wishes sufficed, Russia would have become an economically vibrant democracy several years ago). Also rising from this set of values is an open-minded, but dispassionately skeptical, attitude toward the claims of current reformers about the consequences of their favorite "change of the month."

- *Respect for the capacities and commitments of past and current educators:* this value manifests itself in a willingness to build on insights about how to educate large numbers of children embedded in the collective memories and structures of existing school organizations and educational practices. At minimum, these insights take account of the imperatives in schools that few reformers are either aware of or interested in. This value is a counterbalance for the type of historical ignorance and hubris currently being displayed, for example, by the Ontario government in its efforts to cut education funding in the province.

- *Continuous improvement:* this is an antidote for the sense of being overwhelmed and confused that is fueled by excessively turbulent environments such as those currently faced by schools. A continuous improvement value encourages the seizing of as much local control as central mandates and regulations allow, the determination of manageable priorities for change that make local sense, and systematic, focused initiatives for the improvement of schools through achieving such priorities.

Features of Today's Context: Stimulating the Evolution of Schools

The social, economic, and political contexts within which schools find, and anticipate finding, themselves are obviously crucial considerations in the

design of future schools. However, such considerations are seriously complicated by the conflicting implications for schools of many such contexts.
Nonetheless, the implications of context, including conflicts in the directions they suggest for future schools, provide much of the basis for future
school design.

While there are many contextual forces impinging on the direction of
future school designs, the six examined in this section illustrate (perhaps
even represent) the problems for which educational leaders must seek
solutions. The first two of these forces press schools toward greater centralization, the next two, toward greater organizational decentralization. The
final two contextual forces challenge the institution of schooling more
fundamentally. Each of these three sets of forces engages leaders in what
Watson (1996) refers to as distinctly different "discourses." These discourses
represent loosely coherent frameworks of central values to be given priority
by the organization while still admitting other values in a secondary role. For
example, centralizing trends encourage a discourse that places great value
on control, accountability, and efficiency, whereas decentralizing trends
foster a discourse in which empowerment, cooperation, and continuous
improvement are strongly valued.

Centralizing Forces

End of the "borrow now, pay later" school of public finance. During the 1990s,
developed countries around the world have found themselves seriously
challenged by debt. Furthermore, there is enough public concern for the
long-term consequences of ignoring public debt to make both deficit and
debt reduction politically attractive goals. These debt-reduction programs
arrive as many countries are beginning to experience noticeable increases
in the proportions of their populations that are aging. Such populations
have no direct need for public educational services and so are less willing to
allocate their tax dollars to schools; they are also in greater need of medical
and other social services than they were earlier in their lives (Ng 1992).

The combined effects of government debt reduction programs and
increased competition for public dollars by other social services are significantly eroding the resources allocated to public schooling. This is creating
pressure on schools toward greater centralization. Such centralization, it is
argued, will allow more efficient use of available resources through so-called
economies of scale. Greater centralization of functions such as transportation and purchasing, the combining of programs and institutions, and the
amalgamation of central office structures are all manifestations of responses
to this pressure for centralization as a means of becoming more efficient.

*End of belief that all nontraditional family structures are rare enough to be safely
ignored by schools.* There was a time, not very long ago, when a good many

teachers resented the "intrusion" of their students' unmet social, emotional, and even basic physical needs into the school's primarily intellectual curriculum. With some justification, these teachers complained that responding to such needs was the proper role of parents and social workers. It was not the role of teachers.

Teachers with this complaint often assumed that most of their students came from the kind of functional, two-parent nuclear families that, in Western cultures, were widely believed to be both typical and ideal. Indeed, this was the kind of family around which schools were originally designed, families which were (and still are) thought to provide reliably the "social capital" which James Coleman (1987) has demonstrated is an essential foundation for children to acquire if they are to cope productively with the intellectual challenges for which schools historically have been considered responsible.

Few teachers still feel confident in assuming that their students come from such families and possess the psychological robustness that is at the core of Coleman's meaning of social capital. While many children still do, of course, evidence concerning the widespread existence of alternative family structures has become too pervasive to ignore (Oderkirk 1994). At the heart of the problem for children, of the widespread emergence of what Elkind (in an interview with Marge Scherer) has called "postmodern permeable family" (Scherer 1996, 6), is the erosion of the kinds of familial educational cultures directly responsible for social capital development. These cultures are built on an unqualified acceptance of the child's worth and include, for example, high value awarded education in the home, encouragement, and direct help available from adults in the home for children with their school work, and physical space available for study and homework. Herbert Walberg (1984) has referred to these features, together, as the "alterable curriculum" of the home.

To be more precise, however, it is not alternative family structures themselves that are responsible for an erosion of family educational cultures and, as a result, social capital. Rather, the erosion is due, in part, to the enormous amount of time that many parents now have to devote to work and to further developing work-related skills in order to make certain that their children are provided for (Scherer, 1996). The erosion is also a product of the economic disadvantages that often accompany some forms of the postmodern family structure. For example, while single parent families are quite capable of providing stimulating educational cultures in the home when they are not also suffering undue financial hardship, a very large proportion of single parent families do suffer such hardship (Oderkirk and Lochhead 1992).

What a great many teachers and other educators now believe, that they did not believe before, is that development of social capital is something for which they must take some responsibility. There is also a belief that schools by themselves are not very well equipped to do this job. So this has become a force for engaging, for example, in partnerships with other social agencies to better position their students for success at school. Full service schools and other forms of service coordination in which schools play a role (Smylie and Crowson 1996) indicate how this has become a centralizing force for schools.

Decentralizing Forces

End of society's willingness to assign major decision-making authority to professional expertise. This is a force or a trend being experienced widely throughout the professions. Most professions acquired their status through a willingness on the part of large segments of society to cede them considerable responsibility and authority for decision making. Such willingness was based on the assumption that members of the professional group possessed privileged technical knowledge and skill unavailable to nonprofessionals about a set of problems of critical importance to a large proportion of the public.

While the status and autonomy in decision making awarded to school professionals never matched that of medicine or law, professionals of all types have been experiencing a rapid decline in the public's willingness to continue ceding such power. As Bryk explains, there is "a renewed belief in the power of democratic activity to pull societal institutions from the quagmire of professional control" (1988, 232). This belief is a consequence of, for example, generally higher levels of public education, greater access by the public to information previously possessed largely by members of the professions, and a growing perception that many professionals have betrayed the public trust.

Widespread initiatives by governments around the world to award parents more direct control over schools by establishing either advisory or decision-making roles for parents on school councils (Murphy and Beck 1995) are the most obvious manifestations of this decentralizing force on schools.

End of the public school's technological naivete. A second decentralizing force is evident in the recent trend among schools to adopt more rapidly current electronic technology and to integrate it more fully into the educational and administrative work of the school. While availability and integrated use are not the same thing, it is telling that between 1983 and 1994 the number of U.S. schools with at least one computer rose from 18 percent to 98 percent (Mehlinger 1996). Serious use of electronic technology has been a long time coming and until quite recently seemed anything but inevitable. Even now, many mature technologies (TV's, VCR's) have achieved only marginal status in schools in spite of what was perceived by their advocates, at least, to be of "revolutionary" potential.

However, the computer, has become ubiquitous in our society, and such widespread use has brought pressures and incentives for schools to adopt it from many sources in a meaningful way. For example: the Education Summit held by the U.S. president and governors in April 1996 resulted in a resolution to ensure that all U.S. schools have access to the Internet within six years. When AT&T recently introduced its Internet access service, it offered a discount to schools, presumably with the aim of capturing a substantial share of what the company believes will be a huge market (Gurley 1996). Increasingly, schools make use of microcomputer technology to report on their own work and to maintain existing and achieve new educational goals (Weiss 1996).

While providing access to information is by no means all that schools do (nor computers either, of course), it is a significant part of their current function. Mostly, they bring twenty-five or thirty students together at the same time and in the same place to do it. The reasons for such an arrangement are no longer compelling, however. At least part of the time, students can now access information and discuss it with teachers, fellow students, and others without being in the same physical location. As video-conferencing technology becomes more available and of higher quality, the reasons for students to be always in the same place at the same time will erode even further. This is one of the reasons that at least conventional classroom structures should not be an assumed feature of future schools.

De-institutionalizing Forces

Contemporary understandings of how learning occurs "Constructivism" is the label most often used to describe understandings of learning that have emerged from the work of contemporary cognitive scientists (McLaughlin and Talbert 1993). A good many curriculum and instructional initiatives are premised on such theory. Lampert's (1990) work on the teaching of mathematics and Scardamalia and Bereiter's (1986) work on the teaching of writing composition are examples of instructional applications. California's curriculum frameworks are examples of curriculum applications.

As long as constructivist theory is applied to the teaching of literacy and numeracy, as they are in elementary schools, its implications are largely restricted to increasing the size and to changing the nature of teachers' instructional repertoires. However, the implications, are much more profound as such theory is brought to bear on the teaching of domain-specific knowledge, especially in secondary schools confronted with the task of preparing students for transition to work or to tertiary education. Such schools are frequently criticized because they provide their students with "inert knowledge," to use John Bransford's (1993) term.

Inert knowledge is acquired in contexts separate from those in which it is expected to be applied (e.g., schools). As a consequence, those who possess it have considerable difficulty even recognizing instances in which it would be relevant to use, never mind having the capacity to use it to guide their actions. To be of actual use, cognitive scientists suggest that knowledge needs to be both "situated" and "proceduralized" (e.g., Brown, Collins, and Duguid 1989; Rogoff 1984; Wagner 1987).

When people learn in the context in which their knowledge is subsequently to be used, they acquire much more than the explicit knowledge that is part of the planned curriculum. They also acquire the "tacit" (Polanyi 1967) or "everyday" knowledge that, in combination with the explicit knowledge, provides the depth of understanding and the skill required for practical problem solving. Authentic learning of useful knowledge then depends on involvement in solving real problems within some domain of practice.

However, schools, were created with the express purpose of separating students from such "messy" involvement in order to pour a pristine form of knowledge into their heads. Historically, this has been a form of knowledge largely useless for all but the playing of trivial pursuit using a form of instruction that does not recognize the need for students to personally construct their own meaning. Most efforts to solve the inert knowledge problem in secondary schools involve, already, modest forms of de-institutionalization (cooperative education is perhaps the best-known North American example). Many of the school-to-work transition initiatives associated with the "new vocationalism" (Goldberger and Kazis 1996) also entail the provision of significantly more workplace contexts for formal education.

Widespread recognition of the need for lifelong learning. In her proposed new agenda for education, Judith Chapman (1996) refers to "the learning society and knowledge economy" (1) as the broad policy context within which future schools must be designed. This is a context that acknowledges lifelong learning as instrumental to a rapidly changing job market as well as to opportunities for individuals to choose from "a rich range of options, from which they may construct a satisfying and enriching pattern of activities and life-enhancing choices for themselves" (3). According to Chapman, future schools also must be designed in recognition of a context that privileges those with the capacities to access, make sense of, and use both sources and quantities of information unimagined until quite recently.

Widespread commitment to lifelong learning is a de-institutionalization force on schools since it clearly implies the involvement of people in systematic education at all stages of their lives. Present school designs, in contrast, respond to a set of requirements that were relevant (and to some extent remain so) for those at pre- and early-adult stages in their lives. These requirements include custodial care, physical security, limited life experiences, uncertain motivation for learning the formal curriculum, and immature levels of cognitive development. To the extent that meeting such requirements is irrelevant in the education of adults, the traditional design of schools cannot be justified. Furthermore, many adults do not depend on formal institutions of any kind for their learning, relying instead on personal reading, practical experience, deliberation with colleagues, and the like. Therefore, just redesigning existing school organizations is not obviously a solution.

The Design of Future Schools

Broad Values to Be Represented in the Design of Future Schools

Taken together, these conflicting forces for change begin to suggest at least three broad sets of values that will need to be represented in the designs of future schools: inclusiveness, efficient reliability, and "generativity." First, future schools will need to be more inclusive or participatory in their decision making and more comprehensive in terms of the dimensions of student growth (social and emotional, as well as intellectual) for which they consider themselves at least partly responsible. This criterion responds to the diversity of student needs rising from alternative family structures and the desire for greater non-professional control of schools. An image of future *schools as communities* begins to address this value.

A second value to be represented in the design of future schools is efficient reliability. Schools need to accomplish more reliably the outcomes for which schools traditionally have been held accountable with virtually all of their students and to do so as efficiently as possible. The importance of this value emerges most obviously from the sometimes dramatic reductions in public funding allocated to schools, reductions likely to continue for some time into the future, along with persistent calls for greater public accountability. Imagining *schools as high reliability organizations* is a means of realizing this value.

As a third value, future schools will increasingly need to be capable of continually examining the systems within which they are embedded, anticipate needed changes, and initiate actions to make those changes. Senge (1990) refers to this as a process of "generativity." Not only are expectations for schools changing, but also they are becoming more ambitious as is evident in the pressures on schools to help develop students who will be able to function well in a technologically sophisticated world. These changing expectations are being accompanied by new instructional practices (those rising from new understandings of how learning occurs, such as cooperative learning strategies) that teachers must master and that school organizations need to determine how to support both structurally and culturally. This predictable and unending stream of changes in expectations and practices recommends the design of schools as learning organizations.

Inclusivity and School as Community

A school modeled as a community, according to Bryk and Driscoll, "is a social organization consisting of cooperative relations among adults who share common purposes and where daily life for both adults and students is organized in ways which foster commitment among its members" (1988). As Selznick further explains, its function is "to regulate, discipline, and especially to channel self-regarding conduct, thereby binding it so far as is possible, to comprehensive interests and ideals," and its favored form "is the small, intimate, person-centered structure where solidarity is most effective and most genuine . . . where persons are created and nurtured, where they become situated beings and implicated selves" (1992, 369).

A conception of schools as communities begins to indicate in what ways they might provide students with the social capital that, in the past, schools could more safely assume was being provided to their students through some combination of their immediate families and the networks of relationships available in the lives of students outside their immediate families. Social capital consists of the norms, obligations, and trust that are developed among people through such relationships (Coleman 1987) and the sense of stability, security, and positive self-concept typically engendered in individual children who participate in such relationships. Social capital thereby offers many of the personal and social prerequisites for successful mastery of the challenges provided by the school's curriculum. Claims Gamoran, "when such relations are flourishing, social capital can serve as a resource supporting the cognitive and social development of young people" (1996, 2). The trend toward integrated social services in schools also is an organizational response to the need for children to be provided with the conditions necessary to further develop social capital.

The social capital provided through schools designed as communities has been cited by many as the explanation for apparent achievement of students in some types of schools (e.g., Coleman and Hoffer 1987; Bryk, Lee, and Holland 1994; Wehlage et al 1989), especially for students from disadvantaged backgrounds.

In sum then, several forces shaping the evolution of schools warrant more attention to inclusivity in the design of future schools. In this context, inclusivity is a broad category of values encompassing related values such as

- caring and respect for others: as Starratt explains, caring requires "fidelity to persons, a willingness to acknowledge their right to be

who they are, an openness to encountering them in their authentic individuality, a loyalty to the relationship . . . This value is grounded in the belief that the integrity of human relationships should be held sacred" (1991, 195). Walker (1995) coded words such as *compassion, generosity,* and *dignity* as instances of this value.
* participation: this encompasses Hodgkinson's (1978) values of consensus. It also reflects the concerns for freedom, equality, and social justice in schools rooted in Dewey's concept of the 'democratic school' and given expression currently, for example, in Giroux's (1992) concept of 'leader as transformative intellectual.'

Efficient Reliability and Schools as High Reliability Organizations

While much has been written about the appropriateness of schools as communities, a conception of schools as highly reliable organizations (HROs) has not yet received much consideration. This image has some of its roots in earlier research on effective schools, especially the work of Stringfield who has spearheaded the effort to apply to schools the notion of high reliability originally developed in nonschool organizations (1992, 1995).

Like efforts to develop more "effective" schools (e.g., Mortimore et al. 1988), the motivation for exploring how schools could become more reliable can be traced to concerns about the development of basic skills. This concern is focused especially on those young students either not well served by traditional school practices or enrolled in schools where the context has seemed to erode the systematic use of such practices. Under such circumstances, students' development of reading skills, in particular, is retarded, and so, as a consequence, is their opportunity to master other aspects of the school curriculum that depend on the application of these skills. Early failures in the development of reading skills then often cascade into increasingly serious problems affecting a broad range of school achievements.

Stringfield uses hydroelectrical power grids and air traffic control systems as examples of HROs to demonstrate some of the characteristics that schools need to acquire in order to be more reliable. HROs of this sort accomplish their goals more or less *all of the time,* and the failure to do so would be considered a disaster by the public. According to Stringfield this public perception is a critical precondition for the emergence of HROs, and, until quite recently, the public had not considered failure to learn to read to be such a disaster.

Evidence is mounting, however, indicating that this perception is changing. One such piece of evidence is the persistence in calls for school reform, calls that have been sustained now in North America since at least

1983 when *A Nation at Risk* was first published. Calls for school reform, while common throughout this century, have never persisted for more than a few months to several years at a time. Stringfield argues (personal communication) that the reason for this persistence is growing public awareness of the significant negative financial consequences of a failure to successfully complete school, both for individuals (reduced lifelong income, unemployment) and for society (reduced tax revenues, increased welfare, and unemployment insurance costs). So the perception-of-disaster precondition to support the emergence of schools as HROs would appear to be at least in the formative stages.

From the dozen or more attributes associated with HROs (Stringfield 1995), one example serves to illustrate one of the small but significant changes that would be required for a traditional school to qualify as an HRO: "HROs are alert to surprises or lapses. The experience of HROs is that small failures can cascade into major system failures and are hence monitored carefully" (Stringfield 1995, 87).

By way of contrast, in the context of schools, there is compelling evidence that dropping out of high school can be predicted reasonably accurately from levels of student classroom participation as early as the third grade (Lloyd 1978). Yet schools rarely conceive of third-grade students' off-task behavior as a potential future disaster and so rarely either track it very closely or take extraordinary steps to reduce it.

Application to schools of the full set of HRO characteristics identified by Stringfield would result in an organization with many of the same structural features of a traditional school but with, for example, the following: more flexible, varied, and task-dependent sets of professional relationships; greater commitment by staff to a clearer and more precisely focused sets of goals; much greater attention to evidence about the effects of selected teaching practices; and meticulous attention to the maintenance of the equipment and technology considered important for achieving the instructional purposes of the school.

When the concerns for reduced expenditures on education are coupled with a concern for reliability, as described here, the meaning of efficiency must be understood from a longer-term perspective as well. For example, short-term savings of money achieved through reduced support for early childhood education, as in the case of the current Ontario government, must be placed in the context of their long-term effects on school success, resources needed for remedial and special education, dropout rates, loss of employment, loss of public taxes, and the dampening effects on national competitiveness of a less than optimally educated work force.

As a broad category of values, efficient reliability encompasses specific values such as the following:

- equity: in this context, equity means equal access to knowledge on the part of students rather than equal access to educational resources. The goals of a high reliability school will be achieved only through inequitable distributions of those resources (some children will need much more of those resources than others);
- knowledge: in this case, the knowledge of greatest concern is about the effectiveness of educational practices used by the school in accomplishing the purposes for which they are intended, in the context in which they are used;
- dependability: almost a synonym for reliability, valuing dependability means rewarding people for unfailingly implementing those practices the school judges to be most effective for its purposes;
- persistence: this value recognizes that to be reliable, in accomplishing outcomes as complex as those addressed by schools, will often require recognizing the failure of initial attempts to accomplish some of those goals and a willingness to change one's approach and try again, perhaps many times.

Generativity and Schools as Learning Organizations

In a future context of declining resources, escalating expectations, and turbulent environments, schools will need to be designed so that changing is considered an ordinary activity rather than an extraordinary event. At the heart of an organization's capacity to change is the individual and collective learning of its members (e.g., Peterson, McCarthy, and Elmore 1996). Appreciation of the importance of such learning has given rise to a venerable body of research on collective or "organizational learning" processes in nonschool organizations (for a comprehensive review of this literature, see Cousins 1995). More recent literature has popularized some of these ideas in the concept of the 'learning organization' (Senge 1990; Watkins and Marsick 1993). According to Fiol and Lyles, "Organizational learning means the process of improving actions through better knowledge and understanding" (1985, 203). A learning organization has been defined as "a group of people pursuing common purposes (individual purposes as well) with a collective commitment to regularly weighing the value of those purposes, modifying them when that makes sense and continuously developing more effective and efficient ways of accomplishing those purposes" (Leithwood and Aitken 1995, 63).

Morgan's (1986) use of the brain as a metaphor for the organization is a productive way of quickly glimpsing the promise of the learning organization. Bureaucracies, he notes, behave "with brains"; those at the top of the hierarchy think on behalf of the organization (they are the organization's brains) and transmit messages to those lower in the hierarchy about what to do. Learning organizations, in contrast, behave "as brains"; responsibility for thinking is widely distributed throughout the organization. As their environments become more complex, less predictable, and demand more rapid responses, organizations with brains become overloaded with problems that they cannot possibly have enough information or processing power to solve. Organizations behaving as brains, in contrast, are able to take full advantage of the information collection and problem-solving capacities residing in each of their members, many of whom will be interacting with those environments on a daily basis.

The principal challenge facing those designing schools as learning organizations is to determine the organizational conditions that foster individual and collective learning and to build those conditions into the school. Only recently has attention been devoted to discovering what these conditions might be. Leithwood, Jantzi, and Steinbach (1995) report that such conditions include, for example, a widely shared vision of what the school is trying to accomplish; a professional culture which encourages considerable collaboration among staffs on matters of teaching and learning with strong norms of continuous professional growth, structures that allow for frequent interaction and authentic participation in key decisions in the school, and policies and resources that support professional learning initiatives.

An image of future schools as learning organizations is particularly attractive because it does not require especially accurate predictions about the circumstances that future schools will face or the practices that would be most functional in response. The only prediction required is that schools will face a steady stream of complex problems, a prediction that places a premium on continuous improvements in school staffs' individual and collective problem-solving capacities.

As a category of values associated with schools as learning organizations, generativity encompasses at least specific values such as:

- openness to new ideas: learning is fostered as organizational members discard preconceived beliefs about where useful ideas might originate;
- tolerance for divergent points of view: too much consensus leads to group-think (Janis 1978). Learning organizations need just enough consensus to carry out their work and no more;
- tolerance for strategic failure: valuing failure as a source of learning rather than something to be avoided is a productive value in relation to issues where mistakes do not create disasters for the organization. (Sitken 1992, 199)

- questioning of basic assumptions: Argyris and Schön (1978) refer to this as "double loop" learning.
- speculative thinking: encourages people to imagine plausible future states, anticipate the challenges that those future states may create, and prepare to address them rather than simply responding or adapting to them when they arise;
- personal mastery: as Senge (1990) defines it, personal mastery values the effort of individual members of the organization to become as skilled and knowledgeable as possible about how to carry out their individual responsibilities in the organization as well as how to contribute to collective efforts;
- interconnectedness: Senge's (1990) fifth discipline, interconnectedness or systems thinking, encourages organizational members to appreciate the complex nature of the relationships among different aspects of the organization.

Toward a Comprehensive Image of Future Schools

Not only do the three images of future schools described to this point depend on the expression of different sets of values, but they also are based on quite different assumptions. Each image, though, contains a partial response to the forces shaping the evolution of schools. So a synthesis of these images in the design of future schools would be productive. I think such a synthesis is also feasible.

Table 2.1 captures a sample of the differences in some of the assumptions on which each of the three images depend, in this case, assumptions about human learning, motivation, and organizational mission and goals. With respect to learning, an image of organization as community is based on developmentalist views of the sort reflected, for example, in Piagetian theory. Members of the community, it is assumed, learn what they need to know and be able to do "naturally" and relatively effortlessly from participation in a suitable community setting, much as developmentalists believe children learn in unstructured ways from a stimulating educational setting (Scardamalia and Berciter 1989). However, HROs reflect an information-processing view of learning, one in which there are clear learning goals and a set of powerful procedures available for their achievement. Systematic development by individuals of the skills required to use such procedures is one of the central tasks of organizational members. Finally, learning organizations assume that learning and problem solving are both individual and collective acts (Cohen 1996); such learning is often aimed at unclear goals; and knowledge is socially constructed through interactions among the cog-

Table 2.1 Examples of assumptions underlying three future school designs

	ASSUMPTIONS ABOUT HUMAN LEARNING	ASSUMPTIONS ABOUT HUMAN MOTIVATION	ASSUMPTIONS ABOUT MISSION AND GOALS
SCHOOL AS COMMUNITY	-active -developmentalist explanation (effortless) -depends on stimulating environment & opportunity -group based	-focus is on meeting esteem and affiliation needs	-equity -may be vague -emphasis on personal and social goals -promote adult commitment -provide intrinsic rewards
SCHOOL AS HRO	-active -information processing explanation (effortful but predictable) -depends on practice, coaching & direct instruction -individually based	-focus is on meeting achievement needs	-excellence -predetermined, clear -gateway achievements -foundational competence
SCHOOL AS LEARNING ORGANIZATION	-active -constructivist explanation (effortful but open-ended) -depends on authentic experiences & "situated cognition" -both individually & socially based	-focused is on self-actualization	-quality -complex, evolving -higher order

nitive resources of individual members as they work toward making sense of new problems and information (Weick and Roberts 1996).

The three images of future schools also vary considerably in their assumptions about human motivation. Using Maslow's needs hierarchy (1954) to illustrate, schools as communities most obviously address peoples' affiliation needs. HROs appear to address peoples' achievement needs most directly, whereas self-actualization needs are most obviously met within the context of a learning organization.

As a final illustration of just how different are the assumptions underlying the three images of future schools, table 2.1 also summarizes the most likely mission and goals each type of organization would be capable of realizing. With their overriding concern for inclusion and diversity, schools designed as communities are most likely to view *equity* as their mission and place considerable emphasis on social-emotional goals. The main instrument for change is likely to be organizational members' commitments to students and to the school and its mission. A widely distributed version of *excellence* appears the most obvious mission to be addressed by HROs, along with a core set of traditional goals for schools, goals included in McGregor's concept of 'gateway achievements' (1994, 26). Continuous quality improvement would be a likely contender for the primary mission of the learning organization. Although "quality" is eventually judged in terms of service to students, the first order of business is the processes used to provide such service and the capacities needed by organizational members to refine and implement increasingly effective processes. Continuous improvement, while not ignoring the improvement of processes designed to develop gateway achievements, would be focused especially on higher order, more complex student outcomes, those for which well-codified processes do not already exist.

These examples of different assumptions underlying the three images of future schools illustrate two important points. First and most obviously, these three images really do represent fundamentally different school designs. Less obviously, but central to the purposes of this chapter, there is an important sense in which all of these assumptions can be justified at some point in time, for some people, in some contexts. For example, consider the assumptions about human learning. While these assumptions are quite different, each reflects quite closely the nature of learning under some circumstances: developmentalist assumptions reflect the ways in which most people learn a first language and the informal and implicit nature in which tacit knowledge is acquired in most domains of practice; information-processing assumptions describe reasonably well the cognitive processes associated with learning well-codified, explicit knowledge and skill; and constructivist conceptions of learning are useful in understanding how people make sense of situations in which significant amounts of interpretation are required of them and where there are multiple possible "correct answers."

The same general case made for the appropriateness of each of the three perspectives on learning also can be made for the alternative sources of human motivation and the different organizational missions and goals described in Table 2.1. This suggests that a synthesis of the three images of schools, described separately to this point, offers a comprehensive and potentially workable design for future schools. School as community acts as a foundation for the organization by providing the psychological stability and sense of mutual trust required for organizational members to be willing to risk making changes in their practices. School as HRO offers the conditions to ensure that students achieve the basic capacities or gateway achievements that parents and the wider community have always expected, and continue to expect, schools to develop. Finally, school as learning organization provides those conditions necessary to accomplish the ambitious and/or novel student outcomes for which schools have not, as yet, developed reliable and effective practices.

Conclusion—the Challenges for Leadership Development

From this synthesis of clearly independent designs for future school has emerged a more comprehensive and more fully adequate design, the school *as high reliability learning community*. Such a design responds reasonably well to a wide array of forces currently shaping the evolution of schools.

At the outset, it was argued that future school designs should be capable of growing out of the design of today's schools since the most likely process through which future schools would develop would be an incremental one. This seems possible for the high reliability learning community, at least, when each component of this more comprehensive design is considered separately. The seeds of high reliability are clearly evident in many of today's schools that have responded to research evidence concerning effective teaching strategies and the correlates of effective schools. Stringfield (1995) reviews evidence about specific school programs as well as schoolwide initiatives in support of this claim. Evidence of existing schools with well-developed community features can be found in Sergiovanni (1994) and recent evidence reported by Louis and Kruse (1995). As well, Leithwood and colleagues (1995), Sharrat (1996), and Leonard (1996) report significant amounts of organizational learning in selected schools responding to major policy initiatives.

The high-reliability learning community then appears to be a plausible design for future school organizations because it addresses quite directly the forces for change currently impinging on schools and because it takes into account critical constraints on the implementation of school change. But to create and sustain such a school design would require the practices of stakeholders in the school, especially perhaps the practices of those offering leadership, to be governed by a complex array of values. Meeting this requirement confronts those responsible for leadership development with two central challenges.

The first challenge is to assist present and future leaders to become more sensitive particularly to the crucial, "professional" values on which the design of high-reliability learning communities are dependent. Some of the values that have been identified as important in this chapter already are being exercised by practicing school leaders, according to the available evidence (Walker 1995; Leithwood, Begley and Cousins 1992). This is the case, for example, with respect to caring and respect and participation (associated with inclusion) and equity and knowledge (associated with efficient reliability). The practices of current school leaders also are governed by respect for the capacities of their colleagues. Such values might be termed "personal" since, for the most part, they seem equally salient to all aspects of one's life.

Most of the remaining values identified as important in support of the high reliability learning organization appear not to be internalized by many of today's school leaders, however. This is particularly the case for generativity and its related values, values required to support conditions fostering organizational learning. Also not common among today's school leaders, according to the available evidence, are two values critical to efficient reliability—dependability and persistence—and a value especially important for productive incremental change, carefulness, and a constructively critical perspective. Increasing the sensitivity of present and future school leaders to the importance of these values, some of which are decidedly "professional" in nature, would be essential to implementing the sort of school design advocated in this chapter.

This increase in sensitivity is not likely to happen, however, by continuing to ground the treatment of values in leader preparation in moral philosophy. Moral philosophy gives greatest attention to those personal values already evident in the practices of many school leaders and has nothing useful to say about those important professional values largely absent from such practices. Furthermore, moral philosophy is largely concerned with values that develop over the course of one's lifetime in response to pervasive and sustained personal influences such as religious beliefs, parents, spouses, and adult friends (Raun and Leithwood 1993). At least formal leadership preparation experiences are unlikely to have much effect on the development of these values (W. Greenfield 1985). In contrast, the more professionally-oriented values identified in this chapter as important but missing from the repertoire of present school leaders also seem more amenable to influence through such professional experiences as mentorship and on-the-job leadership opportunities over which leadership developers do have some influence (Raun and Leithwood 1993).

A second challenge facing those responsible for leadership preparation is to assist present and future leaders in exercising their values in a sensitively contingent manner. At different points in time the school will need to give more priority to the development or maintenance of one aspect of its design (community, for example) than to others. This also entails giving priority to one set of values over others (inclusivity, for example). Being sensitively contingent in this way demands a level of awareness about one's values and an understanding of how to use them constructively in solving organizational design problems that is only evident, at the present time, among those with especially high levels of overall problem-solving expertise. Assisting in the development of such expertise may be one of the most productive avenues to contingent sensitivity in the exercise of values by school leaders.

References

Argyris, C., and Schön, D. 1978. *Organizational learning: A theory of action perspective.* Reading MA: Addison-Wesley.

Bast, J., and Walberg, H. 1994. Free market choice: Can education be privatized? In *Radical education reforms,* ed. C. E. Finn, Jr., and H. Walberg, 149–72. Berkeley: McCutchan.

Begley, P. 1988. The influence of personal beliefs and values on principals' adoption and use of computers in school. Toronto: University of Toronto. Unpublished doctoral thesis.

Bransford, J. D. 1993. Who ya gonna call? Thoughts about teaching problem solving. In *Cognitive perspectives on educational leadership,* ed. P. Hallinger, K. Leithwood, and J. Murphy, 171–91. New York: Teachers College Press.

Brown, J. S., Collins, A., and Duguid, P. 1989. Situated cognition and the culture of learning. *Educational Researcher* 18, 1: 32–42.

Bryk, A. S. 1988. Musings on the moral life of schools. *American Journal of Education* 96: 231–55.

Bryk, A. S., and Driscoll, M. 1988. An empirical investigation of the school as community. University of Chicago: Unpublished manuscript.

Bryk, A. S., Lee, V. E., and Holland, P. 1994. *Catholic schools and the common good.* Cambridge, MA: Harvard University Press.

Chapman, J. 1996. A new agenda for a new society. In *International handbook of educational leadership and administration,* ed. K. Leithwood. The Netherlands: Kluwer Academic Press.

Cohen, M. D. 1996. Individual learning and organizational routine. In *Organizational Learning,* ed. M.D. Cohen and L. S. Sproull, 188–94. Thousand Oaks, CA: Sage.

Coleman, J. S. 1987. Families and schools. *Educational Researcher* 16, 6: 32–38.

Coleman, J. S., and Hoffer, T. 1987. *Public and private high schools.* New York: Basic Books.

Cooperman, S. 1994. The new American schools development corporation. In *Radical education reforms,* ed. C. E. Finn, Jr., and H. Walberg, 21–28. Berkeley, CA: McCutchan.

Cousins, J. B. 1995. Understanding organizational learning for educational leadership and school reform. University of Ottawa. Unpublished paper.

Davis, Jr., O. L. 1996. The pursuit of marginal improvements. *Journal of Curriculum and Supervision* 11, 3: 201–4.

Dewey, J. 1916. *Democracy and Education.* New York: Macmillan.

DiMaggio, P. J., and Powell, W. W. 1991. The iron cage revisited: Institutional isomorphism and collective rationality. In *The new institutionalism in organizational analysis,* ed. W. W. Powell and P. J. DiMaggio, 63–82. Chicago: University of Chicago Press.

Epps, E. G. 1994. Radical school reform in Chicago: How is it working? In *Radical education reforms,* ed. C. E. Finn, Jr., and H. Walberg, 77–94. Berkeley, CA: McCutchan.

Feiman-Nemser, S., and Floden, R. 1986. The cultures of teaching. In *Handbook of Research on Teaching,* ed. M. Wittrock, 505–27. New York: Macmillan.

Fiol. C. M., and Lyles, M. A. 1985. Organizational learning. *Academy of Management Review* 10, 4: 803–13.

Gamoran, A. 1996. Student achievement in public magnet, public comprehensive, and private city high schools. *Educational Evaluation and Policy Analysis* 18, 1: 1–18.

Giroux, H. 1992. Educational leadership and the crisis of democratic government. *Educational Researcher* 21: 4–11.

Goldberger, S., and Kazis, R. 1996. Revitalizing high schools: What the school-to-career movement can contribute. *Phi Delta Kappan* 77, 8: 547–54.

Greenfield, W. 1985. The moral socialization of school administrators: Informal role learning outcomes. *Educational Administration Quarterly* 21, 4: 99–119.

———. 1995. Toward a theory of school administration: The centrality of leadership. *Educational Administration Quarterly* 31, 1: 61–85.

Gurley, W. 1996. It's the end of the net as we know it. *Fortune* 133, 8: 181–82.

Hodgkinson, C. 1978. *Towards a philosophy of administration.* Oxford: Blackwell.

Janus, I. 1978. Groupthink. Boston: Houghton Mifflin Co.

Lampert, M. 1990. When the problem is not the question and the solution is not the answer: Mathematical knowing and teaching. *American Educational Research Journal* 27, 1: 29–64.

Leithwood, K., ed. 1996. *International handbook of educational leadership and administration.* The Netherlands: Kluwer Academic Press.

Leithwood, K. and Aitken, R. 1995. *Making schools smarter.* Thousand Oaks, CA: Corwin Press.

Leithwood, K., Jantzi, D., and Steinbach, R. 1995. An organizational learning perspective on school responses to central policy initiatives. *School Organization* 15, 3: 229–52.

Leithwood, K., and Steinbach, R. 1995. *Expert problem solving.* Albany, NY: State University of New York Press.

Leithwood, K. A., Begley, P. T., and Cousins, J. B. 1992/94. *Developing leadership for future schools.* London: Falmer Press.

Leonard, L. 1996. Organizational learning and the initiation of school councils. University of Toronto: Unpublished doctoral dissertation.

Lindblom, C. E., and Braybrooke, D. 1970. *A strategy of decision.* New York: The Free Press.

Lloyd, D. 1978. Prediction of school failure from third-grade data. *Educational and Psychological Measurements* 38: 1193–1200.

Lortie, D. 1975. *Schoolteacher: A sociological study.* Chicago: University of Chicago Press.

Louis, K. S., Kruse, S., ed. 1995. *Professionalism and community.* Thousand Oaks, CA: Corwin Press.

Maslow, A. H. 1954. *Motivation and personality.* New York: Harper.

McGregor, E. B. 1994. Economic development and public education: Strategies and standards. *Educational Policy* 8, 3: 252–71.

McLaughlin, M. W., and Talbert, J. E. 1993. Introduction: New visions of teaching. In *Teaching for understanding,* ed. D. Cohen et al., 1–10. San Francisco: Jossey-Bass.

Mehlinger, H. D. 1996. School reform in the information age. *Phi Delta Kappan* 77, 6: 400–7.

Meyer, J., and Scott, W. 1983. Centralization and the legitimacy problems of local government. In *Organizational environments,* ed. J. W. Meyer and W. R. Scott, 199–215. Beverly Hills: Sage.

Mickelson, R. A., and Wadsworth, A. L. 1996. NASCD's odyssey in Dallas (NC): Women, class, and school reform. Educational Policy 10, 3: 315–41.

Morgan, G. 1986. *Images of organization.* Beverly Hills: Sage.

Mortimore, P., Sammons, P., Stoll, L., Lewis, D., and Ecob, R. 1988. *School matters: The junior years.* Somerset, UK: Open Books Publishing.

Murphy, J., and Beck, L. G. 1995. *School-based management as school reform: Taking stock.* Thousand Oaks, CA: Corwin Press.

National Commission on Excellence in Education. 1983. A *nation at risk: The imperative of educational reform.* Washington, DC: U. S. Government Printing Office.

Ng, E. 1992. Children and elderly people. *Canadian Social Trends* 25:12–15.

Oderkirk, J. 1994. Marriage in Canada, 1600–1990. *Canadian Social Trends* 33: 2–7.

Oderkirk, J., and Lochhead, C. 1992. Lone parenthood. *Canadian Social Trends* 27: 15–19.

Peterson, P. L., McCarthey, S. J., and Elmore, R. 1996. Learning from school restructuring. *American Educational Research Journal* 33, 1:119–53.

Polanyi, M. 1967. *The tacit dimension.* Garden City: Doubleday.

Powell, W. W., and DiMaggio, P. J. 1991. *The new institutionalism in organizational analysis.* Chicago. University of Chicago Press.

Raun, T., and Leithwood K., 1993. Pragmatism, participation, and duty: Value themes in superintendents' problem solving. In *Cognitive perspectives on educational leadership,* ed. P. Hallinger, K. Leithwood, and J. Murphy, 54–74. New York: Teachers College Press.

Rogoff, B. 1984. Introduction: Thinking and learning in context. In *Everyday cognition: Its development in social context,* ed. B. Rogoff and J. Lave, 1–8. Cambridge, MA: Harvard University Press.

Saavedra, E. R., and Anderson, G. L. 1996. Transformative learning in organizational settings. Paper presented at the annual meeting of the American Educational Research Association, New York City.

Scardamalia, M., and Bereiter, C. 1986. Research on written composition. In *Handbook of research on teaching,* ed. M. Wittrock, 778–803. New York: Macmillan.

———. 1989. Conceptions of teaching and approaches to core problems. In *Knowledge base for the beginning teacher,* ed. M. C. Reynolds, 37–46. Oxford: Pergamon Press.

Scherer, M. 1996. On our changing family values: A conversation with David Elkind. *Educational Leadership* 53, 7: 4–9.

Scott, R., and Meyer, J. 1991. The organization of societal sectors: Propositions and early evidence. In *The New Institutionalism in Organizational Analysis,* ed. W. Powell and P. DiMaggio, 108–42. Chicago: University of Chicago Press.

Selznick, P. 1992. *The moral commonwealth: Social theory and the promise of community.* Berkeley: University of California Press.

Senge, P. M. 1990. *The fifth discipline.* New York: Doubleday.

Sergiovanni, T. J. 1994. *Building community in schools.* San Francisco: Jossey-Bass.

Sharrat, L. 1996. The influence of electronically available information on the stimulation of knowledge use and organizational learning in schools. University of Toronto: Unpublished doctoral dissertation.

Sitken, S. 1992. Learning through failure: The strategy of small losses. In *Research in Organizational Behavior* 14, ed. B. M. Straws and L. L. Cummings. London: JAI Press.

Smylie, M. A., and Crowson, R. L. 1996. Working within the scripts: Building institutional infrastructure for children's service coordination in schools. *Educational Policy* 10, 1: 3–21.

Starrat, R. J. 1991. Building an ethical school: A theory for practice in educational leadership. *Educational Administration Quarterly* 27, 2: 185–202.

Stringfield, S. 1992. Research on high reliability organizations. Paper presented at the International Congress for School Effectiveness and Improvement. Victoria, British Columbia.

———. 1995. Attempting to enhance students' learning through innovative programs. *School Effectiveness and School Improvement* 6, 1: 67–96.

Wagner, R. K. 1987. Tacit knowledge in everyday intelligent behavior. *Journal of Personality and Social Psychology* 52: 1236–47.

Walberg, H. J. 1984. Improving the productivity of America's schools. *Educational Leadership* 41, 8: 19–27.

Walker, K. D. 1995. Perceptions of ethical problems among senior educational leaders. *Journal of School Leadership* 5, 6: 532–64.

Watkins, K. E., and Marsick, V. J. 1993. Sculpting the learning organization. San Francisco: Jossey-Bass

Watson, T. J. 1996. How do managers think? *Management Learning* 27, 3: 323–41.

Wehlage, G. G., Rutter, R. A., Smith, G. A., Lesko, N., and Fernandez, R. R. 1989. *Reducing the risk: Schools as communities of support.* London: Falmer Press.

Weick, K. E., and Roberts, K. H. 1986. Collective mind in organizations: Heedful interrelating on flight decks. in *Organizational Learning,* eds. M. Cohen and L. Sproull. Thousand Oaks, CA: Sage.

Weiss, A. M. 1996. System 2000: If you build it, can you manage it? *Phi Delta Kappan* 77, 6: 408–15.

Willower, D. 1996. Inquiry in educational administration and the spirit of the times. *Educational Administration Quarterly* 32, 3: 344–65.

CHAPTER THREE

Value Orchestration by the Policy Community for the Learning Community: Reality or Myth

Olof Johansson and Paul V. Bredeson

Public education in Sweden and the United States has long been viewed as a critical social investment that fires the engines of economic productivity and social progress. As each country deals with the allocation of scarce resources to meet various economic, political, and social demands, educational policy makers at national, state, and local levels are pressed by their constituents to reconcile public expenditures with measurable outcomes. Despite differences, particularly in national and local political and educational contexts, both Sweden and the United States have shared many of the same school reform agendas. For example, the development of national standards and curricula, educational restructuring, the decentralization of authority, and the use of standardized assessment practices are among the reform initiatives put forth to improve education and make educators more accountable.

The purpose of this chapter is to describe educational leadership as a transformative link between two distinct, yet interdependent, communities: the school policy community (state and federal legislatures and officials) and the school learning community (all professionals and other staff members who work in schools) (O. Johansson 1996). Our presentation is primarily grounded in a theoretical argument supported by selected descriptive frameworks. Our discussion addresses values orchestration, decision making, policy implementation, organizational cultures and change, and leadership theory. To support our argument, we will use findings from two investigations that examined the impact of educational reform initiatives in Sweden and in the United States on superintendents' leadership. These cross-national studies of the superintendency addressed the following questions:

- In what ways have educational reform initiatives in Sweden and the United States affected educational leadership in school districts?
- How have various school reform initiatives affected the work-role priorities of educational leaders?
- In what way(s) have educational reform initiatives affected superintendents' traditional sources and use of power in their districts and communities?

- Have changes in superintendents' traditional sources of power as educational leaders affected superintendents' ability to plan and implement school reform initiatives locally?

Empirical Base: Two Studies of Superintendents

Three hundred ninety-seven superintendents in a large Midwestern state and 280 superintendents in Sweden participated in the study. Each completed a three-page written questionnaire. A total of 326 surveys, representing 82.1 percent of district administrators in the state, and 207 (74.2 percent of all superintendents in Sweden) returned survey data for analysis. The questionnaire was developed, piloted, and refined in earlier studies of the superintendency (Bredeson 1996). The questionnaire consisted of four types of survey items: demographic information, open-ended queries, Likert-scaled items, and rank-order responses. For use in Sweden, the questionnaire was translated, piloted, and revised for the mailed survey.

Because school governance structures and the work of superintendents share many similar features, we were able to translate all survey items and aggregate the two data sets for meaningful cross-national comparisons. Data analysis was completed in stages. First, we examined each data set separately. After preliminary analyses of each data set, we then made cross-data set comparisons. Numeric data were analyzed using descriptive statistics, correlations, and tests of difference where appropriate. Content analysis and constant-comparative data analysis were used to analyze open-ended responses.

The role of the school superintendent is deeply rooted in the history of public education in Sweden and the United States. Despite the importance of this formal leadership position, researchers describe the superintendency as an under-researched area (Glass 1992; Crowson and Glass 1991). This is not to say research on the superintendency is nonexistent. Recent studies include investigations of leadership skills (Hoyle, English, and Steffy 1990); the discretionary choices of superintendents (Lidstrom 1991); gender, politics, and power relationships (Brunner 1995a, 1995b; Tallerico, Burstyn, and Poole 1993); demographic profiles, career patterns, preservice preparation and training, and work roles (Glass 1992; Carter, Glass, and Hård 1993; Murphy 1994; Wimpelberg 1988; Crowson 1987); and the instructional leadership of superintendents (Bredeson 1996; Cregård 1996; Faber 1994; Floden, et al. 1988; Johansson and Staberg 1996; Johansson and Kallos 1994; and Murphy and Hallinger 1988). From these investigations rich descriptions and better understandings of the work of school superintendents are emerging. However, there continues, to be a paucity of empirical research on contributions of superintendents as instructional leaders in their districts. There are only limited descriptions of superintendents' beliefs about their work and how they put those beliefs into practice within highly dynamic and often highly politically charged environments. Our chapter focuses on educational leadership, especially that of the superintendent, as the transformative link between the school policy community and the school learning community.

Public education as a social institution is supported by two major communities: the school policy community and the school learning community. We use the term *community* to describe a set of orientations aimed toward a special set of social objects and processes. Both are guided by democratic values. Communities change over time, and the building of democratic communities, policy and school, is an ongoing process linked to the development of the larger society. As formal educational leaders, superintendents and principals are part of the learning community because their main task is not to create policies but to implement policy decisions made by the policy community. A persistent myth apparent in the reform literature and implicit in the initiatives of state and federal governments is that policymakers, because of their legal authority and hierarchical structures, have the capacity to govern local school learning communities and that policy decisions directly influence and are tightly linked to the dominant values and actions of educational professionals and the educational process. We do not question whether the policy community affects schools and the people in them, especially through their fiscal control and powers of mandates. However, we believe, that the dominant values and norms that govern daily life in schools are created within the educational community and transferred to the political policy community. The policy community very seldom has sufficient knowledge and information on how to confront and convince the prevailing school culture of the benefits of reforming the schools. The reforms that have been successful are those that were formulated by, and came out of needs in, the learning community (Johansson and Staberg 1996; Sarason 1995). It is clear that educational values remain rooted in the particular roles that leaders and educators inhabit and that the ideals and commitments of the educational activities are governed by the local school culture. If one accepts this notion of a relationship between the school policy community and the school learning community, then the role of the educational leadership—superintendents and principals—becomes very central in understanding how educational reforms and policy decisions are promulgated and subsequently implemented. Accordingly, we now address the role of the political cultures and core values and their potential for influencing the work of educational leaders.

Political Cultures and Core Values

The way in which the term *political culture* is defined, when studies of educational leadership are designed, strongly influences the extent to which political effects on the school community can be detected. The "simpler" the definition of the term used, the more likely that we will find evidence of transmission of certain basic rules for coexistence in a learning society. According to socialization research, the process of socialization, leading to an individual's knowledge, values, and behavior in response to political issues, can be explained by a number of personal and contextual relationships. The following groups of independent factors are usually identified: agents, contextual variables, and individual characteristics. This is a complex field of research, and most of the variables within each group are interrelated (Johansson 1991). In addition, each of these variables can influence some specific component of the political culture. In analysis, the mutual relationships between the factors give rise to conflicting interpretations of the situation in the dependent variable *political culture.* As a consequence, it can be difficult to identify "clear" relationships and to verify general patterns. The results are always based on a scientific reduction of the real world (Johansson 1995; Inglehart 1990).

It is difficult, but perhaps not impossible, to determine which of these independent variables influence an individual's political culture. However, it is even more difficult to explain how, for example, political orientations arise in general. The same problems occur if the intent is to explain the nature of school culture instead of political culture. School culture must be viewed as a subculture within the political culture of a country, region, or city and maybe also as a local unit (Berg 1995).

We can also identify the influence of other subcultures on the school culture. These include subcultures such as the parents' culture, the youth culture, the local culture, the regional culture, the national culture, and the international culture, as well as, recently, the Internet culture. As these subcultures interact, there is an interplay among the values each holds.

All these subcultures influence each other and, in turn, the local school culture. Despite the complexity of all these different effects and interactions, we can distinguish core values, values near the core, and values distant from the core (Lundmark 1995). Core values are understood as those values that define the essence of any culture. Values near the core are values that are not accepted universally within a culture. They may be expressed as core values by different groups, but they are not viewed as core by all (see figure 3.1). These near-core values are advanced from time to time in different policy documents. Near-core values are in a constant struggle to become core values. For example, a typical core value in education can be that good reading and mathematical skills are important for all students. A near core value might be the idea of school democracy. School democracy as an idea is accepted by most people working in schools, but too often it can be described in terms of true and false consensus (Lundberg 1996). Expressed in another way, it is politically correct to support school democracy

Internet

*School
Community*

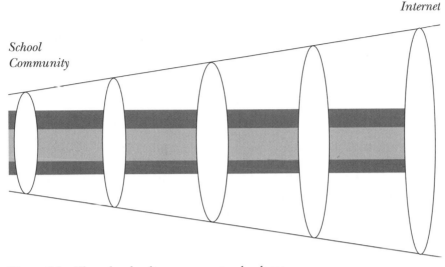

Figure 3.1   The school culture seen as a subculture
Note: Core values, values near the core, and values far from the core

as an idea, but it may not be easy to practice it in one's own classroom. In addition to these two groups of values, there are those values that are distant from the core. Such values sometimes challenge the democratic order or beliefs that most people hold in a society. These often represent major philosophical and paradigmatic realignments. Values that underlie our understanding about the relationship among racial groups are an example in this sector of the model. Radical changes in these values dramatically alter social norms, structures, and individual belief systems. Next, we discuss the interplay of values between the school policy community and the school learning community and its impact of school reform.

Values, Policy Making, and School Reform

Theories of democracy will highlight core values such as freedom of thought, freedom of speech, freedom of political ideas, and the right to vote in open and free elections. These preconditions for democracy must be fulfilled before we can talk about a democratic system. We see democracy as a method to make decisions. In the same way, binding decisions for schools are made by the school policy community. Some of the decisions are decided at national levels, while others are made at regional or local levels. The basic idea is that a policy decision leads to implementation and that what results from the implementation of the policy is what the policy maker originally intended. This is an idealistic way of looking at political decisions or what we call "the myth of democratic culture." This value orchestration model can work only if the policy community and the learning community embrace identical values and the same culture. Only then is it likely that policy and practice are isomorphic (O. Johansson 1996). Though certainly possible, it is generally unlikely. Thus, we need to examine how to bridge the distance between the two communities. The strength of this bridge, transformative educational leadership, is of vital importance to the outcomes of the policy implementation process in education.

If one were to focus only on the content of decisions, it would appear that most decisions from the policy community do not focus on values. However, policy-level decisions, do tend to be value-based, and this is what makes educational reform initiatives so difficult to implement. In the myth of the democratic culture described previously, we argued that in an ideal situation the school policy community and the school learning community would share the same values and culture. This would establish a value bridge between the two communities. There is much empirical evidence that demonstrates that this is not the case. In reality, what occurs is illustrated in figure 3.2: the political community makes a policy decision. This decision is then passed on to the school learning community. If the learning community has a different set of values and culture, it thus views the original policy through a different set of lenses. These lenses change the substance and perhaps even the intent of the original policy. Our visual represents this transformation in terms of white to gray. What is clearly a white policy from the perspective of the policy community is varying shades of gray to professionals in the school community. The effect of the gray learning community

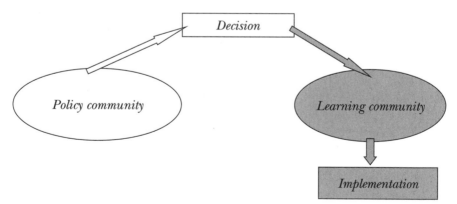

Figure 3.2   Value orchestration by the policy community for the educational
community

culture is that the decision is implemented as gray, not white as originally intended by the policy community.

Certain decisions by the policy community are least likely to be implemented in the intended way. These are decisions that challenge existing values and norms of the school learning community and its culture (Johansson and Kallós 1994). Specific examples might include policy decisions such as those requiring teachers to work in teams, teachers being expected to promote pupil democracy, matters relating to student diversity, special program mandates for children with disabilities, and standardized curricula. These examples are issues that the policy community has argued about for many years. For example, in Sweden, the discussion on democracy in schools has been on the political agenda for the last fifty years and as late as last year there was a Government Commission on the subject (utbildningsdepartment 1997:57). What kind of reforms are readily accepted by the learning community? Many times these reforms are those that are academic in character, for example, more lessons/curriculum directed toward specific topics. In the United States, policy makers have asked schools to address pressing social problems such as environmental contamination, drugs, violence, and sexual behavior and morals. These are areas that have received significant attention in schools both in Sweden and in the United States in the last ten years. However, what may be seen as a clearly stated policy by policy makers, one that is unfunded or simply poorly resourced, plays out quite differently within unique school learning communities across the countries. As each of these issues is examined through the lenses of local values, what becomes evident is that there commonly is a disconnection between the policy community and the school learning community. Even an educational policy issue that should be less hotly contested, the introduction of computers and instructional technology (IT), for instance, can have great difficulty surviving the journey from policy to practice. When computers were first introduced into schools about fifteen to twenty years ago, their presence was often very threatening to teachers. Not surprisingly, the first attempts to enrich classroom experiences by introducing computers in schools was largely a failure. About ten years later, however, the members of the school learning community, not to mention the larger society, had become increasingly familiar with computer technology in their everyday lives and were less threatened by it (Luke 1996). Despite personal limitations, most educators have now come to see the importance of introducing and using computers in schools. Today IT is integrated into most school curricula. The important lesson here, from our point of view, is that the original policy decisions to introduce computers into the work of teachers and children was problematic and remained only modestly implemented until the school learning community decided it was ready, able, and committed to the use of computers in schools.

Is the intention of the policy maker
to implement the decision?

		Yes	No
Does the learning community believe that the policy makers want to implement the decision?	**Yes**	A Real Decision	Symbolic decision seen as a RD
	No	RD seen as a symbolic decision	A real symbolic decision

Figure 3.3   Typology of political decisions

Next we would like to consider the way school professionals view the intentions of the policy makers (Gustafsson 1983). Figure 3.3 is a typology representing two dimensions influencing the successful implementation of policy into practice. The horizontal dimension represents whether or not it is the intention of the policy maker to really implement the decision or, whether the decision was only symbolic and largely politically expedient. The vertical dimension represents educational professionals' beliefs about the intentions of policy makers.

Figure 3.3 describes four different relations between the policy maker and professionals in the school learning community. Only one cell contains a real decision, that is, the policy maker intends to fully implement the decision, and the school learning community believes the policy maker intends to implement the decision. An example of a real decision might be the decision to provide extra financial support to schools to benefit children with special needs. The policy is clear, financial support follows, new practices are implemented, and the results are monitored by policy makers for fine tuning and improved practice. We believe real decisions are ones that most closely align policy initiatives with school-level practices. The remaining three cells represent decision situations with less promising outcomes. Unfunded mandates, often employed by policy makers to influence other communities, are examples of "real-symbolic" decisions. Special education legislation, personnel policies in the United States and in Sweden, and internationalization and cooperation between industry and schools are all examples of real-symbolic decisions. Both policy makers and practitioners know that the decisions are more rhetoric than real. One of the interesting features of political systems that rely heavily on real symbolic decisions is the proliferation of policy statements. Real symbolic decisions are the currency of profligate politicians. Politicians find it easy to add on more and more goals and objectives to the list of what the learning community should be doing especially when they do not need to provide the money for goal fulfillment in relation to their decisions. In addition, policy makers can tell the general public that they have dealt with the issue, leaving schools holding the proverbial bag. Later, when politicians need to find someone to blame, schools and the professionals who work in them become easy scapegoats.

More problematic are the two remaining cells of the model. Let us illustrate by taking one of the symbolic decisions mentioned above, cooperation between school and industry. In reality, the policy community has no intention of implementing its decision nor does it provide any funds to the schools to do so. However, in some schools there are professional educators who take the policy charge seriously and believe the policy makers truly want full implementation of this initiative. For example, a local superintendent and principals might be very interested in questions relating to cooperation between schools and industry. The administrators, believing that the policy maker wants to implement the decision, will work hard to be successful despite the lack of funding to support it. Administrators will find money in their own organizations and even reallocate funds from other activities in their schools to implement what they believe the policy makers want. This is an example of a symbolic decision seen as a real decision. Finally, there are real decisions seen as symbolic decisions. Here, the professionals in the school learning community incorrectly assume that the policy maker is acting symbolically, they ignore the intention of the policy. In such cases, teachers and other school professionals feign interest, but they cleverly avoid implementation. Educators have grown used to policy makers who lose interest or lose track of various initiatives, and there is no point in redesigning their work to conform to a short-lived, symbolic policy gesture.

Gustafsson used this model and found that "The insufficiency of public documents as sources of information about real intentions creates problems for the analyst trying to identify and analyze symbolic policy ingredients. Different members of a decision-making body might, for example, have various feelings about a decision and, as a consequence, vary with regard to seriousness, which makes it hard to offer a relevant general interpretation regarding the policy intentions of a decision-making body" (1983, 277). These are results that we also can verify in our survey data.

Leadership and School Change

Our discussion to this point has examined the impact of culture, values, perceptions, and intentions on the relationships between policy making and policy implementation. Next, we will examine the role of the educa-

TODAY   FUTURE

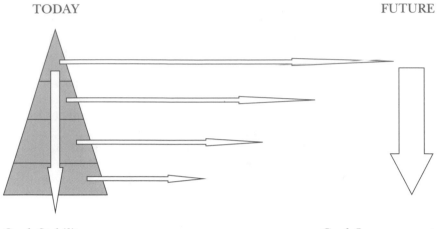

Goal: Stability   vs.   Goal: Improvement

Figure 3.4   Administering stability or leading change

tional leader and his/her role(s) in dealing with various policy initiatives and how (s)he translates those directives into local school change initiatives. Figure 3.4 illustrates the relationship between educational leadership and organizational change. Every school organization can be described in hierarchical terms: the school board at the top, then the superintendent, followed by the principal, teachers, other staff, and students. Organizational theorists often describe schools as maintenance-type organizations. In general, their primary purpose is to preserve and pass on to future generations existing social values and structures. Thus, schools inherently tend toward stability, with most of their resources, activities, and decisions used for that purpose. The policy community often sees organizational stability as good education. With stability as its guiding principle, good education is often reduced to an equation calculated in terms of satisfied parents and pupils, a balanced school budget, and satisfied teachers. This creates a paradox for schools. They are genotypical institutions dedicated to social stability and the maintenance of extant social mores, while, at the same time, they are seen by policy makers as catalysts for change. This creates an interesting set of contradictions for educational leaders. How does a leader simultaneously maintain stability and create initiatives for school improvement and change? The development of national standards and curricula, educational restructuring, the decentralization of authority, and the use of standardized assessment practices are among the reform initiatives used to improve education and make educators more accountable. Yet each contains the seeds of contradictions. Within dynamic educational reform environments, the formal and informal roles of educational leaders, including both the superintendents and the principals in Sweden and the United States, continue to change from management roles to educational leadership roles. The traditional management roles and power relationships that have long governed the work of superintendents in public education are being renegotiated and reshaped. Begley and Johansson (1998) show that both Canadian and Swedish principals are still thinking as managers. In a study, they found that when solving critical school-related situations, by a six to one ratio principals used managerial arguments over educational arguments.

We stated above that every school organization can be described in hierarchical terms. The school board at the top, then the superintendent, the principal, and other school participants. The higher one's position in the hierarchy of the school organization, the greater responsibility that person has for future education improvements at the school.

If it is clear to people at the base of the organizational pyramid that they have as good ideas and knowledge about the need for future improvements as the people at the top of the organization, then the leaders have a problem of legitimization. In many local school organizations, a legitimization gap between the school board and the educational professionals can be observed. In the Swedish case, the new curriculum from 1991 gives more responsibility to the political boards of the school sector. One question that can be asked is Can these new tasks of creating local goals for the schools in a local school plan (LSP) as a part of the national steering system really be executed in an acceptable manner by the lay-leaders on political school boards? Johansson and Kallós (1994) argue that this is not the case. They discuss examples of local school plans from different municipalities and conclude that most of the plans do not follow the intention in the law. In another study, Johansson and Lundberg (1998 forthcoming) found that in 60 percent of all LSPs there was no connection between the goals described in the LSP and the school budget, also decided by the school board.

Against this background, it is obvious that the superintendent, who must be viewed as a senior leader in the organization, will have great problems if (s)he cannot control the board. In cases where the lay-people on the school boards accept the advice of the superintendent, the knowledge gap between the board and the professionals can be minimized or even hidden. Our data also point to the fact that most superintendents work too much, according to their self-reports, at practical administration and devote too little time to thinking about the future of their schools. The focus of the goals of the boards can best be described in terms of stability rather than improvement. Nevertheless, in a reform context, the visionary role for the superintendent is very important and, under most circumstances, is the foundation of developmental processes in schools. Most improvements in schools are incremental and do not occur as large revolutionary changes

(Fullan 1993). In such a context, the leadership capacity of the superintendent becomes very significant. In most school systems, the person holding
that position will be the guarantee for both stability and improvement. Our
survey data indicate that the instructional/visionary role of superintendents
is the least emphasized sets of leadership tasks. Of four primary instructional leadership types identified, the instructional visionary was the dominant leadership role for only 14 percent of Swedish superintendents and 12
percent of those in Wisconsin. The three most common instructional leadership roles for superintendents in Sweden and Wisconsin respectively were
instructional supporter (36 percent and 36 percent), instructional delega-
tor (33 percent and 26 percent), and instructional collaborator (17 percent
and 26 percent).

It is of vital importance that the superintendent or the principal have
an accurate perception of the work load of the professionals in schools
when visions and goals for school activities are being established. Unfortunately, all too often schools get into situations that can be described as an
overload of goals and objectives. In the Swedish case, it is very clear that
since the mid 1980s there has been an increase in goals and objectives for
schools, and, during the same period, there has been a decrease in budget
allocations to schools. Schools have been asked to do more with less money.
Within such a fiscally constrained environment, teachers are being asked to
improve pedagogical methods and pupils' performance.

To illustrate our point we will describe the Swedish system of goal
production for the national school system. The fundamental goals of the
national Swedish school system were set out in chapter 1 of the Swedish

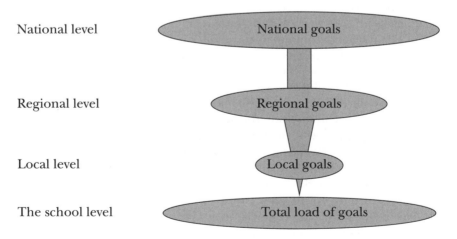

National level	National goals
Regional level	Regional goals
Local level	Local goals
The school level	Total load of goals

Figure 3.5   Overload of goals and objectives

School Act of 1985. The legislation states that education within each type of school shall be equivalent, irrespective of where in the country it is provided. In partnership with the home, education for young persons shall support the harmonious development of youth so that they become responsible persons and productive members of society. Education also shall take into account those pupils who have special needs. The School Act also contains regulations on pupils' rights and the obligations of municipalities regarding education.

In the old school system in Sweden, it was very clear that the principal was the key person for ensuring the availability of an equivalent school experience for all children. Principals were employed by the state, and their duties were highly regulated in laws and formal documents. The decentralization of the school system that has occurred since the mid-1980s has altered the role of principals. As a result of decentralization, principals continue to be responsible for national school standards and curriculum, but they are employed and evaluated by local authorities. Thus, the leadership role of the principal has changed dramatically. In the old system, the principal could always rely on support from the state for his or her decisions. When conflicts over curriculum and program issues occurred at the local level, principals could always fall back on the fact that various directives and policies were promulgated by the State and they were simply carrying out national curriculum mandates. Today, principals and superintendents spend considerably more time helping their local school board interpret and implement national curriculum standards, for the most part, without any real help from the State. If, for example, the municipal authority makes a decision to cut the budget for schools in such a way as to negatively impact children, the principal is caught between national standards and local control. Thus, administrators need the political skills to convince decision makers that their policy choices are having deleterious effects on the education of children in the municipality. The new decentralized educational system demands a greater political role for superintendents and for principals than did the old system.

The best way to illustrate the import of these changes is to consider the way in which the 1994 Curriculum for the schools describes the governing process. This curriculum policy document states that the goals and guidelines for education specified in the School Act, the curriculum, and the syllabi shall be elaborated in the local planning. The measures the municipality intends taking in order to attain national goals for the school should be clearly stated in the School Plan to be approved by the municipal council. Important to keep in mind here is the fact that the School Plan is approved by the municipal council and not by the school board. The school board is an appointed body of politicians at the municipal level, but the council is the only elected body at this level.

The School Plan is supposed to describe the measures that the municipality is going to pursue in order to implement the national goals. However, most school plans do not address the measures to be taken. Instead, most municipalities are identifying goals for the local school system in the School Plan, according to the Swedish superintendent study of 1995 (Johansson and Lundberg 1998 forthcoming). In only a few municipalities is there a direct correspondence between the school budget and the School Plan. The same study found that this is even more the case when the school plan has been developed by administrators rather than politicians.

In Sweden, the principal has the responsibility of guaranteeing that the school plan is actually applied in his or her school. A Local Work Plan is also required for the individual school, which should describe how goal-focused activities will be organized and carried out. This document and the School Plan tend to have a long shelf life but little correspondence to the daily activities in schools. Most of the time, the teachers do not accept the local documents as governing documents for their school. They see their existence at the local level more as compliance with a national policy mandate than as a guide to their pedagogy. This is a problem that some municipalities have now recognized and are trying to change (Johansson and Staberg 1996). Using research on successful strategies for policy implementation, some municipalities are beginning to redefine their responsibilities in relation to school plans and the national curriculum. Rather than spending so much of their resources on steering and control (managerial activities), they are shifting their emphases toward instructional leadership activities, school development, follow-up studies, and support. This shift represents an attempt to steer control away from the politicians based on research findings around the implementation process. Survey data (Bredeson and Johansson 1997) indicated that Swedish superintendents identified school development as their top administrative task. However, when they reported how they spent their time, school development was their third most important administrative task.

Finally, in the 1994 curriculum policy document, the state gave teachers the responsibility of drawing up learning goals together with the pupils, which in combination with the needs and preconditions of different groups of pupils provides the basis for selecting different working methods. We would argue that this is the most important planning in the school system. The learning goals are very seldom documented in a formal way and in most cases stay a private document for the teacher to share with pupils' and their parents when they are visiting the school. We would argue that even when the running of the schools of today is a responsibility of the municipalities, most teachers continue to look to the State for guidelines and support. Local municipalities' power over the schools is today linked to budgets and organization but not to the basic values and tasks of the school.

This might change in the future but, to achieve this, local politicians need to change from the traditional notion of political control to a political control based on a dialogue with school professionals around the School Plan and the Local Work Plans for the schools.

The myth that hierarchical governing works best in a system with control and evaluations of the professionals is too often contra-productive when it comes to school development and improvements of pedagogical methods and pupils performance (Johansson and Kallós 1996). The favored solution to these governance problems often has been decentralization. Why decentralization? There is no easy answer to this question. One answer can be the official one, which is based on knowledge from implementation studies that show that the state cannot regulate a school organization strictly, as the old system did. Even with centralized control and different governing bodies, it was difficult to uphold the national goals for the system because the conditions in the schools varied greatly. The argument put forward was that if the schools had clear goals and were to implement these goals without too many restrictive rules, the implementation result would likely be much better than in a tightly regulated system. A common argument here is also that decentralization is good for the local democracy because important decisions are moved closer to the people involved and sometimes are made with their participation. Another reason decentralization was appealing, one not often discussed in the political arena, is that the state could no longer afford a system where the law regulated how much money different schools should be given. The solution to that problem was to frame laws that provide block grants to the municipalities. In the block grant system, the portion intended for the school sector is unspecified. Through this tactic, the State has managed to lower the state cost for education and has forced the municipalities to take on a greater financial responsibility for education. The problem today is that, in many cases, the municipal board cannot afford to take on full responsibility. The result is a large variation in the budgets different schools receive. The education budget varies by location in the country and, of course, by the size of the municipality. A third reason the state moved to decentralize education was that it simply ran out of ideas about how to steer and govern schools. It had no good strategies for achieving school change in accordance with the decisions of the policy community. The learning community has become increasingly unresponsive to the old hierarchical top-down model of governance. The learning community has become too independent, and the goals of the state policies are no longer seen as important. Many of the policies are also challenging the old values of the school. For example, the state might mandate that teachers work in teams, a mandate that challenges the professional norms of privacy and autonomy. Another example might be a policy stating that schools need to increase parent involvement in the planning of all education. Thus, the only alternative left to the State is to focus on national curriculum goals and objectives for the education process and leave the governance and operation of schools to local authorities.

We know from research that the best way to induce teachers in schools to work toward a common goal is to show that educational leaders are interested in the project (Seashore Louis 1994). In a goal-driven model, the important task for the educational leader is to show interest in the work that the teachers are doing and often ask participants in the group how the process is developing. The focus of the leader who works in this way is on the process side rather than on the control side. To focus on control is to work from a top-down approach and concentrate attention on how decisions are implemented. Common questions in this perspective include the following: Are goals being accomplished? Are the professionals working in the way expected? Evaluations become a primary administrative monitoring tool for the State. However, such evaluations generally provide too little information too late to affect what local schools are doing. Thus, such monitoring by the state has done little to accomplish national curriculum goals. The official reason for political boards to link evaluations to their decisions is often that they would like to control the goal fulfillment of their top-down decision. We would offer another explanation, one seldom expressed openly, that is, *the primary benefit of evaluation is for protection of the decision made!* However, when politicians demand an evaluation, they are, at the same time, protecting their own decision and can always rely on the fact that their decision will be evaluated and that they can comment on the goal fulfillment in relation to those results.

Control of this kind has little to do with school improvement. If the role of the policy community and the educational leaders in the educational community has shifted from top-down control to providing support to enhance local success, the possibilities are greater that the work of leaders will effect the goal fulfillment of the educational process. The role of the leaders then is to transform the goals at different levels into their leadership roles so they can motivate the members of the learning community to work with the goals of the policy community.

Our focus in figure 3.6 is on developing the learning community. We would argue that too much emphasis has been put on the control side and too little discussion has concentrated on what kind of support processes are needed for successful implementation of different educational reforms or decisions. The figure represents a top-down model, but one with a more demanding focus on leadership. For a leader to exercise this kind of leadership, the figure posits that she must actively take part in the goal implementation process and also use the leadership position for a clear instructional purpose. A large part of this leadership must focus on goal motivation and

Figure 3.6   Transformation of goals via the leadership

vision building for schools. This form of leadership for change and school improvement is more difficult than bureaucratic leadership with a primary focus on organizational stability and control. To move away from a traditionally passive, top-down model toward a more active-support, top-down model of governance has implications for the way decisions are made. In an active supportive role, the leader will recognize and/or be told about problems and obstacles to the implementation of the policy decision. The leader then needs to take active part in the solution of the problems at hand. This will involve the leader in the process and she will realize that in some cases the only way to deal effectively with the situation is to become engaged at the political level. The leader then confronts political decision makers and describes how their decisions have negatively affected schools. The arrows in the figure suggest a reciprocal exchange of influence between the policy community and the school learning community. The exchange is mediated through the leadership of school superintendents and principals. Policy makers working without a close connection to the realities of school cultures very seldom have adequate knowledge and information on how to confront and convince the prevailing school culture of the benefits of re-forming the schools. The reforms that are successful are those that are formulated by, and out of needs in, the learning community (Johansson 1996; Sarason 1995).

Given that political reform decisions often fail to be implemented effectively and that there is considerable policy drift from the original intentions of political leaders, we suggest combining the ideas of the top-down

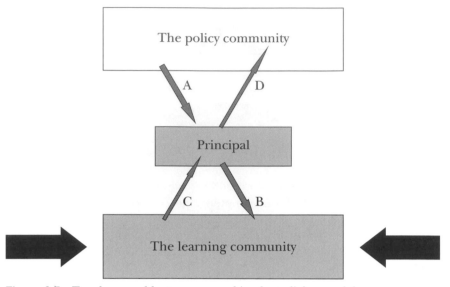

Figure 3.7   Top-down and bottom-up combined—a dialog model

and bottom-up analysis in a dialog model. In the dialog model, the policy community, in one way, gives away power because it commits itself to listen to ideas and proposals from the school learning community. When it finds ideas appropriate, it makes decisions that are supportive of proposals put forward by the school learning community. Research indicates that successful educational reforms are those that are formulated by, and out of, needs in the school learning community. Thus, decisions formulated in a reciprocal dialog between the two communities will have a greater possibility of attaining their intended educational goals. Much of the power over agenda setting and progress of the school community will still be in the hands of the policy community. However, a better understanding of the needs and interests of the learning community will increase the likelihood that political decisions are appropriate policy directives for the school learning community and that the policies will be successfully implemented, thereby bringing about the types of changes and improvements needed to enhance teaching and learning.

It is clear that educational values are rooted in particular roles that leaders and educators inhabit and that the ideals and commitments of educational activities are governed by local school culture. The school learning community can be seen as a closed community with a special culture, special rules, and special codes of conduct, which become insulating shells around the core of the culture. Political decisions that are made without knowledge of these cultural norms and values threaten the existing culture and, as a result, very seldom manage to penetrate those protective outer shells. Policy decisions not threatening to the culture and often with an academic focus are the kind of policy decisions that manage to penetrate the protective outer shells of the school learning culture.

Let us return to examples cited earlier in this chapter: policy decisions that stipulate curriculum content in the areas of environmental education and in drug and alcohol awareness. Since these decisions typically have had the support from politicians, top-down influence, and from parents, there was a much greater likelihood of the decisions penetrating the core of the school learning community. Decisions made regarding the introduction of instructional technology (IT) were less successfully implemented early on because there was not the combined force of top-down and community support forces required to penetrate the core of the school learning community.

When the first political decisions came in the early 1970s to introduce computers in schools, the decisions were often real decisions by the policy community, money for investments was supplied by the policy community, and money was also often set aside for in-service training of teachers. Despite all these prerequisites for high goal fulfilment of the decision, very little happened. In Sweden, many computers were bought but very few were used, and after some time computer rooms were moved to basements and forgotten. The explanation for the failure to successfully integrate IT into schools was that the learning community was not ready for the change (K. Johansson 1996). Interviews with educational leaders in Sweden suggest that in the 1970s very few teachers saw themselves as change agents, nor were they yet believers in computers in schools. However, when the last wave of policy decisions in IT came in the 1980s and early 1990s, the situation was very different. Children from middle-class homes already had computers at home. They already knew how to play games with computers, use graphics, write letters, and research papers on their favorite topics, produce their own newspapers, and, of course, surf the Internet. Again, we find a situation where the pressure to change is most expressed from parents and school children, that is, horizontal change forces. Those horizontal change forces created a thunderstorm-like effect in terms of the implementation of IT. The pressures from the side created demands for action at the top, and, in this case, not thunder but decisions and support for real change in schools. With the combined forces for change coming from the top (politicians) and from parents and students (horizontal) the demands for change and improvements became greater than the forces for stability (compare figure 3.4). Our point is that parents as a group have the ability to bring about changes if they use their horizontal force for the best interests of their children. In doing so, they also look for a different style of leadership from school administrators: leadership that supports educational change decisions rather than one that attempts to control all aspects from the top.

Conclusion

Let us return to the questions that guided our research. In what ways have educational reform initiatives in Sweden and the United States affected educational leadership in school districts? How have various school reform initiatives affected the work role priorities of superintendents and principals? The role of educational leaders in implementation processes is not only the application of formal power or control measures. As our model and discussion have shown, much more emphasis needs to be focused on the importance of school culture to successfully implement of educational policy. Superintendents and principals as educational leaders are the transformative link between the two communities that support and carry out public education—the policy community and the learning community. Superintendents are members of the learning community, and they are the chief educational officers responsible for implementing decisions made by the policy community. A dialogue and basic understanding between the two communities/cultures are prerequisites for successful implementation of current educational reforms.

References

Begley, P. T., and Johansson, O. (1998) The values of school administration: Preferences, ethics and conflicts. *The Journal of School Leadership*. 8, 4:399–422.

Berg, G. 1995. Skolkultur—Nyckeln till skolans utveckling, Göteborg, Förlagshuset Gothia.

Bredeson, P. V. 1996. Superintendents' roles in curriculum development and instructional leadership. *Journal of School Leadership* 6, 3: 243–64.

Bredeson, P. V., and Johansson, O. 1997. Leadership for learning: A study of the instructional leadership roles of superintendents in Sweden and Wisconsin. Paper presented at Annual Meeting of the American Educational Research Association, Chicago, IL, April 1997.

Brunner, C. 1995a. By power defined: Women in the superintendency. *Educational Consideration* 22, 2: 21–26.

———. 1995b. The promising intersection of power and ethics: The superintendency as transformed by Euro-American women. Paper presented at the 1995 Convention of the University Council for Educational Administration in Salt Lake City, Utah.

Carter, D. S. G., Glass, T. E., and Hård, S. M. 1993. *Selecting, preparing and developing the school district superintendent*. Washington, DC: The Falmer Press.

Cregård, A. 1996. Skolchefers arbete. Om chefskap och styrning inom skolsektorn. Göteborg: CEFOS.

Crowson, R. L., 1987. The local school district superintendency: A puzzling administrative role. *Educational Administration Quarterly* 23, 3: 49–69.

Crowson, R. L. and Glass, T. E. 1991. The changing role of the local school district superintendent in the United States. Paper presented to the annual meeting of the American Educational Research Association in Chicago, IL.

Faber, R. Z. 1994. Superintendents' involvement in curriculum development: Issues of influence in leadership. Unpublished doctoral dissertation, University of Wisconsin-Madison.

Floden, R. E., Porter, A. C., Alford, L. E., Freeman, D. J., Irwin, S., Schmidt, W. H., and Schwille, J. R. 1988. *Educational Administration Quarterly* 24, 2: 96–124.

Fullan, M. 1993. *Change forces.* London: The Falmer Press.

Glass, T. E. 1992. *The 1992 study of the american school superintendency.* Arlington, VA: American Association of School Administrators.

Gustafsson, G 1983. *Symbolic and Pseudo Policies as Responses to Diffusion of Power in Policy Science* 15, 269–87. Amsterdam, Elsevier Scientific Publishing Company.

Hoyle, J. R., English, F. W., and Steffy, B. 1990. *Skills for successful school leaders.* Arlington, VA: American Association of School Administrators.

Inglehart, R. 1990. *Culture shift in advanced industrial society.* Princeton, NJ: Princeton University.

Johansson, K. 1996. Nulägesbeskrivning av IT i undervisningen. Umeå Research Report, Center for Principal Development: Umeå University.

Johansson, O. 1991. Youth and Mass media: On the co-variation between mass media use and democratic values. *Politics and the Individual* 1, 1. Hamburg: Verlag Dr. R. Krämer.

———. 1995. Swedish reactions to the assassination of the Swedish prime minister Olof Palme. *Scandinavian Political Studies* 18, no. 4. Oslo: Scandinavian University Press.

——— . 1996. Value orchestration by the policy community for the learning community: Reality or myth. Paper presented at the Toronto Conference on Values and Leadership, October.

Johansson, O., and Kallós, D. 1994. Om rektorsrollen vid målstyrning av skolan. In *Segerstad (red) Skola med styrfart û en antologi om styrning av skolans verksamhet,* af Anita Hård. Uppsala: Rektorsutbildningen.

———. 1996. Tänk utveckling om effektivitet och kvalitet ur ett ledarperspektiv. In *Tänk utveckling û en antologi om skolans kvalitet och effektivitet û vad kan ledaren göra?* af Johansson and Kallos. Rektorsutbildningens skriftserie, nummer 3. Umeå, Umeå Universitets tryckeri.

Johansson, O., and Lundberg, L. 1998. Decentralization by the policy community to the learning community—A changed role for educational leaders. In *Local Education Policy: Comparing Sweden and Britain,* ed. A. Lidstrom, and C. Hudson. Houndsmills: Macmillan (forthcoming).

Johansson, O., and Staberg, U. 1996. Kommunal skolutveckling möjlig via den kommunala skolplanen? In *Tänk utveckling û en antologi om skolans kvalitet och effektivitet û vad kan ledaren göra?* af Johansson and Kallós. Rektorsutbildningens skriftserie, nummer 3. Umeå: Umeå Universitets tryckeri.

Lidstrom, A. 1991. *Discretion: An art of the possible.* Umeå, Sweden: Department of Political Science, University of Umeå.

Luke, C. 1996. Ekstasis cyberia. In *Discourse: Studies in the cultural politics of education* 17, no. 2. Oxford: Journals Oxford Ltd.

Lundberg, L. 1996. En skola som lär för livet. In *Tänk utveckling—en antologi om skolans kvalitet och effektivitet - vad kan ledaren göra?* af Johansson and Kallós. Rektorsutbildningens skriftserie, nummer 3. Umeå, Umeå Universitets tryckeri.

Lundmark, C. 1995. Towards a green democratic theory. Umeå, Department of Political science, Lic-dissertation.

Murphy, J. 1994. The changing role of the superintendency in restructuring districts in Kentucky. Paper presented at the Annual Meeting of the American Educational Research Association in New Orleans, LA.

Murphy, J., and Hallinger, P. 1988. Characteristics of instructionally effective school districts. *Journal of Educational Research* 81, 3, 175–81.

Sarason, S. 1995. The predictable failure of educational reform: Can we change course before it's to late? San Francisco: Jossey-Bass.

Seashore Louis, K. (1994) Beyond managed change: Rethinking how schools improve. *School Effectiveness and School Improvement* 5,1, 2–24.

Tallerico, M., Burstyn, J. N., and Poole, W. 1993. *Gender and politics at work: Why women exit the superintendency.* Fairfax, VA: The National Policy Board for Educational Administration.

Utbildningsdepartementet. 1997. *Värdegrundad Skola—idéer om samverkan och möjligheter.* Stockholm: Nordstedts Tryckeri AB.

Wimpelberg, R. K. May, 1988. Instructional leadership and ignorance: Guidelines for the new studies of district administrators. *Education and Urban Society* 20, 3: 302–10.

CHAPTER FOUR

Beyond the Veil:
Moral Educational Administration
and Inquiry in a Postmodern World

James Ryan

For many men and women in this day and age, the act of choosing, of selecting one or more options from a range of particular alternatives, is not as simple as it once was, or so it appears. Many who live in Lola, Montana, would probably support this view, although the respective combatants in the battle over the content of the school curriculum would have little hesitation in telling others which position one should choose (Anderson 1990a). In this small rural community battles lines were drawn over the teaching of values. On the one side were those who favored a values-clarification approach. On the other side were the fundamentalists. The former felt that providing a survey of value positions rather than indoctrinating students into one or more of these orientations was the way to go, while the latter believed that the teaching of "global perspectives" instead of patriotism and "moral reasoning" as opposed to traditional Christian and American principles was a subversive act and that those who taught these things were enemies of society.

Lola, however, is not the only place where value choices are complicated. Ryan and Wignall (1996), for example, describe a situation in a Canadian city where a school administrator must resolve an issue that involves value orientations with which she is not completely familiar or in complete agreement. While both she and her school district feel that practices of new Canadians, those who have recently immigrated to the country, ought to be honored, to do so in this particular case would violate some of her basic moral principles. While people in power eventually, and with obvious difficulty, came to decisions in both of these cases, there were no easy or straightforward solutions. To be sure, issues associated with these apparently irreconcilable positions will surface again. It goes without saying that, given the character of the times, as reflected in these and many other such messy, ambiguous situations, educators and those interested in education will increasingly be making moral judgments in a world where traditional ethical guidelines are often of little assistance in the matters at hand.

Judging from these and other similar situations in education and in other spheres, the context for making value choices is undergoing a shift. Where once humanity seemed to spend comparatively little energy sorting the preferred courses of action from the less attractive options, the range of potential alternatives now open to us and the increasing complexity of the choice-making process have impeded decisive and sure-footed action. Uncertainty rather than sureness and ambivalence, as opposed to faith, appear more and more to be the norm in what some would refer to as a "postmodern" world. Bauman, for example, maintains that it is precisely this uncertainty that characterizes what he describes as the "postmodern moral crisis."

> Ours are the times of strongly felt moral ambiguity. These times offer us freedom of choice never before enjoyed, but also cast us in a state of uncertainty never before so agonizing. We yearn for guidance we can trust and rely upon, so that some of the haunting responsibility for our choices may be lifted from our shoulders. But the authorities we may entrust are all contested, and none seems to be powerful enough to give us the degree of reassurance we seek. In the end, we trust no authority, at least, we trust none fully and none for long—we cannot help being suspicious about any claim to infallibility. This is the most acute and prominent practical aspect of what is justly described as the "postmodern moral crisis." (1993, 21)

Bauman (1993; 1995) goes on to say that this condition is not a new one. He maintains in fact that it has been with us for centuries, even though men and women have never quite realized it. One reason that the (privileged sectors of the) Western world have only recently become aware of what appears to be an increasingly ambiguous moral condition is that over the years certain individuals worked to cover up it up. Legislators played a significant role in these activities. Passing laws and making rules, these men were able to weave a veil over a chaotic world, deflecting attention from its increasingly fragmented and uncertain character. Men and women were, to a point, eager to believe their promises for an orderly utopia and accept that the thin film of order that they currently experienced was but a small measure of what was to come. Philosophy and science also played an important part in promoting the illusion of an orderly existence. Many at the time looked to scientists and philosophers in the belief that their conceptual schemes and techniques would be able to deliver on the promise of orderly and thereby moral conduct in states, institutions, and organizations. Not quite as apparent was the fact that acceptance of these supposed ambivalent schemes also served to mask the moral character of this order-producing agenda.

Until recently, such an approach to inquiry dominated the study of educational administration and organization. In the modern tradition and under the guidance of the tenets of the "theory movement" (see Greenfield 1986; Evers and Lakomski 1991), empirical research in the field for years revolved around supposed value-free methods of inquiry that were part of an order-producing quest to control the actions of men, women, and children (Ryan 1995). Many at the time believed that these methods were the only ones that were capable of generating the objective knowledge that morally neutral administrators needed to run and improve their respective organizations. Over the last couple of decades, however, as the belief in the possibility of fashioning a universal moral order dissipated and the veil lifted on a rather chaotic world, the popularity of this particular approach has declined. Despite the fact that there currently exists no shortage of approaches to and methods of inquiry in the field, a vacuum of sorts has surfaced. It revolves around at least two unanswered or open questions about values: What is, or should be, the purpose of inquiry in the field? And How does it or should it relate to the moral nature of administration and organization of schools in an increasingly fragmented, ambivalent, and uncertain world? This chapter is organized around a response to these two questions. In the end, I conclude that inquiry in the field needs to be organized around efforts to help administrators provide the conditions that will allow all individuals and groups in their school community and in the wider community to *search out, understand, critique* and *create* moral forms of life.

Before I get to this task, however, I provide some background detail. First, I trace the emergence of instability in the move from a premodern to a modern world. Reactions to this uncertainty are also noted. Next, I show how efforts to legitimize inquiry in educational administration followed the patterns established in these reactions and how work by Greenfield (Greenfield and Ribbins 1992) and Hodgkinson (1978; 1983) led the way in piercing this veil of order. A description of contemporary conditions and an account of their influence on the emergence of the postmodern moral crisis, referred to by Bauman (1993), follows. Finally, I offer one option to help educators deal with the difficult value issues that they face and outline the role that inquiry can play in such a process.

From the PreModern to the Modern

For most premodern individuals, morality did not constitute a problem, nor was it generally something upon which they reflected (Bauman 1993). People of this time did not concern themselves with value issues for at least two reasons. The first was that the range of choices open to men and women was decidedly limited. This was particularly true in tribal societies. Groups in these societies operated as small, relatively cohesive units. They took part in comparatively limited (as least by later standards) life-sustaining activities, and their socialization practices were generally successful in inducting the young into unambiguous and uncomplicated social orders (Durkheim 1964). The oral manner in which they passed on their traditions, interpreting the past from the prism of their particular version of the present, allowed these people to avoid the dissonance that was to plague literate societies of the future, which would come to rely on permanent records (Goody and Watt 1968). As premodern societies evolved from hunting to farming pursuits, the range of options for men and women increased but nevertheless continued to pale in comparison to those that would be open to future generations.

Another reason that morality was not a going concern was that individuals believed that life as a whole was first and foremost a product of Divine creation (Bauman 1993). Spirits, gods, or God presided over human pursuits. Free will was not always a luxury afforded individual men and women. Traditional nomadic hunting groups, for example, did not attribute the actions of individuals—whether they contributed to the welfare of the group on not—to individuals themselves. Rather, they believed that in the final analysis it was the spirits who made these acts possible (Henrikson 1973; Ryan 1988; Riddington 1989). The premodern Christian world also saw morality as divinely determined. According to Bauman (1993), free will, if it existed at all, meant the freedom to choose wrong over right, that is, breach God's commandments, depart from the way of the world as God had ordained it. However, being in the right was not a matter of choice. Indeed, following the customary way of life actually meant avoiding choice.

As the modern era dawned, morality increasingly became a concern, at least in some circles. This was due, at least in part, to the exploding range of choices available to men and women and the declining power of spiritual beliefs. Many of these changes can be traced to technological developments. Technology made possible large-scale changes in the means of production and advancements in communication and travel. The migration of people to towns and cities and ocean-going travel brought together men and women from very different traditions, exposing them to ways of doing things that were often very different from their own and of which they were not previously aware. More than this, however, the routine mass production of goods was to disrupt forever the relatively stable and enduring life patterns and cycles that had existed in the past. Marx (1954) contends that capitalism engendered a way of life that was inherently unstable and unpredictable. The competitive nature of the market system, he believes, encouraged producers to constantly seek out new markets, new sources of raw materials, fresh labor power, and new sites for production. Indeed, the struggle to maintain profitability sent capitalists off to explore all kinds of possibilities. The innovation that was part of this process in turn exacerbated instability and insecurity as producers shifted masses of capital and workers from one production line to another in the race to sustain a competitive edge in fulfilling perpetually changing consumer wants, tastes, and needs (Ryan 1995).

The move to a more secular world view also had an influence on awareness and attitudes toward morality. As new explanations about existence surfaced, some capable of predicting the future, the divine world view faded. Many now believed that divine powers had considerably less power over human conduct than was previously accepted. As the modern era bloomed, "man" was born (Foucault 1970). In others words, people, at the time, came to believe they were self-conscious, autonomous beings, endowed with free will and capable of acting on their own. Gods no longer pulled the strings or provided clear-cut sets of alternatives for beliefs and practices. Now, many men and women accepted the fact that they were responsible, to a much greater degree, for their own actions and choices (Bauman 1993). These developments proved to be a cause for concern among certain groups. Indeed, the expanding diversity in the seventeenth and eighteenth centuries produced anxiety, particularly among certain privileged individuals who stood to lose their wealth, their land, and their power. They were convinced that the volatility of ordinary people's erratic habits represented a serious threat to their interests. As a response to this perceived danger, these people and their sympathizers stimulated and circulated a discourse of fear, one that prepared the way for legislators to create order by passing laws that were designed to regulate the actions and the morality of populations on a comparatively large scale. Bauman refers to the fear mongering associated with this legislated morality.

> This is what the fear-mongering age of legislation prepared us to expect. The strategy of order-building inevitably spawns a no-alternative, without-us-a-deluge policy. It is always our type of civilized life, or barbarism. A replacement for this order is total randomness, not another order. Out there is a jungle, and the jungle is frightening and unliveable because in the jungle everything is allowed to happen. But even that unspeakable horror of the free-for-all was represented by the fear-mongering propaganda of the civilized order as "the law of the jungle." In the age of built-up order as and of order-building, the entity most difficult, nay impossible to contemplate was a world in which there was no "order"—however spurious, contorted or perverse. (1995, 36)

Scholars also played a role as they responded to the fears of the builders of a now godless order. They looked not to legislation but to systems of thought to provide order and hope for humanity. These European men set about this task by, among other things, seeking out universal forms of morality and securing them with foundations. They also proceeded with their order-producing agenda by generating schemes that supposedly would allow humanity to control its natural and social environment. The scholars of the time believed that scientific techniques eventually would provide men and women with the power to predict and control the future so that they would be able to secure this universal morality, and in so doing, achieve human emancipation and enrich daily life. As we all know, however, science has not yet lived up to its promises. In the interim, though, science and the legislation designed to create order have managed to cover up the diversity that some believe threatens the human condition. Along with society, institutions, routines, images, structures, and managerial principles, the hope that accompanies science's promises and its conceptual apparati, have for years cast a thin veil of order over what Bauman (1995) believes is an inherently diverse, if not chaotic, world. Science has played a role (if not practically, then conceptually) in quashing this diversity, ironically by purporting to produce objective, that is, value-free knowledge. In doing so, however, it disguised the moral nature of administration and organization and the sources of its moral power. Nowhere has this been more apparent than in management studies, and by extension, inquiry in educational administration.

Creating and Piercing the Veil

Herbert Simon's (1945) classic work *Administrative Behavior* was to play a decisive role in casting a veil over the fundamentally moral and often chaotic world of educational organizations as scholars in educational administration looked to his ideas to help them explore the world of administration. While Simon accepted the place of value in the world, he believed that the value side of life was not amenable to study. His solution then was to split values from facts and study only the facts. He believed that factual research, was possible if social scientists would concentrate on revealing how organizations worked, rather than formulating value-laden prescriptions for administrators, as a number of his contemporaries were in the practice of doing. Researchers then would convey this scientific, and thereby objective, knowledge of how members of institutions generally responded to various organizational arrangements to the administrators who would be expected to act on this information.

However, underlying Simon's scheme, was a particular view of organization and administration that ignored its contingent, often chaotic, and always moral nature. Simon assumed that organizations displayed an inherent order, although this may not have always been apparent to those who worked in organizations. Thus, it was left to social scientists to deliver on the promise of orderly institutions by uncovering the persistent patterns of organizational behavior. Simon also cast administrators in the role of morally neutral actors or moral ciphers. He assumed that as a matter of course they would apply the information that social scientists supplied, in their efforts to make their organizations more effective and efficient. He believed that there was little, if any, room for deliberation or choice in these matters, since he considered effectiveness and efficiency to be universal values. As this approach came to dominate inquiry in educational administration after its introduction through the "theory movement" in the 1950s, social scientists paid little attention to the moral side of administration. Many of them believed that to do so would have jeopardized the supposed objectivity of their inquiries and contaminate the results they produced. Instead, social scientists proceeded merrily along under the illusion that administration was primarily a rationale enterprise and that scientific inquiry into it would eventually help administrators engineer an orderliness that achieved the ultimate ends of efficiency and effectiveness.

The cracks in the foundation of this approach appeared early, although they were not always apparent to many social scientists blinded as they were by its supposed power and promise. Those who first noticed its impotence were administrators in the field who had contact with this new scientific vision. As Blumberg (1984) maintains, many practitioners who were aware of this science simply dismissed its findings outright. Among other things, they found it difficult to identify with the sterile characterizations of organizations displayed in these studies. In most cases, administrators discovered that these portrayals were a far cry from their messy school environments where they were required to constantly confront moral issues. While some of the architects of the theory movement later expressed their doubts about it (see for example, Halpin 1970), it was not until later in the 1970s that serious critiques of the underlying assumptions of the movement would emerge to pierce the veil that deflected the efforts of social scientists from the contingent and value-laden world of administration. At the forefront of this critique were Greenfield (Greenfield and Ribbins 1993), and Hodgkinson (1978, 1983).

While their respective emphases on varied aspects of administration may have differed, Greenfield and Hodgkinson were of a single mind about one aspect of administration—they both stressed that it is first and foremost a moral endeavor. Greenfield and Hodgkinson both emphasized that to ignore the moral side of administration is to seriously misconstrue the very character of administration. They believed that even though certain administrative acts may have a technical side, they also necessarily have an ethical side. To be sure, every decision an administrator makes involves some sort of value choice. And while empirical knowledge generated about organizations or administration, conducted within Simon's framework or not, may be helpful, this and other information always will be considered in the context of an administrator's value orientations before he or she comes to a decision.

Greenfield (Greenfield and Ribbins 1993) also looks to dispel the illusion implied in the theory movement's conceptual orientation that organizations display an underlying order. His argument is straightforward. If organizations are not things but social constructions, if men and women know few limits in their constructions and thus are likely to construct their realities (and organizations) in quite different ways, and act on values which not all share, then organizations would display anything but the unity and coherence that those working in the scientific tradition look to discover. While Greenfield would probably stop short of endorsing organizations as little more than settings for "wars of all against all" in the Hobbesian sense, he nevertheless sees them as resembling more closely battlefields than smoothly oiled and well-running machines. Because there is ultimately no consistent determining agency, men, women, and children in school organizations will not always follow constant and regular patterns of behavior. Each and every one of us possesses a unique nature, and as such, there can be no assurance that we will believe in, or do, the same kinds of things that our friends and colleagues do. Nor can there be any guarantee that we will do the same things from day to day, or respond to similar situations in consistent ways. To a large extent, we make our own realities and live them in our own particular, peculiar, and haphazard ways (Ryan 1997). In this regard, Greenfield (Greenfield and Ribbins 1992) maintains that "we live in separate realities. What is true for one person is not for another. In that sense we live in different worlds. Each of us . . . is an island universe" (127).

While critiques mounted by Greenfield, Hodgkinson, and others (Gronn 1982; Bates 1980) initially met with considerable resistance, the substance of their remarks eventually took hold. Today, most scholars in the field take for granted the notion that administration, along with inquiry into it, is a value-laden practice and that organizations do not necessarily conform to the orderly schemes designed by scholars. Social scientists are also more likely to acknowledge the heterogeneity of life not only in organizations but also in the field of inquiry and in life generally. As differences continue to explode around us, it is at long last evident to most scholars and practitioners that we are now well beyond the veil that once obscured the contingent, fragmented, and uncontrollably diverse nature of modern existence.

Beyond the Veil

Over the last two decades or so, changes in the social circumstances of many in the Western world continue to undermine efforts to promote a universal set of ethical standards. Technology is at least partly responsible for changes that enhance, rather than diminish, diversity. Among other things, technology has facilitated the circulation of people, goods, and services to and from all parts of the globe; made possible the increase in the production and circulation of knowledge; and given rise to the current consumption practices. Changes in communications and transportation capabilities and the development of a global market place now make it easier for men and women, products and services to cross what, at one time, were impenetrable boundaries. Now, more than ever, people are traveling from their countries of birth to take up residence in new lands. Increasingly, countries of the West are the recipients of immigrants from Asia, Africa, and South America. In particular, Great Britain (Owen 1994), Australia (Australian Bureau of Statistics 1995), the United States (United States Bureau of the Census 1995), and Canada (Statistics Canada 1993) continue to admit more and more people from these continents.

Also, material goods and services that were once native to other parts of the world are now available to those in the West. Most Westerners, for example, now have the opportunity to sample cuisine from all parts of the world. However, the West has exported its own products abroad; for example, MacDonald's restaurants provide fast food to citizens of many countries around the world. While these so-called differences are certainly visible to most Westerners, the various perspectives and values that accompany them continue to demand a legitimacy previously not extended to them. Now, more than ever, people from previously marginalized sectors--immigrants, people of color, aboriginal people, women, and so on—are speaking out, and their views and practices are increasingly being honored (Ryan 1995).

Technology also has has played an important role in the production and circulation of knowledge. Increasing numbers of scientists and social scientists now have access to instruments and techniques, which they believe can help them explore new areas in novel ways. They also have at their disposal the means to circulate their results to their colleagues and the general public. The electronic and print media frequently oblige scientists by broadcasting, telecasting, or printing results in which they feel their listeners, viewers, or readers would be interested. However, this process has not produced a unified body of knowledge. Rather, it has generated information that can be confusing and downright contradictory. Hargreaves maintains that

> the knowledge explosion . . . has led to a proliferation of expertise; much of it contradictory and competitive, all of it changing. This has begun to reduce people's dependence on particular kinds of expert knowledge but also created a collapse of certainty in received wisdom and established beliefs. Sunshine is good for you, then it is not. Alcohol is assumed to be detrimental to one's health until it is announced that modest levels of red wine actually *reduce* cholesterol levels. The reported release by the Colombian drug cartel that cocaine is high in fiber, is a joke that points to the disconcerting pervasiveness

and perversity of such scientific certainties. Science no longer seems able to show us how to live, at least with any certainty or stability. (1994, 57)

Complicating knowledge associated with science are the various other sources available to us. Magazines, tabloids, novels of all sorts, talk shows, radio call-in programs, soap operas, documentaries, sitcoms, news programming, infommercials, made-for-television movies, movies available in the cinema and on video, live theater, sports events, rock videos, and the Internet, to name a few of the more obvious sources, all provide us with various and often conflicting perspectives and views. The electronic media, and in particular, television, contributes as much as any of the other sources to the increasing diversity. They do so, not just by the sheer number of available networks and programs but also through the ways in which they finance themselves through the commercial programming that they run. In order to sell products, advertisers often deem it necessary to present and sequence images that may be interpreted in a number of different ways. Andersen (1995) maintains that a certain amount of ambiguity in meaning is necessary to excite and engage the viewer. Without gaps of significance, desire has no place to invest itself. Neutral or definite representations do not always hold our interest.

However, heterogeneity is not just the consequence of a surplus of meaning. The reason for the contemporary explosion of differences can also be traced to the fact that producers actively exploit the instabilities associated with diversity (Ang 1995). Indeed, the current culture of consumerism is founded on the idea that the constant transformation of identities through consumption is pleasurable. This state of affairs has emerged with the change in the nature of social hierarchies over the past century. The fact that identity is no longer tied as it once was to stable patterns of status such as class, for example, means that men and women are now impelled to perpetually reconstruct themselves (Ang 1995; Taylor 1991). For many, lifestyle provides the opportunity to shape one's identity and, in the process, acquire status and emotional fulfillment (Featherstone 1991). Now that lifestyle is no longer tied to traditional patterns of class, for example, consumption of the *symbolic* quality of material goods and services that constitute the adoption of a particular lifestyle provides men and women with the means to fulfill their deepest desires. More than ever before, men and women acquire pleasure from the act of carefully choosing, arranging, adapting, and displaying goods, services, and other pastimes. They acquire a degree of fulfillment as they become part of what their houses, clothes, professions, and leisure pastimes, including the television programs they watch, signify. However, producers scramble not only to search out new markets, but to create, often through advertising techniques, desires in consumers, which they then satisfy, or claim to be able to satisfy, through the products and services that they sell.

Responding to Diversity

The plain fact of the matter is that men, women, and children will increasingly have to come to terms with "otherness" and the accompanying diverse value perspectives that abound in the contemporary world. Schools, perhaps more so than many other institutions, will be at the heart of this encounter. We can see the beginning of it as more and more diverse constituencies within school communities vie for recognition and legitimacy and educators continue to find it more difficult to rely on traditional and/or universal standards to guide their actions. How then are educators, including administrators, to find their way in a legitimately diverse world? And what role are social scientists to play?

Evers and Lakomski (1991) provide us with one alternative to this dilemma. Like the Enlightenment pioneers, they believe that science eventually will be able to generate knowledge that will rescue humankind from the abyss. Accordingly, they feel that practitioners of their coherentist version of science will provide the basis for solving ethical dilemmas in a world where administrators must live with "a welter of conflicting moral viewpoints and the sheer complexity of administrative decision-making." Evers and Lakomski insist that "we justify or improve our values . . . by justifying or improving our total or global theory of the world" (1991, 185) In other words, as more and more theories of the world cohere with one another, they leave us with more and more reliable knowledge—knowledge that we can use to adjudicate one value position from another. While such theories are not in evidence today, Evers and Lakomski are confident that eventually humankind will build up a bank of these coherent theories to the point that they will be able to accomplish this task. In time, the knowledge generated by these theories will, supposedly, provide administrators with an appropriate normative framework within which they can sort out the value issues that arise.

Evers and Lakomski's ambitious effort falls short on a number of counts. Aside from the problems associated with the potentially infinite number of interpretations one can attribute to the concept of 'coherence,' particularly in this day and age, the questionable practice of lumping ethical and empirical claims together, and the appeal to empirical findings in support of all moral claims, their thesis demands that readers have faith in a future that seems to recede further by the day and that administrators (and educators) only play a marginal role in the value scenario. The expectation that science will eventually produce cohering theories appears questionable at best. If we look around, quite the opposite seems to be the case. The increasing number of theories about the world instead offer increasingly contradictory claims. Educational administration provides a good example. At one point, one perspective dominated the heuristic landscape. Now those interested in exploring the world of educational administration can employ any number of perspectives, many of which display irreconcilable differences with one another. Given this fact, one may well be justified in questioning whether coherentism has the ability to deliver on its rosy promises for the future.

While Evers and Lakomski differ from Herbert Simon in that they acknowledge the centrality of value in the administrative process, they also share with him his idea that the basis for action lies not with practitioners but with social scientists. Like Simon they believe that it is social scientists and not practicing administrators who will generate the knowledge that will help the latter make the best decisions for their organizations. Since we cannot rely on "folk theories," they expect practitioners to act on what they learn from social scientists and their more reliable scientific theories. Unlike Simon, however, Evers and Lakomski believe that this heuristic activity will show us the way to better values. Indeed, as social scientists build on their stock of theories that cohere with one another, they will produce knowledge capable of adjudicating value claims. However, assigning practitioners what seems to be a fairly minor role in adjudicating value positions would seem to ignore well thought-out criticisms that have been directed at the theory movement. Indeed, Greenfield (Greenfield and Ribbins 1993) and Hodgkinson (1978; 1983) have emphasized that neither technologies, techniques, nor methods, in themselves, can make decisions for us, nor can they sort out the right values from the wrong ones. This task, they maintain, will always rest with men and women. It would seem then that inquiry in the field of educational administration ought to acknowledge the primary role of practitioners in establishing and acting out value preferences. If anything, research in the field should be organized around efforts to help not only administrators but all those involved in the educational process to approach, understand, critique, and establish ethical principles rather than doing this for them.

Into the Postmodern

However, alternatives to a coherentist approach to morality in a postmodern world, seem often to be mired in an "us verses them" polarization. Adherents of one position commonly characterize opponents in ways opponents would not necessarily agree. Soper makes reference to such a caricature:

The caricature presents us on the one side with the dogged metaphysicians, a fierce and burly crew, stalwartly defending various bedrocks and foundations by means of an assortment of trusty but clankingly mechanical concepts such as "class", "materialism", "humanism", "literary merit", "transcendence" and so forth. Obsolete as these weapons are, they have the one distinct advantage that in all the dust thrown up by the flailing around with them, their wielders do not realize how seldom they connect with the opposition. On the other side stands the opposition, the feline ironists and revelers in relativism, dancing lightheartedly upon the waters of difference, deflecting all foundationalist blows with an adroitly directed ludic laser beam. Masters of situationist strategy, they side-step the heavy military engagement by refusing to do anything but play. (1995, 19)

Neither characterization would apply to most contemporary perspectives. In educational administration, for example, few today would employ religiously the "clanky mechanical concepts" referred to by Soper in their inquiries. Rather, many, like Evers and Lakomski (1991) and Willower (1994) to name just two, incorporate elements of positions critical of logical empiricist approaches to advance their own "softer" postpositivist perspectives. While adherents of various versions of so-called scientific approaches to the study of social phenomenan may feel that their ideas have been misinterpreted, this misrepresentation often pales in comparison to the ways in which so-called postmodern perspectives have been (mis)understood. Granted, (mis)representations of this sort are inevitably political in that they are designed, at least in part, to discredit the opponent's position while advancing one's own ideas. Even so, embedded in these characterizations may well be some genuine misunderstandings.

Perhaps the biggest misunderstanding may be that what are considered to be postmodern theories or ideas can be neatly grouped, like most other genres, by virtue of their most obvious characteristics. Perhaps more so than other "types" or "categories," a postmodern designation resists classification and the boundaries that accompany it. This is because many who are labeled in this way display many differences among each other. For example, there are many fundamental and irreconcilable differences among Foucault (1977; 1980), Baudrillard (1981; 1998; 1993), Lyotard (1984), Rorty (1982), and Bauman (1993; 1995)—scholars who commonly fall under the postmodernist label. While some (Squires 1995; Roseneau 1992; Burbules and Rice 1991) may attempt to separate broadly the various positions into extreme (strong, skeptical, antimodern) and moderate (weak, affirmative, postmodern) versions, these divisions fail to do justice to the complexities of the various positions contained therein.

Another common myth revolves around the idea that most postmodern approaches advocate an "anything goes" view (see, for example, Squires

1995). Advocates of more traditional scientific approaches, who are also critics of postmodern ideas, often pursue this line of critique. Adopting "either/or" stances, some reason that if scholars do not recognize or support universals or absolutes then they must by default see or advocate a meaningless world devoid of any sort of morality. If one cannot rely on universal values, the argument goes, then one must necessarily be thrust into a world where there are no standards of any sort. However, advocates of an "anything goes" philosophy are not easy to find, whether they are describing the contemporary human condition or speculating on the future. Baudrillard (1981) probably comes closer than most in this regard. Even so, in accounting for the current media-dominated condition, he describes not a world mired in chaos, but more-or-less persistent patterns of human interaction. He even goes so far as to recommend a particular course of action, although he is skeptical that it will have much impact (Baudrillard 1998; see also Ryan, 1998). Others, such as Foucault, Bauman, Lyotard, and Rorty, are even more definite about the history and current state of the world and with suggestions for action, although some of their arguments may well contain contradictions.[1]

Perhaps what alarms critics the most and prompts them to level the anything goes charge is that the above scholars insist that there are no foundations to which one can appeal to verify or substantiate a particular view or position. Indeed, the latter often expend much effort in dispelling the idea that there is a neutral, external touchstone or Archimedean point to which all claims can be referred for ultimate adjudication or a solid footing upon which conceptual edifices can be built. In making their case, they maintain that, to date, appeals to foundations have not yet, nor will they ever, settle outstanding value issues. What Foucault (1977; 1980) and others leave us with in the world of *Realpolitik* is that it is not appeals to foundations or cogent arguments in themselves that determine right and wrong, but power relationships between and among individuals, groups, and institutions. What this means is not that people cannot believe deeply in certain positions, or that there are no persistent moral standards, but that the prevailing values or arguments for them will always be tied to particular contexts where relationships of power operate.

One last misconception revolves around the notion that scholars or commentators on the postmodern condition can somehow remove or distance themselves from the power struggles that take place in the real world. If this is the case, then it is only the privileged that have this opportunity. Soper, for example, maintains that those who may hesitate in engaging in political quests may only do so because they

> know that the allure of a pragmatic dystopianism is a fantasy in which it is much easier to cocoon oneself if one is already enjoying comforts which figure

only in the utopian dreams of the African peasant, the street child in Rio de Janeiro or Iraqi political prisoner. They know that in reveling in the loss of progress is a Western metropolitan privilege which depends on living in a certain state of grace, a condition where no one is starving you, no one torturing you, no one even denying you the price of a cinema ticket or tube fare to the conference on postmodernism. (1995, 21)

The lesson to be learned here is that postmodern scholars, teachers, administrators, and most people in this day and age are engaged, through their actions, in some sort of political activity. No one can place himself above or apart from the rest of the world. We are all on the ground, so to speak, caught up in struggles to promote our views and to realize our interests, working—sometimes unconsciously—to maintain a status quo from which we profit or to change a system that oppresses us. Scholar or administrator, everyone takes a position and necessarily must speak from somewhere. However, all such positions and the values to which they are tied display characteristics that must be taken into consideration when helping educators, to deal with the difficult value issues that arise in the contemporary world. When providing options for educators we must keep in mind that moral positions are shaped by men and women, involve power relationships, and manifest themselves in particular contexts. Each of these conditions is elaborated below.

All values, moral standards, and ethical positions are human creations. This view follows from the idea that men, women, and children are responsible (often to varying degrees) for constructing the world in which they live. However, this perspective, is not, by any means, a new one. It has been around for some time. The idea that humans create their own world did not gather force, until championed by Enlightenment thinkers anxious to dethrone aristocrats and religious powers by illustrating that sources other than the divine were implicated in the actions of men and women. In time, social scientists and philosophers such as Weber (1968), Schutz (1967), Mead (1932), Berger and Luckman (1966), and others would lay the foundation for Greenfield (Greenfield and Ribbins 1993) and many in educational administration to emphasize that organizations were human inventions. If we are to follow this logic to its end, then we cannot but conclude that morality, like all other aspects of reality, is a human creation. Foucault maintains "What is good, is something that comes through innovation. The good does not exist, like that, in an atemporal sky, with people who would be like the Astrologers of the Good, whose job is to determine what is favorable nature of the stars. The good is defined by us, it is practiced, it is invented. And this is a collective work" (Weeks 1995, 190).

Following Foucault, Weeks (1995) contends that it is a mistake to seek the "truth" of values ethics and morality in history, theory, science, or some extraterrestrial source. On the contrary, he states, we constantly invent or re-invent moralities to face the contingencies of the present and the veiled landmarks of the future. Like Foucault, Weeks also stresses the collective nature of this process. Our notions of good are given meaning and validated not by single individuals acting on their own, but by traditions of belief and practice. In this regard, they are reviewed, reconstructed, and invented through collective experience. And because there are many different tradi-tions and collectivities, there are also many notions of the good.

All moral stances and value positions are the products of power relationships. If morality is a human construction, fashioned as men and women interact with one another, then it follows that those things that influence the out-come of these interactions will play a key role. Since power is one of, if not *the* central organizer of human interaction, it follows that power will deter-mine, to a great extent, the values that will take precedence in various contexts. Nietzsche was among the first to acknowledge this relationship. He maintains that "the judgment *good* does not originate with those to whom the good has been done. Rather it was the 'good' themselves, that is to say the noble, mighty, highly placed, and high minded who decreed themselves and their actions to be good, i.e., belonging to the highest rank, in contradistinction to all that was base, low-minded and plebeian. It was only the *pathos of distance* that authorized them to create values and name them" (1956, 160).

Bauman (1993) also emphasizes the role power plays in establishing morality. He contends, for example, that to be accused of immorality, and for the charge to stick, one first has to be defeated. In making his point, he cites cases where certain states were able to commit widespread atrocities and because of their powerful and/or victorious positions escape condem-nation. But power need not be seen exclusively as something that individ-uals or groups can possess.

Another way of looking at power is in terms of discourse. Foucault (1978; 1980), for example, believes that power works in many important ways through discourses, that is, through particular configurations of sym-bols, signs, and word patterns. In this view, power works not only on men and women as they become immersed in various discourses but through them as they use and act on the various associated terms, meanings, and values. In this sense, power infiltrates the thoughts, words, and deeds of people, shaping how they see themselves and the moral positions to which they subscribe, in ways of which they are not always fully aware.

Values and moral standards are always expressed and enacted within particular contexts. A final consequence of the socially constructed nature of life is that values are inevitably context-dependent. Social existence is such that moral-

ity is necessarily acknowledged, talked about, and put into practice in particular situations. The fluidity and increasing complexity of the contemporary
world dictates that contexts and the resulting meanings that are attributed
to any and all general moral principles can, and will, differ considerably
from situation to situation. Thus, while Smith (1988) feels that everything
participates in value, she nevertheless rules out the existence of unfalsifiable
use values, transcendental aesthetic values, or ultimate moral goods. She
insists that there are no statements of value that are not statements of
particular needs, desires, or preferences, whether of individuals or of
groups who find themselves in particular situations. "All values are entirely
contingent, always in the process of being transacted in the multiple over-
lapping economies of needs, desires and wants which make up human life
and history" (Connor 1995, 38). And while particular cultural groups may
display a certain limited form of regularity in patterns of social evaluation,
there will always be a certain degree of heterogeneity or "scrappiness" of
human interests that can never be simplified into any single principle of
value (Smith 1988).

Efforts to devise and impose such principles are likely to fall on the
rocks. At one time in Ontario, for example, the government established a
set of goals designed to reflect and guide the character of education in the
province. While many in the province probably would have agreed with
most of them, their general, and thus vague, nature meant little to those
who were responsible for acting on them at the school and classroom level.
Administrators and teachers who represented a wide range (of sometimes)
conflicting approaches to education inevitably could interpret them in
whatever way they saw fit (Ryan 1997).

Dealing with Moral Issues

The fact that educators have to make choices in a world where there are no
guarantees—where morality is a human creation dictated by past and current power relationships and manifested in fluid contexts of action—does
not mean that all value positions are meaningless. Quite the contrary. People and groups of people will continue, as they always have, to feel strongly
about various issues. What it does mean, however, is that we have to acknowledge that these positions are the products not of some transcendental or
external forces but of a series of contexts to which men and women have
been exposed to over a life time. What people believe in arises out of both
the immediate and more distant, invisible social relationships in which they
have participated and continue to engage—early socialization patterns,
educational experiences, peer associations, media sources, discourses, and
so on. One important task for educators in an increasingly legitimate plural-

ist postmodern world then is to recognize, understand, and critique the invention and articulation of morality and to help others, particularly those who may be at a disadvantage in such matters both in the school community and beyond, with these processes and with the act of actually creating morality.

Recognizing values. Recognizing particular values or systems of morality is not as easy or as straightforward as one might think. This is because much of what we do in our daily activities is a matter of routine, what Schutz (1967) sees as the product of our "natural attitude." What he is saying here is that we take much of our social activities for granted. Seldom do we pause to reflect on the nature and consequences of our everyday acts. And when we do choose to notice things or reflect on them, we can be very selective. As a consequence, only certain kinds of activities or events will merit our attention. In this regard, Anderson (1990) notes that throughout American history certain groups of often underprivileged people and their associated positions have been rendered invisible. He maintains that with a few exceptions more privileged sectors of the United States have failed to acknowledge the plight of African Americans and homeless people, among others. In his own work he has noticed how educators failed to acknowledge the salience of racial issues in their schools, even though he saw it as a pressing issue. The point I am trying to make here is that educators, like everyone else, often fail to recognize or acknowledge particular values because they seem to be a natural part of our social landscape. It is thus important for administrators, teachers, students, and others in educational communities to recognize the sometimes hidden or taken for granted values that guide their actions and the actions of others and which may have a substantial impact on everyone's lives.

Academics have much to offer educators in this quest, even though such assistance might not always revolve around social scientific inquiries. Social science nevertheless can provide useful information for educational communities. In particular, studies conducted from unique vantage points can provide them with new ways of looking at things (Anderson 1990b). Genealogies, for example, can provide practitioners with vantage points from which they can explore and reflect on various previously taken for granted values (Foucault 1984). The humanities also can provide educators with insight in these matters. They have the capacity to provide men and women with the opportunity to step back and critically examine surroundings that they may have previously taken for granted, and in doing so, view not only educational organizations but life itself, from new and exciting perspectives (Ryan 1994). Academics also can help educators by organizing or helping to organize activities that allow educators to undergo new or different experiences that allow them to reflect on their situations. While

Greenfield's (Greenfield and Ribbins 1992) idea of immersion in foreign life ways, as in the case of living for an extended period of time in a monastery, may be a better way of achieving this goal, long-term in-service that prompts individuals to examine their own place in the world may be the next best option.

Understanding and critiquing value systems. Critiquing various moral positions requires first not only that are individuals able to recognize them but also that they have the capacity to come to some understanding of the *processes* associated with the invention and articulation of these positions. Given that these are social processes, educators would do well to familiarize themselves with power dynamics which Foucault (1980), Bauman (1993), and others maintain often obscure the sources of morality. School communities can profit only by understanding the variety of ways in which power works on, and through, men and women as it disguises and produces value positions. Effective critique also involves an understanding of the outcomes of this process, that is, the consequences of certain moral stances. How, for example, might favoring European-based perspectives in the curriculum affect students who are not of this same heritage? Analyzing consequences in this day and age, however, is no easy manner. This is because, as Foucault (in Dreyfus and Rabinow 1982, 189) maintains, "People know what they do. They frequently know why they do what they do. But what they do not know is what they do does." In other words, we cannot always know what the ramifications of our actions are. Extending this line of thought, Bauman (1993) believes that moral impulses can easily lead to immoral consequences. He also contends that technology complicates our actions even more by displacing the means from the end. By feeding, clothing, and caring for our children in morally acceptable ways today, for example, we may well be bequeathing to them and their children a polluted, desiccated, depleted, and overheated planet.

Critical research has much to offer educational communities in their efforts to understand the processes associated with the construction of value. By looking to expose power relationships and the oppression that often accompanies them, critical researchers can offer a view of life that departs from portrayals that (sometimes implicitly) legitimate or provide support for the dominant way of seeing things. Researchers who are themselves members of marginalized groups or those who employ approaches that allow previously silenced voices to be heard can provide school communities with a take on the value-construction process from a perspective that is not always acknowledged (Kirby and McKenna 1989). However, efforts of this sort, should not always be conducted exclusively by academics. Instead, collaboration between scholars and practitioners can give way to a process over which the latter has a measure of control and which ideally can generate information that can be of practical use (Ryan 1995). Practitioners might want to combine these sources of knowledge with what they hear from those in their own communities, including those whose voices are not always acknowledged. The challenge for both academics and practitioners then is to design situations that might encourage a wide variety of different and sometimes contrary views to emerge. Only in this way can school communities take a hard look at the value options open to them and, after careful analysis, choose those that will benefit all members of the community.

Resisting and/or creating morality. Given that morality is a social construction, individuals and groups can resist and/or create the values by which they live. One way of initiating the resistant/creative process within the context of the considerable differences that characterize contemporary value positions within school communities is to engage in dialogue. Communicating with one another in this fashion provides a way for different positions to be circulated, analyzed, and discussed. While dialogues also may constitute an important part of critiquing value positions, the negotiations often associated with attempting to grapple with many different and conflicting positions can form the basis both for the resistance to certain value positions and the establishment, and eventual acceptance, of others. Weeks (1995) for example, maintains that morality is something about which we have to argue. Rorty (1982), Habermas (1987), Burbules and Rice (1991), and Beck (1995) also see value in continuing conversations, working towards ideal speech situations and dialoguing across differences. Among other things, Burbules and Rice (1991) believe that participants in these kinds of interchanges can develop a capacity to (1) construct one's identity along lines that are more flexible, (2) broaden one's understanding of others, and, through that, an understanding of oneself, and (3) foster more reasonable and sustainable communication practices. However, simply engaging in dialogue, however, is no guarantee that all positions will get the same hearing. One reason for this is that all dialogue takes place through the medium of discourses and institutional arrangements that reflect particular configurations of power. Such configurations often confer advantages on some participants while depriving others of a medium that allows them to adequately pursue their interests. It is up to the participants in these dialogues, and in particular the ones who enjoy certain advantages such as administrators, to constantly interrogate these communicative practices, searching out any potential disadvantages and making efforts to ensure that all individuals and positions get fair hearings. While there can never be any guarantees that all positions will be treated fairly or that agreements will always be reached, educational communities that undertake such a process will probably be better prepared to engage in negotiations, formulate policies, and eventually translate these into practices that work in the interests of all sectors of the community.

Academics have a role to play here as well. Among other things, they can provide information for educational communities on the dynamics of these communication processes. Researchers can generate knowledge about success, failures, facilitators, and barriers, including the often subtle ways in which certain groups and individuals get marginalized in such processes. Academics also can get involved with educational communities in organizing, monitoring, and evaluating efforts to include the various constituents of such communities in dialogue.

Conclusion

The increasing awareness and legitimacy of diversity in the contemporary world will continue to offer up many challenges for educators. Central among these challenges are issues that revolve around morality and value. Practitioners and scholars in education are now required to make decisions in, what is generally perceived to be an increasingly ambiguous moral climate. This does not mean that educators are powerless to act or that they cannot subscribe or refer to various resources. While they should view ready-made formulas for action with caution, educators would do well to follow a number of principles when making decisions in their respective constituencies. First, they need to keep in mind that moral positions are shaped by men and women, involve power relationships, and manifest themselves in particular contexts. With these things in mind, they can then work to recognize, understand, and critique the invention and articulation of morality and to help others, particularly those who may be at a disadvantage in such matters, both in the school community and beyond, with these processes and with the act of actually creating morality. These steps are not always easy or straightforward, and it is in this regard that academics have an important role to play in assisting practitioners in these endeavors. While these actions will not necessarily guarantee solutions to moral dilemmas, they nevertheless represent a starting point for educators as they attempt to come to grips with an increasingly morally ambiguous world.

Notes

1. Lyotard (1984) in fact may be accused of promoting a "nothing goes" position that contains an obvious contraction. On the one hand, he promotes a resistance to all attempts at closure. On the other hand he Lyotard imposes his own closure of sorts in the more-or-less consistent set of meanings that emerge from his own writings (See also Haber 1994).

References

Andersen, R. 1995. *Consumer culture and TV programming.* Boulder, Colorado: Westview.

Anderson, G. 1990b. Toward a critical constructivist approach to school administration: Invisibility. *Educational Administration Quarterly.* 26, 1: 38–59.

Anderson, W. A. 1990a. *Reality isn't what it used to be.* San Francisco: Harper.

Ang, I. 1995. *Living room wars.* London: Routledge.

Australian Bureau of Statistics. 1995. *1995 Year Book Australia.* No. 77. Canberra: Australian Bureau of Statistics.

Bates, R. 1980. Educational administration, the science of sociology and the management of knowledge. *Educational Administration Quarterly* 16, 2: 1–20.

Baudrillard, J. 1981/1994. *Simulacra and simulation.* Ann Arbor: University of Michigan Press. *Selected Writings.* Poster, M. Ed. Stanford: Stanford University Press.

Baudrillard, J. 1998 Selected writings. Stanford, CA, Stanford University Press.

———. 1993. *Baudrillard live: Selected interviews.* London: Routledge.

Bauman, Z. 1993. *Postmodern ethics.* Oxford: Blackwell.

———. 1995. *Life in fragments: Essays in postmodern morality.* Oxford: Blackwell.

Beck, C. 1995. Educating for moral and ethical life. In *Critical conversations in philosophy of education,* ed. W. Kohli, 127–36. New York: Routledge.

Berger, P., and Luckman, T. 1966. *The social construction of reality.* New York: Doubleday.

Blumberg, A. 1984. The craft of school ddministration and some other ramblings. *Educational Administration Quarterly* 20, 4: 24–40.

Burbules, N., and Rice, S. 1991. Dialogue across differences: Continuing the conversation. *Harvard Educational Review* 25, 3: 393–416.

Connor, S. 1995. The necessity of value. In *Principled positions: Postmodernism and the rediscovery of value,* ed. J. Squires, 31–49. London: Lawrence and Wisehart.

Culbertson, J. 1983. Theory in educational administration: Echoes from critical thinkers. *Educational Researcher* 12, 10: 15–22.

Dreyfus, H., and Rabinow, P. 1982. *Michel Foucault: Beyond structuralism and hermeneutics.* Brighton: Harvester Press.

Durkheim, E. 1964. *The division of labor in society.* New York: Free Press.

Evers, C., and Lakomski, G. 1991. *Knowing educational administration: Contemporary methodolgical contraversies in educational administration research.* Toronto: Pergamon.

Featherstone, M. 1991. *Theories of consumer culture and postmodernism.* London: Sage.

Foucault, M. 1970. *The order of things: An archeology of the human sciences.*

———. 1977. *Discipline and punish: The birth of the prison.* New York: Pantheon Books.

———. 1978. *The History of Sexuality: An Introduction.* New York: Vintage.

———. 1980. *Power/knowledge: 1972–1977.* New York: Pantheon Books.

———. 1984. Nietzsche, genealogy, history. In *The Foucault reader,* ed. P. Rabinow, 76–100. New York: Pantheon.

Goody, J., and Watt, I. 1968. The consequences of literacy. In *Literacy in traditional societies,* ed. J. Goody. Cambridge: Cambridge University Press.

Greenfield, T. B. 1986. The decline and fall of science in educational administration. *Interchange* 17, 2: 57–80.

Greenfield, T. B., and Ribbins, P., ed. 1993. *Greenfield on educational administration.* London: Routledge

Gronn, P. 1982. Neo-Taylorism in educational administration? *Educational Administration Quarterly* 18, 4: 17–35.

Gronn, P., and Ribbins, P. 1993. The salvation of educational administration: better science or alternatives to science? *Educational Management and Administration* 21, 3: 161–69.

Haber, H. 1994. *Beyond post modern politics: Lyotard, Rorty, Foucault.* New York: Routledge.

Habermas, J. 1987. *The theory of communicative action.* Boston: Beacon Press.

Halpin, A. W. 1970. Administrative theory: The fumbled torch. In *Issues in American Education,* ed. A. M. Kroll, 156–83. New York: Oxford.

Hargreaves. A. 1994. *Changing teachers, changing times.* Toronto/New York: OISE Press, Teachers College Press.

Harvey, D. 1989. *The condition of postmodernity.* Cambridge: Blackwell.

Henrikson, G. 1973. *Hunters in the barrens: The naskapi on the edge of the white man's world.* St. John's: Memorial University. Newfoundland Social and Economic Studies No. 10.

Hodgkinson, C. 1978. *Towards a philosophy of administration.* Oxford: Basil Blackwell.
———. 1983. *The philosophy of leadership.* Oxford: Basil Blackwell.

Kirby, S., & McKenna, R., 1989. *Experience, research, social change: Methods from the margins.* Toronto: Garamond.

Lyotard, J. 1984. *The postmodern condition.* Minneapolis: University of Minnesota Press.

Marx. 1954. *Capital* 3. Moscow: Progress.

Mead, G. H. 1932/1980. *The philosophy of the present.* Chicago: University of Chicago Press.

Nietzsche, F. 1956. *The genealogy of morals.* Trans. Francis Golffing. New York: Doubleday.

Owen, D. 1994. *Population trends.* No. 78, Winter. Office of Population Censuses and Surveys OPCS London: HMSO 23–33.

Riddington, R. 1988. Knowledge and power in the subarctic. *American Anthropologist* 90,1: 88–100.

Rorty, R. 1982. *The consequences of pragmatism.* Minneapolis: University of Minnesota Press.

Roseneau, P. 1992. *Postmodernism and the social sciences: Insights, inroads and intrusions.* Princeton, NJ: Princeton University Press.

Ryan, J. 1988. Disciplining the Inuit: Social form and control in bush, community and school. Unpublished doctoral thesis, University of Toronto.

————. 1994. Transcending the limitations of social science: Insight, understanding and the humanities in educational administration. *Journal of Educational Thought* 28, 3: 225–44.

————. 1995. Order, anarchy and inquiry in educational administration. *McGill Journal of Education* 30,1: 37–59.

————. 1996. Putting Humpty Dumpty together again: Order anxiety and systemic reform. *International Journal of Educational Reform* 5, 4: 453–62.

————. 1997. Understanding Greenfield. *International studies in educational administration* 25,2: 95–105

————. 1998. Critical leadership for education in a postmodern world: Emancipation, resistance, and communal action. *International Journal of Leadership in Education.* 3(1)257–278.

Ryan, J., and Wignall, R. 1996. Administering for differences: Dilemmas in multiethnic schools. In *School Administration: Persistent Dilemmas in Preparation and Practice,* ed. S. Jacobson, E. Hickcox, and B. Stephenson, 47–62. Westport, CT: Greenwood.

Simon, H. 1945/1957. *Administrative behavior: A study of decision-making process in administrative organizations,* 2nd Edition. New York: The Free Press.

Smith, B. H. 1988. *Contingencies of value: Alternative perspectives for critical theory.* Cambridge, MA: Harvard University Press.

Soper, K. 1995. Postmodernism, subjectivity and the question of value. In *Principled Positions,* ed. J. Squires 17–32. London: Lawrence and Wisehart.

Squires, J., ed. 1995. *Principled positions: Postmodernism and the rediscovery of value.* London: Lawrence and Wisehart.

Statistics Canada. 1993. *Ethnic origin.* Ottawa: Ministry of Industry, Science and Technology.

Taylor, C. 1991. *The malaise of modernity.* Concorde, Ontario: Anasi.

The United States Bureau of the Census. 1995. *Statistical abstract of the United States: 1995,* 115th ed. Washington, DC: U.S. Bureau of the Census.

Weber, M. 1968. *Economy and society: An outline of interpretive sociology.* New York: Bedminster.

Weeks, J. 1995. Rediscovering values. In *Principled positions: Postmodernism and the rediscovery of value,* ed. J. Squires, 189–211. London: Lawrence and Wisehart.

Willower, D. 1994. Whither educational administration? The post postpositivist era. *Journal of Educational Administration and Foundations* 8, 2: 13–31.

CHAPTER FIVE

Administrative Science, the Postmodern, and Community

William Foster

Some thirty-odd years ago, Dell Hymes (1972) asked the question, "If anthropology didn't exist, would we have to invent it?" In the same fashion, thirty-odd years later, I want to ask the question, "If administration did not exist, would we have to invent it?" Perhaps, but not administration as we have to come to know it historically. Administration does exist, but perhaps it needs to be re-invented. This is what I am calling my "postadministration hypothesis";—that it is time to move beyond those models of administration that have dominated the discipline in this century and to begin to consider other ways of conceiving the field.

It is clear that our conventional understanding of administration and administrative research has been under some attack. Not only do our understandings not inform the practice of administration, but they often misinform it. This is to say that often the intellectual establishment of a field will later find expression in the activities and world views of its practitioners; the general's orders are carried out by foot-soldiers. Giddens asks, "Why . . . do seventeenth century theories of the state retain a relevance to social or political reflection today? Surely exactly because they have contributed to constituting the social world we now live in" (1984, xxxv). In much the same fashion, those theories of administration regnant in the twentieth century have contributed to the constitution of administrative practice as we know it. In talking about twentieth-century "administrative Progressives," Tyack and Hansot found that they were "linked in networks that combined university leaders with influential superintendents and foundation officials . . . [and] sought a form of private power: they gained, as did leaders in other occupations, authority to define what was normal or desirable" (1982, 7).

What was desirable, if not normal, was for the field of educational administration to become a science, indeed, a social science, but a science nevertheless. Such ambition revolved around attempts to accumulate knowledge based on "rigorous" procedures, to conduct quasi-experiments intent on unfolding the laws of human behavior in organizations, and to move administration from intuition and into rationality.

In this regard, Fenwick English observes,

> Educational administration remains solidly anchored in scientific empiricism. As such, the professors and practitioners who make up the field overwhelmingly appear to support the objectivist view of truth. The majority appear to

hold the view that truth can be considered apart from the context and culture in which it has been "discovered." Like Plato's ideals, truth represents fixed properties and relations between properties outside of life's temporal habitat. (1994, 89)

I would then like to begin to dispute this administrative attitude by looking first at the nature of science and truth in administration and then at some postmodern observations.

Essentially Contested Concept

Gallie uses the phrase essentially contested concept to describe and to distinguish philosophical concepts from their scientific brethren. Such concepts are to be "understood historically, as a phase in an inherited and unending intellectual task" (1986, 8). Such concepts, it is important to note, have rival versions of the truth and thus, in many ways, precede the postmodernist arguments, yet, in many ways, advance them. Essentially contested concepts, then, are those that have no governing laws that define them, nor do they have agreed-upon definitions of what they are about. Rather, they tend to present themselves in "schools of thought" "ways of thinking," and so on.

While the natural sciences may, indeed, develop hard and fast "rules" and laws regarding the predictability of events—such as at what temperature water will boil—social sciences generally do not. Indeed, the attempt to define and restrict such undefinable and essentially contested social concepts winds up in their trivialization. MacIntyre, for example, finds that "the expected consequence of the attempt to render certain areas of social and political inquiry amenable to scientific procedure ought to be the utterance of trivial generalizations about a subject matter other than that in which we were originally interested" (1973, 8).

Thus, with essentially contested concepts, we need to decide whose case is stronger, which side we believe in, and where we stand. We need, in fact, to be seduced by the texts and the narratives. With administration, this means a seduction that comes from various sources: from business, from education, from political science. Gallie provides seven conditions to determine the contestability of concepts (1968, chapter 8).

First, the concept must be "appraisive" in its content, meaning that it reflects something of significance and value. To exert and practice leadership and administration under contemporary conditions certainly meets this test, insofar as they are valued as good and noble things.

Second, the concept must be internally complex. Administration certainly is—no simple definitions of what it is are readily available.

Third, the concept must allow for rival and plausible descriptions of its internal dimensions. For Gallie, this means that "the accredited achievement is *initially* variously describable" (1968, 161). Educational administration, with its history of various approaches and different stresses would also seem to meet this condition.

Fourth, the concept must be "open" in character, meaning that it is open to modification as times change and thinking evolves. We have seen how this is true with respect to the concept under consideration.

A fifth condition is that the various schools of thought centered around the concept recognize each other *but* attempt to promote their own version of the truth. With the idea of administration, this is clearly the case, as a reading of the history of the field demonstrates: from efficiency to behaviorism, to critical theory, and so on.

Two more conditions inform Gallie's use of 'essentially contested concepts'. One is the derivation of such a concept from a historical exemplar. While this is more problematic in the case of examining administration, I think a case can be made that the term entered the language at a particular time and, on entry, stood for a way of looking at the world. The term became an accepted part of our linguistic repertoire and, while not fully developed, served to influence subsequent users of the term.

Finally, Gallie suggests that "the continuous competition for acknowledgment as between the contestant users of the concept enables the original exemplar's achievement to be sustained or developed in optimum fashion" (1968, 168). This, in looking at the idea of administration, is indisputable. The concept occurs, enters into common parlance, and then various ways and means of defining and redefining the term happen, all of which promote the viability of the original concept: that such a thing as administration might exist and might influence the course of human events.

The point I make here is that many concepts in the social sciences are contested concepts. There are rival explanations of each variant of the concept, and each rival clashes upon ideological fields for supremacy. In educational administration, the "paradigm wars," the theory debates, the different versions of inquiry all suggest that the concepts embraced in the field of educational administration not only are contested but will be contested forever. There is a reason for this: social science concepts are inherently unstable; they reflect the actions and activities of the agents who derive them and are intimately tied up with current style. This is to say, they lack predictability. Unlike natural science concepts, social science ones, including those in educational administration, do not lend themselves effectively to prediction nor to control. This, as I will discuss, results in their fundamental reliance on issues of power and social separation.

The idea of predictability is fundamental to natural science. Were water to boil at one temperature today and a different one, under the same conditions, tomorrow, science as we know it would be impossible. But in the social science, predictability is but a throw of the dice. There are, according to MacIntyre (1984), at least three basic reasons for this. The first is that claims to generalizable knowledge in the social sciences exist peacefully and side-by-side with recognized counterexamples. Thus, the idea that increasing centralization provides increasing efficiency, while often true, is not always true, and many times is demonstrably false. Second, such generalizations in the social sciences lack what MacIntyre labels "scope modifiers," that is, statements that tell us the precise circumstances under which the generalization may apply. Thus, a particular scientific law may be said to hold under all conditions except when x and y apply; these modify the law but are themselves of such specificity to enable us to predict the application of the law. Third, social science generalizations are unable to specify those conditions under which generalizations do not apply, as can scientific laws. The generalization that leadership is a function of *motivation times ability,* for example, cannot tell us when leadership might not occur even when such conditions apply.

Yet the idea of the administrative expert, who uses scientific observation, reigns supreme in Western society. It is an idea that presupposes that administrators can, by their will, impose order and rationality on what is otherwise an unordered chaos. Administrators and managers, though, are much like the rest of us; sometimes their suasion works, and sometimes it does not. The idea of the administrator as an "expert" again is a moral fiction because "the kind of knowledge which would be required to sustain it does not exist" (MacIntyre 1984, 75). This means, simply, that the social and administrative equivalent of a physics of administration and management is not now present and virtually unattainable in the future. The nightmare that writers have had of the totally managed state, with its capacity for total control, is only true under principles of coercion, not of science.

Again, the social sciences, including those concerned with administration, lack any kind of predictability. If a science is to have any legitimacy, then it must be able to say that under certain conditions, x will happen. The social sciences cannot do this. Their lack of predictability concerns the basic nature of human life: that people can choose, and with these choices they can defy what social science might believe.

There are certain conditions of social life that argue against the formation of administrative science and managerial expertise. One is that innovations in social life are themselves unpredictable—to predict the invention of the wheel is indeed to invent it. Thus, prediction of the future, at least a radically new future, is not possible because to predict it is, in fact, to invent it.

Other sources of unpredictability lie in the "game" nature of social life, where individuals make choices based on their assessment of current events and previous choices, and these remain unpredictable. Whether to use American or Delta, in my choice of flights, is inherently unpredictable because certain events could emerge that might make neither carrier the preferred one. Normally, and in the statistical probability of events, it can be shown that I will board one flight because I have made reservations, I like the airline (or hate the other one), and so on. But this probability can be thrown askew by all kinds of events, and the certainty implied by the observation that water will boil at a certain temperature is a certainty not found in the social sciences.

The unpredictability argument is an important one. It is important because it brings into question the basic epistemological assumptions of social science and thus those of administrative or managerial science. If a social science cannot approach those avenues of lawlike generalization demanded of other sciences, then its status, as a science, is considerably undermined, and "the salient fact about those (social) sciences is the absence of the discovery of any law-like generalization whatsoever" (MacIntyre 1984, 89). This means, in essence, that the overlay put on their theory by both the management and administrative theorist to provide meaningful and predictive generalizations about human behavior in organization is shown to be a basically false assumption, which only shores up the power and status of university professors, highly paid consultants, and other "imagers" of managerial expertise.

If such arguments are, on the face, adequate ones, where does that leave us? It leaves us with a noncertainty, nontruth, and nonabsolutist view of organizational relationships. This is where the postmortem agenda appears particularly welcome. The postrnodernist movement developed primarily in literature and philosophy but has a certain application to the social sciences.

In the postmodernist approach to knowledge, "history is not the progress of universal reason. It is the play of power rituals of power, humanity advancing from one domination to another" (Dreyfus and Rabinow 1983, 110). History, for the postmodernist, is a series of ruptures, and it is through the tracing of family resemblances—the genealogy—that we begin to understand our origins and the story of human domination as classes struggle for power and control.

Each rupture is characterized by the development of a "metanarrative," a story that presents a given reality. It is through language and discourse that the powerful can present their story as the "right" one, as the one that reflects the "true" nature of society and of social relationships. In the modern period, the metanarrative has been of the power of science, to explain, and to predict. The scientific metanarrative certainly has guided the field of educational administration during most of this century and indeed can be taken as the guiding metaphor for the social sciences in general. But it remains only a narrative, albeit one that hides as much as it reveals.

A critical historical rupture occurred, in this way of thinking, in the movement from traditional modes of governing to "enlightened" modes, where the rise of capitalism and industry required a regulated and docile citizenry. The development of social science, including theories of criminology, demographics, and administration, served to rationalize procedures of control and contribute to the narrative of the modern state.

According to Dreyfus and Rabinow (1983, 136–42), there were several historical ruptures that led to the modern conception of the state and of its administration. Traditionally, political theory was concerned with the idea of the "good life" and how the practice of politics could lead to the achievement of both goodness and justice. Ancient philosophers preached the value of mortals engaging each other in a quest to find the right way to live and the good way to live. With the emergence of the Renaissance, however, a different type of political theory emerged, that of considering the most effective ways to harness power to protect the sovereign. This form of Machiavellianism was a rupture with the past. No longer concerned with the achievement of the good life, it looked only to a variety of political strategies that could be used to protect the ruler. The third and final phase was the emergence of the power of the nation-state itself. In this phase, "political rationality no longer sought to achieve the good life nor merely to aid the prince, but to increase the scope of power for its own sake by bringing the bodies of the state's subjects under tighter discipline" (Dreyfus and Rabinow 1983, 137). This was the emergence of what Foucault labels "biopower," the ability of the modern political apparatus to control the physical and mental functioning of its subjects.

This approach suggests that the state apparatus evolved the means to internalize power over its subjects. External threat and coercion were no longer the sole means to secure control. Rather bureaucratic authority and a wide-ranging institutional structure, supported by accepted metanarratives, developed a citizenry whose acquiescence became more and more widespread. Control over the body through institutional structures, such as the prison and the school, was also control over the mind. Foucault writes:

> In the seventeenth and eighteenth centuries a form of power comes into being that begins to exercise itself through social production and social service. It becomes a matter of obtaining productive service from individuals in their concrete lives. And in consequence, a real and effective incorporation of power was necessary, in the sense that power had to be able to gain access to the bodies of individuals, to their acts, attitudes and modes of everyday behavior. Hence the significance of methods like school discipline, which suc-

ceeded in making children's bodies the object of highly complex systems of manipulation and conditioning. (1980, 125).

In this view, administration serves as one means for controlling the physical presence of the citizenry, thereby offering opportunities for ideological indoctrination and the enhancement of state power. The institutional control of individuals, as seen in prisons and schools, is, for Foucault, a form of biopower, power exhibited in the control of the biological presence of such individuals. And it is through the administration of such institutions that biopower can reach its fullest expression.

Social science, that is, the "disciplines" of sociology, economics, political science, and so on, thus can be seen to be in the service of the state, in providing more and more rational ways of securing the power of the state, of exerting "discipline" over the population. Administration, in this view, is a "discipline" only to the extent that it too can exert disciplinary control over the state's subjects.

But this is an ad hoc process, not a scientific one. That is, institutional structures of control emerge and evolve and exert real power, but they do not do so in any calculated, rational, and scientific fashion. Rather, they reflect the will to power of the powerful, the need to develop discourses which reflect the interests of those in power.

Thus, the social science disciplines emerged from the daily practices of the ruling elite over the masses. However, this history, this relationship with structures of control, becomes lost in the narrative discourse of the social sciences themselves. They become victim to the narrative of "science" and begin to see themselves as objective, value-free predictors of human behavior. But, as Dreyfus and Rabinow (1983) note:

> Thus, while in the natural sciences it is always possible and generally desirable that an unchallenged normal science which defines and resolves problems concerning the structure of the physical universe establish itself, in the social sciences, such an unchallenged normal science would only indicate that an orthodoxy had established itself, not through scientific achievement, but by ignoring the background and eliminating all competitors. It would mean that the basic job of exploring the background of practices and their meaning had been suppressed. (1983, 163–64)

In this view then, the idea of a social science that parallels that of the natural sciences is but a false representation that masks, first, the inability of the social, including the managerial, sciences to actually predict anything about human behavior in any kind of lawlike fashion, and, second, the intimate connection between such sciences and the legitimation of the State.

Applying Postmodernism to Administration

Postmodernism makes the following claims, which are significant to an understanding of the myth of a management science:

1. Knowledge is nonfoundational. This means that we act in our organizational worlds as if we had a solid knowledge base to guide our decisions; that, indeed, there is an accepted foundation for what it is that we do. Postmodernists argue the opposite: knowledge is always produced in specific contexts, which are time and space dependent. Thus, what we know is not what we know universally; rather it is only what we claim to know in a specific setting with the parameters defined by our history and culture.
2. Further, the agreement that we develop about the meaning of "true" knowledge is intimately related to the distribution of power in a society. The powerful, in other words, support a particular form of knowing (of what counts as knowledge, of what is valued and what is not), which reinforces their position in a society.
3. The resulting outcome is the development of what poststructuralists call "grand narratives" or widely accepted stories that construct reality for most of us and that serve to maintain the existing system of privileges and power. For example, Reed argues that in poststructuralist organizational theory:

> Belief in an independently existing and objective "organizational reality," knowable through scientific reasoning and discourse, is replaced by a conception of theories as self-justifying representational forms or "intelligible narratives" which allow groups or communities of researchers and scholars to make shared sense of their collective engagement with a predefined phenomenon. (1992, 11).

Culler summarizes the argument nicely when he says that "structuralists are convinced that systematic knowledge is possible; poststructuralists claim to know only the impossibility of this knowledge" (1982, 22).

Postmodernist arguments generate four problematic areas that thought about leadership will have to confront. Schwab (1989), reviewing various postmodernist ideas and analyzing Frank's (1989) arguments, suggests that there are four themes characteristic of the postmodern position: order, metaphysics, representation, and history. An analysis of each of these begins to suggest how and in what ways administration becomes a contested terrain.

The problem of order deals with the question of whether the order observed in social structures is merely an arbitrary way of designing realities that systematically discriminate against the possibility of other, and equally plausible, orders of the universe. Thus, the order one observes "naturally" in social systems conceals the other possible orders that, as well, may be aspects of the social structure—or there may be no order at all. In many theories of organization, of course, the problem of order is not a problem at all; rather, order is presupposed and the theory then begins to explain how order works. There is certainly a connection between the presumptions of leadership and the need for order, if only that one function of leadership is to create order or to re-create order. Thus, the revolutionary leadership of a Lenin can certainly be seen as an attempt to establish a new, if also repressive, order. The problem of order is such that in a hard and real world there emerges a contest for whose order will dominate, and the winners of that particular contest are our leaders.

A second area that Schwab (1989) suggests that postmodernists reject is the concept of 'metaphysics,' which is, he claims, "the ideology of order" (1989, xvi), and which serves to provide an external explanation of why things are ordered as they are. Thus, whether one believes in God, universal laws, or natural science as creating the condition under which most of us labor, a metaphysic stands behind our belief in our reality, in our ordered universe. Such a metaphysic is rejected by postmodernists, who look more to the arbitrary nature of social constructions. Yet the metaphysic of order is also the metaphysic of leadership, to the extent that leaders attempt to perpetuate their rule by establishing some sort of belief system. The leader then looks for fidelity to this system and relies on managers to implement its tenets.

Language use is another theme found in postmodernist thought. Schwab, using the term *antirationalist* to suggest postmodern ideas, expresses this theme this way:

> At the least radical level, anti rationalists doubt that conceptual thought (and language) is an adequate means to represent or express the basic truths of our world and our conception of it. A reality that is basically chaotic cannot be rendered conceptually, or it will be violated in the process. The language of concepts is consequently abandoned in favor of expressive, poetical, highly metaphorical, often overtly inconsistent forms of discourse. More radical is the idea that language and thought do not carry representational power at all, that is, do not relate to anything over and above the events of thinking and speaking. This idea applies the anti rationalist opposition to order to the field of thought and language, thus integrating the *medium* of our attitude *toward reality into* the reality as anti rationalism conceives of it. (1989, xvi, italics in original)

Language, in this position, seems to be less a conceptual way of ordering the world than a way of reacting to linguistic situations, of judging things in the here and now. Language and thought here are reflections of cultural antics and a means of attempting to order the world. And this, of course, is what leadership does best. It is through the use of language that leaders search for followers, and it is through the use of language that leaders attempt to *re-order* the world.

Finally, the postmodern position provides a position on history. History, in this reading, appears as discontinuities, as epochs, each of which has little or no relationship to each other. Rather than seeing history as the episodic unfolding of events, each related in some way to the other, postmodernist thought sees history as reflecting "breaks and ruptures." This view of history is compatible with the idea of leadership as a contested terrain, for history is the drama of contests, of power struggles, and of breaks from past practices. The various revolutions of the modern era reflect this, as does any serious inquiry into the development of leadership.

Poststructuralist or postmodernist thought, then, reflects an analysis of language and society that accepts their dependence, that acknowledges that power relates to language use, and that asserts that the many divisions a society accepts—between classes, races, genders, and so on—are related to the way the "power elite" can dominate the signifiers in a language. In other words, postmodern thought suggests that there is no final or ultimate position that one can come to through one's research or analysis—it "all depends" on the power of the arguments, on the acceptance of these by the power elite, and on the symmetry of the words with the times.

Postmodern thought, combined with an analysis of modern social science, suggests then that there is no foundation or ultimate position for theories of management or administration. Indeed, such theories in management science represent attempts to solidify the power base of those presenting them. Such theories represent ways to socialize the student into the mystifications of management science or administrative behavior. Such theories reflect a more basic preoccupation with how economics drive the social sciences. Such a pessimistic view of administrative science is not meant to impugn the many people who work in this area; rather it is to suggest that they perhaps labor under conditions of false consciousness, where they do in fact believe in the power of social science.

Gergen (1992) would place the administrative or managerial scientist in the period he calls "modernism." He finds that modernist approaches to organization include a belief in the power of reason and observation, a belief in foundations or essentials, faith in progress and development, and "absorption in the machine metaphor" (211). With postmodernism, however, these concepts become exposed, not as being neutral signifiers of one organizational reality, but as weapons in the fight for organizational control.

Why, then, do we continue to believe in the myth of managerial expertise, this evidence to the contrary? Perhaps, only because we have few or no other meaning systems to sustain us, bureaucracy demands that we acquiesce to the idea of expertise and to the idea that we can, in fact, control events to our liking. But what if we cannot? What alternatives remain?.

Both the nonpredictability argument and that of postmodernism suggest that the structures that we do create are ones that tend to support the dominant relationships in a society. The language used, the images evoked, and the metaphors used all tend to re-create the kind of society that rewards those in power and disenfranchises those without. In educational administration or management science, the images of power and control, of an ability to make sense of organization, and of a talent to shape the organizational future contribute to a myth of performance unsupported by results. Yet it continues, unabated. The reason must lie in a generalized cultural myth, carefully built up and reinforced over generations, rather than in palatable results. This is, indeed, the claim that both MacIntyre (1984) and the postmodernists make, though each arrive at this conclusion from different routes. For MacIntyre, "managerial effectiveness functions much as Carnap and Ayer supposed God to function. It is the name of a fictitious, but believed-in reality, appeal to which disguises certain other realities; its effective use is expressive" (1984, 76).

Consequently, management scientists turn to the social sciences for their legitimacy and, using a particular construction of social science as objective, valueless, and rational, create a mythology of expertise, the role of which is to conceal the conceptual inadequacies of the metanarrative. More than this, the mythology is seduction: it seduces the reader/practitioner into thinking of the contested concept as an uncontested one.

Take, for example, a concept common to the discourse of educational administration—that of 'leadership'. The seduction of leadership is a seduction of power. Calas and Smircich (1991), through an analysis of some of the major texts that address leadership, show how leadership becomes a discourse aimed at concealing more than revealing. This means that the idea of leadership itself becomes a means for establishing or maintaining those power relationships that allow certain privileged persons in a society to concretize their power over others. By allowing the term to stand as a surrogate for power, such leaders seduce us into acquiescing to their demands. Here, leadership and seduction are the same thing; leadership is the seduction of others into a system of power relationships whose benefits go to those in power. *Leadership,* they show, often becomes a term designed to veil the masculine dominance in a society, to seduce the rest to follow.

In another sense, the texts on leadership also seduce. Each presents a conception of leadership designed to convince the reader to believe in the authority, legitimacy, and truthfulness of the writer. Such texts are seductive. Thus, a business professor's text on leadership conveys a message designed to seduce us to his or her way of thinking about the topic. An anthropologist's study of leadership conveys another way of attempting to seduce the reader. One might read the various texts on leadership and come to a conclusion that leadership is a science, an art, a personal quality, a gift of God, and so on. The idea of leadership is a seductive idea because it is an attempt to solve the problems of order, metaphysics, language, and history. To solve those very postmodernist problems, leadership must seduce. In our era, it does so through the text. That is, the contests regarding leadership are battles now fought in print. The text attempts to convince us, as Nielsen puts it:

> Texts are not simple mirrors of reality. All textual meaning must be con-structed. . . . *The text creates the meaning structure which it conveys.* The illusion is a necessary condition for meaning to come into being. Thus, it is not possible in fact to see the seductive dimensions of the text as something separate from its message. The seduction is not a beautiful candy-coating for the pill as it slides down the throat; 'seduction' is an integrated part of the text's meaning. No meaning without seduction. (1995, p. 8).

Thus, the leadership texts attempt to convey to us, the readers, a way of construing not only the concept but the world. The text is a way of convinc-ing us of the rightness of the author's view.

A major consideration then in examining metanarratives, such as ad-ministrative effectiveness and leadership, is the issue of power. "The concept of power," Bertrand Russell is said to have observed, "is to the social sciences what energy is to physics" (Russell 1938, cited in Burns 1978, 12). The idea of power is a fundamental concept in the social sciences, one used to explain a variety of social differentiations, to discuss the politics of social life, and to examine such phenomena as management and leadership.

Despite its usefulness as an explanation of hierarchies and of social distinctions, it remains a concept largely taken for granted as something that is just there. Power is such a ubiquitous part of social life that dimen-sions of power often remain unexplored, and alternative conceptions of the notion go unnoticed. Yet disciplines such as political science, business ad-ministration, educational administration, sociology, psychology, and so on could hardly do without it.

The concept of power might largely be an essentially contested con-cept, that is, a construct in the social sciences about which different and rival explanations could be secured. Unlike some fundamental notions in the physical sciences, many social science concepts open themselves up to com-prehensive, rational, yet competing definitions. Basic stock in the social sciences such as "leadership," "authority," "community," and so on could legitimately lend themselves to differing and, in their own way, rational, definitions.

Were one to do an exhaustive treatment of the issue of power in the social sciences, one would likely find differing, and defensible, treatments, each of which disagreeing with the other on basic premises. In Gallie's terms (1968), such competing definitions each have a comprehensible set of assumptions about what the definition encompasses, a compelling set of arguments based in those assumptions, and a rational construction and conclusion of how those definitions are achieved. The idea of power is, I think, an appropriate candidate for the notion of an essentially contested concept.

There are probably two dominant approaches to power in the literature today. Each reflects a competing view on the nature of the subject. The first reflects a behavioral, management orientation, where the origins and distribution of power are largely unexamined. Instead, attention is turned to descriptions of power and strategies on gaining and using power. Perhaps the classic prototypical example in this genre of research on power is that developed by French and Raven (1959); this typology tends to be the backbone of those limited discussions of power that occur in the typical "organizational behavior" textbook. Their typology suggests five "types" of power: legitimate, reward, coercive, expert, and referent. The descriptions of these are largely self-explanatory and need not be detailed here. However, it is, worth noting that this particular analysis of power takes the presence of power as a given and as a natural part of organizational and social relations, in no way questioning the uses, abuses, and origins of this concept. Indeed, power is an uncontested notion that plays a particularly important role in reaffirming social structures.

An examination of power as might be used in this type of analysis tends to look at questions of how power can be attained, how it is a "good" to be used, and how it can reflect other dimensions of social life (such as status, control, achievement, and so on).

A more sophisticated analysis of the concept of power is found in the literature of political science. Here, power is considered part of "a system of social causation" (Burns 1978, 13), wherein the holder of power can "cause" the recipient of power to act in a way in which she or he may not have chosen to act. Power turns into leadership when the recipient becomes the willing recipient of such power acts. This definition of power—that A can cause B to perform in such a way even though B would not have done so absent the power relationship—is a common one in the political science/ sociology literature, traceable at least back to Weber's thinking. In a somewhat more global way, Giddens defines power "as the use of resources, of whatever kind, to secure outcomes. Power then becomes an element of action, and refers to the *range* of interventions of which an agent is capable" (1995, 214).

Such power can be coercive, of course, yet it often finds recipients of power who are both willing and able to carry out orders and directives. The agent of power must, for Burns (1978), have both motive and resources; the recipient only the ability to comply. This version of power then refers to a largely individual ability to amass resources, to use them to achieve personal goals, and to control others in the course of the exertion of power prerogatives. These views of power tend to share the following assumptions about the issue of power: First, power is assumed as a social fact, a good to be sought after. It is also largely a function of individual ability, in the sense that the "powerful" are identified as individuals who have attained positions of control. Then the idea of power is considered as a *largely political* function, an idea that reflects how individuals scale ladders of success in order to exert political influence over their supporters.

It is possible, however, to examine power from a more macro perspective—to engage in a postmodern analysis of what power is in modern societies. Here, the notion of power is linked to issues of control, of legitimacy, and of belief.

Power and Knowledge

In this analysis, power is not the seamless web of authority that modern texts seem to suggest. Rather, it is a more *fractured* concept, one whose uses and definitions change according to the dominant issues of the age. Such forms of power are both hopeless and hopeful: *hopeless* in the sense that as systemic knowledge of and control over natural systems increases, fractured power is accumulated through a worldwide concentration of media, advertising, and related control-oriented endeavors; *hopeful* in the sense that pockets of resistance are both available and viable and can use knowledge as a means for illumination and edification. The project then is not the final and ultimate victory over forces of coercion and domination; perhaps it lies more in the recognition of domination and the development of strategies designed to make our limited lives more meaningful. That is, in a postmodern world, power and domination will always exist, and pure emancipation is, perhaps, deceptive, but we do what we can.

James Ryan has stated that

> resistance practices that are based on liberating an enduring transcendental subject will not work in this view, since individuals can become only what the surrounding circumstances allow them to be. Subjects will always display a multiple and dispersed character that inevitably experiences a degree of (self) constraint. The challenge here will be to not only understand the multiple and changing ways in which subjects are constituted, and as a result entrapped, but also to devise strategies that resist this entrapment. (1996, 15)

Postadministration

Postmodernism relies to some extent on an analysis of power and the effects of power over the individual. It is the self-forming, autonomous individual who is determined by postmodern politics and power relations, it is such an individual who is *administered*. Educational administration has taken as its goal the structuration and control of institutional life, which forms the autonomous individual but which has formed such individuals within wider structures of domination and inequality. Perhaps it is necessary for educational administration to cast a wider net, to begin to see itself as an oppositional tendency within the structures of control. This is what I would call "postadministration."

But such a conception of administration requires an acknowledgment of the importance of community. Haber writes, "Since the subject is an effect of multiple community formation, alternative subjects can only be formulated within the discourses of alternative communities. This is to claim that there are no individuals, in the traditional sense and that the traditional autonomous subject must be replaced by the concept of subjects-in-community" (1994, 108). Further, she writes that "we have vocabularies (though not only one vocabulary) only as a member of *some community or other,* and so *it is only as a member of some community or other that we are empowered"* (121). The genealogy of knowledge, insofar as it speaks only to the sanitized individual, does not allow us to trace the language of difference and to empower communal groups based on that difference. The ethics of administration then have to do with the denial of the universilization of oneness and with the empowerment of difference. The ethics of administration must speak not just to the conduct of office but to the practices of life.

What agenda then can be built for educational administration in the few years left to this century? It is fitting here to note Thom Greenfield's observation that if students of administration should study anything, it should be law, history, and philosophy (Greenfield & Ribbins, 1993). Each of these is important in the formation of consciousness about ourselves and about the other. In addition, however, I think the practice of the field should be involved in the creation of spaces for the development of communities of understanding and spaces undominated by the legacy of economics and efficiency. We might also look to see how administrators can be bridge builders and border crossers, providing opportunities for the reconstruction of a meaningful public life for all. The administrative coat should be a coat of many colors.

Jerry Starratt summarizes some feelings about administration:

Within the postmodern mood, we discover a series of insights concerning the nature of knowledge as a social and cultural construct, the understanding of learning as involving the learner in knowledge production, the understanding of learning as inescapably involving the self's own narrative, the relation of learning/knowledge to cultural production, the relation of learning to self-realization and self-creation, and the relationship of learning to communities of language and communities of memory, and hence to the meta-narratives of communities. (1996, 53)

Administration is about learning and knowledge, about community and self, and mostly about our children and their worlds.

References

Burns, J. M. 1978. *Leadership.* NY: Harper Torchbooks.

Callas, M. B., and Smircich, L. 1991. Voicing seduction to silence leadership. *Organizational Studies* 12, 4: 567–602.

Culler, J.D. 1982. *On deconstruction: Theory and criticism in the1970s.* Ithaca, NY: Cornell University Press.

Dreyfus, H. L., and Rabinow, P. 1983. *Michel Foucault: Beyond structuralism and hermeneutics,* 2nd. ed. Chicago: University of Chicago Press.

English, F. W. 1994. *Theory in educational administration.* NY: Harper Collins.

Foucault, M. 1980. *Power/knowledge: Selected interviews and other writings, 1972–1977,* ed. C. Gordon. NY: Pantheon Books.

Frank, M. 1989. *What is neostructuralism?* trans. S. Wilke and R. Gray. Minneapolis: University of Minnesota Press.

French, J., and Raven, B. H. 1959. The bases of social power. In *Studies of social power,* ed. D. Cartwright. Ann Arbor: Institute for Social Research.

Gallie, W. B. 1968. *Philosophy and the historical understanding.* 2nd ed. NY: Schocken Books.

Gergen, K. J. 1992. Organization theory in the postmortem era. In *Rethinking organization: New directions in organization theory and analysis,* ed. M. Reed and M. Hughes, 207–26. Newbury Park, CA: Sage.

Giddens, A. 1984. *The constitution of society.* Berkeley and Los Angeles: University of California Press.

Greenfield, T., and Ribbins, P. 1993. *Greenfield on educational administration.* London: Routledge.

———. 1995. *Politics, sociology, and social theory.* Stanford: Stanford University Press.

Haber, H. F. 1994. *Beyond postmodern politics.* NY: Routledge.

Hymes D. H. 1972. Reinventing Anthropology. Ny: Pantheon Books.

MacIntyre, A. 1973. The essential contestability of some social concepts. *Ethics* 84: 1–9.

———. 1984. *After virtue,* 2nd ed. Notre Dame: University of Notre Dame Press.

Nielsen, H. B. 1995. Seductive texts with serious intentions. *Educational Researcher* 24, 1: 4–12.

Reed, M. 1992. Introduction. In *Rethinking organization: New directions in organization theory and analysis,* ed. M. Reed and M. Hughes, 1–6. Newbury Park, CA: Sage.

Ryan, J. June 1996. Critical leadership for education in a postmortem world: From emancipation to resistance. Paper presented at the Annual Conference, Canadian Society for the Study of Education, St. Catherines, Ontario.

Schwab, M. 1989. Foreword. In *What is neostructuralism?* x–xliv, M. Frank. Trans. S. Wilke and R. Gray. Minneapolis: University of Minnesota.

Starratt, R. J. 1996. *Transforming educational administration: Meaning, community, excellence.* NY: McGraw-Hill.

Tyack, D., and Hansot, E. 1982. *Managers of virtue.* NY: Basic Books.

Part II

Values Theory:
Debates and Developments

The Place of Values in Theories of Administration

Paul T. Begley

A recent review of the existing values literature* reveals that the discourse on the function of values in administration remains clouded by conceptual difficulties and epistemological wrangling. In particular, prevailing notions of theory and scientific evidence continue to constrain the consideration of values as an influence on administrative action by perpetuating the separation of fact from value. Perhaps the best-known articulation of this posture in the field of educational administration is Simon's conception of the value-neutral administrator (1965, 58–59), ethical matters being associated with policy, and factual matters being the domain of administration. Examples of alternate perspectives include those derived from Kuhn (1962) and Greenfield and Ribbins (1993). Positions more recently articulated include Lakomski and Evers (chapter 9), their critics Allison and Ellett (chapter 10), and Campbell (chapter 8). These opposing views fuel controversy by raising objections to traditional empiricism and questioning the existence of hard data. Others are employed to underwrite or attack, depending on the author, arguments in support of coherentist, subjectivist, or relativist world views. However, all these theoretical postures share one quality—they more readily embrace notions of personal value, will, or intent as influences on administration.

Those determined to reconcile the more philosophical issues associated with administrative values may be most attracted to the work of Evers and Lakomski (1991; 1996; chapter 9 of this book). Evers and Lakomski mediate the epistemological battleground by arguing that the weaknesses in traditional administrative science can be traced back to foundationalist epistemological assumptions embedded therein. They critique the paradigm approach associated with Kuhn (1962) and Feyerabend (1981), asserting that it promotes critical immunity from one methodological paradigm to another. In simpler terms, this means that the adoption of relatively polarized positions on the nature of administrative values largely eliminates the need to defend or reconcile the fundamental assumptions implicit in these positions. Thus, critical theorists need not justify what, to a functionalist,

---

* Portions of this chapter describing the place of values in administration were previously published in P. T. Begley, 1996. "Cognitive Perspectives on Values in Administration: A Quest for Coherence and Relevance," *Educational Administration Quarterly* 32, 3: 403–26.

appears to be a utopian view that ignores the practical necessity for an incremental approach to social change. Conversely, functionalists, within the protective armor of their paradigm, need not defend their apparent unquestioning acceptance of established power relationships within organizations that, as their critics contend, perpetuate the agendas of particular vested interests at the expense of certain minority groups. As an alternative to the foundational or paradigmatic metatheories of administration, Evers and Lakomski propose *criteria of coherence* (1991, 96) as their contribution to the development of a general theory of administration. However, these coherentist applications still have their critics, including Maddock (see Evers and Lakomski 1996) and Allison and Ellett who present their case in chapter 10.

Hodgkinson (chapter 7), an important critic of empiricism, like Simon, advocates the separation of fact from value but considers values fundamental to the nature and practice of administration. In sharp contrast to Simon's position, which appears to place the values dimension outside the usual domains of administrative practice, Hodgkinson concludes that facts are the domain of science and that administration is fundamentally value-laden humanism.

Finally, there are those whose interests and research have been more pragmatically aligned toward applied administrative practices as opposed to philosophical or theoretical fidelity. Foremost among these scholars is probably Willower (see chapter 6), but this category of scholarship also includes Begley (chapter 12), Leithwood (chapter 2), and Roche (chapter 13), as well as Strike (1990), Campbell-Evans (1991), and Sergiovanni (1992). By narrowing the locus of inquiry to an organizational or professional perspective, these scholars reduce the necessity of participating in much of the epistemological debate. The individualistic values of personal preference and transrational principles (Hodgkinson 1978) are not so much denied an existence as conceptually set aside in favor of the firmer ground of collective social values and moral decision making. What becomes highlighted is the mainstream administrative domain of social accountability, consequence-focussed and/or consensus-based decision making. Moreover, it is no coincidence that these value types are those most readily justified through rational processes or empirically verified through research.

References

Campbell-Evans, G. H. 1991. Nature and influence of values in principal decision-making. *The Alberta Journal of Educational Research* 37, 2:167–78.

Evers, C. W., and Lakomski, G. 1991. *Knowing educational administration.* Toronto: Pergamon Press.

————. 1996. *Exploring educational administration.* Toronto: Pergamon Press.

Feyerabend, P. K. 1981. *Philosophical papers 1 & 2.* Cambridge: Cambridge University Press.

Greenfield, T., and Ribbins, P. 1993. *Greenfield on educational administration.* New York: Routledge.

Hodgkinson, C. 1978. *Towards a philosophy of administration.* Oxford: Basil Blackwell.

Kuhn, T. 1962. *The structure of scientific revolutions.* Chicago: University of Chicago Press.

Sergiovanni, T. J. 1992. *Moral leadership.* San Francisco: Jossey-Bass.

Simon, H. 1965. *Administrative behaviour,* 2nd ed. New York: Free Press.

Strike, K. A. 1990. The ethics of educational evaluation. In *Teacher evaluation: Assessing elementary and secondary school teachers,* ed. J. Millman, and L. Darling-Hammond, L. 356–73. Newbury Park, CA: Sage Publications.

CHAPTER SIX

Values and Valuation: A Naturalistic Inquiry

Donald J. Willower

Plato held that the ministry of education was the greatest of all the offices of the state. Whether or not that office is taken to be greater than others, few would dispute the importance of education. However, the reality is that the problems associated with education are often difficult and commonly ongoing. For instance, questions such as the directions that ought to be taken by schools remain as persistent as they are urgent. They are not questions that pertain only at higher levels of governance; they can be asked about a neighborhood school or even about a particular classroom or student. In a democracy, such questions are not just the business of educators, they are the business of every citizen. Hence, there is an abiding social and community right to express preferences about educational aims and directions.

At the same time, those who work in the schools, administrators and teachers alike, often face moral choices that can affect students and others. Education is a profoundly moral activity in terms of both its possibilities and its everyday practice.

Values, Writing, and Polemics in Educational Administration

In philosophy, the study of values traditionally has dealt with what is good or desirable, with the kind of behavior that one should engage in to be virtuous. The history of philosophy provides numerous examples. Plato's idea of the Good was the highest of his ideal forms—forms believed to be real and immutable, transcending temporal phenomena. For Aristotle, rationality was a defining human quality, and its cultivation through contemplation and moderation exemplified the good life. Spinoza believed that goodness could be achieved through the intellectual love of God, defined pantheistically and identified with nature. Kant's touchstone in ethics was his categorical imperative, which asserted that one should act as if that action were to become a universal law. Jeremy Bentham's guide to morality was the greatest happiness of the greatest number. Nietzsche envisaged a "superman" devoted to a creative and heroic life unfettered by conventional precepts of good and evil.

More recent philosophers have continued to examine virtue, justice, and values. They have been concerned with issues such as the proper grounding of ethical principles and the problems of their application in human affairs. While the proper role of government has been part of ethical thinking since the time of the Ancient Greeks, its contemporary importance has been underscored by concerns about individual freedom, justice, and equity in the context of an array of social problems made vivid by the pervasiveness of mass media.

Given all this, one would expect that discussions of values in educational administration would deal with the various kinds of ethical theories that seem most appropriate and the way in which such theories might be applied in situations of practice. However, far too much of the discussion has been devoted to statements averring that there has been a lack of attention to values in educational administration, along with denunciations of those believed to be responsible. T. B. Greenfield (1986), for instance, blamed positivism, mindlessly technocratic administrators, and Herbert Simon. Neo-Marxists and critical theorists (e.g., Bates 1980) attacked positivism and also the dominant and privileged classes, the latter not for ignoring values, but for being concerned only about values that helped maintain the status quo and their power.

Subjectivism and neo-Marxist critical theory both came into educational administration well after they had become important in fields of the social sciences and humanities. By the time they entered educational administration in the late 1970s and early 1980s, they had already gained a near dominant position in, to give one example, sociology (Alexander 1988). A conventional feature of Marxism was its ideological emphasis and political agenda. In Greenfield's hands, subjectivism, too, took an ideological turn, and his writing was often even more polemical than that of the critical theorists, many of whom conformed to the Marxist tradition of political disputation.

While subjectivism and neo-Marxism are poles apart philosophically, in educational administration and often elsewhere, both groups attacked similar targets such as positivism, quantitative studies, and sometimes scientific inquiry itself. In this they had allies in some of those who espoused identity politics and pursued agendas devoted to the promotion of a particular interest group, often held to be oppressed, or at least, failing to get a sufficient share of societal recognition and rewards. More recently, postmodernists and those identifying with the mostly French version of the view, poststructuralists, have joined in with their special brand of nihilistic relativism. Postmodernism is philosophically not very compatible with either subjectivism or neo-Marxism, and subjectivist scholars (e.g., Van Manen 1994) and critical theorists (e.g., Habermas 1987) have vigorously attacked postmodernism.

Despite the philosophical differences in these views, some writers in educational administration, and other areas of education, mix features of the perspectives and sometimes add identity politics. For example, a science-bashing epistemology arguing that knowledge is subjective and relative is combined with an oppression-oriented social philosophy and a radical reformist political ideology. Such mixing is necessarily highly selective but not in itself invalidating as long as contradictions are avoided. However, a mixture of the kind given in the example is often mainly a political statement rather than a philosophical analysis. The epistemology is typically weakly developed with attacks on a long-dead positivism, the kind of sweeping attacks that Phillips described as showing "an embarrassing degree of philosophical illiteracy" (1992, 95). Further, the social philosophy is rarely considered in detail or contrasted with alternatives.

Generally speaking, the level of discourse on values in educational administration is too often uninformed and merely polemical. Villains abound. They range from an allegedly monolithic research establishment to an allegedly monolithic societal power structure, both depicted as dominant and with single-minded devotion to stamping out contrary opinions, all this with reference to universities, and usually to American society, the chief societal scapegoat in such polemics. That both happen to be especially free and open is simply ignored.

In educational administration, a related polemical ploy is the exaggeration of the influence of the philosophy of logical positivism and of functionalist sociological theory. This distortion has been advanced to support the contention that there was/is a single dominating philosophy and a single dominating theory in the field. The falsity of that contention is documented elsewhere (Willower 1996).

When the diversity that actually has characterized thought and research in educational administration over the years is ignored, it is easy to fall into dualistic traps and simplistic divisions. A common example is that of the valiant few fighting against the entrenched dominant position, presumably held by everyone else. This was illustrated in Greenfield's "there are two fundamental ways of looking at the world" (1975, 74), a stance he never abandoned, and in the division of human kind into oppressors and the oppressed, a view traditionally held by Marxists and frequently by postmodernists.

Such thinking degrades discourse on ethics, but it does fit the spirit of the times. Relativism and political advocacy have gained a following, especially in the academy, even though they depreciate inquiry and the search for insight and knowledge. While the politics of academics in the social sciences and humanities is often to the left of prevailing social opinion, the broader cultural context and times can complicate the picture. Just as Farber (1959) noted how Heidegger's influence could be explained by cultural receptivity to irrationalism, Merton and Wolf (1995) remark the current association of increased societal dissensus and disciplinary fragmentation in sociology.

Conflict within a field of study also can lead to efforts to rewrite the field's history. For instance, in sociology Lipset (1994) showed how radical activists starting in the 1960s incorrectly portrayed the leaders of the discipline as a reactionary establishment devoted to the status quo. This is not surprising since, as Klatch (1994) points out, the history of that period was written by radical scholars. I have already indicated that the influence of positivism and functionalism in educational administration has been wildly exaggerated. It remains to add that the attention given to values in educational administration in the past has been downplayed by some writers who apparently see advantages in depicting the field as deficient and defective prior to their own pronouncements, a ploy similar to that of Lipset's activists.

The fact of the matter is that values have been an important part of the intellectual scene in educational administration from the beginning but have been emphasized to varying degrees over different times and places. W. T. Harris, one of the field's earliest practitioner-scholars, founded and for many years edited the *Journal of Speculative Philosophy*. He developed a reputation as a Hegelian scholar but was also a practical empiricist. Travers reported that Harris, like Horace Mann, believed that the collection of facts and statistics was vital to school improvement but that, unlike Mann, Harris "loved compilations of statistics" (1983, 36). This illustrates how difficult it is to type people, just as it is difficult to typify eras. The burden of proof is on anyone making a sweeping generalization about a field's history. Exceptions and variations frequently are found when the particulars are examined.

As Culbertson (1988) pointed out, early scholars in educational administration were committed both to science as they understood it and to the pursuit of ideals. This description seems to apply across time as well. Values such as equity are central to work in school finance, with the foundation plans of the 1920s aimed at attaining basic per pupil expenditure levels an early example (Guthrie 1988). Equity and rights have always been at the forefront of school law. Philosophic statements of purpose such as "the development of the capabilities of each student to the fullest" have abounded for years in the literature and as school district objectives.

Even empirical work intermixes science and values. Studies of democratic administration, popular after World War II (Campbell et al. 1987) and various forms of participatory management to today's empowerment and restructuring are all oriented to school improvement. The turn toward the social sciences in the late 1950s and early 1960s was similarly grounded in the idea that if schools were to become better, we needed to improve our understanding of how they worked.

It is true that the beginning of this period in educational administration featured discussions of the normative-descriptive dichotomy emphasized by logical empiricists. Actually, the literature in the field had become so hortatorical that the linguistic distinction between 'ought' and 'is' statements needed to be stressed. This kind of linguistic clarity did not abrogate the recognition of the significance of values or the existential fusion of the 'ought' and 'is' in administration, and the debates on school issues and educational policy simply continued. Then, as now, moral issues were more likely to be defined in terms of specific educational problems, without much attention to the niceties of ethical theory. Even in preparation programs, values often were treated in the context of concrete cases, typically using the well-developed case books of the time (e.g., see Sargent and Belisle 1955; Culbertson, Jacobson, and Reller 1960). A recent study of values in preparation programs was done by Beck and Murphy (1994). In a relatively small sample of universities, this study found cases, formal courses, issues courses, and other approaches to ethics being used, but there was no dominating approach, and some institutions made no systematic provisions beyond the treatment provided in courses that explore alternative choices and futures.

In the literature of the earlier period, there was a concern about values as a philosophical matter (e.g., see Graff and Street 1957; Willower 1964; Ohm and Monahan 1965), although this kind of scholarship in educational administration was limited in amount compared with empirical and theoretical studies. My claim here is a modest one and easy to defend. It is that work on values in educational administration was ongoing during the period from the late 1950s to the late 1970s or early 1980s, the approximate time frame typically cited by those claiming otherwise. The allegation that values were ignored is as out of touch with reality as the allegation that philosophical positivism and sociological functionalism dominated the field. Of course, the allegations are related, in the sense that they serve the David and Goliath fantasies of those making them; but they are also miseducative because they are too often naively accepted in educational administration, a field that, like many others, exhibits a surprising amount of philosophical and sociological innocence.

I confess that I do not give a high priority to writing about the past when there is so much to be done in the present. I do so because there have been so many farfetched distortions and because more accurate renditions of history can hold useful lessons for the present. Among such lessons is that, at least in the social sciences and related fields, one person or one movement alone rarely changes a whole field of study in fundamental and dramatic ways. Even ideas that catch on are typically abetted by multiple causes and circumstances and often by broader societal or environment factors.

The Present: Some Contenders and Problems

Now I turn to some contemporary problems in the area of values and valuation in educational administration. Elsewhere I suggested (1988) that an increased concern with values is one of a number of trends in the literature of educational administration. It is a trend that I welcome, and I readily acknowledge that writers I have criticized, as well as others and the spirit of the times, helped fuel this increased concern. In this part of the paper, three approaches to values that have gained some attention in educational administration will be briefly and critically examined. They are subjectivistic ethics, emancipatory moral perspectives, and the notion of caring as a key to ethical choice.

Consideration of these approaches will be limited mainly to their generic qualities. Claims of newness can draw attention and sometimes facilitate career advancement, but the core problems of ethics, and of philosophy proper, are essentially long-standing and familiar, as are the strong and weak points of the various efforts to address them.

To be sure, the world and life are ever changing. New experiences and thinking are found everywhere, varying by time, place, and specific individuals and groups. Still, the big questions such as What is good and right? and How should one make moral choices? endure, just as the broad types of answers given to such questions have endured. Hence, the focus on generic qualities, with particular emphasis on the weak points or generic flaws of each of the views considered, something also done later for the naturalistic approach I see as the most justifiable available.

Subjectivism in Ethics

Subjectivism in philosophy usually has been a form of idealism. Hence, the expectation that subjectivist ethics will always be highly individualistic and relativistic is incorrect. Often subjectivist ethics reflect the belief that there are certain ideals that are immutable and absolute and that adherence to these ideals is moral conduct.

In educational administration, while T. B. Greenfield correctly emphasized the obvious, the importance of values for the field, he did not articulate a position on values or valuation. This task was done by Hodgkinson (e.g., 1991), a substantive scholar, who has completed four books on ethics and administration in education. Writing within an idealist-subjectivist frame of reference, Hodgkinson presented a hierarchy of values based on personal preferences, appeals to reason, and principles described as having a quality of absoluteness, which were at the pinnacle of the hierarchy. Hodgkinson is a skillful writer, and many of the examples he gave made intuitive sense.

However, there are, several generic problems in such a view. One is the source of absolute principles. Do they emanate from some form of transcendental insight given to the author, from an authoritative being, from an ancient or special writing invested with a sacred quality, or some other source? Further, how does one decide whether a value is absolute, only reasonable, or merely a personal preference, especially in the case of values near the dividing points in the three-part hierarchy? Another problem is the possibility, even the likelihood, that there will be conflicts between absolute values in the context of particular moral choices. This would present a dilemma for anyone who takes the absolute character of both values seriously, a dilemma unresolvable within this framework (Evers and Lakomski 1991).

A broader point in connection with absolute values is that they lend themselves to closed-minded dogmatism. The answers are in hand and only need to be mechanistically applied or imposed. The latter term is added because history is replete with instances of evil committed by zealots in the name of fixed principles held to be true and worthy of universal acquiescence. Positions that ground principles in experience, leaving them open to new evidence and logical argument, seem far less easy to use to support extremism of whatever sort. While those who accept the notion of fixed and absolute values are frequently tolerant and compassionate persons, the history lesson remains.

Emancipatory Moral Perspectives

As used here, *emancipatory moral perspective* refers to the various Marxist, neo-Marxist, and Marxist-related views on the subject. Critical theory, the version most popular in educational administration, derived historically from the effort of the so-called Frankfurt School to revise and revitalize Marxist thought (Held 1980), which had lost ground because of its erroneous predictions and the vitality of liberal democracies where workers failed to develop class consciousness, let alone foment revolution. Today's far Left has the added problem of the demise of Marxist and Marxist-oriented governments after being roundly rejected by their citizens, including the working classes. Social radicalism has, more than ever, become the domain of intellectuals located in the academy, some of whom have even taken to calling themselves "culture workers."

Wallerstein wrote of "the era of a thousand Marxisms" (1986, 1302). More recently Davies (1995) used "post-Marxist" to cover thinkers having a Marxist lineage but who eschew some Marxist tenets and blend a radical agenda with postmodernist ideas, and with gender, and racial politics, going beyond the traditional emphasis on class. Variation here often has been like doctrinal disputes within a church, with much argument over particular points of belief and ideology, as in the recent reproduction-resistance debates.

Beyond these internal debates, neo-Marxists tend to be clearer on what they oppose than what they support. Much of their writing is social commentary, often in the form of attacks on institutions and groups thought to be the sources of inequity or oppression. Dominant classes or interests are typically assumed to be monolithic and controlling. In addition to politically conservative views and liberal ideas, positivism is also a frequent target. 'Positivism' is used as a catchall and pejorative term, despite its demise in philosophy many years ago.

The term *emancipatory* was used here because it is favored by neo-Marxists and other social radicals in the academy. It is usually broadly employed to refer to the freeing of the oppressed. The latter include not only the economically deprived, but also an array of groups believed to suffer inequities because of ascribed, rather than achieved, status. Radical academics have not been reluctant to become self-appointed spokespersons for those they refer to as the "silenced" or the "voiceless." This is not unrelated to Davies' comments on the assumption that "only critical theorists know what ordinary folk really desire" (1995, 1472), an assumption he sees fitting the Marxist tradition which projects the movement's political aspirations as objective interests of disadvantaged groups.

In any event, such issues are rarely defined as empirical ones. Even the growing collection of studies frequently referred to as critical ethnography is usually oriented explicitly to social change rather than to scientific inquiry (Anderson 1989). This brings us to a generic flaw of extreme political movements that has something in common with transcendentalism. Here, political ideology takes the place of absolute values and is given a privileged status. Ideologues of neither the Left nor the Right present their views as hypotheses to be tested; they have pregiven solutions. Unlike those who subscribe to a set of absolute values, however, emancipatory thinkers tend to put their faith in a political agenda that has a temporal dimension—hence, the many in-house debates within the broader ideological framework. Just as transcendentalists can differ about which values are absolute, emancipatory thinkers can differ about ideological interpretations and priorities. However, these differences are usually not over specific issues of ethics in the formal sense. They tend to be about the ideological fit of various concepts and ideas. The reproduction-resistance debate noted earlier, for instance, was about whether an emphasis on reproduction stinted the ardor of the oppressed for radical reform and should be replaced by an emphasis on resistance. Much of the energy of scholars writing in the Marxist tradition has been expended in two broad areas: one, in attacks on oppressors as indicated previously, the other, in internal debate. The reproduction-resistance dispute is just one recent example. An ongoing task has been to account for the failure of workers and others to rally to the cause, with elaborate treatments of the causes for false consciousness a major pre-occupation.

Whatever the reason, there is a dearth of formal philosophical work on values within this tradition. Equality and emancipation are favored terms, and the direction of desired radical reform (revolution is no longer in vogue) is clear at least in general terms, but there appear to be no systematic treatments of valuation, to take one example of a crucial area in ethics. Critical theorists might argue that philosophical issues are less urgent than issues of social justice, a well-meant point. Nevertheless, there are many general questions the Marxist tradition neglects. One example is When should equality be of opportunity or when of outcomes? Another set of questions concerns what should be done when the will of a popular majority clashes with radical political objectives. On the latter issue, the Marxist legacy is a dismal one, in need of contemporary treatment.

A related generic flaw that extreme political views share is their tendency to ignore "means" in favor of "ends." History is replete with examples of this sort of thing, especially once extremists attain power. On this, the Marxist legacy is, in some cases, far worse than dismal, it is malefic.

Caring

The concept of 'caring' has become a more significant one in the literature on ethics. Its rise appears to be associated with the increased influence of feminists in society and across a variety of academic disciplines. In educational philosophy, caring is associated with the work of Noddings (1984) and in educational administration with that of Beck (1994). There have even been some descriptive studies of the relationship of caring and administrative practice (Marshall et al. 1996).

An ethic based on caring has much to recommend it. Motivation and intentions are significant parts of moral behavior. Indeed, a caring attitude, which presumably includes empathy and acceptance, can of itself have positive effects for recipients. However, caring shares the generic flaw of ethics of good intention. While good intentions may be a facilitative, and, in many cases, even a necessary condition of doing good, they are not a sufficient condition. After all, students of education are all too familiar with cases of school administrators and teachers who genuinely cared and wanted to do good by helping students grow and learn, but whose efforts somehow ended in failure and frustration.

Caring and good intentions do not appear to be the central problems of contemporary education. Commitment to the welfare of students is often cited by educators as a major reason for their career choices and successes with students are frequently given as key sources of career satisfaction. On the whole, educators seem to exhibit relatively high levels of caring already.

A more fundamental problem is how to translate caring and good intentions into outcomes that actually benefit others. This is one of the basic concerns of ethical theory, a concern that is stinted by ethical theories that de-emphasize the processes of making moral choices in concrete situations.

Naturalistic Ethics

A naturalistic approach to ethics is concerned with just such a problem. Its emphasis is on the use of the best available ideas and methods to deal with moral problems. It is concerned not just with intentions, but with outcomes, with how well thought-through applications of ideals in real situations unfold and work out.

Much academic writing is the repackaging or creative application of ideas gleaned by studying the work of others. Hence, it is helpful to place one's views in context. The version of naturalism I present is philosophically influenced by critical naturalism and instrumentalism, and in some respects, by pragmatism and empiricism. Dewey (1922; 1938) and Farber (1959) are major sources, acknowledged though occasionally contravened.

The view is science friendly, aware that the methods of inquiry have worked better than authority, tradition, faith, or intuition in confronting human problems. Science is seen as a human creation with an important subjective component as well as a public verification side and as a fallible, often inadequate process that can provide only tentative explanations about nature, including human behavior, but as the best we have in an imperfect world. Science's blend of curiosity, openness to new ideas, and disciplined skepticism is taken as basic to the resolution of problems, including social and ethical ones. From a naturalistic perspective, positivism, subjectivism, critical theory, and postmodernist approaches are all seen as flawed, although each may offer some tenable ideas.

In terms of theory of knowledge, Dewey's (1938) definition of truth as warranted assertibility is appropriate, with warranting seen in terms of criteria of adequacy, such as explanatory plausibility and empirical credibility. Theory of knowledge in naturalistic philosophy is thus tied to inquiry and understanding, both seen as historically conditioned because they change and are self-rectifying over time. A conception of knowledge and knowledge getting is basic to this perspective's ethical theory because moral problems are addressed in the same general way as other important problems.

Moral problems were separated by logical positivists from scientific methods and results, a view held today by many subjectivists, critical theorists, and others. However, as actually experienced, issues of ethical desirability are intermixed with descriptive observations and interpretations. Further, genuine moral choices occur in concrete situations, and, if wise choices are to be made, judgments about the probable outcomes of alternative courses of action are required. The best available means are what Dewey (1922; 1938) variously called the "methods of inquiry" or "reflective methods," or sometimes, "deliberation," "intelligence," or "scientific methods." That such methods can facilitate the implementation of valued purposes makes sense, but an issue is the status of values and ethical principles in a naturalistic perspective.

Values and Principles

There is substantial agreement, in the abstract, about the worth of a large number of values and the lack of worth of others, often the negative poles of the former. For example, there would be high agreement about the desirability of liberty, love, kindness, justice, learning, health, adventure, and curiosity, and on the undesirability of subjugation, enmity, cruelty, ignorance, injustice, and so on. While the term *value* is usually used to connote conceptions of the desirable, other terms such as *ideal* and *virtue* are also current. Such terms also refer to desirable qualities, although 'ideal' may suggest difficulty of attainment, and 'virtue' sometimes indicates a personal characteristic.

Ethical principles, in a naturalistic framework, are well-established values that attain that status through use and experience. They result from cumulative ethical inquiry and knowledge and are crucial guides to moral choice, but they are not treated as absolutes. Fixed choices block reflective evaluation and can separate ethics from realities. Ethics divorced from the existential is not ethics at all, as illustrated in Dostoyevsky's malady of modern politics—love of humanity and hate for individuals.

The ethical individual is seen as one who strives to make wise moral decisions and who exemplifies the Deweyan (1922) concept of 'character', that is, the internalization of reflective methods and a devotion to human growth and attainment. In terms of social philosophy, this implies a society that fosters such methods and purposes. For Dewey, who advocated such a society, one of the failures of his times was that the methods of inquiry were rarely brought to bear on social problems, while pregiven solutions and inflexible ideologies were common. This, of course, is a failure that has remained with us.

This sketch of naturalistic ethics has been brief. I have treated that topic (1994b) and Dewey's thought (1994a) more extensively elsewhere, but in the space left, I want to turn to educational administration more specifically and then examine some generic flaws of the view presented.

Applications in Educational Administration

Many decisions in school organizations, whether made by administrators or teachers, or through some sort of participative arrangement, do not require moral assessment. They are minor, routine, or noncontroversial. Even some relatively significant moral issues can be resolved readily, if the competing values in the case are clearly of unequal moral force. It is when choices are between closely competing goods or the lesser of evils that moral valuation comes into play, in what administrators sometimes call the "gray areas." That writing on values in an applied field such as educational administration has not given greater attention to valuation, or the process of making moral choices, is unfortunate. Indeed, the separation of values from valuation is indefensible. It divorces values from critical thinking and reflective analysis, the very processes needed to abet moral choice.

An emphasis on valuation gives life to values, which are so often honored in a ritualistic way with verbal commitment rather than concrete action, a real danger in organizations such as schools, whose goals are complex and neither easily attained nor measured. Such an emphasis also underscores the importance of praxis, or thoughtful practice, in administration, just as it exposes the futility of packaged answers or quick fixes.

Valuation

The concept of 'valuation' as used in the present context refers to the application of the methods of inquiry to moral problems. Such problems can take a number of forms. A common one in administration is the problem that is thrust upon the administrator. Something happens that involves competing values. For example, a teacher's personal problems might seriously reduce teaching effectiveness, or a group of parents might demand that a classic work they find offensive be removed from the library. Another kind of problem is originated by administrators or others who want to improve some aspect of organizational work or outcomes. A curriculum change geared toward certain new and desirable learnings, or the implementation of a program designed to reduce drug use or some other dysfunctional student behavior are examples. For more elaborate illustrations, see Willower (1994c).

The first type of problem is one that demands attention even when one might wish to avoid it, the second requires an awareness of present circumstances and of possibilities for improvement. Persons of sensitivity and vision might readily imagine desirable possibilities, but a number of straightforward strategies are available to everyone. Seeking wide input on desirable school futures, scanning for gaps between goals and realities, reviewing lists of commonly accepted values and ideals to suggest directions that might be overlooked, and searching for organizational maladies such as routines or other structures that may no longer be relevant or effective are a few of the ways one can scan for desirable futures. Both received and originated problems are concerned with competing values and moral choices. A major difference is that originated problems are initially products of deliberate hopes and plans for more desirable futures.

Both kinds of problems require moral valuation. The steps to be taken are simply the methods of inquiry applied in a decision situation: the problem is formulated, alternative solutions are devised, the probable consequences of each alternative are conceptually elaborated, and a course of action that seems likely to achieve the valued outcomes sought is agreed upon.

This approach recognizes that moral choices occur in contexts. As such, a choice that benefits one person or group might harm others. The elaboration and analysis of probable consequences can help to anticipate negative consequences and to reduce unanticipated and unintended ones. When the potential negative consequences of a moral choice can be foreseen, they can be headed off or mitigated, which is itself a moral activity. Consequence elaboration and analysis, including the reduction of negative consequences as part of a larger moral choice, are thus taken to be important features of valuation. That there is little discussion in the literature on values in educational administration concerning such points suggests a certain irrelevance and lack of attention to the kinds of concrete moral problems that educators face.

Consequence analysis is an effort to see forward and to predict what will happen in a given situation. Obviously, it is a very chancy activity that will have its fair share of mistakes and occasional fiascoes. Even so, to ignore the probable outcomes of actions that affect others seems morally irresponsible. Hence, an aim should be consequence analysis that is informed and thoughtfully carried out. In this connection, relevant concepts and explanations, usually from the social sciences or education, that help us understand human behavior in organizations, can be of great utility. Knowledge of special contingencies in the particular setting is also valuable.

An issue in consequence elaboration is how far it should go. Consequences for various individuals and groups can be considered, and consequences can be formulated in educational, psychological, sociological, political, fiscal, and other terms, just to mention a few of the more obvious possibilities. However, deliberation cannot be endless, and choices have to be made. The purpose of consequence analysis is to facilitate moral choice, to help get to the heart of the matter at hand, and to abet a wise choice.

Here, reflective choices will simply have to be made. That available and relevant understandings and evidence were drawn upon rather than ignored is a kind of justification and a sign of thoughtful administration.

Since a naturalistic ethics uses the methods of inquiry to address moral problems, the same limitations that are characteristic of science are relevant here. The methods are fallible and uncertain, all the more so when applied to human activities and to problems occurring in particular settings with their own histories and contingencies. Still, there appear to be no better alternatives, although an inquiry-oriented perspective is always open to one, if its utility can be demonstrated.

Some Generic Flaws

Next, a few generic flaws of generally naturalistic approaches to ethics are considered. A common complaint is that there are no standards for good and evil in such a framework because absolute values are rejected. The point that principles, in that framework, derive from experience and cumulative moral inquiry was made earlier. The argument is similar to that used with regard to foundationalism in epistemology but applied to ethical knowledge.

That there is reasonably good agreement on general goods and evils or general principles is a sign of cumulative moral knowledge. That which principles apply, and how they are to function as guides, has to be worked out in concrete situations, is a sign of the importance of valuation.

In any event, it cannot be demonstrated that absolute values have extra-experiential grounding. Obviously, one could argue that human experience shows some values to be so important that they should never be violated and hence are absolute. Such an argument is understandable but would be more compelling if "never" were "only in the most unusual circumstances." This is necessary because of situations in which there are exceptions, as when someone must kill to save lives. However, exceptions are inadmissible for those who insist on an absolute standard. In the end, the demand for an absolute standard beyond that provided by intelligent reflection and moral inquiry is essentially unproductive, leading to endless argument and infinite regress. Hence, this "flaw" does not appear to be a fatal or even serious one.

The second generic flaw considered is more formidable. Here, a philosophy or ethics that stresses the methods of inquiry is seen as naive and overly optimistic. The idea that people would use such methods to deal with everyday or even serious problems is derided as unrealistic. Further, it is pointed out that such methods could be put to use to serve nefarious ends and that altruism in human affairs is rare, while its opposite is more frequent. History is often evoked to illustrate the darker side of the human condition.

The essential accuracy of much of these criticisms has to be granted. What they show is already well known—reason and ethical deliberation and judgment have never been the first coins of the realm. Most naturalistic perspectives recognize the centrality of emotion and cultural bias and argue that reflective methods should be internalized at the level of individual and institutionalized at the level of the organization or society (see Willower 1994a; 1994b). Further, they typically also see the gaining of more desirable futures through the use of the methods of inquiry as an ongoing struggle with no guarantees of success. However, a degree of optimism is often helpful in such struggles (as most administrators seem to know).

The frailties of the human condition beset all philosophical positions. Some, such as existentialism with its emphasis on anguish and despair, and postmodernism with its confused, narcissistic aversion to reason, appear to have given up hope. Obviously, hopes for the future need to be blended with a realistic understanding of the uncertainties and pitfalls sure to be met along the way. A philosophy grounded in inquiry seems less likely than some to be naive or unrealistic, but the generic flaw noted should serve as a warning. In human affairs, few worthwhile things come easily and events often have a kaleidoscopic quality, unfolding in unexpected directions. Nevertheless, when moral choices work, when consequence analysis leads to positive outcomes while minimizing negative ones, philosophy gains concrete, rather than abstract, justification.

Concluding Comments

I have presented a view of ethics that can be useful to those making moral choices. If one dismisses extreme ideologues and advocates for a particular interest group or political agenda, there is probably a considerable amount of common ground among those espousing different moral frameworks, especially when it comes to actual situations. The concrete, existential elements of moral problems in school settings and the constraints faced by educators in real organizations and communities would likely elicit reflective responses influenced by the particulars. Utopian schemes presumably would fade in favor of doable improvements that might actually benefit students, and abstractions about values would be eclipsed by concern about their attainment in the case at hand (Willower 1973).

All this is a warning of the dangers of ethical philosophy too far removed from day-to-day human experience. It also suggests that philosophy can serve practitioners in education best when it provides tools that sharpen the processes of ethical decision, rather than a fixed and impractical ideology.

If ethical ideals are to have meaning for educational practice, they should have plausible connections to genuine problems of educational policy and conduct. However, it is well to keep in mind that policy issues are not the sole province of practitioners, academics, or other specialists. Even internal school decisions can be legitimately questioned by citizens. Issues of policy and conduct can be illuminated by philosophy, although that does not happen very often. Indeed, philosophy seems less in evidence in public affairs than it once was, perhaps because so many academics espouse ideas that are, for want of a better term, merely academic.

The naturalistic view presented is one that is relevant to the issues of policy and practice in education. It provides methods geared toward the resolution of moral problems, and it insists on the importance of ethical principles and ideals while rejecting absolutes that ignore context.

I hope that the significance of valuation has been sufficiently emphasized. An approach to values divorced from valuation is of little use. It would be salutary if the debates about values in educational administration would begin to pay greater attention to valuation. In so doing, they might become more relevant to the kinds of pressing problems currently besetting education. The same methods of valuation are, of course, relevant to problems of all kinds, including broader societal ones and those faced by individuals in everyday life.

References

Alexander, J. C. 1988. The new theoretical movement. In *Handbook of sociology*, ed. N. J. Smelser, 77–101. Newbury Park, CA: Sage.

Anderson, G. L. 1989. Critical ethnography in education: Origins, current status, and new directions. *Review of Educational Research* 59: 249–70.

Bates, R. J. 1980. Educational administration, the sociology of science and the management of knowledge. *Educational Administration Quarterly* 16: 1–20.

Beck, L. G. 1994. *Reclaiming educational administration as a caring profession.* New York: Teachers College Press.

Beck, L. G., and Murphy, J. 1994. *Ethics in educational administration leadership programs.* Thousand Oaks, CA: Corwin Press.

Campbell, R. F., Fleming, T., Newell, L. J., and Bennion, J. W. 1987. *A history of thought and practice in educational administration.* New York: Teachers College Press.

Culbertson, J. A. 1988. A century's quest for a knowledge base. In *Handbook of research on educational administration*, ed. N. J. Boyan, 3–26. New York: Longman.

Culbertson, J. A., Jacobson, P. B., and Reller, T. L. 1960. *Administrative relationships: A case book.* Englewood Cliffs, NJ: Prentice-Hall.

Davies, S. 1995. Leaps of faith: Shifting currents in critical sociology of education. *American Journal of Sociology* 100: 1448–78.

Dewey, J. 1922. *Human nature and conduct.* New York: Henry Holt.

———. 1938. *Logic: The theory of inquiry.* New York: Henry Holt.

Evers, C. W., and Lakomski, G. 1991. *Knowing educational administration.* Oxford: Pergamon.

Farber, M. 1959. *Naturalism and subjectivism.* Springfield, IL: Charles C. Thomas.

Graff, O., and Street, C. 1957. Developing a value framework for educational administration. In *Administrative behavior in education,* ed. R. Campbell, and R. Gregg. 120–52. New York: Harper.

Greenfield, T. 1986. The decline and fall of science in educational administration. *Interchange* 17:57–80.

Greenfield, T. B. 1975. Theory about organizations. In *Administering education: International challenge,* ed. M. Hughes, 71–99. London: Athlone.

Guthrie, J. W. 1988. Educational finance: The lower schools. In *Handbook of research on educational administration,* ed. N. J. Boyan, 373–89. New York: Longman.

Habermas, J. 1987. *The philosophical discourse on modernity.* Oxford, England: Oxford Press.

Held, D. 1980. *Introduction to critical theory: Horkheimer to Habermas.* Berkeley and Los Angeles: University of California Press.

Hodgkinson, C. 1991. *Educational leadership: The moral art.* Albany: State University of New York Press.

Klatch, R. E. 1994. The counterculture, the new left, and the new right. *Qualitative Sociology* 17:199–213.

Lipset, S. M. 1994. The state of American sociology. *Sociological Forum* 9: 199–220.

Marshall, C., Patterson, J. A., Rogers, D. L., and Steele, J. R. 1996. Caring as career: An alternative perspective for educational administration. *Educational Administration Quarterly,* 32: 271- 94.

Merton, R. K., and Wolf, A. 1995. The cultural and social incorporation of sociological knowledge. *The American Sociologist* 26: 15–39.

Noddings, N. 1984. *Caring: A feminine approach to ethics and moral education.* Berkeley: University of California Press.

Ohm, R. E., and Monahan, W. G., eds. 1965. *Educational administration: Philosophy in action.* Norman: University of Oklahoma.

Phillips, D. C. 1992. *The social scientist's bestiary.* Oxford, England: Pergamon.

Sargent, C. G., and Belisle, E. L. 1955. *Educational administration: Cases and concepts.* New York: Houghton-Mifflin.

Travers, R. M. W. 1983. *How research has changed American schools: A history from 1840 to the present.* Kalamazoo, MI: Mythos Press.

Van Manen, M. 1994. Pedagogy, virtue, and narrative identity in teaching. *Curriculum Inquiry* 24: 135–69.

Wallerstein, I. 1986. Marxisms as utopias: Evolving ideologies. *American Journal of Sociology* 91: 1295–1308.

Willower, D. J. 1964. The professorship in educational administration: A rationale. In *The professorship in educational administration,* ed. D. J. Willower and J. A.

Culbertson, 87–105. Columbus, OH: University Council for Educational Administration.

———. 1973. Schools, values and educational inquiry. *Educational Administration Quarterly* 9: 1–18.

———. 1988. Synthesis and projection. In *Handbook of research on educational administration,* ed. N. J. Boyan, 729–47. New York: Longman.

———. 1994a. Dewey's theory of inquiry and reflective administration. *Journal of Educational Administration* 32: 5–22.

———. 1994b. *Educational administration: Inquiry, values, practice,* rev. ed. Lancaster, PA, and Basel, Switzerland: Technomic.

———. 1994c. Values, valuation and explanation in school organizations. *Journal of School Leadership* 4: 466–83.

———. 1996. Inquiry in educational administration and the spirit of the times. *Educational Administration Quarterly* 32: 344–65.

CHAPTER SEVEN

The Will to Power

Christopher Hodgkinson

Why should administrators or executives spend any of their valuable and high-priced time on philosophy? Such a question is neither trivial nor rhetorical. Administrators are already fully occupied with the nuts and bolts of organizational life. Where, if anywhere, would philosophy fit in all of this?

Well, in the first place, we are talking about administration rather than management,[1] and about practical wisdom rather than academicized philosophy. It is not that the general sweep of philosophical interests, academic or otherwise, is irrelevant to administration—far from it—but that our focus is upon the business of administration and leadership and all the human ramifications that that entails. The motives for studying this kind of philosophy are at least threefold: superficial, deep, and profound or, let us say, light, dark, and heavy.

The light reason for doing administrative philosophy is that it yields *sophistication.* This word derives from the Greek school of Sophists and has the connotation of *worldly* knowledge, knowledge about the way things and people really are, about motivation and the pathologies of people in organizations. The pay-off here is self-evident: sophistication trumps innocence.

The dark or deeper reason for doing administrative philosophy is that it leads, or can lead, to greater *understanding.* There is a significant difference between knowledge and understanding. The latter implies a depth and comprehension that can be ascribed to wisdom rather than to cleverness, mental agility, technical competence, or professionalism. Here, too, it can be argued, there would be much profit for the leader, for the practical executive, and for all who are embroiled in policy making and administrative action. Understanding trumps sophistication.

Last, the heavy reason, which is not for all, but for some it is incontestable. For those who have been once infected with the intellectual fascination of the study of human nature and the human condition (as this nature and condition is manifested in organizational life), there is no turning back. One does administrative philosophy because one can do no other—for its own sake, *sui generis, ars gratia artis.* Even apart from these motives or values there is a plain matter of fact: administrators cannot help *doing* philosophy because administration is philosophy in action.[2] The question then becomes, *Will they do it well or badly?*

Granted then that the discipline of administrative philosophy has some credibility, let us turn to the topic before us. It is a difficult one. It has vexed the greatest minds for millennia and therefore needs to be approached with some temerity. Consider the following linked sequence of propositions.

Propaedeutic Propositions

1. Leadership is an incantation for the bewitchment of the led.
2. Leadership is an attempt to determine the future, and hence *folie de grandeur.*
3. The best leadership is often followership.
4. Leadership and powe are coterminous. Impotent leadership is an oxymoron.
5. Power is the first term in the administrative lexicon.
6. Leader power is the ability to impose one's will.
7. Will is ubiquitous, but free will is a rarity.
8. Will supervenes reason.
9. The resolution of the conflict of wills is called "history."
10. A will is a value.

These propositions deal, in descending order, with the central administrative concepts of leadership, power, and will. Of these three basic elements, the central or linking concept is power. Power is the mediating factor between leadership and will.

Without defining (or confining) this primal concept of power, it may be said that it is the human analogue of the term *energy* in physics, that is, the ability to do work. In human affairs, however, as opposed to the simplicities of physics and mechanics, power is much more than that. It is above all the ability to impose one's will. Physical events are not the same as human events. In science, one presumes a determinism of cause and effect, a law of causation. (Let us ignore quantum phenomena for the moment.) In human events, a new factor appears: the concept of 'will' or 'voluntarism'. Thus, the human agent in the total equation of determining forces is "felt" to possess a freedom of choice. Of course, as we shall see, that sense of freedom may be a mere epiphenomenon, a psychological by-product of unconscious vectors, which are the *real* determinants. However, administration cannot function without either the illusion or the reality or both. Science itself stops short at the edge of voluntarism, at the frontiers of conscious choice and of mind, as opposed to brain. For this reason, a distinction between administration and management is essential:[3] the former opening upon the limitless horizons of philosophy, the latter upon the restricted field of vision right and proper to science and technology.

It follows that administration is a form of life in which wills enter into a complex domain of conflict, reconciliation, and resolution. In other words, administration is politics, that is, the creating, organizing, managing, monitoring, and resolving of value conflicts—where values are defined as concepts of the desirable with motivating force. In principle or in theory, the accomplishment of administrative ends, goals, targets, aims, purposes, plans, and objectives is no more than the imposition of a putative collective will upon the resistant and countervailing forces of matter, circumstances, materials, resources, and contending wills. To be without will would be to be without power, and, conversely, to have power is the ability to impose will. Of course, the more tender-minded might prefer the term *influence* to *impose*, but this is only to say that the imposition may be accomplished by more congenial and/or politically correct means.

Will to Power

The concept of 'will to power' extends beyond strictly administrative considerations and is generally associated with the philosopher Friedrich Nietzsche.[4] Its origins can be traced back through Nietzsche's mentor Schopenhauer, where it appears as the Will-to-Life to Vedantic Indian philosophizing about the life force and the eternal dynamic of creation, preservation, and destruction.[5] At considerable risk of oversimplification, it can be taken to refer to the primal maxim: self-preservation is the first law of nature. This maxim I have represented elsewhere as the first of the administrative meta-values.[6] However, self-interest in administration is always modulated by group and collective interest. Here, will becomes the will of the collectivity, and hence, in this sense, corporations, organizations, and nations can be said to be imbued with the will to power. From this, too, is born a foundational myth in administration. It is this: the leader represents and embodies the good of the whole and thus has the authority and power of a legitimized will. *L'etat, c'est moi*. Yet, despite this myth and the assumptions and presumptions of the textbooks, administrative reality is less a field of honor than a battleground of wills, a domain of confused, confusing, and conflicting values, a "darkling plain . . . where ignorant armies clash by night."[7]

On this darkling plain, victory is a function of will. Teh concepts of will and power, the will to power, are correlative; they are aspects of one another. But the will always encounters circumstantial and existential opposition, the so-called reality constraints. It is here that we tend to delude ourselves about the freedom of our will because we are not *conscious* of the extent to which we are mechanistically determined or programmed by external, subjective, and objective factors. Our capacity to shape events, for ourselves and others, is much less than we might think. There is nothing new in this. The Romans said it, *Fata viam inveniunt*, things happen by themselves. In complex circumstances, things just *happen,* and consequently the honorific of leadership (or administration) is often falsely attributed to an actor who is simply in the right place at the right time. Fate has smiled upon him. His plan has worked out. His enterprise has been successful. All of which speaks neither to his virtue nor to his will.

> The Roman people often refused to mark great and beneficial victories because the qualities of leadership of the commander were inferior to his good luck. In this world's activities we often notice that Fortune rivals Virtue; she shows us what power she has over everything and delights in striking down our presumption by making the incompetent lucky since she cannot make them wise. She loves to interfere, favoring those performances whose course has been entirely her own. That is why we can see, every day the simplest amongst us bringing the greatest public and private tasks to successful conclusions.[8]

Or to jump from ancient Rome to modern quantum physics and brain science:

> It may well be argued that each of our actions is ultimately determined by our inheritance and by our environment—or else by those numerous chance factors that continually affect our lives. Are not *all* of these influences 'beyond our control', and therefore things for which we cannot ultimately be held responsible? . . . The legal issue of 'responsibility' seems to imply that there is indeed, within each one of us, some kind of independent 'self' with its *own* responsibilities—and, by implication, rights—whose actions are *not* attributable to inheritance, environment, or chance.[9]

So, there we have it. There *may* be a self that constitutes some "missing ingredient" or "will," known to the law but presently unknown to science.[10] Let us now consider this prospect from a different angle.

Values and Organizations

Proposition 10 asserts that a will is a value. What does this mean? It follows from the definition of value[11] that all of our values are label for desire. What are desires but wills seeking gratification? In this sense, our selves are not unitary but instead complexes of competing and conflicting desires (to drink or abstain, to choose this wallpaper over that wallpaper, to be naughty or nice, to be or not to be), and the value that wins out in any situation is *ipso facto* the strongest desire or will, a will that we are then conditioned to regard as our free will or our free choice.

This logic is illustrated by figure 7.1.

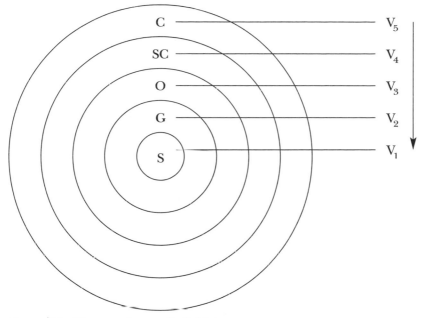

Figure 7.1   The morphogenetic field

This illustration shows how values themselves are not unitary or homogeneous but exist hierarchically as concepts of the desirable, with motivating force at different levels: the levels of culture (C), subculture (SC), organization (0), group (G), and individual (S), in a downward impress from, respectively, V_5 to V_1. Our much-cherished freedom of will is here shown to be, at the very least, attenuated and, at the most, totally conditioned (albeit unconsciously) by the contending wills of the morphogenetic field. The concept of 'morphogenesis' is drawn from biology and evolutionary theory as exemplified particularly in the work of Sheldrake and Goodwin.[12] A simple life illustration would be the wearing of backpacks and the de rigueur uniformity of backward baseball caps among the youth of the day. At a more sinister level would be the enormous influence of political correctness and its "tyranny of virtue."[13]

Notwithstanding the impress of cultural, social, and organizational values upon us, we cling, by virtue of the will to power, to the notion of the autonomy and unity of the individual self. We would make the world in our own image, and the organization wherein we work and upon which our careers and livelihood depend (V_3), closer to our own administrative-political desires. This individual aspect of will to power is captured in the centrality of self or V_1, but this in turn can be enucleated or analyzed as shown in figure 7.2.

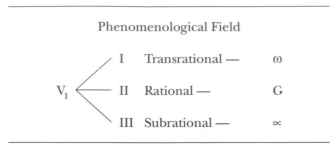

Figure 7.2

Here values are analyzed as they occur within the realm of subjective experience. At level III they are preferences rooted in our emotional or basic alpha nature. At Level II they are rationalized values based either on group consensus or on some form of utilitarian cost-benefit or pleasure-pain calculus. In any event, they invoke the intelligence or G factor as opposed to affective impulse or alpha. Finally, at level I, values transcend the psychological faculties of cognition and affect and exhibit an apparent transcendent quality of will (Ω). Type I values go beyond reason in that they are integral to the individual will to power. They are not subject to negotiation or compromise. One could say that one lives or dies by them. Examples are martyrdom, terrorism, nationalism, patriotism, religion and, in general, any overriding life commitment to an ideological cause. A clear type I pattern, for example, emerges from even a superficial examination of the Unabomber manifesto.[14] Type I values or type I will to power thus represent the largest challenge an administrator may have to encounter; they also represent a countervailing force to the general morphogenetic impress.

This latter constitutes a complex of value forces, an ecology of interests and will, which forms the axiological context of practical administration (praxis). It also allows us to identify the central value conflict in organizations and suggests the hypothesis that the root conflict is not the conventional idiographic contest between V_1 and V_3. Rather, it is a dual conflict between, first, individuals (V_1) and their organizations (V_3)—the orthodox idiographic-nomothetic dissonance—and second, between culture (V_5) and its component corporate units (V_3) where the interest conflict can be specified in economic terms—the greed of the parts being in opposition to the welfare of the whole.

As society becomes increasingly an *organizational* society with large, complex, bureaucratic, and corporate entities increasingly dominant, and as it becomes increasingly international and global in scope, the phenomenon of the individual deriving psychological *identity* from the organization dominating that individuals's life, as the source of livelihood and career, becomes more and more the norm. Saul has defined the term *corporation* as "any interest group: specialized, professional, public or private, profit-oriented or not." The one characteristic assured by all corporations is that the primary relationship of individual members is to the organization and not to society at large. In their own relationship with the outside world, corporations deal, whenever possible, with other corporations, not with individuals. The modern corporation is a direct descendant of the medieval craft guild.[15] The more one is beholden in a hierarchical structure, the more one is in the power of one's immediate superiors, as well as one's peers!

In Saul's view, corporatism represents the triumph of fascism over democracy; democracy here taken in the romantic Athenian or practical Swiss sense—fascism here taken in its proper original sense as a collectivity of V_3 interests bound together by the State—the emblem of which was the bundle of sticks (fasces) bound together around an axe and carried before the Roman senators by the lictors as a symbol and reminder of the common good. (One can easily break one stick, but the bundle together is unbreakable.) Examples of contemporary sticks (and feudal identities) are the professions, the bureaucracy, and the corporations of industry, trade, commerce, and entertainment. Rather thick sticks, one must admit, but by them we come to identify ourselves *to* ourselves not as individuals, not as *persons,* but rather as doctors, lawyers, civil servants, educators, or administrators—as what we do rather than what we are. Thus we leach our individuality, our wills, and our very consciousness into the roles provided by the organizational forms.

The administrative implication of this malaise is that it tends to exacerbate the imperative to fight one's own corner, whatever that corner might be: the department, division, company, corporation, or private practice. The larger good is always decided elsewhere, if at all—increasingly *if at all.* Our eyes are on the next prize, and prizes are bestowed close to home. One is not rewarded for blowing the whistle in the greater interest. In this state of value affairs, our consciousness of ourselves is defined and limited by our roles and our wills are weakened by corporatist and subcorporatist myopia. What is good for General Tobacco may or may not be good for the nation, but it is certainly good for the CEO. And as to democracy, that great catchword, what difference to the good of the commonwealth does one-man-one-vote make in a mass electorate of millions? What is one vote among a million? What power attaches to a drop in the ocean? What is one will against the blind will to power?

A possible answer to this rhetorical question is indeed philosophically intriguing. It is that the one will (of the individual) is conscious, or at least susceptible of being conscious, while the will of the mass is not conscious in any way that we can sensibly interpret. It is Leviathan, but we do not feel ourselves to be programmed robotic machines, and we do feel we can resist social, peer group, and organizational pressures, if only very modestly and occasionally. To some extent at least, we feel we can be cause rather than effect. Yet Professor Penrose is exceedingly tentative on this point. In his work on the science of consciousness he questions the whole concept of cause.

> I shall argue that when a 'cause' i, the effect of our conscious actions, then it must be something very subtle, certainly beyond computation, beyond chaos, and also beyond any purely random cause. . . . If it were not for the puzzling aspects of consciousness that relate to the presence of 'awareness' and perhaps of our feelings of 'free will', which as yet seem to elude physical description, we should not need to feel tempted to look beyond the standard methods of science for explanation of minds as a feature of physical behavior and brains.[16]

Where does all this leave the philosophically minded administrator? With three options; namely, the extremes of determinism and voluntarism embracing a middle position of potentiality. The thrust of my argument has been to show the very powerful deterministic and mechanistic world views deriving from contemporary science. The reactionary extreme to this is the now somewhat faded rubric of existentialism (sometimes characterized as irrationalism), which insists upon the essential human experience of choice and, usually with tragic overtones, the consequent burden of responsibility. Administrative experience will be sympathetic to this philosophical standpoint because of the centrality of decision making in administrative practice, but serious reflection upon any decision or policy-making process will again return us to the question of the actual *freedom* of this process. Does not the strongest vector always decide?

Finally, there is the middle ground. *Via aurea mediocritas!* The human actor is conceived of here, as, at least, a potentially conscious entity, albeit with a transient and elusive self, who has the *potential* for making conscious and free choices, despite conditioning, and who therefore is capable of (and hence responsible for) altering the world from what it otherwise might be, to however minor a degree. This would then be the true will to power and the very crux of leadership. Furthermore, this human potentiality is capable of self-development. One can grow, fail to grow, or simply wither on the vine; one can become more or less mechanical, more or less conscious, more or less a will. From this, it would follow that the onus of leadership, the philosophical White man's burden of administration (if I can be forgiven a political malapropism) is to advance the human potential within the prescribed field of organizational life.

The Education of the Will

The will to power is an abstraction. Nietzsche himself refused to advance positive characterizations of the will to power. It was simply that which "resides at the most basic level of intelligibility,"[17] in other words, the primal motivation. It becomes reality as it is embodied and manifested in the *individual*. Moreover, it must be understood that, at the individual level, will (intention) is a faculty distinct from either thinking (cognition) or feeling (affect). As has been shown above, what commonly passes for will is not that at all but is simply an unconscious result of competing affective preferences or vectors (impulses) in which the strongest wins out and is thereafter rationalized (if it is thought about at the conscious level) as an act of will. Actually, this is the act of an automaton. Let us discriminate then between apparent will and real will, between mechanical will and free will. The question before us then becomes Is it possible to acquire the latter? To become free? Or, to put it another way, Can one achieve self-mastery?

The general answer to this question is yes. But the education or training necessary to achieve this affirmative is unlikely to be found in the schools of leadership, management, and administration in the West.[18] The military disciplines of leadership training practised in officer schools of both West and East, while they clearly confront part of the problem through ego-submission techniques, do not thereby educe *freedom* of the will. On the contrary, it could be argued that such education is moral programming or conditioning rather than any inducement to the Socratic examination of the self or the questioning of authority. With reservations, much the same might be said of elite schools of administration generally. Indeed, short of adopting oriental, monastic, or Zen principles of character development and training, all that can be reasonably said or done is to analyze the psychological principles implicit in these more esoteric methods of will education and present them for reflection and consideration wherever the affirmative answer is seriously sought.

The essential element and primary ingredient in all such 'will' methodologies would appear to be introspection. In contemporary society, administrative man or woman is continuously engaged in action of some kind—in affairs, in gossip, in the hurly-burly and abrasive rough and tumble of organizational politics, in busyness, calendars, schedules, meetings, conferences, and the multiplicity of human contacts, which, if not always stressful, are always demanding of energy. In consequence, the psyche is pressured. Any spare time is occasion for guilt that there should even be spare time. When such time is to be found, it is not generally conceived as retreat, as space for solitary reflection or the inward look of contemplation. Such time is more generally regarded as opportunity for well-earned egoistic self-indulgence (and possibly yet more wear and tear). Now, from the standpoint of the education of the will, I would argue that both excessive 'action' and excessive 'recreation' are detrimental. Action and contemplation may be at opposite ends of some psychic continuum, but in administrative philosophy they need to be balanced. Either one without the other falls short. The will to power requires both.

This would be verifiable not in the empirical scientific mode but in the phenomenological mode, that is, by individual experience and personal experimentation. The hypothesis is that some form of reflection, introspection, or self-observation can lead to an inner understanding, which is accompanied by increased awareness or consciousness of one's own being and willed actions. This sensibility is then directly applicable to others because it increases the capacity for what the Germans call "*Mitfühlung*," a sort of empathy and insight into the motivations of one's fellows. One becomes a "*Menschenkenner*," in that one senses or knows what makes people "tick." Such knowledge is power. Moreover, there is a further power hypothesis in this line of reasoning: consciousness and will are correlative.[19] The increase of the former creates at least the potential for a corresponding increase of the latter.

At a minimal level then, any new curriculum with the radical objective of the independence of the will would have to aim at self-discipline and self-mastery in the domain of *emotion*, particularly *negative* emotion. Given the assumption that one can control increasingly one's emotions, one can become 'detached'. Kipling's "If one can keep one's head while all about you are losing theirs," is an attribute of obvious appeal in the administrative art.

To realize authentically one's will to power would be to have acquired sufficient strength of will to be 'unimpressed' (literally so) by all value levels above V_1. Such a degree of freedom does not mean that those levels would be disparaged or discounted but that it would allow the leader to use the levels V_2–V_5 to the end of the common, organizational, or higher good without being used *by* them. Such a leadership agenda would be neither unconscious nor reactive. It would be a function of will and consciousness. It would imply at least the inclusion of some type I values. Such leadership might also be, indeed is likely to be, politically incorrect. This follows because this leadership would be authentically individual and a challenge to social norms and hence not without risk. In the ideal, it would embrace a full comprehension and sensibility of the entire V_1–V_5 range but yet with an independent autonomous V_1 interpretation, which, while often held in restraint to subserve the consensus, nevertheless at its greatest moments becomes in truth a triumph of the will.

Conclusion

I shall now conclude with a balancing set of propositions that derives from this philosophical expedition but which has a more practical and perhaps therapeutic import than its propadeutical predecessors.

Therapeutic Propositions

1. There is never any shortage of leadership positions.
2. There is never any dearth of aspirants for leadership positions.
3. Therefore, the problem is now, as it has always been, *curricular.*
4. The administrative curriculum is lifelong.
5. The managerial side of this curriculum is currently adequate, the administrative or leadership side, inadequate.
6. Knowing what and knowing how are less important than nothing why.
7. Knowing why can be define d as axiology: the philosophical theory of value in general, embracing ethics or the philosophical theory of morality, but extending far beyond it to include aesthetic, technical, prudential, hedonic, and other forms of value. Any field of human discourse in which the value-terms *good* and *ought* figure falls within the range of axiology, even that of scientific method with its principles about the degree of belief we *ought* to give to a hypothesis in the light of a given body of evidence.[20]
8. Hence, the emergent curriculum would include consideration of the problem of the will, the problem of the common good, *Realpolitik*, social critique, and bureau pathology in all its forms.
9. At a minimum the emergent curriculum would incorporate practical training in the art of commonsense, logic rhetoric, and polemic.
10. Administration proper is a high-risk, high-reward vocation, the fine art of discovering, developing, and deploying power and imposing will upon the world.

The point of the exploration has already been made, but, to reiterate, it is the peculiar onus upon those who would aspire to leadership in the truest sense to achieve the maximum degree of self knowledge and self-mastery. This may sound idealistic, but it is my conviction that it is neither ethereal nor impractical, but rather an *ultra*-practical or even *hyper*-practical suggestion. That it is avoided as often as not is merely the mark of malaise, of the flight *into* reason rather than *beyond* it. *Will supervenes reason.*

Notes

1. C. Hodgkinson. (*Towards a Philosophy of Administration.* Oxford: Blackwell. 1982) Prop.6: 21.
2. Ibid. Prop.1, 202.

3. Sir Geoffrey Vickers. (*Public Administration.* 1979, 57: 229).

4. Considering the administrative theorists' concern with power, it is somewhat curious that Nietzsche is so rarely cited in the literature. See the English text *The Will to Power.* trans. Walter Kaufmann and R. J. Hollingdale, New York: Vintage. 1968).

5. Nietzsche sees it as an ultimate driving force in the economies of life and nature, extending beyond merely human affairs. "Life itself is *essentially* appropriation, injury, overpowering of what is alien and weaker; suppression, hardness, imposition of one's own forms, incorporation and, at its mildest, exploitation. . . . Life simply *is* will to power." (*Beyond Good and Evil.* trans. Walter Kaufman. New York: Penguin.1976, 211).

6. Hodgkinson. 1982. 180ff.

7. Matthew Arnold. (Dover Beach).

8. Michel de Montaigne. (*Four Essays.* trans. M. A. Screech. London: Penguin. 1995, 57).

9. Roger Penrose. (*Shadows of the Mind.* New York: Oxford University Press. 1994, 36).

10. Ibid.

11. Christopher Hodgkinson. (*Administrative Philosophy.* Oxford: Pergamon. 1996, 110–11).

12. Rupert Sheldrake. (*A New Science of Life.* London: Paladin.1981); Brian Goodwin. *The Evolution of Complexity.* New York: Simon and Schuster. 1994).

13. Richard Bernstein. (*Tyranny of Virtue.* New York: Knopf. 1994).

14. "The Unabomber Manifesto," private copy. (Available via U.S. libraries, but applicants are liable to be listed on FBI computer files.)

15. John Ralston Saul. (*The Doubter's Companion.* Toronto: Viking. 1994, 74).

16. Penrose. Op. cit. 36, 50.

17. Alphonso Lingis. (The Will to Power. In *The New Nietzsche.* ed. D. Allison. New York: Delta 1977, 37–63).

18. The Matsushita School of Government and Management Tokyo is, from the author's experience, a clear illustration of the contrary. (Cf. PHP Institute, Osaka, Japan.)

19. Christopher Hodgkinson. (*The Philosophy of Leadership.* Oxford: Blackwell. 1983, 229).

20. Lord Quinton's definition. (*Dictionary of Modern Thought,* 2nd edition. London: Fontana. 1988).

CHAPTER EIGHT

Ethical School Leadership: Problems of an Elusive Role*

Elizabeth Campbell

It is highly improbable that one would encounter, in either the theoretical educational literature or discussions with practitioners and students en-rolled in administrator preparation programs, the suggestion that school administrators should not be ethical leaders. On the contrary, much of the current literature emphasizes the need for a heightened awareness of the ethical dimensions of educational leadership, and lively classroom debates engage students who seem inclined to seize on the practical significance of these dimensions. On the one hand, the issue appears noncontestable; it is a given that educational practitioners should fulfill their professional obliga-tions in ways that are moral and ethical. On the other hand, the conceptual complexities of translating theoretical prescriptions into practical action seem, at times, insurmountable.

To imply, as the title of this chapter does, that the desirable role of the ethical school leader is an elusive one is not to suggest that it does not exist or that principals necessarily do not strive to be moral leaders. However, it does suggest that, what ethical or moral leadership actually means in practice is seemingly difficult to identify, define, describe, achieve, and comprehend; an elusive concept is one that may signify many and differ-ent things to many people. The quality of elusiveness in this case is com-pounded and complicated further by the pervasive, contemporary accep-tance of moral or value relativism.

To explore this thesis, the purposes of this chapter are to review briefly some recent literature that focuses on the ethical nature of schooling and educational administration and criticizes the lack of attention given to ethics in professional preparation courses, to propose that it is ironic and ultimately paralyzing to assert the need to enhance ethical practice in schools while continuing to advance relativist and subjective interpretations of ethical values, and to provide a discussion of the place of ethics in admin-istrator preparation programs based on my own practice and the theories of others. The chapter concludes that, while the acknowledgment of the ethi-cal dimensions and dilemmas of school leadership is valuable and essential,

* Originally published May 1997 in *Journal of School Leadership* 7, 3: 287–300. Lancaster PA: 1997 Technomic Publishing Co., Inc.

the links between theoretical reflection and practical application have yet to be established in this complex philosophical area.

The New Imperative of Ethical Leadership

Contemporary theoretical and empirical literature increasingly has addressed the necessity for educators to regard their professional responsibilities as basic moral and ethical imperatives. Moral agency, moral purpose, and the moral authority of accountable practice in education are highlighted (Fullan 1993; Grace 1995; Hodgkinson 1991; 1995; Holmes 1992;; 1992b; Marshall 1992; Sergiovanni 1992, 1996; Sockett 1990; 1993; Strike and Ternasky 1993; West 1993). Closely related to these is the growing emphasis on building moral communities in schools (Sergiovanni 1996) and the demand that schools stand for and reflect valued principles (Cohen 1995; Etzioni 1990; Lickona 1991; Wynne and Ryan 1993). These concepts correspond well with an interest in uncovering and describing the moral character of schools and the ethical dimensions of schooling (Jackson, Boostrom, and Hansen 1993; Kirschenbaum 1994; Sockett 1993).

Central to much of this literature is the argument that educational leaders must develop and articulate a much greater awareness of the ethical significance of their actions and decisions, be they the unintentional outcomes of their daily practice (Jackson, Boostrom, and Hansen 1993) or the deliberate goals they establish based on an inherent moral authority (Sergiovanni 1994). Sergiovanni (1992; 1994; 1996) regards the work of leadership to be a type of stewardship in which shared purposes, values, beliefs, and commitments supply the roots for school community building. He argues that morally based leadership is a desirable substitute for value-neutral managerial and bureaucratic "frames" of leadership that traditionally have informed educational administration theory.

Similarly, Hodgkinson criticizes organizational bureaucracies, such as schools, for their "loss of ethics" (1991, 37), and complains that, "values, morals, and ethics are the very stuff of leadership and administrative life, yet we have no comprehensive theory about them and often in the literature they receive very short shrift" (11). He recommends that school leaders and other aspiring and incumbent administrators gain self-understanding and knowledge through the close examination and questioning of the values they reflect and uphold.

Clearly, it is important for educators to contemplate the essence of their work, the values they transmit formally and informally in their daily practice, and the implications of these values for those with whom they are engaged. However, while it may be conceded that "the unexamined value is not worth holding" (Hodgkinson 1995, 80), it should be noted also that the process of deep and genuine reflection does not necessarily make a value more morally and ethically desirable. So, for school leaders faced with moral conflicts and ethical dilemmas, solitary reflection of the inherent value principles is crucial but may not imbue them with the level of objective certainty needed to translate theoretical concepts into correct action.

In her account of educational values for school leadership, West notes that this lack of guiding principles needed to inform individual decision making is a new societal reality as much as a school one. She notes that the "loss of common purpose and shared values in our society encourages a tendency to turn away from the immeasurable areas which are concerned with values or ethics and to substitute for such considerations a reliance on the apparently neutral language of technical and operative mechanisms" (West 1993, 152). This assumed neutrality of technical and managerial orientations to educational administration characterizes organizational conceptions so criticized by Hodgkinson and Sergiovanni, among others.

Conclusions drawn from empirical studies of principals' decision-making practices support the claim that ethical considerations are subordinated by instrumental ones related to policy and strategy. This is not to suggest that principals necessarily do not behave ethically or that policy-driven choices cannot also be morally sound. However, if ethical means and ends are merely the happy coincidence of leadership choices rather than the focused aim, then the vision of ethical leadership and the building of morally based school communities, so recommended in the literature, is obscured.

In a study of twenty-three principals who were asked to describe their professional experiences involving moral conflict, Kirby, Paradise, and Protti (1992) reported that the majority of principals functioned at an "institutional" or "societal" level in which decisions were based primarily on policy and prevailing norms of behavior, even when they conflicted with personal ethical reasoning.

In concluding that decision making in schools is dominated by strategic rather than ethical concerns, Strike (1993) defines strategic choices as those that seek "to achieve certain ends, but tend not to appraise the ends sought, address potential conflicts between different ends, or constrain the pursuit of these ends by any moral principles" (1993, 103). Ethical choices, by contrast, appraise decisions to determine the rightness or wrongness of actions. While the two are not necessarily unrelated, they are distinguishable from each other.

Similarly, in a study of teachers' and principals' moral dilemmas, Campbell (1992) noted that the principals frequently denied that their problems were ethical in nature; instead, they characterized them as being strategic, practical, professional, and political. Ethical dilemmas were seen often as "other people's" problems in which principals are called on to mediate using decision-making and conflict resolution strategies and techniques that are perceived to be reasonably value neutral.

In another research study of situations that school administrators consider to be ethical dilemmas, Marshall notes that administrator training programs emphasize "the technical, social, and conceptual dimensions of administration, usually neglecting questions of values" (1992, 369). Consequently, ethical dilemmas arose because "there was no clear and sensible guidance from policy or a professional code" (376). They tended to be handled by principals in highly subjective ways based on personal judgment, beliefs, and the kind of "moral human beings" (376) they thought themselves to be. Marshall concludes, "Seat-of-the-pants ethics does not work; it gives us stressed administrators unable to make decisions with any sense of professional guidance or support" (383).

Despite, or perhaps because of, such empirical evidence, the call for more ethically aware leadership in schools is intensifying. A brief survey of recent literature confirms this new imperative. However, the dilemma, persists in how to bridge theory and practice. Stating clearly, as Hodgkinson does, that "we must stop doing those things we ought not to do and begin doing those things we ought to do" (1995, 75) does not seem specific enough to be useful. And stating with conviction, as MacIntyre (1981) does, that we should adopt the guiding principles of justice, truth, and courage does not seem to be easily interpreted and translated into action. While agreement with these virtues in the abstract may be achieved fairly easily, consensus on their application in practice may remain beyond our reach. Furthermore, current attention to the ethical dimensions of school leadership, while theoretically significant for our ongoing quest for improved practice, is constrained by the prevailing climate of value relativism in which our discussions evolve.

If Everything Is Relative, Then Nothing We Do Is Wrong—or Right

A certain irony characterizes the heightened attention directed at the ethical dimensions of school leadership. It is that efforts to raise theoretical awareness of the role and to enhance practice in this area are evolving within a societal and organizational context that continues to advance a normative belief in moral or value relativism; and it is this very context that constrains these efforts to promote the concept of 'ethical leadership'. I have argued elsewhere (Campbell 1994, 1996) that moral and ethical dilemmas in administrative practice persist because, in accepting value relativism as a viable substitute for traditional moral and ethical philosophy defining "the good life," individuals have lost the ability to pursue, with any certainty beyond their own subjective feelings, objective right in the course of their professional lives.

Reviewers of my arguments against moral relativism have suggested that, in this philosophically "sticky" area, relativism, in fact, may provide functional alternatives to dogmatism and absolutism that indeed carry with them their own sets of potentially dangerous assumptions. I agree with this caution against fervent doctrines that refuse to tolerate alternative points of view on issues so complex as those concerning ethical behavior. However, I am not satisfied that, in our efforts to define and uphold ethical principles, we have only relativism or dogmatism from which to choose. This implies an assumption that any attempt to describe ethical behavior in anything but a relative way, consistent with the specifics and peculiarities of a situation, population, or experience, is dogmatism. If this is the case, then there seems little point in acknowledging that ethical school leadership, in any general and applicable sense, is even definable.

I am similarly unconvinced that some who support in an objective, if not universal, sense virtues such as fairness, justice, honesty, and integrity necessarily have a monopoly on dogmatism. Some supporters of perspectives more closely associated with variations of relativistic ideology may advance their positions with equivalent fervor, even though the irony of asserting the "rightness" of relativism has been noted throughout history and by philosophers at least as early as Plato.

In his criticism of relativism, Bricker, writing from an Aristotelian perspective, defines relativists as those who "dismiss moral debate as no more than idle rationalizing" (1993, 13). Similarly, Strike, Haller, and Soltis describe relativistic school administrators as "manipulators of others, unconcerned about the ethics of school administration . . . (who) renounce their responsibilities of evaluating the moral worth of objectives and policies" (1988, 106). According to other contemporary critics, the climate of relativism is pervasive in organizational life.

In one critique, Ternasky refers to the "widespread acceptance of common moral relativism in educational circles" (1993,118) and refutes the argument that no universally true moral norms exist. Ryan blames the plight of today's schools, which lack any sense of common and agreed-upon moral principles, on the "currently voguish notion that as members of a pluralistic society we have few shared values" (1993, 5). Hare claims that reference to ethics or general virtues and qualities primarily is "met with some resistance and scepticism" (1993, 1) by those who believe that such "high-minded idealism" ignores the daily realities of schooling, even though such realities are inevitably and inherently value-laden. In their discussion of relativism and education, Delattre and Russell criticize the current climate for producing many educators and students who "do not know what a genuinely moral standard is and who mistakenly believe that moral standards do not in any way transcend individual commitments or personal preferences" (1993, 24). Many of these critics of relativism support the universality of basic principles such as "fairness, equity, justice, integrity, honesty, and trust" (Covey 1992, 18). However, given the organizational and societal climate described above, it is difficult to project exactly how such principles are to be interpreted and adopted in practice to provide the necessary framework for improved ethical leadership.

From a British perspective, Grace notes that headteachers who "have historically been expected to give moral and professional leadership in responding to (social and school) problems" (1995, 152) are now challenged by the fact that many moral certainties of the past have been publicly questioned and rejected. In the absence of anything that might fill the gap left by such moral relativism, headteachers "had no access to a formal moral charter to guide their decisions on moral dilemmas" (150). Grace concludes that "moral, ethical and professional value dilemmas in school leadership have probably never been as sharp and complex as they are now" (155). West makes similar observations and urges headteachers and other school leaders "whether they relish the prospect or not" (1993, 153) to establish with colleagues and other stakeholders what values should be conserved or retrieved.

Efforts to accomplish goals that identify and enhance the moral and ethical climate of schools may be rendered futile in the face of relativism. How can we assert the necessity for addressing moral and ethical values in administration and offer practical alternatives for correct action while we remain reluctant to acknowledge a level of value objectivity?

Most people of good will do not wish to be or to be seen as dogmatic or doctrinaire absolutists. While the primary moral support for their conceptions of ethics is derived from their own relative and subjective beliefs, they may be hesitant to impose these values in the name of ethical leadership for fear of interfering with others' similarly supported subjective and relative beliefs. Thus, they end up either imposing nothing known with any certainty to be right or allowing others to impose everything, including possibly wrong values, without any clear moral base beyond their own individual and subjective judgments. I am not sure which of the two is more troublesome and potentially dangerous, but both defeat the aim of enhancing ethical awareness and practice of school leaders.

In his discussion of professional ethics in education, Soltis argues that "the specter of ethical subjectivism needs to be dispelled if we as a profession are to have an ethic and be genuinely ethical practitioners" (1986, 2). An obvious place to initiate the pursuit of heightened ethical school leadership is in administrator preparation programs. Yet, as will be explored in the subsequent section, personal observation and practice suggest to me that given the pervasive contemporary climate of relativism, discussions of ethics in such programs inevitably retrench the opinion that these values, when applied to school practice, are largely subjective and individually determined. This opinion, in turn, constrains further discussion of the role of the ethical school leader.

The Challenge of Preparing Ethical School Administrators

It is not surprising that many of those who write about the ethical role of school leaders also discuss the crucial need for administrator preparation programs to emphasize the moral and ethical dimensions of educational administration and to explore ways of anticipating and resolving value-laden dilemmas relevant to professional practice (Bricker 1993; Grace 1995; Hodgkinson 1991; Kirby, Paradise, and Protti 1992; Kirschmann 1996; Marshall 1992; Strike, Haller, and Soltis 1988; Strike and Ternasky 1993). Most complain that "few management courses in education address ethical dilemmas" (Grace 1995, 143), even though professional interest in the ethics of education and schooling has been increasing over the past decade (Bull 1993). Strike and Ternasky conclude that, unlike other professions, "education, it seems, has neither deliberate and systematic instruction in ethics nor an enforceable code of ethics" (1993, 3).

General agreement is expressed in the literature about the minimal usefulness of formal ethical codes in both administrator preparation and teacher education programs. Some critics define such codes as platitudinous and perfunctory (Strike and Ternasky 1993, 2) or inadequate, bureaucratic, and legalistic (Watras 1986, 13); others accept that a working knowledge of the codes may be valuable in an abstract way to establish professional foundations for decision making. However, most agree that "one does not become an ethical professional simply by learning an ethical code" (Soltis 1986, 2). Codes of ethics therefore do not constitute a significant part of the programs' curriculum (Strike and Ternasky 1993, 3), and it is widely acknowledged that instruction in professional ethics must go beyond exposure to formal ethical codes (Suom 1989).

Some recommend that the case study method of instruction is the most effective and desirable way to acquaint educators, be they student teachers or future administrators, with the moral and ethical realities and dilemmas in schools (Howe 1986; Kirby, Paradise, and Protti 1992; Kirschmann 1996; Soltis 1986; Strike 1993; Strike, Haller, and Soltis 1988; Strike and Soltis 1985). Strike and Ternasky (1993) argue that ethical instruction must move beyond abstract courses in philosophy to examine the realities of daily organizational life. Case study methods, which present students with realistic scenarios depicting the ethical complexities of practice in education, engage students in a level of "critical reflection" (Howe 1986, 5) that should inform their decision making as future school leaders. This kind of reflection, to which Hodgkinson (1991) alluded, should allow students to connect practical dilemmas and theoretical ethical principles that underlie those dilemmas. The process of reflection, it is hoped, should increase students' awareness of the ethical dimensions of their future roles and encourage them to anticipate dilemmas so as to be better equipped to deal with them.

While fully supportive of case study instruction as a preferred means to examine the ethics of school administration with students preparing for leadership roles, I have two reservations. Both stem from the challenges of sustaining useful dialogue about ethics within the current social and organizational context of moral or value relativism. First, it is not possible to anticipate and explore, through case study instruction, every potential scenario and dilemma relating to school administration and to take into consideration all likely contingencies, situational realities, and desirable courses of action. Therefore, the use of case studies should provide an opportunity for students to discern the larger ethical principles inherent in the dilemmas and then apply this theoretical knowledge to other, new dilemmas. These may differ in specific practicalities, but embody similar principles such as justice and truth. In this respect, both processes of induction and deduction are employed. However, moral or value relativism undermines our ability to discern ethical principles that, in order to be widely identified, interpreted, and applicable in practice should be seen as objective in the sense that they transcend individual preference or belief. Even when agreement in an abstract sense can be reached regarding the ethical certainty of a principle, such as justice or care, it is inevitably challenging to ascertain exactly how the principle is effected in practice. Thus, discussions about the ethical dimensions in case studies frequently conclude with the dismissal of principles as personal beliefs, individuals' convictions, relative value interpretations, and judgment calls. In administrator preparation courses, this further constrains students' efforts to relate overall philosophical principles to the practical realities of school leadership.

My second reservation about case study instruction in administrator preparation courses rests on an uneasy suspicion that the very process of case study analysis can become a variation of values-clarification education, which is typified by relativism and subjective interpretations of ethics. Thus, if students reflect on the dilemmas from a relativist position, rationalize their responses to the ethical dimensions, and conclude that they are satisfied with the resolutions they recommend for particular isolated situations, then it must be acknowledged that ethical choices have been made. Yet, in this way, individual and subjective reflection becomes the primary justifiable moral base, and students gain little direction for future decision making beyond the confirmation of their own convictions. Watras (1986) raises similar concerns about case method as values clarification, and recommends against its use as a form of applied ethics instruction.

Despite these two reservations, I believe that case study approaches in administrator preparation programs provide future school leaders with a singularly valuable opportunity to confront the complexities of ethical decision making in realistic and potentially controversial and confusing value-laden situations. As individuals grappling with contemporary relativistic orientations to ethics and very few solid guidelines to facilitate their professional responsibilities, students in these programs can benefit by elevating their awareness of the ethics of administration. This, at least, is infinitely better than ignoring this critical aspect of school leadership.

In my own practice, teaching policy and philosophy courses to preservice teachers, in-service teachers, and school administrators enrolled in educational administration programs, I have used the case study approach to instruction in educational ethics in two ways. First, students read and respond to cases depicting ethical dilemmas written by others. Kirschmann (1996), Strike, Haller, and Soltis (1988), and Strike and Soltis (1985) provide excellent examples. Second, students discuss and write about specific experiences they have had in their own professional practice that have confronted them with ethical dilemmas. In both cases, students analyze the scenarios and possible alternatives to resolve the dilemmas based not only on their own opinions and beliefs but also on a grounding in principles of moral and ethical philosophy. Thus, they consider the dimensions of the case studies from various perspectives such as utilitarianism, consequentialist and nonconsequentialist ethical theories, or teleology and deontology. They discuss interpretations of basic principles such as justice, honesty, and trust. For example, they may debate the meaning of equity that, by no means, enjoys uncontested definition, especially when translated from the abstract to the practical.

Contemporary perspectives that offer alternative frameworks from which to explore ethical issues also should be assessed as students struggle with the practicalities of their decisions and seek to clarify the origins of their beliefs. For example, do their responses to dilemmas reflect principles associated with critical theory, the feminist ethic of caring, postmodernism, secular humanism, or liberal democracy? Students need to be engaged in the ethical debate that has been expanded and nuanced by various schools of thought. Therefore, alternative perspectives on ethics, including those that are essentially sympathetic to variations of relativistic beliefs, should be invited into the debate, so that the issues may be viewed through a multidimensional lens.

The complex area of human values and ethics does not comprise a series of variables that can be mapped out on a managerial grid in an effort to deduce a formulaic "best way" to resolve our dilemmas. Thus, rationalistic models that define teleology as a concern with administrative efficiency and deontology as adherence to bureaucratic principles embodied in school rules and policies (Malloy and Hansen 1995) do little to address issues of basic virtue, right, and wrong that have presented philosophical challenges for thousands of years. Thus, administrator preparation programs should not treat ethics as another management strategy; instead, they should struggle with the challenges of determining what is right, not just what is best under specific circumstances.

These philosophical challenges that have such significance for the practice of school leaders are compounded by the pervasive climate of relativism. For how can we make choices, either about our own behavior or our support for one or more of the often conflicting perspectives on ethics including relativistic perspectives, with any degree of conceptual certainty within a context where such certainty is elusive?

In my own teaching experience, I encounter students who are able to relate with insight personal accounts of their professional dilemmas and who can identify with depth and philosophical precision the confusing ethical dimensions of their situations. Some can also abstract the dominant principles and apply them to similar cases. However, when the point comes for them to resolve their dilemmas, make decisions about how principles translate into right action, and project how ethical school leaders would respond to future challenges, propositions inevitably involve the following phrases: "I don't really know if this is right," "This is just my opinion," "Everything is a personal judgment call," "No one can tell others what's right and wrong," "You've got to go with what you believe is right," "Whose values should inform this decision?" These discussions reflect the relativistic uncertainty they face in trying to reconcile their own values and interpretations of ethics with those of parents, students, colleagues, educational systems, and with the various philosophical theories of ethical principles. They frequently appeal to a need for firmer policy guidelines to help them with their dilemmas, although many suspect that formal policy in this area would be as ineffectual as ethical codes.

The challenges described in this section affect not only students of administrative theory but also their instructors, current school leaders, other practitioners, policy makers, and philosophers for we all live and work within societal and organizational contexts influenced by relativist perspectives on ethics. Sometimes, the gray areas seem to become even more gray. Nonetheless, if we are to support the increasing demand that school leadership be seen as fundamentally an ethical role, then inquiry into this often confusing area must be pursued in both theoretical and practical ways.

Summary

One of the intentions of this discussion has been to emphasize how recent and current educational literature has identified the ethical dimensions of schools, schooling, professional practice, and leadership as issues in need of significant, even urgent, consideration. I share with many theorists and practitioners the belief that the place of ethics in education should be elevated, that awareness of this area should be enhanced through rigorous inquiry and debate, and that preparation programs for future school leaders should develop more comprehensive approaches to address this fairly neglected area in ways that link theory and practice.

It is for this reason that I conclude this discussion with a certain level of personal frustration by acknowledging that no philosophically and practically useful solution is being offered here. This somewhat pessimistic acknowledgment is a result of the conceptual argument that, given the pervasive climate of moral or value relativism, the role of the ethical leader is an elusive one to identify; thus, efforts to equip future school leaders for this role are fraught with challenges. These challenges engage us in reflective discussions of ethical principles that often serve to confirm relativist orientations and provide few recommendations for improved practice beyond the requirement that individuals explore, analyze, and understand their own and others' subjective beliefs. As Hodgkinson notes, "Leadership is a function of self-knowledge and of values. How they are held and why they are held" (1995, 80). Yet will this knowledge, while important to achieve, offer us any assurance that truly ethical leadership practice will ensue? Could we even identify it, as the literature exhorts us to, as long as subjective and relative definitions of ethics in practice dominate our interpretations of theoretical ethical principles? It has been the related intention of the discussion to examine this conceptual point in the contexts of the literature and my practical experience.

Popular wisdom maintains that acknowledging a problem is the first step to resolving it. This may be true. At least by acknowledging the ethical complexities of school leadership, theorists and practitioners can expand the discussion of a significant area in ways that might connect a substantive vision of ethical leadership with the daily dilemmas and realities of life in schools. Nonetheless, a nagging feeling persists that this expanded discussion may not get us very far in realizing this aim to develop enhanced ethical leadership as long as we continue to teeter on the edge of reflecting ourselves further into the relativist corner.

References

Bricker, D. C. 1993. Character and moral reasoning: An Aristotelian perspective. In *Ethics for professionals in education: perspectives for preparation and practice,* ed. K. A. Strike and P. L. Ternasky, 13–26. New York: Teachers College Press.

Bull, B. L. 1993. Ethics in the preservice curriculum. In *Ethics for professionals in education: perspectives for preparation and practice*, ed. K. A. Strike and P. L. Ternasky, 69–83. New York: Teachers College Press.

Campbell, E. 1992. Personal morals and organizational ethics: how teachers and principals cope with conflicting values in the context of school cultures. Unpublished dissertation, University of Toronto, Canada.

———. 1994. Suspended morality and the denial of ethics: how value relativism muddles the distinction between right and wrong in administrative decisions. Paper presented at the 8th International Intervisitation Program, Toronto, Canada, and Buffalo, U.S.A., May.

———. 1996. Suspended morality and the denial of ethics: how value relativism muddles the distinction between right and wrong in administrative decisions. In *School administration: Persistent dilemmas in preparation and practice*, ed. S. Jacobson, E. Hickcox, and R. Stevenson, 63–74. Westport, CT: Praeger.

Cohen, P. 1995. The content of their character: educators find new ways to tackle values and morality. *Curriculum Update,* Association for Supervision and Curriculum Development, 1–8.

Covey, S. R. 1992. *Principle-centred leadership.* New York: Simon and Schuster.

Delattre, E. J., and Russell, W. E. 1993. Schooling, moral principles, and the formation of character. *Journal of Education* 175, 2: 23–43.

Etzioni, A. 1990. *The moral dimension: Toward a new economics.* New York: Macmillan Publishing Company.

Fullan, M. 1993. *Change forces: Probing the depths of educational reform.* London: Falmer Press.

Grace, G. 1995. *School leadership: Beyond education management.* London: Falmer Press.

Hare, W. 1993. *What makes a good teacher.* London, Ontario: Althouse Press.

Hodgkinson, C. 1991. *Educational leadership: The moral art.* Albany: State University of New York Press.

———. 1995. Towards an axiology of leadership. *Journal of educational administration and foundations* 10, 2: 72–83.

Holmes, M. 1992a. Moral education: Emancipation and tradition. *Curriculum Inquiry* 22, 4: 339–44.

———. 1992b. The revival of school administration: Alasdair MacIntyre in the aftermath of the common school. *Canadian Journal of Education* 17, 4: 422–36.

Howe, K. R. 1986. A conceptual basis for ethics in teacher education. *Journal of Teacher Education* 37, 3: 5–12.

Jackson, P. W., Boostrom, R. E., and Hansen, D. T. 1993. *The Moral Life of Schools.* San Francisco: Jossey-Bass.

Kirby, P. C., Paradise, L. V., and Protti, R. 1992. Ethical reasoning of educational administrators: Structuring inquiry around problems of practice. *Journal of Educational Administration* 30, 4: 25–32.

Kirschenbaum, H. 1994. *100 ways to enhance values and morality in schools and youth settings.* Boston: Allyn and Bacon.

Kirschmann, R. E. 1996. *Educational administration: A collection of case studies*. Englewood Cliffs: Merrill.

Lickona, T. 1991. *Educating for character: How our schools can teach respect and responsibility*. New York: Bantam.

MacIntyre, A. 1981. *After virtue: A Study in moral theory*. London: Gerald Duckworth and Company.

Malloy, D. C., and Hansen, H. 1995. An holistic model of ethical decision-making for educational administration. *Journal of Educational Administration and Foundations* 10, 2: 60–71.

Marshall, C. 1992. School administrators' values: A focus on atypicals. *Educational Administration Quarterly* 28, 3: 368–86.

Ryan, K. 1993. Why a center for the advancement of ethics and character. *Journal of Education* 175, 2: 1–11.

Sergiovanni, T. J. 1992. *Moral leadership: Getting to the heart of school improvement*. San Francisco: Jossey-Bass.

———. 1994. The roots of school leadership. *Principal*, November: 6–9.

———. 1996. *Leadership for the schoolhouse: How is it different? Why is it important?* San Francisco: Jossey-Bass.

Sockett, H. 1990. Accountability, trust, and ethical codes of practice. In *The Moral Dimensions of Teaching*, ed. J. Goodlad, R. Soder, and K. Sirotnik. San Francisco: Jossey-Bass, 224–50.

———. 1993. *The moral base for teacher professionalism*. New York: Teachers College Press.

Soltis, J. F. 1986. Teaching professional ethics. *Journal of Teacher Education* 37, 3: 2–4.

Strike, K. A. 1993. Teaching ethical reasoning using cases. In *Ethics for professionals in education: Perspectives for preparation and practice*, ed. K. A. Strike and P. L. Ternasky, 102–116. New York: Teachers College Press.

Strike, K., Haller, E., and Soltis, J. 1988. *The ethics of school administration*. New York: Teachers College Press.

Strike, K., and Soltis, J. 1985. *The ethics of teaching*. New York: Teachers College Press.

Strike, K. A., and Ternasky, P. L. 1993. *Ethics for professionals in education: Perspectives for preparation and practice*. New York: Teachers College Press.

Strom, S. M. 1989. The ethical dimension of teaching. In *Knowledge base for the beginning teacher*, ed. M. C. Reynolds. 267–76. Oxford: Pergamon Press.

Ternasky, P. L. 1993. Coping with relativism and absolutism. In *Ethics for professionals in education: Perspectives for preparation and practice*, ed. K. A. Strike and P. L. Ternasky, 117–31. New York: Teachers College Press.

Watras, J. 1986. Will teaching applied ethics improve schools of education? *Journal of Teacher Education*, 37, 3:13–16.

West, S. 1993. *Educational values for school leadership*. London: Kogan Page.

Wynne, E., and Ryan, K. 1993. *Reclaiming our schools: A handbook on teaching character, academics and discipline*. New York: Macmillan.

CHAPTER NINE

Values, Socially Distributed Cognition, and Organizational Practice

Gabriele Lakomski and Colin W. Evers

Naturalistic Coherentism and Organizational Practice

Our work to date has mapped out the philosophical-epistemological groundwork for a new, postpositivist science of educational administration (see Evers and Lakomski 1991; 1996). Naturalistic coherentism, or Australian naturalism, as our program is also known, grew out of our early argument that educational administration's most damaging legacy for both its theory and its practice was its persistent misidentification of science with the empiricist conception of science, often loosely called "positivism." The consequences of this misidentification shaped even those approaches that offered alternatives to the (positivist) science of administration, such as Greenfield's subjectivism, Hodgkinson's humanism, Bates and Foster's version of critical theory, and Sergiovanni and others' interpretive-cultural perspective, in that they continued to accept an empiricist version of science as valid (in the realm of nature) and explicitly rejected any science of administration as inappropriate. As a result, alternative views in educational administration maintained empiricism's strict fact/value dichotomy and thereby undercut their own claims to have advanced the cause of values, ethics, and effective practice over and against positivist administrative science.

Employing the insights of modern philosophy of science and epistemology, we endeavored to show that both empiricist and alternative conceptions of educational administration are incoherent in that their claims outstrip the epistemological resources they have to defend them. A major source of incoherence is the poor coupling that exists between claims to knowledge on the one hand and the human capacity to acquire it or to learn on the other hand. This is exemplified by empiricism's narrow view of the mind and human reason whose characteristic postbehaviorist feature was believed to be its linear symbol processing ability.

The idea that human rationality was to be identified with linguistic representation became enshrined in the famous distinction of "knowing that" and "knowing how" and provided the grid through which practice in educational administration and elsewhere was studied. But the point of practice is that most of the time it cannot be externalized in linguistic-symbolic form. We just know how to do something, like identify a face or interpret a situation, or make judgments. The very conception of the nature of human cognition as symbol processing then prevents a causal under-standing of practice. It thus also mitigates against a better understanding of the nature of ethics and values, the invisible "ought" of the is/ought dichotomy, which has occupied writers from the theory movement to the present day.

But, since we are finite beings endowed with certain cognitive capacities and means of computation, the core of our naturalism is the modest requirement that claims to knowledge need to be on a par with claims about our ability to learn. According to what we take to be the current best scientific knowledge developed by modern cognitive science's connectionist accounts of brain functioning, we do not acquire knowledge or process information according to the physical-symbol system hypothesis (see Newell and Simon 1976; Hutchins 1996, 358). A neural network account of parallel distributed processing makes it possible, for the first time, to consider the representation of practice in terms of prototype activation patterns.

In this chapter, we continue our naturalistic explorations in educational administration by examining the important issues of ethics and leadership in order to demonstrate how our naturalism might solve some of its key difficulties and thereby improve our knowledge of organizational practice.

A Naturalistic Approach to Ethics: Empiricism and the Fact/Value Distinction

Several features of our approach to knowledge and its justification have a direct bearing on how we view ethics. The first feature, and one that will serve as a point of entry to others and their consequences for ethics, is what is known as "semantic holism." According to the strand of logical empiricism most influential in the development of educational administration, cognitively significant claims are either analytic or synthetic. Analytic claims, such as tautologies, or logical truths, are true by virtue of the meanings of their terms, and hence their justification can proceed without explicit appeal to empirical evidence. However, synthetic claims are empirical but also exhibit the dual nature of evidence in meaning and justification. The specific range of sensory experience that serves as evidence for justifying a particular claim serves as part of an account of the basis for its meaning. Articulated systematically by A. J. Ayer in *Language, Truth and Logic* (1936; 1946) as the principle of verification, the meaningfulness, or cognitive content of synthetic propositions, was identified with the range of observations that would provide either evidence for truth or evidence for falsehood (Ayer 1946, 35–41).

Applying this standard of meaningfulness to ethics, Ayer (1946, 108) explores why it is impossible to find a criterion for determining the validity of ethical judgments. This is because they have no objective validity whatsoever. If a sentence makes no statement at all, there is obviously no sense in asking whether it is true or false. Observation is relevant to what is or is not the case, to the empirical facts. For Ayer and many other traditional empiricists, ethics ends up being merely about our attitudes to those facts, expressions of feeling that do not say anything or make a statement.

The reason this view became so influential in the development of educational administration during the 1950s and 1960s was because it was given expression by Herbert Simon in his account of values in *Administrative Behavior* (1946) and played a major role in his conception of a science of administration and his analysis of the structure of decision making.

Ethics and Holistic Meaning and Evidence

In more recent times, the relationship between observational evidence and the claims it is meant to justify is regarded as much more complex. The principal difference concerns the holistic nature of justification. We now know, thanks to the early work of W. V. Quine (1951; 1960), that there are at least three important reasons why observational evidence distributes its empirical support globally, across an entire theory, rather than statement by individual, synthetic statement as logical empiricism assumed. First, observations are theory-laden, being made from the vantage point of some perspective or another. More technically, the observational sentences that figure in justificatory inferences always contain some theoretical terms. This thesis is of a piece with the claim that all experience is interpreted experience, filtered through the mind of the perceiver. Second, the claims our theories make about the world, because they are couched in general terms, always outrun any available observational evidence. Theory is always underdetermined by experience. This means that the same observations can verify different theories. Finally, because the empirical testing of claims is complex, we have some methodological choice in relocating the blame for an alleged empirical failure away from the hypothesis being tested and onto some other assumption in the complex of background conditions required to conduct and interpret the test.

Because the resulting shift toward holism in justification spills over into a corresponding holism about meaning, traditional empiricism's way of specifying cognitively significant claims, indeed of drawing the cognitive/noncognitive distinction, will no longer work. With the aid of some further philosophical machinery, we conclude that ethical statements can be as true or as false as any paradigm empirical statement and as meaningful in exactly the same sense.

Some writers have seen holistic considerations as ushering in an era of subjectivism, because they seem to detach, altogether, questions about the merits of theories from the once-assumed secure foundation of observational evidence (Greenfield and Ribbins 1993). In reply, our argument has been that we need to use criteria of theory choice that are more suitable in these circumstances: criteria that make use of normative holistic notions such as coherence applied to the epistemological domain. When it comes to ethics, we claim that using these criteria permits the justification of ethical statements to be conducted in the same way as for other statements. So, just as empirical assertions are justified by considering the coherence their inclusion confers on a wider system of assertions, we think that considerations of system are equally relevant in assessing the warrant for moral values. (See P. M. Churchland 1989, 297–303; 1996, 91–108.)

To understand the effect of adopting a theoretical basis for making observations, consider a number of cases. An expert's view of an x-ray photograph is mediated by a substantial amount of medical theory acquired through experience and training. Fractures, or changes in bone density, for example, hidden from the novice can be seen easily with suitable training. Discerning detail, or even making sense of observations mediated by scientific apparatus, is likewise a theoretical endeavor, as is identifying features embedded in music, art, or literature. Theory, when construed broadly (as epistemology requires) will permit the construction of culture-laden examples of observation and the role of interpretation and assumed background understandings behind natural and social events. Thus, describing a sequence of behaviors as "bidding at an auction" or as "giving offense to the host" can reveal more cognitively significant content and lead to greater predictive success than the use of rival descriptions.

Observation can be value-laden in a similar way. An account of patterns of behavior as "murder," "unfair," or "generous", can reflect deep familiarity with a network of interrelated concepts that are essential for a person to navigate successfully through the social world, anticipating correctly the responses of others in the course of pursuing their own theoretically motivated goals. Systematic positions on social justice, respect for persons, the good life, and many context-dependent particular moral judgments can be part and parcel of this conceptual network. In every case, there is no question that the moral theory being used to drive perceptions of the world around is also enmeshed in a wider fabric of theory articulated through practice, culture, "commonsense," and with bodies of knowledge grouped into familiar specialisms such as biology, mathematics, or politics. We can add that the apparent distance of ethics from the observational data of empiricist confirmation and disconfirmation is a result of the distilled nature of ethics, rather than to any purported epistemological distinctness.

One significant limitation on the extent to which ethical statements can be enmeshed into a more global theory, whose merits can be determined by the application of coherentist criteria, is the belief that, despite the surface appearance of an admixture of fact and value among ethical terms, these two elements are logically distinct and can never be combined. On this view, murder, for example, consists of some empirical state of affairs—the factual component—and a separate evaluative component to do with imputing wrongness. Empirical evidence is relevant to establishing the facts concerning a killing, but beyond that, moral approbation is left over as a feeling or an expression of sentiment toward the facts, in effect attempting to close the gap between 'is' and 'ought'. In the course of developing accounts of moral justification, a number of writers within the cognitivist tradition of ethics have sought to close this gap. John Rawls in his celebrated *Theory of Justice* (1972) seeks to enmesh principles of justice within a theory of rationality. The basic strategy is to defend principles by showing that they would be chosen by rational persons acting under conditions of impartiality. Habermas (1972) is another writer who employs this Kantian strategy. He seeks to enmesh moral principles in an account of what is presupposed by any act of human communication. Background to each speech act is thought to reside in an ideal speech situation, which includes imperatives such as truth-telling or the right to fair participation in the speech community.

Although the sense of 'ought' being sought is broader than mere affect, being located in a view of what 'oughts' are embedded in human reason or communication, we are skeptical of this Kantian enterprise. In general, we think that attempts to establish presuppositions of all thought, or all thought on a particular topic, are, in practice, attempts to establish the assumptions behind some particular theory, perhaps a theory of reason or a theory of communication. That is, theory-ladenness invests the Kantian enterprise. In Habermas' case, we find the branch of science that deals with communication in an information theoretical way more plausible, with its requirement for statistical regularity rather than truth. And in Rawls's case, maximizing reasoning—always hedging against the worst possible outcome—ignores the complexities of rational, context-sensitive risk taking. Normative accounts of human reason cannot be so readily detached from empirical studies of human cognition.

Another influential approach to ethics that attempts to enmesh the ethical and the factual is hedonistic utilitarianism, which seeks to define good naturalistically, in terms of human happiness. However, there has been a long debate in ethical theory about whether any attempt to produce a definition that equates a moral term with a set of nonmoral terms commits a fallacy—the so-called naturalistic fallacy (see Smith 1995, for a guide to the recent literature and debates). Our position in this debate is on the side of naturalistic definitions (Evers and Lakomski 1991, 166–77). Following Quine (1951) we think that semantic holism can be extended to blur not just the distinction between factual and theoretical synthetic statements but also the distinction between analytic and synthetic statements. (A key part of Quine's argument appeals to the complexity of test situations where he claims that any statement in a theory can be rendered immune from empirical revision, and hence analytic, by methodologically choosing to revise other statements in the theory.) This latter distinction can be deemed unimportant for ethical theory because usual attempts to formulate the naturalistic fallacy argument require that a definition be analytic. For example, if it is assumed that a definition is analytic, then we get G. E. Moore's famous "open question argument," which runs as follows. If an analytic statement cannot be questioned intelligibly, and for every purported naturalistic definition of "good" we can intelligibly ask, "But is 'good' really (say) 'the greatest happiness for the greatest number'?" then there cannot be a naturalistic definition of 'good'. (Evers and Lakomski 1991, 169–72, contains a more detailed discussion.)

Once we accept enough of semantic holism to blur the analytic/synthetic distinction (and we emphasize that we do not see conceptual role as the sole arbiter of meaning), we are able to adopt a less restrictive account of definition. For example, in science we may come to accept the definition of force as mass times acceleration (F=ma), because of its theoretical centrality in the most coherent global account we can give of certain phenomena. The definition will fail the open question argument, but so what? Its acceptability resides in the excellence of the theory in which it is embedded. Our point is that the same reasoning applies in the case of ethics. A naturalistic definition of 'good', or any other ethical term, will owe its plausibility to the extent to which it figures centrally in a theory of human conduct and behavior that meshes with the most coherent account we can give of experience. If versions of hedonistic utilitarianism are to be found wanting, it will not be because of failure of analyticity. It will be because they fail to organize considerations of human motivation, cognition, judgment, and intelligent action in an epistemically satisfactory way.

While any number of different approaches within naturalism may emerge as enjoying more of the advantages of system than rivals, our own approach takes note of the provisional, fallible, and experimental nature of all knowledge, as emphasized by Dewey and Popper. To solve our problems, relate satisfactorily with others in the pursuit of our individual and collective plans, and navigate our way around the natural and social world with the possibility of success better than chance, there is a premium on good theory. Whatever the final shape of a systematic naturalistic account of ethics, one central organizing feature we assume, following Dewey, will be an articulation of the virtue of promoting the long-term growth of knowledge. We see this as a touchstone virtue in the sense that it is shared by a very wide range of perspectives and hence is more likely to turn up as a vital part of almost any attempt to build a most coherent global theory. So, instead of appealing to a priori accounts of rationality, or communication, in order to understand the conditions under which the growth of knowledge can occur, we appeal to empirical theories of learning. The result, we believe, will include some of the ethical aspects of human modes of association relevant to individual, organizational, and social learning.

Maintaining that knowledge is valuable and that our capacity to know is limited and fallible places a premium on the development of knowledge acquisition processes. In much of the administration literature, where the emphasis is on decision making, concessions to fallibility manifest as accounts of bounded rationality. In our view, the process of learning is more basic. Most work on human cognition in the rationality tradition is based on a view of the human mind as a symbol processor. Indeed, rationality is identified with the rule-based manipulation of symbolic structures (Newell and Simon 1976). However, recent work on cognition in the human learning tradition takes as its focus models of brain processes, particularly the study of artificial neural networks. According to this approach, which is sometimes referred to as the "new cognitive science," cognition is primarily a matter of pattern processing, with symbols appearing as just one kind of pattern from among many present in the environment. (For details, see, P. S. Churchland, 1989; Rumelhart and McClelland 1986; Grossberg 1988; Port and van Gelder 1995.)

Against Moral Rules

While more detail relevant to educational administration can be found elsewhere (see, for example, Evers and Lakomski 1996, 104–28; Evers, forthcoming) we highlight three consequences for ethics. First, for a very large proportion of our knowledge, and most of our day-to-day practical knowledge, we have no symbolic, languagelike representations at all. This knowledge, or know-how, although regular and patterned, cannot be represented plausibly by linguistically formulated rules. Examples include judging whether the milk has gone off, when to change gear as the car goes uphill, whether some purchase would make an appropriate present for someone, whether a child might benefit from a special curriculum, or a thousand other humdrum to major matters with which we deal every day. And to this list we would add ethical judgment (Churchland 1995, 123–50).

Attempts to codify moral knowledge into a linguistic representation present two key problems. First, the desire for generality results in the loss of guidance in any particular case. At the extreme, to advise "Do good and avoid evil" is not to advise at all unless some specification of what counts as good and evil is given. But second, giving such a specification makes for particularity, leading to a failure to advise beyond time, place, circumstance, participants, and issue. The usual trade-off is to describe instances at some intermediate level of description and advise to act in such-and-such a way in relevantly similar situations. We suggest that in practice the problem is dealt with by the brain learning to extract prototypes of moral situations from experience. Prototypes, which capture the statistically central features of experience, serve as nonbrittle templates for the identification of patterns of similarity and relevance in the flux of moral life.

Ethics, Error, and Feedback

In his political theory, Karl Popper (1945) advocated open, free, and democratic societies as these possess the requisite features for the organized testing of social theories. Fallible knowledge can be improved only if there exists the machinery for putting its claims to tests. While concurring with his general point, Popper's account of theory revision and error elimination needs to be augmented with an account of how coherence constraints function in selecting the most epistemically progressive possibilities for revision. The improvement of theory occurs best in the context of a particular set of social arrangements regulated normatively by ethics whose key features include tolerance of diverse viewpoints, freedom of speech and association, and respect for persons.

From studying neural network models of individual cognition, we believe that significant natural learning occurs, including the building up of prototypes, through the processing of feedback according to the coherent application of multiple soft constraints. In light of experience we appear constantly to adjust our inner representation of knowledge in an effort to realize the most reliable path through the possibilities and options presented. Where experience can be summarized into useful linguistic formulations, these are able to serve as proxies for our own efforts, thus providing an efficient way of learning from others. However, again there is the same premium on particular ethical infrastructures for learning: those characterized by tolerance of alternative viewpoints, openness to criticism, willingness to foster freedom of expression and forms of association that permit the free exchange of ideas.

In attending to the ethics required to promote learning and the growth of knowledge, we have tended to focus on limits to human cognition. However, the new cognitive science does suggest some natural strategies for ameliorating these limits. The strategy that is of most importance to the ethics of educational administration is what is known as 'the externalization of cognition'. Limitations to memory can be partly overcome by keeping records—writing things down—and then, when this becomes extensive, using a retrieval system. What is more important, very difficult, or perhaps very complex learning tasks can be dealt with by distributing the cognitive load socially, as a mode of organization, a point we will revisit later.

The possibility of more effective problem solving by resort to organization dovetails nicely with the point that individuals can comprehend patterns in modes of association, locating themselves coherently within such patterns. Having a sense of structure, a sense of neighborhood relations, and a grasp of a modest portion of the task seems sufficient to permit the off-loading of much individual cognition onto a mostly external division of cognitive labor.

In the next section, we comment further on organizational structures construed as patterns of distributed learning and emphasize that there is again an ethics embedded in these structures. We focus on the question of leadership, traditionally the most important aspect of structure.

A Naturalistic Approach to Leadership: Influential Approaches to Leadership

Although the study of leaders and of leadership has a history that dates back to the 1940s, there is general agreement among leadership researchers, in education and elsewhere, that the empirical and theoretical efforts expended to date to clarify this organizational phenomenon far outstrip the results achieved. We do not yet have an answer to the fundamental question of what leadership is and what makes for an effective leader.

Some of the main concerns raised by critics (e.g., Bridges 1982; Howe 1994) regarding leadership include competing or inconsistent definitions, incompatible methodological approaches, and a paucity of theoretical and conceptual developments. These difficulties apply both to traditional leadership studies which dominated the field until the early 1980s and to what Bryman (1986) calls the "New Leadership," whose beginnings can roughly be identified with the publication of McGregor Burns's (1978) landmark study (see especially Bass 1985; Avolio and Bass 1988; Bass and Avolio 1994 whose transformational leadership conception heavily influenced educational administration; examples of good discussions are Hunt 1991 and Bryman 1986).

Since the beginnings, leadership scholars have assumed that there is a linkage between leadership and organizational effectiveness and considered it a "commonly accepted theorem" (Bowers and Seashore 1973, 445). In the same vein, good leadership, based on what Landsberger (1967–68, 3) calls the "happiness-efficiency correlation," was considered to be democratic and employee-centered and paid more attention to social relations than to bureaucratic rules (see Perrow 1986, 85). The supposition that good leadership will lead to increased morale which, in turn, will lead to increased effort and higher productivity, has remained an unquestioned cornerstone of both traditional and new leadership studies, despite the lack of robust empirical evidence and theoretical support for it (see Lawler and Porter 1967; Perrow 1986).

The New Leadership, while maintaining a basic belief in the "happi-ness-efficiency" correlation, focuses "rather less upon the effects of the puta-tive leader's behavioral style and rather more upon their role in defining, articulating, reinforcing, and changing basic values and beliefs of the led (e.g., Bennis and Nanus 1985)" (Bresnen 1995, 496–97). What has thus come into focus more sharply is an emphasis on values and organizational norms in the attempt to define leadership, where the leader is generally identified with the top executive. A top-down approach is thus characteristic of the new mode (Bresnen 1995). But despite the claims of encouraging empirical results regarding the effects of transformational leadership, re-ported by some researchers (see Leithwood 1994; Leithwood and Steinbach 1995), Avolio and Bass point out that "very little is known regarding the process by which individuals become energized and under what circum-stances a transforming leader will be most effective. In our opinion, this is one of the most important questions raised by Bass's model" (1988, 46). We concur and attempt here to outline some possible answers.

Problems of Theory, Methodology, and Cognitive Assumptions

In our view, what creates major problems for the study of leaders and of leadership is its theoretical empiricist framework which is ill-equipped to provide a satisfactory account of leadership. In particular, empiricism's hypothetico-deductive structure of knowledge acquisition, together with its narrow view of the human mind and of cognition, makes claims for leader-ship and leaders it cannot in principle uphold. Since we have examined the structure of both hypothetico-deductive accounts of knowledge and leader-ship in detail elsewhere (Evers and Lakomski 1991; 1996) and considered the model of the brain as symbol processor earlier, we would like to make a few comments regarding the gathering of evidence in leadership studies.

Researchers in both the traditional and New Leadership modes rely heavily on questionnaires and quantitative-statistical methodology to gather data and provide evidence for the existence of leadership. This raises two critical issues. First, what has been measured, so it has been argued, are the cognitive structures of whatever "followers" believe leadership is, that is, their implicitly held leadership theories which are already deeply ingrained in our culture (e.g., Gronn 1995). The issue of attribution then is most critical because it characterizes leadership as an after-the-event rationaliza-tion to explain effective (or ineffective) practice, as the case may be (Bres-nen 1995, 498; Perrow 1986). Second, quantitative methodologies are good at picking up patterns in large specifiable sets of computations and linguis-tic representations but are powerless to represent the kinds of things at which leaders are said to excel: making plans, judging, and understanding the needs of followers and/or circumstances. These capabilities are not amenable to linguistic representation. Neuronal patterns of activation, the mode in which experience is represented, do not have syntactic structures but exhibit causal sequences only (Tienson 1990). Thus, their representation cannot possibly be accomplished by means of statistical machinery.

What emerges from the preceding comments is (1) that leaders are leaders only through the eyes of those who see/interpret them as such; leadership is a relational concept, and one cannot be a leader in a social vacuum, and (2) that whatever evidence we can find for leadership or leading has to be based on the real cognitive capabilities of human agents, individually and in groups, and in their interaction with their variously structured physical and social environments.

It is here, we believe, that recent accounts of human cognition and information processing provide the most incisive insights. While the function of linguistic representation remains important, it is no longer misidentified with all human cognition, knowledge, and reason. In addition, there is also an increasing awareness by connectionist researchers that cognition is a cultural process. This means that a research focus on individual cognition is shifting to include the cognition of groups. This is a highly relevant development for the study of leadership as an organizational phenomenon, as we will next sketch.

Cultural or Distributed Cognition

Leaders, as portrayed in traditional and the New Leadership studies, have tended to be considered epistemically privileged individuals whose superior knowledge flows down and through the organization. The knowledge of other organization members, while not explicitly denied, has not been theorized as playing any part in leadership and organizational practice. This seems to have its clearest expression in hierarchical organizational structure where there are no feedback loops going "back up" from the various levels in the organization. Much is thus expected of the cognitive abilities of the individual leader.

We are quite accustomed to speak of the physical division of labor as evidenced in the organizational structures and arrangements of schools, or any other place of work in modern society. But the idea that such division might imply a cognitive division of labor, is not one with which we are familiar. Considered from an evolutionary point of view, however, such cognitive distribution is highly sensible for creatures with finite cognitive capacities (Resnick 1991).

The assumption that cognition is restricted to one individual's mind or brain recently has been challenged by scientists from different disciplines. Alternate conceptions have been described variously as "socially shared cognition," "situated cognition," or "situated learning" (see the collection of articles in Resnick, Leride, and Teasley 1991). These are attempts to break down this assumption and to consider knowledge "as distributed across several individuals whose interactions determine decisions, judgments and problem solutions" (Resnick 1991, 3. For examples of ethnographic studies on how people reason and learn in concrete settings see Lave 1991; Rogoff and Lave 1984; Levine and Moreland 1991; Hutchins 1996). In her discussion of apprenticeship learning, to cite just one example, Lave (1991, 69) argues that becoming a "knowledgeably skilled" practitioner or "old-timer" does not appear to happen through planned organizational processes. Rather, novices become skilled practitioners "through a social process of increasingly centripetal participation, which depends on legitimate access to ongoing community practice" (Lave 1991, 68). She points out that apprentices learn not by being formally taught but by being broadly exposed to ongoing practice, which, she argues, is "in effect a demonstration of the goals toward which newcomers expect, and are expected, to move." In being so exposed, knowledge and skill are developed as an integral part of the process of becoming a master practitioner within a community of practice (Lave 1991, 71). Similar points are made by Hutchins (1996) in his study of ship navigation.

In his book, thoughtfully entitled, *Cognition in the Wild,* Hutchins argues, "Culture is not a collection of things, whether tangible or abstract. Rather, it is a . . . human cognitive process that takes place both inside and outside the minds of people." Delimiting cognitive systems in terms of the inside/outside boundary as has been sanctioned by classical cognitive science, and considering all intelligence as being located on the inside of that boundary, has the major disadvantage of overattribution. As a consequence, we might erroneously "attribute the right properties to the wrong system or (worse) invent the wrong properties and attribute them to the wrong system" (Hutchins 1996, 356). Studying "cognition in the wild" is the best way to understand the mutually interacting cognitive properties of the sociocultural system and the cognitive properties of humans who manipulate these elements (Hutchins 1996, 362).

Human cognition and computation plainly do not equate with what Clark calls the "filing cabinet" view of mind where "the mind [is] a storehouse of passive language-like symbols waiting to be retrieved and manipulated by a kind of neural central processing unit" (1997, 67). Such a model is more akin to a computer's linear way of thinking than a human's, and although we have learned to manipulate symbols, their formal manipulation does not exhaust our cognition and computational capacities.

Perhaps the most important implication for leaders and leadership so far is that we are now in a position to appreciate the magnitude of the attribution error spoken of in traditional and New Leadership models. If cognition is distributed as discussed, and since it does not equate with the symbol-processing model but rather consists in associative pattern recognition and completion (e.g. Tienson 1990; Clark 1996; 1997), we suggest that a more productive approach to leadership is to be found precisely in studying the reciprocal interrelationships of human cognition and organizational processes and structures. The complexities of leading as described above become complexities of the interactions not of leaders and followers as merely individual brains but of the social organization of distributed cognition.

In order at least to catch a glimpse of how this might be accomplished, some further comment on the extension of basic human cognition might help to explicate advanced and distinctive features of human reason such as planning and problem solving (all believed to be part of a leader's repertoire).

The Scaffolded Mind

Since cognition is not simply bounded by skull and skin (although thoughts originate in an individual brain), it "leaks" (Clark's colorful phrase) into the world and creates, maintains, and interacts with external structures, both symbolic and social institutional. What is the role of such external "scaffolding"? In Clark's definition, scaffolding "denotes a broad class of physical, cognitive, and social augmentations—augmentations that allow us to achieve some goal that would otherwise be beyond us" (1997, 194–5). Such "external structures function so as to complement our individual cognitive profiles and to diffuse human reason across wider and wider social and physical networks whose collective computations exhibit their own special dynamics and properties" (Clark 1997, 179). Important problem-solving work is delegated to external social and institutional structures and processes, and that means the role of public language now becomes more prominent (Clark 1997, 180). Moreover, the role and function of public language in such accounts is controversial and can be noted only in the present context. In order for us to have advanced cognition—being able to plan, run a country, lead a school—we have to be able to dissipate reasoning; that is, the brain has to create its own external props and labor-saving devices. A simple example may make clear what seems highly abstract or merely speculative. Consider long multiplication. We can easily learn to know at a glance that $7 \times 7 = 49$. We do it "in our heads." But when asked to multiply 4756×7625, we would take pencil and paper or reach for a calculator to solve the problem. As Clark points out, "resorting to pen and paper is a reduction of the complex problem to a sequence of simpler problems beginning with 2×2. The external medium is used to store the results of these simple problems, and by an interrelated series of simple pattern completions coupled with external storage, we get to the solution" (1997, 61). This is a very good example of symbol processing, which demonstrates that the external environment is in fact an extension of our mind. What goes on is a kind of computational bootstrapping through the interactions of our basic pattern-completing abilities with complex and well-structured environments. Just as pen and paper served as the external medium, which imposed certain behaviors on us given the practice of long multiplication, so, at a more complex level, organizations and institutions provide the external resources in which we behave given their policies, practices, and norms.

Linguistic artifacts, including ever-important administrative rules, regulations, and policies, thus play the part of other external structures. They help us reshape some cognitive tasks into formats that are better suited to our basic computational capacities. Thus, the role of language goes beyond the facilitation of communication. It represents a kind of tradeoff between "culturally achieved representations and what would otherwise be . . . time-intensive and labor-intensive internal computation" (Clark 1997, 200). It helps us store memory externally in terms of texts, provides labels with which to navigate our environments successfully, allows us to coordinate action with others and with ourselves, serves to manipulate our own attention by inner rehearsal of speech, and, last but not least, lets us communicate.

What then are some of the implications of the scaffolded mind for leading as an example of organizational practice?

Decentralized Cognition/Decentralized Structure

The conclusion we draw from what we now know about the cognitive computational capacities of human agents for leadership and organizational structure is this: decentralized cognition can begin to serve as the basis for a systematic approach to decentralized structure. Let us fill this out a little as a conclusion, pointing to some prospects and problems for future research.

The notion of isomorphism between theory and organizational structure (Evers and Lakomski 1996, chapters 5, 6), evident in traditional and New Leadership conceptions, also can be extended to naturalistic leadership. In the former case, the hypothetico-deductive account with its implied conception of rational symbol manipulation and linear computation sanctioned a hierarchical structure. In the latter case, a naturalistic account of leadership based on scaffolded pattern completing reason raises the possibility of a very different organizational structure whose major feature is decentralization. The complexities involved in delimiting an appropriate structure to maximize cognition are extraordinary in scope and remain the work of the future. However, it appears advantageous to advocate nonhierarchical, participatory structures in social organizations such as schools, for example, to facilitate greater cognitive input in decision making and generate a greater variety of possible interpretations of problem solutions, coupled with the creation of double feedback loops, as advocated by Argyris and Schön (1996). There are nevertheless complexities here, too, insofar as more communication among groups is not always better and more heads do not always know more (on the effects of different types of social organization on group communication, see Levine and Moreland 1991; Hutchins 1991, 1996).

What seems to be beyond doubt given the preceding discussion is that leaders, while they may be formally in the top position, are inextricably embedded in the cognitive economy of the groups, whose cognitive patterns, in turn, are shaped by the specific and local cultural processes and structures of their organization. It follows that theory building of how distributed cognition works in social organizations, such as schools, begins from the bottom up, since how agents solve their everyday problems depends on activating locally effective strategies of pattern recognition in response to some external event. These, in turn, will leave their traces and will be integrated into the overall cognitive fabric of the organization.

Adopting a naturalistic account of organizational practice implies that what makes for effective practice will differ from context to context and may not be able to be summed across several contexts. However, guided by the general design principle of enhancing learning, promoting the solving of problems, and contributing to how we individually and collectively achieve our theoretically motivated purposes, the pursuit of effective practice is no longer a means distinct from an external moral goal. Rather, moral goals become embedded in the construction of epistemically progressive practices, and the path traveled becomes as important as the destination.

References

Argyris, C., and Schön, D. A. 1996. *Organizational learning II*. Reading, MA: Addison-Wesley.

Avolio, B. J., and Bass, B. M. 1988. Transformation leadership, charisma, and beyond. In *Emerging leadership vistas,* ed. J. G. Hunt, B. R. Baliga, H. P. Dachler and C. A. Schriesheim. Lexington, MA: Lexington Press.

Ayer, A. J. 1936. *Language, truth and logic*. London: Victor Gollancz.

———. 1946. *Language, truth and logic,* 2nd ed. New York: Dover.

Bass, B. M. 1985. *Leadership and performance beyond expectation*. New York: Free Press.

Bass, B. M., and Avolio, B. J., ed. 1994. *Improving organizational effectiveness through transformational leadership*. Thousand Oaks, CA: Sage.

Bowers, D. G., and Seashore, S. E. 1973. Predicting organizational effectiveness with a four-factor theory of leadership. In *Readings in organizational behavior and human performance,* ed. W. E. Scott and L. L. Cummings. Homewood, IL: Richard D. Irwin.

Bresnen, M. J. 1995. All things to all people? Perceptions, attributions, and construc- tions of leadership. *Leadership Quarterly* 6, 4: 495–513.

Bridges, E. M. 1982. Research on the school administrator: The state of the art, 1967–1980. *Educational Administration Quarterly* 18, 3: 12–33.

Bryman, A. 1986. *Leadership and organizations.* London: Routledge & Kegan Paul.

Burns, J. M. 1978. *Leadership.* New York: Harper & Row.

Churchland, P. M. 1989. *A neurocomputational perspective: The nature of mind and the structure of science.* Cambridge, MA: The MIT Press.

———. 1995. *The engine of reason, the seat of the soul.* Cambridge, MA: The MIT Press.

———. 1996. The neural representation of the social world. In *Mind and morals,* ed. L. May, M. Friedman, and A. Clark. Cambridge, MA: The MIT Press.

Churchland, P. S. 1989. *Neurophilosophy: Toward a unified science of the mind/brain.* Cambridge, MA: The MIT Press.

Clark, A. 1996. Connectionism, moral cognition, and collabortive problem-solving. In *Mind and morals,* ed. L. May, M. Friedman, and A. Clark. Cambridge, MA: The MIT Press.

———. 1997. *Being there: Putting brain, body, and world together again.* Cambridge, MA: The MIT Press.

Evers, C. W. (Forthcoming). Decision-making, models of mind, and the new cogni- tive science. *Journal of School Leadership.*

Evers, C. W., and Lakomski, G. 1991. *Knowing educational administration.* Oxford: Elsevier.

——— 1996. *Exploring educational administration.* Oxford: Elsevier.

Greenfield, T. B., and Ribbins, P., ed. (1993). *Greenfield on educational administration: Towards a humane science.* London: Routledge.

Gronn, P. C. 1995. Greatness re-visited: The current obsession with transformational leadership, *Leading & Managing* 1, 1: 14–28.

Grossberg, S., ed. 1988. *Neural networks and natural intelligence.* Cambridge, MA: The MIT Press.

Habermas, J. 1972. *Knowledge and human interests.* London: Heinemann.

Howe, W. 1994. Leadership in educational administration. In *International encyclope- dia of education: Research and studies,* 2nd ed., ed. T. Husen and T. N. Postleth- waite. Oxford, England: Pergamon.

Hunt, J. G. 1991. *Leadership: A new synthesis.* Newbury Park, CA: Sage.

Hutchins, E. 1991. The social organization of distributed cognition. In *Perspectives on socially shared cognition,* ed. L. B. Resnick, J. M. Levine, and S. D. Teasley. Washington, DC: American Psychological Association.

———. 1996. *Cognition in the wild.* Cambridge, MA: The MIT Press.

Landsberger, H. A. 1967–68. The behavioral sciences in industry. *Industrial Relations,* index to volume 7: 1–19.

Lave, J. 1991. Situated learning in communities of practice. In *Perspectives on socially shared cognition,* ed. L. B. Resnick, J. M. Levine, and S. D. Teasley. Washington, DC: American Psychological Association.

Lawler, E. F., and Porter, L. W. 1967. The effect of performance on job satisfaction. *Industrial Relations* 7, 1: 20–28.

Leithwood, K. 1994. Leadership for school restructuring, *Educational Administration Quarterly* 30, 4: 498–518.

Leithwood, K., and Steinbach, R. 1995. *Expert problem solving: Evidence from school and district leaders.* Albany: State University of New York Press.

Levine, J. M., and Moreland, R. L. 1991. Culture and socialization in work groups. In *Perspectives on socially shared cognition,* ed. L. B. Resnick, J. M. Levine, and S. D. Teasley. Washington, DC: American Psychological Association.

Newell, A., and Simon, H. A. 1976. Computer science as empirical enquiry: Symbols and search. In *The philosophy of artificial intelligence,* ed. M. A. Boden 1990. Oxford: Oxford University Press.

Perrow, C. 1986. *Complex organizations.* New York: Random House.

Popper, K. R. 1945. *The open society and its enemies,* I and II. London: George Routledge & Sons.

Port, R. F., and van Gelder, T., eds. 1995. *Mind as motion: Explorations in the dynamics of cognition.* Cambridge, MA: The MIT Press.

Quine, W. V. 1951. Two dogmas of empiricism. *Philosophical Review* 60: 20–43.

———. 1960. *Word and object.* Cambridge, MA: The MIT Press.

Rawls, J. 1972. *A theory of justice.* Cambridge, MA: Harvard University Press.

Resnick, L. B. 1991. Shared cognition: Thinking as social practice. In *Perspectives on socially shared cognition,* ed. L. B. Resnick, J. M. Levine, and S. D. Teasley. Washington, DC: American Psychological Association.

Rogoff, B., and Lave, J., eds. 1984. *Everyday cognition: Its development in social context.* Cambridge, MA: Harvard University Press.

Rumelhart, D. E., and McClelland, J. L., eds. 1986. *Parallel distributed processing,* I and II. Cambridge, MA: The MIT Press.

Simon, H. A. 1946. *Administrative behavior.* New York: Macmillan

Smith, M. ed. 1995. *Meta-ethics.* Aldershot, U.K.: Dartmouth.

Tienson, J. L. 1990. An introduction to connectionism. In *Foundations of cognitive science,* ed. J. L. Garfield. New York: Paragon House.

CHAPTER TEN

Evers and Lakomski on Values in Educational Administration: Less than Hcoherent

Derek J. Allison and Frederick S. Ellett, Jr.

> To be humane, to escape the fact-driven, calculable world, we must be
> human. . . . And this of course takes us out of the limited world of fact and
> matter, out of synapses and programmed responses into the world of culture,
> into true culture, a world that Evers and Lakomski deny, or accept only as
> an obverse of the physical.
> —Thomas Greenfield, in Greenfield and Ribbins,
> *Greenfield on Educational Administration*

In their recent book, *Knowing Educational Administration,* Evers and Lakomski (1991) present their case for adopting and applying coherentist criteria to choose between competing theories of the world and educational administration in particular. While key elements of their argument fail to satisfy their own criteria, their book is very impressive. They are to be particularly commended for the clarity of the text (especially some of their synoptic summaries) and, more particularly, for the richness of the philosophical discussions presented. Indeed, it would not be overstating our view to say that their book has elevated discussion and argument in the field to higher, previously unattainable yet welcomed levels.

We agree with much of what they say in their book. At the superficial level of text, we largely agree that "an alternative, post-positivist science of educational administration is not only possible but theoretically and practically desirable" (Evers and Lakomski 1991, viii). We further agree that such a science (although we prefer terms such as *disciplined* or *systematic inquiry*) should not be based on foundationalist assumptions, should be fallibalist (but not quite in the sense they often use the term), and should draw on the "extra-empirical," coherentist virtues they champion when choosing between theories (but not in the way they advocate). Where we part company with Evers and Lakomski is on their assessment of inquiry (including science) as a human activity and in their apparently uncritical acceptance of Churchlandian doctrine. In consequence, we find ourselves opposed to their eliminativist project and their, in our view, unjustified "eschewing [of] meaning as an explanatory category" (ix).

In this chapter, we focus primarily on what we see as Evers and

Lakomski's rather dated and restricted treatment of human values and their place in both administrative theory and systematic inquiry. We argue that by concentrating on values as primarily individuated preferences and substantially ignoring the presence and press of *human culture*, they seriously underestimate and misrepresent both the nature of values and their inescapable influences on action and choice both in the ordinary social world and in science.

Evers and Lakomski appear to think that there is a natural world, populated by human beings whose thinking and actions are derived from knowledge acquired through reasoned interaction with the world (social and physical). In consequence, they see the task of inquiry as being to form and refine a set of interdependent theories that ultimately reduce to first-order propositions about the physical world. To progress in this endeavor, they argue that we need to apply a set of extra-empirical criteria to make rational choices between competing theories and thus foster coherence. On our reading, they seem further to think that their coherentist virtues can be applied in a formal and a "rulelike," way. For this reason, we will call their conception of epistemic coherence "Fcoherence."

Our view is that we are more than just human beings inhabiting physical and social worlds, that we are persons who are formed by, and contribute to, the continual re-forming of an additional historical-social-cultural-linguistic reality that gives objective meaning and value to our thoughts and purposive actions. Physical and biochemical realities of the world and the human frame obviously impose mechanical constraints and limits on what we can think and do, and thus accurate and reliable knowledge about such things is desirable. Yet the broad domain of social science cannot sensibly ignore the historical-cultural reality that provides a matrix of meaning for purposeful social thought and actions as, for instance, in administration. We doubt that valid, reliable, and useful knowledge about the sociocultural world, and thus administration, can be reduced sensibly (at least smoothly) to the physical. We agree, nevertheless, that epistemic criteria such as those identified by Evers and Lakomski have a crucial role to play when it comes to choosing between competing theories, be they about the physical, social, or cultural worlds. Yet we do not accept that these standards can be rationally applied in formal and rulelike ways. Because their meaning is contextually embedded in historically formed and socially manifest cultures and domain-referenced subcultures, we see them as superordinate *values* that are used by persons and communities to make informed judgements. This process promotes what we will call "H (for historical) coherence." At the center of our response, then, is our conclusion that while Evers and Lakomski's epistemology may be Fcoherent it is not Hcoherent, and thus fails as a meaningful frame within which to pursue disciplined inquiry into educational administration.

In the pages that follow, we flesh out our view in three main sections. In the first, we locate Evers and Lakomski's position within the broader scope of philosophy, with particular reference to the writings of their declared heroes, Popper, Quine, and the Churchlands. As Evers and Lakomski freely acknowledge, the issues and options under discussion are complex and rapidly evolving—they are also much more highly contested than one might conclude after reading their book. Our overview is thus intended to relate their position to other historical and contemporary viewpoints while laying some cornerstones for our arguments. In the second section, we take a close look at the epistemic values, drawing on a paper by Thomas Kuhn that offers an alternate way of seeing how such a common set of standards promotes rational inquiry. In the third section, we turn to ethical concerns and give our views on three issues discussed in the recent literature and by Evers and Lakomski, namely Hume's is-ought dichotomy, Moore's naturalistic fallacy, and the problem of arbitrating moral values.

Comments on the General Philosophical Stance

We do strongly support Evers and Lakomski's *general* philosophical stance. They call it "naturalism," as do others. But most of the "naturalists" also have been called "pragmatists"! We shall return to the significance of this point later. Naturalism, in the widest sense, is a philosophical approach that is opposed to any and all foundations, *a prioris*, essentialisms, transcendentalisms, universalisms—in short, it is opposed to all forms of epistemic "*privilege*." In other words, "there is no First Philosophy," naturalists regarding such views as either question-begging or inadequately grounded (see Hooker 1987, chapter 3; Margolis 1995, chapter 2).

It is important to understand that the naturalists form quite a heterogeneous group. We have tried to give a sense of the diversity within the naturalistic approach by means of figures 10.1 and 10.2. Figure 10.1 provides a schematic overview of evolving lines of thought contributed by influential philosophers, with the naturalists appearing in the lower center. Figure 10.2 zooms in on the naturalist group and identifies key points and positions in the thinking of central contributors.

Evers and Lakomski seem to have three philosophical heroes: Churchland, Quine, and Popper. As shown in the figures, we have *not* placed Popper among the naturalists. We believe Popper really belongs with the logical empiricists, for his metaphilosophy appears essentially the same as the logical empiricist metastand. In particular, Popper held that there *is* a kind of First Philosophy (See Hooker 1987, chapter 3).

Figures 10.1 and 10.2 help us make three further points. First, Husserl used 'naturalism' as a pejorative term to refer to those philosophers who

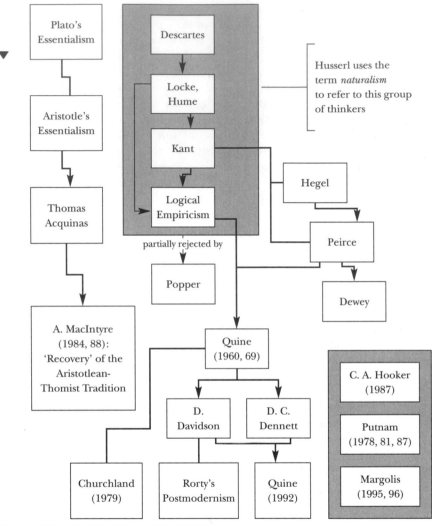

Figure 10.1   A global view of the field

ignore the preformative context of the social-cultural-linguistic life world. He specifically had in mind Descartes, Locke, Hume, Kant, and the early positivists. Husserl meant to sharply contrast such "naturalisms" with his own form of inquiry, "phenomenology." Later phenomenologists, for example, Heidegger and Merleau-Ponty, criticized Husserl for not applying the same critique to his own line of inquiry. Somehow Husserl imagined he could escape his own preformative, cultural context to find what is uncondi-

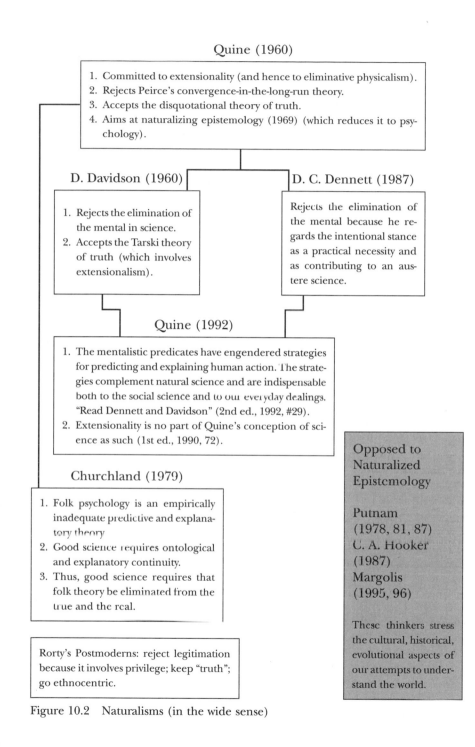

Quine (1960)

1. Committed to extensionality (and hence to eliminative physicalism).
2. Rejects Peirce's convergence-in-the-long-run theory.
3. Accepts the disquotational theory of truth.
4. Aims at naturalizing epistemology (1969) (which reduces it to psychology).

D. Davidson (1960)

1. Rejects the elimination of the mental in science.
2. Accepts the Tarski theory of truth (which involves extensionalism).

D. C. Dennett (1987)

Rejects the elimination of the mental because he regards the intentional stance as a practical necessity and as contributing to an austere science.

Quine (1992)

1. The mentalistic predicates have engendered strategies for predicting and explaining human action. The strategies complement natural science and are indispensable both to the social science and to our everyday dealings. "Read Dennett and Davidson" (2nd ed., 1992, #29).
2. Extensionality is no part of Quine's conception of science as such (1st ed., 1990, 72).

Churchland (1979)

1. Folk psychology is an empirically inadequate predictive and explanatory theory
2. Good science requires ontological and explanatory continuity.
3. Thus, good science requires that folk theory be eliminated from the true and the real.

Rorty's Postmoderns: reject legitimation because it involves privilege; keep "truth"; go ethnocentric.

Opposed to Naturalized Epistemology

Putnam (1978, 81, 87)
C. A. Hooker (1987)
Margolis (1995, 96)

These thinkers stress the cultural, historical, evolutional aspects of our attempts to understand the world.

Figure 10.2   Naturalisms (in the wide sense)

tionally necessary or essential. On our reading, Gadamer extended the Heideggerean view when he insisted that all distinctions, all rational inquiry and claims, obtain *within the bounds of history,* and thus they 'must' be subject to its flux and cannot exit from it (see also Bernstein 1983). In developing his theme, Gadamer "recovers" a positive sense of "prejudice," which becomes the key to his theory of history.[1] As Gadamer put it: "It is not so much our judgements as it is our prejudices that constitute our being. . . . Prejudices are biases of our openness to the world. They are simply the conditions whereby we experience something—whereby what we encounter says something to us" (1976, 9) We suspect that Evers and Lakomski have not grasped Husserl's critique and its implications. It also seems that they have little appreciation of Gadamer's views, which are clearly directed toward an account of the *ontology* of persons. It is true that Gadamer does not spend much time developing and defending the kind of epistemology his view requires, but he does insist that epistemology and ontology must be co-ordinated. Nothing in Evers and Lakomski's chapter "The Cultural Perspective" comes to grips with this basic set of problems. What is more, they assume throughout their book that the issues are epistemological and frequently duck ontological questions. Yet, as we shall see, they do have very strong views about ontology, and about truth. Moreover, it should be clear that the issues before us are not merely or mainly epistemological. Questions about how we can know things are necessarily related to questions about the way the world is. In consequence, a plausible philosophy will co-ordinate epistemology, ontology and a theory of truth.

On the question of what may be known about the world, Evers and Lakomski appear to adopt a Popperian stance. While Popper denied that we can ever know the laws of nature, he had no doubt that there are (universal) laws in physics and sociology. In this he rejected Aristotle's essentialism but maintained a "modified essentialism" that held that one needs universal laws to make sense of science. Evers and Lakomski seem to subscribe to this view and accept the existence of laws in both physical and social science. But both Cartwright (1983) and van Fraassen (1989) have argued plausibly that physical science is a coherent activity without the existence of laws. Davidson (1984) has further argued that there are no laws in the social sciences.

Second, within the naturalist group, there is a rather sharp divide between those who follow, in a broad sense, Quine's version of "naturalized epistemology" and those who do not. For Quine, naturalized epistemology is supposed to reduce the second-order legitimative features of epistemology to some causal explanation in a first-order science (see also Goldman 1992). Evers and Lakomski want to insist that the Quineans are basically correct. Hooker, Margolis, and Putnam have argued repeatedly that Quine has never really defended this view, that it looks implausible, and that there is a better account anyhow. We share the judgement of Hooker, Margolis, and Putnam.

Our third point is that Evers and Lakomski accept and uncritically advocate the views of Patricia and Paul Churchland. The Churchlandian view claims, first, that the conceptual framework of persons and beliefs, values and actions—what has come to be called "folk psychology" in recent literature—is a grossly inadequate empirical theory in terms of its predictive and explanatory success rates. Next, Churchlandians claim that folk psychology (as any good theory should) must be *ontologically* continuous with our other best scientific theories, and, in order to do this, it must be *explanitorily* continuous. Churchlandians take this to mean that the terms of any legitimate science must either reduce to the physical level—which would be neurobiology for human action—or be eliminated. But as Greenwood (1991b) argues, the Churchland group has never really presented any detailed evidence that folk psychology is so grossly inadequate. Indeed, Evers and Lakomski (1991, 90–91) acknowledge that what they call "folk theory" has a "large measure of empirical adequacy" within the realm of ordinary, everyday life. Still, the Churchland view maintains that what they define as good science requires that all terms reduce to some kind of physicalism. This is why Evers and Lakomski can conclude that "folk theory may be both empirically adequate *and false*" (91; emphasis added). Consequently, Churchlandians further conclude that if "inner" human intentions (such as desires, beliefs, and values) do not reduce to physical mechanisms—as all now agree they will not—then the terms should be eliminated from scientific theory. As McDonough explains, "the only way it can be made to appear plausible that one can eliminate content states [intentions] is to engage in the wholesale redescription of human behavior where all reference to human culture-embedded behavior is systematically removed. This is precisely the eliminativist strategy" (1991, 275). We did not expect Evers and Lakomski to mount a full defence of the Churchlandian view; but even Quine (1960) did not really argue for his earlier view either, preferring just to lay out his predilections:

> There remains a thesis of Brentano's . . . that is directly relevant to our emerging doubts over the prepositional attitudes and other intentional locutions. It is roughly that there is no breaking out of the intentional vocabulary by explaining its members in other terms. Our [Quine's] present reflections are favourable to this thesis. . . . One may accept the Brentano thesis as either showing the indispensability of intentional idioms and the importance of an autonomous science of intention, or as showing the baselessness of intentional idioms and the emptiness of a science of intention. My attitude, unlike Brentano's, is the second. . . . If we are limning the true and ultimate structure of reality, the canonical scheme for us is the austere scheme that knows

no quotation but direct quotation and no prepositional attitudes but only the
physical constitution and behaviour of organisms. (1960 220–21)

Since then, the arguments of Davidson and Dennett have lead him to
change his mind. Thus Quine (1992, sec. 29), one of Evers and Lakomski's
heroes, now rejects 'eliminative' physicalism. Another of their heroes, Popper, never accepted it. And, of course, Hooker, Margolis, and Putnam have
repeatedly rejected it.

Yet in their chapter "The Cultural Perspective," Evers and Lakomski
cleave to the eliminativist ideal and in doing so seriously misrepresent the
nature and effects of human culture. They declare, "What makes us 'human' in the cultural perspective, is that we possess 'inner' phenomena such
as motives, purposes and intentions" (1991, 128). This is already a serious
misreading of what the cultural and the intentional involve. As Putnam
(1981) has put it, "meanings are not in the head." McDonough explains
that even in ordinary language usage "we do not generally say that people
have beliefs, and so forth, inside them. We say that persons are *in* states of
belief or desire: 'She did it in the belief that it was best,' and 'They did it in
the desire to win' (1991, 264). McDonough adds, parenthetically, that such
common language usage suggests that "beliefs, and so forth [within which
category we will explicitly include values] are objective things in which
people can share" (265). Evers and Lakomski go on to characterize their
portrayal of intentions as "inner states" posing the dualist problem. Consistent with their project, they maintain that all substance and property dual-
isms between the mental and the physical are mistaken. Yet the problem is
not (or not just) the mind/body problem; we also have to deal with the
culture/nature problem. Here, the character, as well as the content, of
natural languages must be considered. Language cannot be reduced to the
aggregated thoughts and utterances of "individuals" (see Greenwood
1991a; Margolis 1991; McDonough 1991).

Evers and Lakomski's denial of ontological differences between mind
and body, culture and the physical, ignores the view shared by Gadamer,
Foucault, and Margolis (1995), that real persons are historical artefacts
having no nature, only histories. On this account, persons have real, intentional properties that are incarnate in the physical. Persons are entities who
have been "constructed" by being initiated into a specific sociocultural-
linguistic-material world and into sets of more or less distinct subcultures
and their associated subcommunities. The closest Evers and Lakomski come
to considering the key elements and the promise of this interpretation of
the cultural perspective is in their chapter "The Greenfield Revolution."
There, they acknowledge that "Greenfield's approach to organizational theory (and the long tradition of social science in which his approach stands)
admits of no easy reply" (90). Just so. They nonetheless continue un-

deterred with their eliminativist project, dismissing the culturally anchored analyses of science offered by Feyerabend and Kuhn as amounting to little more than "anything goes" and "mob psychology"[2] respectively. This dismissal, we think, is a serious error. In our view, what we will henceforth term the "cultured-folk frame" holds great promise for the future of social science and for disciplined inquiry in educational administration. And contrary to Evers and Lakomski's hope of reducing everything to the physical, we believe the cultured-folk frame offers greater promise for a plausible account of realism in the physical sciences (See Bernstein 1983; Hooker 1987; Margolis 1995).

In sum, although Evers and Lakomski are most often balanced and fair, on the issues discussed above they betray a limited and a mistaken grasp of the problems, the possibilities, and the plausible (or coherent) responses. This leads us to a discussion of the Evers and Lakomski "touchstone" of extra-empirical virtues.

On the Nature of "Epistemic Virtues"

Throughout their book, Evers and Lakomski argue that researchers in educational administration (or at least those who are aware of the demise of positivist-derived empiricism) have been unduly pessimistic about the prospects for scientific (objective) inquiry in the field. They claim that scientific inquiry has available to it a set of extra-empirical standards that inquirers can, and should, be using to appraise research in the field and to choose between competing theories. "Objectivity," they declare, "is a matter of coherence, not [just] hard data" (96). Evers and Lakomski call the super empirical criteria that will promote coherence "touchstone virtues" and use William Lycan's presentation of how they can (should) be applied. Lycan (1988, 130) laid out his scheme as a set of global decision rules, as shown in Table 10.1.

Here then is an interesting set of rules which could be used to appraise theories. But why should one use this set of decision rules? Evers and Lakomski seem to be saying that in a given domain of inquiry there is a truth of the matter, so there must be a way to determine what this truth is. Yet, even if this claim were true (and as we will see Quine, Rorty, and Putnam do not think it is), Evers and Lakomski have not shown us why their set of virtues should be used.[3]

The difficulty facing Evers and Lakomski here is that their account only establishes objectivity for the process by which they would apply their epistemic virtues, and not for the virtues—the choice criteria—themselves. In this respect, they have unwittingly fallen back to a logical-empiricist notion of "objectivity." Still, they are in good company as Paul Hirst (1972),

Table 10.1   Lycan's decision rules, Evers and Lakomski's epistemic virtues, and
Kuhn's epistemic values

Lycan (1988):
Other things being equal·
Prefer Theory 1 to Theory 2, if Theory 1 is *simpler* than Theory 2
Prefer Theory 1 to Theory 2, if Theory 1 *explains more* than Theory 2
Prefer Theory 1 to Theory 2, if Theory 1 is *more readily testable* than Theory 2
Prefer Theory 1 to Theory 2, if Theory 1 *leaves fewer messy, unanswered questions* (problems)
   behind, especially if Theory 2 raises messy, unanswered questions (problems)
Prefer Theory 1 to Theory 2, if Theory 1 *squares better* with what you already have reason to
   believe.

Evers and Lakomski's (1991) epistemic virtues (following Lycan):
Simplicity, Explanatory Power, Testability, Question Resolving Power, Congruence with Existing Beliefs

Kuhn's (1977) epistemic values:
Simplicity, Empirical Adequacy, Internal and External Consistency, Broad Scope, Fruitfulness

---

John Rawls (1993), and Christopher Hodgkinson (1978; 1983) all made the same mistake (see Mackie 1977, chapter 1, section 5).

It is intriguing that Evers and Lakomski do not use William Lycan's own defence of his rules, wherein he holds that some such set of decision standards is innate, hardwired, topic-neutral, and thus formal. And, although they cite a pertinent passage from Quine, they really do not draw out his position (which was given originally in 1960, section 56), which was that these just are the standards that are found (more or less) in all kinds of systematic theorizing, including philosophy.[4] Thus, for Quine, such extra-empirical epistemic virtues provide a plausible account of working values central to doing science (and philosophy) and adjudicating between scientific theories and other accounts of the world. Here then is at least one set of values that has been justified or legitimated. But how?

This leads us to a crucially important point. Essentially, this same set of scientific standards was identified, delineated, and defended by none other than Thomas Kuhn (1977) himself in a paper entitled "Objectivity, Value Judgement, and Theory Choice," originally presented in 1973. There Kuhn identified five characteristics of "a good scientific theory":

> First, a theory should be *accurate:* within its domain, that is, consequences deducible from the theory should be in demonstrated agreement with the results of existing experiments and observations. Second, a theory should be *consistent,* not only internally or with itself, but also with other currently accepted theories applicable to related aspects of nature. Third, it should have

broad scope: in particular, a theory's consequences should extend far beyond the particular observations, laws, or sub-theories it was designed to explain. Fourth, and closely related, it should be *simple,* bringing order to phenomena that in its absence would be individually isolated and, as a set, confused. Fifth, . . . a theory should be *fruitful* of new research findings; it should, that is, disclose new phenomena or previously unnoted relationships among those already known. (321–22; emphasis added).

Earlier, in his important *Structure of Scientific Revolutions*, Kuhn had put the basic points more succinctly: "First, the new candidate [theory] must seem to resolve some outstanding and generally recognized problem that can be met in no other way. Second, the new paradigm must promise to preserve a relatively large part of concrete problem-solving ability that has accrued to science through its predecessors" (1970, 169)

Part of our interest here is the similarity between the Lycan/Evers and Lakomski list of evaluative criteria and Kuhn's epistemic values. The commonalities and key points are summarized in Table 10.1. We think it is clear that Kuhn's values readily subsume the conceptual principles underlying Lycan's rules and that Evers and Lakomski could have no objections to including Kuhn's values of empirical adequacy and fruitfulness among their epistemic virtues. Furthermore, both sets could be augmented with other values that often figure in theory choice, such as elegance and parsimony, for example. Still, we are not interested in specifying a full and definitive list (if that were possible), our main point being to show the existence of a set of epistemic values guiding theory appraisal and selection.

The first of our broader points is that these epistemic values are by no means new. Kuhn has shown that if one looks at what scientists really do (which he held that only a historian was capable of doing) then one finds something like these conceptions of the desirable at work throughout the history of science. In reflecting on this, it is of the first importance to grasp that Kuhn is saying that these values are characteristic of the *collective*—of the scientific culture at large as it has evolved through history. Further, although many, especially logical positivists such as Hempel and Reichenbach, have taken these values to be formal (or content-free or neutral), Kuhn explicitly denies that they are, or can be, sensibly applied as formal rules. Hence they should not be seen to be "fixed once and for all, unaffected by their participation in transitions from one theory to another" (Kuhn 1977, 335–36). Evers and Lakomski seem to hold a contrary view, implying that the epistemic virtues constitute a "theory of evidence" which will do its work of selecting the best theories of the world independent of those theories (1991, 229). Yet, as Hooker (1987) has put it, there can be no double standards here, for what methods are appropriate depend upon what theories we find acceptable.

Kuhn has always admitted that he has "no theory of induction." He has always held that he believes scientific inquiry is rational but has conceded that his task has not been to show why it is rational (or objective). He clearly realized that to assume that science is a paradigm of rationality is either question begging, circular, or arbitrary (see Goldman 1992).

How then do we proceed? It is at this point that we need to recover our earlier remark that almost all naturalists were/are pragmatists. A pragmatist holds that any attempt to justify science "directly" will end up using some form of illicit privilege. What is needed is a holistic (global) defence along the following lines. It seems hard to deny that science has served our interests in prediction, control, and explanation.[5] This gives us good, but tentative, reasons to think that science is in touch with the world. (This is part of Habermas's 1968 thesis). Within the scope of this holistic defence, let us now look more precisely to try to determine what are the salient areas of achievement and why, and let us use the insights we gain to refine and redirect future inquiry. This second step involves what second-order legitimation becomes when one rejects all attempts at privilege.[6] We will likely find, given what we think we know, that these (historically formed, culturally embedded, content full) epistemic values provide a promising framework to us carry forward.

There is one more crucial insight to be gained from Kuhn. (Again, Evers and Lakomski miss it in their work). Once one grasps what the epistemic values involve, one sees that they can easily conflict. A choice can be made only by the exercise of informed judgement, which trades off the conflicting values. There is no higher-level value to appeal to here in seeking to adjudicate the conflict; inquirers must informally, yet intelligently, weigh the evidence and judge. Notice here that it can turn out that well-informed, reasonable inquirers (such as Bohr and Einstein) can disagree and yet both still be reasonable in their judgements. Nor should it be assumed that Kuhn's use of "judgement" in such cases equates with merely subjective "taste" and that theory choice is ultimately "un-discussable" because of this (Kuhn 1977, 336–38). The point is that the best minds in a domain can appraise the best evidence using the best criteria—these being the epistemic values—and reach differing, entirely reasonable, judgements about what appears to be the best scientific theory. This outcome of Kuhn's work has frightened many people.

The important point here is that scientific thinking, which traditionally has been called "theoretical reason," can now be seen as having the same logical form as "practical rationality." In other words, Kuhn helps us reject the traditional dichotomy, found in Aristotle, Hume, and Kant, between theoretical reason and practical reason. The import of Hooker's (1987) latest work is to sustain precisely this point about the form of "theoretical acceptance." The problematic gap between "(theoretical) reason" and "passions" in the traditional view is no longer a problem for practical rationality. This removes any qualitative gap that may have been assumed to exist between scientific reasoning and practical problem processing in social-action domains, including value-saturated domains such as educational administration. The cognitive content involved will obviously differ, vastly in some respects. Scientific inquirers also typically have access to various kinds of specialized data collection instruments and analysis tools (but so do administrators). Yet inquirers even in the most esoteric domain of hard science ultimately interpret and evaluate what they consider to be the evidence relevant to a particular problem much as a practicing school administrator will do in his or hers.

There is one final point to be made before ending this section. As noted earlier, Evers and Lakomski seem to hold that in a given domain of inquiry there is a *unique* truth about the ready-made externalistic world waiting to be discovered. As they say, "a true theory is one which corresponds to, or matches up with, the way the world is" (1991, 42). In this respect, their arguments seem to be a modified version of C. S. Peirce's view that reality will be discerned over the long run as our successive attempts at theory building eventually converge to the uniquely true account, a view that Dewey called a "spectator theory of knowledge" and Rorty, a "mirror theory" of truth. Even while they appear to take Quine as one of their heroes, they have not come to grips with his critique of Peirce:

> Peirce was tempted to define truth outright in terms of scientific method, as the ideal theory which is approached as a limit when the (supposed) canons of scientific method are used increasingly on continuing experience. But there is a lot wrong with Peirce's notion, besides its assumption of the final organon of scientific method and its appeal to an infinite process. There is a faulty use of numerical analogy in speaking of a limit of theories, since the notion of limit depends on that of "nearer than," which is defined for numbers and not for theories. And even if we by-pass such troubles, . . . still there is trouble in the imputation of uniqueness ("*the* ideal result"). (Quine 1960, 23)

Quine holds then that science is indeed the way to truth, "but it affords even in principle no unique definition of truth. Any so-called pragmatic definition of truth is doomed to fail equally." As he has put it more recently, "two epistemically ideal but equivalent theories [can] describe one and the same world. Limited to our human terms and devices, we grasp the world variously" (Quine 1992, 101). Thus, Quine rejects the correspondence theory of truth. Similar considerations also led Rorty (1991b) and Putnam (1981) to reject the mirror theory of truth.

It is at this point that the pragmatists (or naturalists) roughly divide into the two conflicting groups shown in our figures 10.1 and 10.2: the

Davidson-Quine-Rorty group and the Hooker-Margolis-Putnam group. The first group has either no theory or a very narrow theory of the person (or self) and usually remains focused upon sensory and mental states (which seems to be the case with Evers and Lakomski). The second group takes the person to be some kind of historically emergent entity and, where it can, recovers and integrates recent themes from Franco-German thought. We ally ourselves with this second group. Greenfield and Hodgkinson share a strong sense that persons are real entities (Greenfield more so than Hodgkinson, perhaps). Thus, they too could be sensibly linked to the second group. The members of the first group mostly subscribe to an *externalistic* account of knowledge in which the real condition of the world possesses a determinate structure entirely apart from, and unaffected by, the intrinsic conditions of human knowledge, understanding, and inquiry. The members of the second group are inclined toward some post-Kantian, *constructivist* account in which idealism is intertwined with realism.

Part of the import of these first two sections has been our attempt to put the varieties of "naturalism" into clearer focus and to provide a wider set of plausible possibilities for social inquiry. We were also attempting to recover a sense of rigor or objectivity for the epistemic values of scientific inquiry. As we hope to show in the following section, this is important for moral inquiry because many of those who are skeptical about moral values (Mackie 1977, for example, claiming moral values would have to be "queer" to be real) are also those whose arguments undermine the objective values of truth and epistemic goodness in science itself, which, of course, they would not want to do at all. Scientific describing, theorizing, and truth claiming are saturated with the epistemic values and the (normative) value of truth itself. In science, as in other historically formed and culturally informed domains of purposeful human activity, facts and values are inescapably intertwined.[7] In sum, we hope we have managed to sketch a plausible defence of the following quite important claim: Given that there are objective (or real) values in scientific activity, then it is at least possible that there are objective values in moral matters and thus, of course, (educational) administration.

Comments on the Ethical Stance

As we said at the outset, we are, generally, quite sympathetic to the global, naturalistic approach taken by Evers and Lakomski. When it comes to ethics, we stand with them in opposing what they call "'the autonomy of ethics' thesis: the thesis that ethics is somehow distinct and separate from empirical knowledge" (1991, 167). Whereas they are primarily concerned with linking values to physical science, we see the links with culture as most important. Evers and Lakomski tend to place most of their views on ethics and morality (and thus values) in their chapters 8 and 9. There they warn the reader that their thinking is still quite tentative, in flux, and at best suggestive. We hope our remarks can be taken in the same open-ended manner. In what follows, we draw upon the recent approach to providing an account of moral thinking, which has been called "moral realism" or "cultural realism." This approach is critically reviewed by Arrington (1989) and Margolis (1995). We believe that moral realism, broadly understood, can provide a comparatively plausible account of moral objectivity.

Getting an 'Ought' from an 'Is'

As the story goes, a certain M. Holmes (1986, 85), rather straightforwardly said if person *T* were a teacher of seven year olds in the public schools, then person *T* ought to teach them to read (if she can, etc.). To this, a certain C. Hodgkinson (1991, 90) replied that to argue (or reason) in this manner is to make an invalid inference for one cannot legitimately get an 'ought' from an 'is', as was originally demonstrated by none other than the great David Hume himself.[8] However, Hume was not as thoroughgoing as Mackie for Hume claimed no such thing for the term *good*. Hume took reason to be "theoretical reason," of a kind moreover that had yet to discover probability in the sense we understand it today, a point we will take up later.

The is-ought conundrum has generated some debate in educational administration. Evers and Lakomski use some good work by Max Black to help us get over the so-called gap between the two. Using some of the recent work by "moral realists," our argument is more direct and, we think, tremendously more helpful—within the cultured-folk sphere (and thus the domain of administration) we deny that the arguments for the gap are any good at all. In the case of the Holmes-Hodgkinson debate, we maintain that what one gets is the following. teacher *T* is *prima facie* obligated to teach the children to read; so, too, with all shared understandings of role ascriptions and established rule-governed social situations in any given historically formed, culturally anchored, human society. Thus, if a person *is* a teacher, that person *ought* to teach, and in contemporary Western societies the commonly shared understanding is that teachers of young children *should* teach them to read (if they can, etc.); if the traffic light is red, the driver ought to stop; if a male person in the upper strata of sixteenth- and seventeenth-century European society was called a liar by a social equal, he accepted that he ought to demand the satisfaction of a meeting (a duel), and so on and so forth throughout known history.

Now everyone is right in a sense. Mark Holmes and J. Searle (1969) are correct in that their teacher and promise-maker are *prima facie* obligated to live up to their respective commitments in their respective examples. But Hodgkinson, Hume, and Mackie are also correct in that cultural rule observance is only a *prima facie* obligation and is not categorical (or unconditional or absolutely binding). Even so, many people have gone to the stake or to a similar fate because they accepted an obligation associated with their social identity as being, for all intents and purposes, binding.

Our kind of interpretation defuses the primary concern of the is-ought problem. We are still left, of course, with the seemingly important question of whether one can ever show that a certain claim, conclusion, or judgement is ever categorical, unconditional, or absolutely binding. Our answer is in two parts, one geared to the physical frame, the other to the cultured-folk frame. In the first case, if we cannot expect binding compliance to the facts of the matter as interpreted by leading scientists such as Bohr and Einstein—remember Kuhn and reasonable disagreement among the reasonable—we should not expect it in ethics. Second, established practices and authorities in a given society (including, of course, educational administrators in twentieth century post-industrial states), often do expect, and even demand, binding compliance to properly legitimated role and rule expectations, the current buzz-standard of "zero tolerance" providing a convenient example.

Further, we think it prudent to ask whether either Hume's original quibble over the form and application of certain logical arguments or Hodgkinson's subsequent and intransigent global application of the resulting rule to the administrative art is particularly relevant to disciplined inquiry into, and the professional practice of, educational administration. Regardless of the canons of formal logic involved, it is a fact of social life that people frequently do derive oughts from what they take to be the is of a matter, as a moment's reflection on the content of everyday conversations, especially in organizations, will demonstrate. Moreover, it is not stretching the point to say that administrators are *prima facie* obligated to derive what will become official oughts from what they (and others) take to be the given facts of certain types of social situations. This is not to imply, of course, that this will necessarily be simple, mechanical, or even achievable in any given situation. Still, can we not entertain an expansion of Holmes' original challenge? Person *P* is a school principal, and thus *P* (*prima facie*) ought to do all that is prudent, possible, and permitted to ensure that teacher *T* teaches her students to read.

The Naturalistic Fallacy and Moore's Concern with Definitions

We would probably not have to concern ourselves with Moore's "naturalistic fallacy" if it had not found its way into the literature of educational administration through a tendency of some writers to conflate it with the is-ought question. Moore (1903) was concerned with the nature of good, which he saw as the fundamental 'object' of ethics. One of his conclusions was that good is a simple, nonnatural property that cannot be defined in terms of any natural property for any such definition can always be rephrased as an open question. Thus, while a statement such as "teaching children to read is good" accurately captures a prevailing *prima facie* value in contemporary societies, it does not exhaust, still less does it define, the nature of good for one can always ask if the essence of good is teaching children to read, or whatever. Any attempt to define 'good' in terms of a natural property will thus commit what Moore called the "naturalistic fallacy."

By concluding that good was a nonnatural property, Moore was consciously placing the analysis of good beyond the reach of science, as he conceived it, thus bolstering the autonomy-of-ethics thesis. Evers and Lakomski think he failed in this project, and so do we but, as will come as no surprise, for different reasons. From our point of view, we readily agree that good is a nonnatural property in Moore's sense for normative terms cannot be Quinean-naturalized, nor can 'good' be equated with the specific features that make something good. *Prima facie* good will be what people, individually and in collectivities, take it to be within the webs of meaning embedded within the cultures in which they participate. On our view then, everyday social interactions are infused with what people take to be first-level, *prima facie* conceptions of the good, which are informed by and referenced more or less directly to conventions, norms, values, and institutions embedded in and transmitted through historically dynamic cultures.

Administrators, by virtue of their role and responsibilities, are inextricably caught up with the frictions, confusions, and conflicts that will inevitably result as individuals and groups act on their differing conceptions of what is good under the prevailing circumstances. But, more than this, administrators, especially those charged with the administration of state policies, have both legal and moral *prima facie* obligations to enact and uphold official values and moral codes proclaimed in the prevailing systems of order and are empowered to do this through the judicious exercise of the authority granted them for this purpose.[9] There can be no escape from this. Whatever else they do, administrators will arbitrate values and uphold moralities for even a failure to act, in a value-laden social situation, communicates a moral stance. This is particularly so for school administrators who head institutions charged with educating, socializing, and enculturating the young.

In this context, we think Moore's work has little to offer practicing administrators or those who inquire into educational administration, although his famous fallacy has heuristic utility in helping administrators appreciate the impossibility of simply defining absolute good. We were thus somewhat surprised at the amount of attention Evers and Lakomski devoted to Moore's analysis. There is no great concern for definitions in the analysis of meaning *per se* in contemporary systematic moral inquiry (Williams 1985), although this was, of course, a requirement in positivism. Further, Moore was not a naturalist. Indeed, his major conclusion about the nature of good is almost pre-Kantian for he thought good could be perceived only through human intuition, an explanation which is clearly implausible to a naturalist. Still, the most intriguing aspect of Evers and Lakomski's treatment is the first part of their argument against Moore where they draw directly on the centrality of contextualized meanings in ordinary language and thus on culturally embedded norms and values. Their brief consideration of the serviceability of ordinary language conceptions helps to illustrate and support the power of the cultured-folk explanatory frame. Thus, we were disappointed to see them trying to displace it in their tenacious pursuit of their eliminativist project.

Adjudicating Moral Values

In the balance of their chapter 8, Evers and Lakomski go on to outline a theory of value acquisition and morality that they claim "is more coherent than its major rivals" (1991, 172), by which they mean, of course, Fcoherent within their frame. It should thus come as no surprise that the warmed-over version of Quinean behavioralist learning theory, which they advance, fails to acknowledge, let alone accommodate, the broader impress of socially mediated culture (the Life Worlds), with the acquisition of both language and value being treated as merely "individuated" cognitive processes. Given this, the "Normative Framework for Administrative Practice," which they then proceed to erect, is difficult to justify by their own standards. The key norm to be used when adjudicating administrative choice in their framework is that choices should be "in the long term, educative" (1991, 185). But how might this standard be understood, let alone applied, in isolation from historically evolving conceptions of education within human culture? Neither does their attempt to equate education with either "the growth of knowledge" or "problem-solving" really help in getting around the major difficulty for (as was the case with their treatment of the epistemic virtues) they offer no justification for the framework itself, and hence any claims for objectivity remain limited to the standards within the framework. But, while we feel that their attempt to essentially stipulate 'good' in this respect is wrongheaded, we sympathize with their predicament. It seems that there is no simple or straightforward way to proceed that is readily defensible. How might one go about developing naturalistic moral theories that could provide guidance to administrators and policy makers?

Again, building broadly upon moral realism, we think the way to start is by recognizing that what we are after is a form of *second-order critical legitimation,* which will give us acceptably rigorous reasons for making informed choices. In contemplating this, we can be encouraged by the progress made in scientific domains (see the second section above). Of course, science, will never be able to establish that something is categorically or absolutely good. But we also have seen that while science yields serviceably true theories, there is no reason to believe it will ever provide us with the uniquely true account of the world. We also have seen that scientific inquiry is not a special kind of rationality and that it cannot be reduced to sets of formal rules or follow-the-recipe algorithms. Indeed, it seems that the informed yet informal application of a set of objective epistemic values is central to the scientific process, with the result that reasonable scientific decision makers can disagree on theory choice. These, and related considerations, are encouraging for, as we have argued, they show that even scientific reasoning involves a form of second-order critical legitimation. Moreover, the history of science clearly shows that our understanding of the world can change with acceptance, and then application, of new theories—this process being woven into historically rooted changes in how we conceive ourselves, our societies, and our moral obligations. It would seem impossible, then, for any form of inquiry to produce an absolute, categorically binding theory of *any* aspect of the world, including morality. The concept of 'probability' provides an interesting case in point here. As shown by Hacking (1975; 1990) our modern concept of probability does not predate the 1600s yet is accepted today as being central to rationality, as illustrated, for example, in Evers and Lakomski's discussion of modern theories of utilitarianism. Rationality then is itself an evolving, cultural artefact.

How then might a process of critical legitimation contribute to an objective approach to choosing and defending moral values? We would recognize at the outset that such a process would simply not have the resources to defend categorical, binding, absolute moral values and that we would thus have to settle for something less than the "absolute." Further, the rational values that we will need to call upon when making choices in the course of inquiry cannot be derived from first-order, *prima facie* conceptions of the desirable. As in the case of epistemic values guiding inquiry in science, we will need to recruit second-order norms and standards embedded in human culture and apply them in Hcoherent ways. And, of course, a naturalistic inquirer will have to renounce all forms of epistemic privilege— as we said in the beginning, all foundationalisms, *a prioris,* essentialisms, transcendentalisms, universalisms, and so forth.

How might such an inquirer proceed? He or she could sensibly begin with an understanding of the basic non-moral sensibilities and beliefs of persons in a given socio-cultural context. In this respect, it seems important to recognize that there appear to be widespread (but not universal) human sensitivities to the suffering of others, especially to the extreme and pro-longed suffering of others. This is not yet a moral sensitivity; it yields directly no moral criterion of right or wrong.[10] As a next step, our inquirer could look to see if people, again in a given cultural context, have any clear sense of their prudential needs and interests. Given that there is such a *prima facie* obligation to satisfy one's prudential needs, they are also bound to have a rather clear sense of what would be needed for (or highly conducive to) the survival and moderate well-being of their newly born. There is a *prima facie* obligation to provide for such needs—for food, shelter, and a good-enough education for the young, for example. It also appears that there is a *prima facie* obligation to conform to the conventional norms of the social groups to which people belong. More specific prudential needs and associated obliga-tions will likely be evident in particular historical societies. In societies of the kind in which we live, for example, there is a *prima facie* educational obliga-tion to teach, or otherwise help, members to be literate, as well as to under-stand cultural norms at a level higher than the merely tacit.

Inquiry of this kind will yield a sense of the cultural norms of various societies, especially one's own. To this could be sensibly added a review of the positions advocated by influential moral ideologues,[11] for example, Aristotle, Kant, and, to bring us up-to-date, thinkers such as K. O. Apel (an *a priorist*), J. Habermas (1990), and J. Rawls (1993) (universalists), and A. MacIntyre (1984; 1988) (an essentialist). An appreciation of historically dominant ideologies, such as various forms of capitalism, socialism, and feudalism, would provide further useful resources for the last stage of the project. In this final stage, our inquirer would use these resources to build an Hcoherent and Hplausible set of moral principles, which rejects all forms of privilege and which seeks to recover central elements of what appear to have been the best attempts of previous theorists.

Given the resources at hand in the moral domain, we should not be surprised if more than one reasonable and plausible set of principles emerged from such a project. Given that there are no convincing grounds for expecting uniquely true theoretical accounts of the world at large, we should not expect to find a uniquely plausible moral vision. However, at the same time, there are no convincing grounds for construing the incom-patibility of critical (legitimative) sets as a failure of moral reasoning (see the "cultural realism" approach in Margolis 1995).

Finally, it seems clear that any set of moral principles, however crit-ically legitimated, will fail to be "neutral." The poststructuralists and Isaiah Berlin, in particular, are correct on this point. No matter what form a society (including, of course, its educational and administrative systems) may take, some moral good will be favored over others: "Some among the Great

Goods cannot live together. . . . We are doomed to choose, and every choice may entail an irreparable loss" (Berlin 1991, 13).

Some Conclusions and Implications

What does our view imply for inquiry in educational administration and for the prospects of improved practice in this vitally important profession? Quite a lot, we think, but given the length to which this chapter has grown, we trust the reader will tolerate the very sketchy outline that follows.

1. Greenfield was substantially right in his appreciation of the enormously difficult plight of the administrator[12] and the centrality of values and valuing in organizations, but he consistently underestimated the resources and prospects for disciplined, systematic inquiry into administration and organizations.

2. Hodgkinson is also right in recognizing and drawing attention to the centrality of moral philosophy, in thinking about and doing administration. But while his "models of values" are not without interest and have heuristic utility, they can claim objectivity only with respect to the standards of the models themselves. In this and some other respects (especially his treatment of values as internal, individuated phenomena), Hodgkinson's views are closer to Evers and Lakomski's than initially might be assumed.

3. Evers and Lakomski are right to champion the continued pursuit of coherent theory in, and of, (educational) administration, but their eliminativist project appears to perpetuate the goals of the old theory movement by pursuing an unlikely form of rulelike or lawlike explanation. Further, their approach to, and use of, the epistemic virtues establishes objectivity only with respect to the standards set by the virtues themselves. They do not establish the objectivity of these touchstone virtues. A similar weakness inheres in their treatment of ethical/moral concerns and particularly their preferred framework for guiding administrative decisions in education. Although they claim objectivity for the standards within the framework, they have not established the objectivity of the framework itself. They, much like Hodgkinson, fall back on a logical empiricist view of objectivity.

4. Given that the theory movement has failed (at least by the standards set by its founders), there is a pressing need for the field to re-appraise the nature of theory and inquiry and what may be reasonably expected of both. Evers and Lakomski's book helps point the way toward the kinds of discussion that are needed, but they tend to focus too much on epistemology to the neglect of crucial ontological questions and theories of truth.

5. The failure of the theory movement in educational administration

should not be interpreted as signifying either the impossibility or the irrelevancy of disciplined or "scientific" inquiry in the field. Nor should the dethroning of logical empiricism as a doctrine be assumed to invalidate methods of inquiry typically employed in "empirical" research. What is needed is a more careful and informed approach to the selection and application of research methods that seeks to justify methodological choice within the theoretical context of the problems being addressed, while recognizing and accepting the limitations associated with the methods available.

6. More attention needs to be given to values and their legitimation in both the practice and study of educational administration. Although almost self-evident, how this might best be done is not clear. Spending more time discussing the extant "models" and other treatments of values presented in the current literature is an obvious place to begin but may not move us forward very effectively. Seeking ways to actively engage practitioners and trainees to appreciate more the presence and influence of values in social action and what this means for their work and experienced realities may yield greater dividends. We believe much can be gained through discussions (and other activities) modeled on the process of second-order critical legitimation discussed in this chapter.

Concluding Remarks

Let us end by reiterating our sincere admiration for Evers and Lakomski's work. As we sought to reconstruct their intended meanings, we discovered important points of disagreement. Still we hope they will accept our pragmatic kind of second-order legitimation of the epistemic values and will become open to Hcoherence in the cultured-folk frame. If they were to reject this line of argument and to continue to hold that the epistemic values were formal (and hence neutral), then we fear they would be what Husserl called naturalists. Or, to borrow what Gadamer once said of Habermas, they would be "the last of the enlightenment."

Notes

1. We also think the Gadamerian view can be reconciled with Marx's basic doctrine of "praxis" and with many of Max Weber's theories of social-cultural science, thus allowing these also to be recovered and integrated into a modern theory of sociocultural-historical inquiry.

2. Evers and Lakomski do take care to attribute the "mob psychology" tag to Kuhn's unkindly critics, namely Lakatos, whom Kuhn himself reports described his

views as making theory choice "a matter for mob psychology" (Kuhn 1977, 321, quoting Lakatos 1970, 178).

3. Evers and Walker (1983) did attempt to sketch a putative justification, arguing that since the touchstone virtues are common to all forms and domains of knowledge, there is really only one single, inclusive knowledge domain. As well as confusing "a coherent universe of discourse" with "a single domain of inquiry" (and thus failing), this view (i.e., 1993) provides further reasons to conclude that Evers and Lakomski take the epistemic values as being formal.

4. It is in this sense that Paul Feyerabend and others are correct—there is no unique (special) scientific method.

5. Evers and Lakomski may agree. They talk about the (nearly) universal touchstone concerns.

6. Rorty (1991a and 1991b) and Lyotard (1984) are incoherent because they assume that all legitimation must involve privilege.

7. Both Hodgkinson and Greenfield have misplayed the "separate" worlds of fact and value, science and administration. We hold that both scientists and administrators reason and make choices about their domain problems within interpretive frames informed by sets of interrelated, interdependent facts and values.

8. In this passage, Hodgkinson actually declared that Holmes was committing the naturalistic fallacy. But, as Evers (1985) and Evers and Lakomski (1991) point out, Hodgkinson and others often have conflated the is-ought and naturalistic issues. See Lobb's (1993) insightful discussion.

9. Of course, this was one of Weber's main theoretical constructs, especially the notion of systems of order, or more precisely systems of "legitimate order" ((1922/1978, 31–36).

10. Rorty (1991a) could follow this line of reasoning and recant his ethnocentric ways!

11. An ideologue is someone who puts forward substantive moral claims on the basis of some form of (illicit) privilege.

12. This will perhaps turn out to be his greatest legacy for, in showing us this, he also showed us that there can be no science of administration in the sense of theories that would allow administrators to abdicate their moral responsibilities to decide matters. As Weber put the essential point, disciplined inquiry into the socio-cultural domain cannot "presume to spare the individual the necessity of making . . . choice(s), and so it should not even give the impression of being able to do so" (1913/1978, 85).

References

Arrington, R. L. 1989. *Rationalism, realism and relativism.* Ithaca, NY: Cornell University Press.

Berlin, I. 1991. *The crooked timber of humanity: Chapters in the history of ideas.* New York: Knopf.

Bernstein, R. 1983. *Beyond objectivism and relativism: Science, hermeneutics and praxis.* Philadelphia: University of Pennsylvania Press.

Cartwright, N. 1983. *How the laws of physics lie.* Oxford: Clarendon Press.

Churchland, P. M. 1979. *Scientific realism and the plasticity of the mind.* Cambridge: Cambridge University Press.

Davidson, D. 1984. *Inquires into truth and interpretation.* Oxford: Clarendon Press.

Dennett, D. 1978. *Brainstorms: Philosophic essays on mind and psychology.* Cambridge MA: The MIT Press.

Dennett, D. C. 1987. *The intentional stance.* Cambridge, MA: The MIT Press.

Evers, C. E. 1985. Hodgkinson on ethics and the philosophy of administration. *Educational Administration Quarterly* 214: 27—50.

Evers, C. W., and Lakomski, G. 1991. *Knowing educational administration.* Oxford, England: Pergamon Press.

Evers, C. W., and Walker, J. C. 1983. Knowledge, partitioned sets and extensionality. *Journal of Philosophy of Education* 172:155—170.

Gadamer, H. G. 1976. The universality of the hermeneutical problem. In *Philosophical hermeneutics,* ed. and trans. D. Linge. Berkeley, CA: University of California Press.

Goldman, A. 1992. *Liaisons: Philosophy meets the cognitive and social sciences.*Cambridge MA: The MIT Press.

Greenfield, T., and Ribbins, P. 1993. *Greenfield on educational administration: Towards a humane science.* London and New York. Routledge.

Greenwood, J. D., ed. 1991a. The future of folk psychology: Intentionality and cognitive science. Cambridge: Cambridge University Press.

Greenwood, J. D. 1991b. Introduction: Folk psychology and scientific psychology. In *The future of folk psychology: Intentionality and cognitive science,* ed. J. D. Greenwood, 1–21. Cambridge: Cambridge University Press.

Habermas, J. 1969/1972. *Knowledge and human interests.* Boston: Beacon Press.

———. 1990. *Moral consciousness and communicative action.* Cambridge, MA: The MIT Press.

Hacking, I. 1975. *The emergence of probability. A philosophical study of early ideas about probability, induction and statistical inference.* New York: Cambridge University Press.

———. 1990. *The taming of chance.* Cambridge: Cambridge University Press.

Hirst, P. 1972. Liberal education and the nature of knowledge. In *Education and the development of reason,* ed. R. F. Deardun, P. H. Hirst, and R. S. Peters. London: Routledge & Kegan Paul.

Hodgkinson, C. 1978. *Towards a philosophy of administration.* Oxford. Basil Blackwell.

———. 1983. *The philosophy of leadership.* Oxford: Basil Blackwell.

——— 1991. *Educational leadership: The moral art.* Albany: State University of New York Press.

Holmes, M. 1986. Traditionalism and educational administration. *Journal of Educational Administration and Foundations 1 and 2:* 40–51.

Hooker, C. A. 1987. *A realistic theory of science.* Albany: State University of New York Press.

Kuhn, T. 1970. *The structure of scientific revolutions,* 2nd ed. Chicago: University of Chicago Press.

———. 1977. Objectivity, value judgement, and theory choice. *The essential tension.* Chicago: University of Chicago Press.

Lakatos, I. 1970. Falsification and the methodology of scientific research programmes. In *Criticism and the growth of knowledge,* ed. I. Lakatos and A. Musgrave. Cambridge: Cambridge University Press.

Lobb, W. M. 1993. Hodgkinson's values model: A question of ethical applicability. Unpublished thesis, The University of Western Ontario.

Lycan, W. G. 1988. *Judgement and justification.* Cambridge: Cambridge University Press.

Lyotard, J. F. 1984. *The postmodern condition: A report on knowledge,* trans. G. Bennington and B. Massumi. Minneapolis: University of Minnesota Press.

MacIntyre, A. 1984. *After virtue,* 2nd ed. Notre Dame: University of Notre Dame Press.

———. 1988. *Whose justice? Which rationality?* Notre Dame: University of Notre Dame Press.

Mackie, J. I. 1977. *Ethics: Inventing right and wrong.* Harmondsworth: Penguin.

Margolis, J. 1991. The autonomy of folk psychology. In *The future of folk psychology: Intentionality and cognitive science,* ed. J. D. Greenwood, 242–62. Cambridge: Cambridge University Press.

———. 1995. *Historied thought, constructed world. Conceptual primer for the turn of the millennium.* Berkeley: University of California Press.

———. 1996. *Life without principles: Reconciling theory and practice.* Cambridge: Blackwell.

McDonough, R. 1991. A culturalist account of folk psychology. In *The future of folk psychology: Intentionality and cognitive science,* ed. J. D. Greenwood, 263–88. Cambridge: Cambridge University Press.

Moore, G. E. 1903. *Principia ethica.* Cambridge: Cambridge University Press.

Popper, K. 1963. *Conjectures and refutations.* London: Routledge & Kegan Paul.

Putnam, H. 1975. The meaning of meaning. *Mind, language, and reality: Philosophical papers 2.* Cambridge: Cambridge University Press.

———. 1978. *Meaning and the moral sciences.* London: Routledge & Kegan Paul.

———. 1981. *Reason, truth and history.* Cambridge: Cambridge University Press.

———. 1987. *The many faces of realism.* La Salle, IL: Open Court.

Quine, W. V. 1960. *Word and object.* Cambridge, MA: The MIT Press.

——— 1969. Epistemology naturalized. In *Ontological relativity and other essays.* New York: Columbia University Press.

———. 1992. *The pursuit of truth.* Cambridge MA: Harvard University Press.

Rawls, J. 1993. *Political liberalism.* New York: Columbia University Press.

Rorty, R. 1991b. Habermas and Lyotard on postmodernity. In *Essays on Heidegger and others: Philosophical papers 2,* ed. R. Rorty, 164–76. Cambridge: Cambridge University Press.

———. 1991a. On ethnocentrism: A reply to Clifford Geertz. In *Objectivity, relativism and truth: Philosophical papers 1,* ed. R. Rorty, 203–10.Cambridge: Cambridge University Press.

Searle, J. 1969. *Speech acts: An essay in the philosophy of language.* London: Cambridge Press.

van Fraassen, B. C. 1989. *Laws and symmetry.* Oxford: Clarendon Press.

Weber, M. 1978a. Value judgements in social science. In *Max Weber: Selections in translation,* ed. W. G. Runciman and E. Matthews. Cambridge: Cambridge University Press. Originally published 1913.

———. 1978. *Economy and society,* ed. G. Roth and C. Wittich. Berkeley: University of California Press. Original work published 1922.

Williams, B. 1985. *Ethics and the limits of philosophy.* Cambridge, MA: Harvard University Press.

Part III

Research on Values and Leadership: Findings and Implications

Competing Research Paradigms and Alternate Perspectives

Paul T. Begley

Ontological (nature of reality) and epistemological (nature of knowledge) issues are often central sources of debate within the literature of educational administration, as indicated in the introductory chapter to part 2 of this book. However, this debate also spills over into discussions of the methodologies employed to conduct research in the social sciences* and, in particular, research on the values of administration or the valuation processes that occur in various administrative contexts.

Guba and Lincoln present an excellent analysis of the function of values within the distinctive systems of inquiry associated with competing paradigms of research methodology. They begin by defining 'paradigm' as "a set of basic beliefs (or metaphysics) that deals with ultimates or first principles. It represents a world view that defines, for its holder, the nature of the 'world.' the individual's place in it, and the range of possible relationships to that world and its parts, as, for example, cosmologies and theologies do" (1994, 107). Four alternate inquiry paradigms are then identified: *positivism* (the objective or 'received view' that has dominated the discourse in physical and social sciences), *postpositivism* (a contingent positivism that attempts to accommodate the most problematic criticisms of the former), *critical theory* (a blanket term used to describe neo-Marxism, feminism, materialism, and participatory inquiry), and *constructivism* (relativism, subjectivism, and locally constructed realities) (108–109). The main outcome of Guba and Lincoln's analysis, with respect to the function of values in research inquiry within the four paradigms, is the observation that values are either specifically excluded or of central importance to methodology. In the case of positivist and postpositivist research, the function of values is excluded from *methodology* because of the epistemological posture of the paradigm. Although values might very well be the object of inquiry (e.g., Rokeach 1973), positivist methodologies are aimed at objective inquiry in the sense of traditional scientific inquiry that makes a virtue of the claim that they are value-free. The methodological focus is on the empirical and tech-

---

* Some of the material addressing the place of values within research methodologies is taken from P. T. Begley, 1996. "Cognitive Perspectives on the Nature and Function of Values in Educational Administration." In *International Handbook on Educational Leadership and Administration*, ed. K. A. Leithwood, Boston: Kluwer Academic.

nical. In fact, the bulk of research on leadership and administration conducted within this paradigm remains blind, in the case of postpositivists consciously so, to what Barnard (1938) proposes as the moral dimension of leadership. An essentially rational view of the educational administration process is presented: that is, one devoid of feelings, emotions, or affect and full of unexamined values. Gordon conveys this notion by suggesting that the institutional norms recommended by such research are at best the "trappings of thought" (1984, 46) that must be utilized by real people who think in radically different ways depending on how they perceive situations. So school leadership practices, for example, may be portrayed as unidimensional (e.g., Cuban 1986) or multidimensional (e.g., Sergiovanni 1984). Prescriptions for effective administration may be proposed in terms of typical practices (e.g., Kingdon 1985) and effective practices (e.g., Larsen 1987) or as actual roles versus preferred roles (e.g., Gousha 1986). Other researchers, preferring a more contextualized view of school leadership, describe patterns of practice or leadership styles (e.g., Hall et al.1986; Leithwood and Montgomery 1986). However, virtually all these images of effective practice share one persistent limitation. They are founded on research findings that are basically descriptive or correlational in nature. As an outcome, practices may be espoused even when they do not have a good fit in a particular community or leadership context. In an effort to identify an objective generalized truth, positivist research methodologies regularly strip away the details associated with specific contexts. These are often the very details that give meaning or reveal the intents and motivations of particular administrative actions.

Despite these limitations characteristic of positivist and postpositivist methodologies, it is worth noting that the vocabulary and ideas associated with the findings of the effective schools and school improvement modes of inquiry have now become comfortably familiar to the thinking, if not the practices, of many school administrators. These notions are reinforced through the content of formal preparation courses, debated at conferences focused on administrative practice and very much evident in professional literature on school leadership. In many respects, these notions form the foundation of professional knowledge for aspiring school administrators. Much less obvious, however, are the values and intentions implicit within these images of educational leadership.

Although values are explicitly *excluded* from research methodologies conducted in the positivist and postpositivist modes, values are an elemental component of the research methodologies grouped by Guba and Lincoln (1994) in the critical-theory and constructivist paradigms. In critical theory, values, those conceptions of the desirable with motivating force, manifest themselves in an a priori manner. Particular *articulated* value sets virtually shape research findings whose outcomes are aimed at recognizing or promoting particular social, political, cultural, economic, ethnic, and gender values. Research findings are, in effect, consciously value-mediated. Shining examples of such orientations might include Gilligan's (1982) and Shakeshaft's (1987) work on gender issues or Apple's (1990) writing about equal access to educational opportunity and other equity issues. Following a similar pattern, research conducted from the constructivist paradigm also champions the interests and values of the individual, the powerless, or socially unempowered minorities. However, with constructivism, the particular stress is on giving voice to alternate viewpoints and promoting the right to existence of locally constructed and specific realities, rather than championing a particular minority group or repressed social viewpoint.

The crux of the matter, in the context of considering the relevance of values to educational administration, is that the majority of research on school leadership has tended to be positivist and not particularly informative on the intents of administrative action or the underlying and motivating values of the actors. The prevailing domain of research has been focused on the publicly and logically verifiable world of facts. However, as previously asserted, the notion of values extends beyond facts, and the nature of values as influences on administrators has not figured prominently in research.

Two of the chapters included in this section of the book, those by Begley (chapter 12) and Walker and Shakotko (chapter 15), are examples of on-going research studies by scholars who began their research careers during the mid-1980s. Both of these researchers, along with others such as Lang (1986) and Campbell-Evans (1991), were among the earliest Canadian researchers to begin exploring values as influences on administrative action. Whereas their earlier research focused on initial empirical verifications of values-theory models such as that proposed by Hodgkinson (1978), these researchers now write and conduct research with the increased confidence and conviction that values are important influences on leadership and administration. Furthermore, their work has now been augmented by that of several new scholars, a new generation of researchers who are beginning to generate some very interesting findings. This new generation of researchers includes Leonard (chapter 11), Roche (chapter 13), and Grogan and Smith (chapter 14).

Leonard's research reported in chapter 11 considers the influence of personal and professional values on the decision making of teachers and administrators working in an urban Canadian elementary school. Her concern is the lack of clarity, coherence, and relevance between values-theory and educational practice. This is, at least in part, because investigating educational values in school settings poses a notable challenge—a challenge that is rooted in elusive abstraction as well as ontological and epistemological ambiguity. Despite the pedestrian familiarity of the term *value*, its everyday usage contributes more to obfuscate the task of defining and understanding value than it does to clarify its meaning. The situation, then, becomes a methodological challenge as well, inasmuch as a lack of clarity and consensus about what values are makes it difficult for researchers to know not only *what* to look for, but also *how* to look for it. The investigative approach employed by Leonard was influenced by Hodgkinson's (1991) discussion of organizational theory, of the layers of values that comprise organizations and of the importance for educational leaders to have knowledge of members' values at various levels of the organization. This study makes the assumption that school organizations may be studied best by examining them from various perspectives; that is, from the perspective of an individual, of a subgroup, or of the school community as a whole. In particular, the chapter reports those findings related to the educational purposes of schools. In order to better understand this complex phenomenon, the framework for this study focuses on the examination, not only of the value orientations of individual members and groups within an organization, but on the *variations in value orientations* and the *value conflicts* that individuals may have experienced in their daily interactions with others within the school.

Begley (chapter 12) and Roche (chapter 13) report the findings of research on the valuation practices of school administrators. Begley's findings are derived from two separate studies focused on the personal and professional values of school administrators. Two general themes were employed as conceptual organizers for the research: the influence of personal preference and transrational principles on the problem-solving actions of school administrators and the value conflicts that administrators experience in their work. One study was conducted in Umeå, Sweden, in collaboration with Johansson (see chapter 3), the other in Toronto, Canada. A conceptual framework was employed that integrates Hodgkinson's (1991) values theory with information-processing theory. Action-research methods were adopted as a way of overcoming the special problems associated with conducting research on values. Findings suggest that administrators' personal values are significant influences on problem solving. Specifically, the rational-value types of consensus and consequences predominate in the valuation processes of school principals, personal preferences are infrequently articulated, and transrational principles tend to be employed under particular circumstances.

Roche's research, reported in chapter 13, was stimulated by his concern that "the vagaries of the postmodern world present a complex dilemma for school administrators acting in the face of increasing moral confusion and ambiguity." Roche notes that frequently a range of confusing and conflicting values preclude the determination by administrators of any clear choice, action, or decision. His premise is that school administrators routinely confront moral and ethical dilemmas that demand a response.

Roche's recently completed and previously unpublished study moves beyond the usual preoccupation of empirical research with the nature and influence of values, to an investigation of how school administrators actually respond to moral and ethical dilemmas, the most difficult value conflicts they encounter.

The remaining two chapters of this section, those by Grogan/Smith (chapter 14) and Walker/Shakotko (chapter 15), address the work of school district superintendents. Like school principals, superintendents of public schools must respond daily to a wide variety of issues, some of which can become serious moral dilemmas. However, by the time superintendents become involved, the situations are usually extremely complex and any course of action proposed is likely to have far-reaching consequences for members of the greater school community. Grogan's chapter draws on data gathered in the school year 1995 through 1996 in the initial stage of a study done with eleven women superintendents of K through 12 public schools in two U.S. states. The moral dimension of leadership in the superintendency is discussed based on the lived experiences of the study participants, but from the feminist perspective. Interviews were conducted with each superintendent to learn about her approaches in resolving some of the moral dilemmas she faced in the course of her work.

Walker and Shakotko's research, reported in chapter 15, describes the relative importance of value based challenges and issues to Canadian superintendents according to selected demographic variables, such as province. These findings are based on over two hundred Canada-wide survey responses. Highlighted are the pressures and influences coming to bear on executive leaders in district-level educational organizations: the sources of information used, factors or forces making a difference to work-related ethical decision making, and the perceived role of professional codes and ethics.

References

Apple, M. W. 1990. Creating inequality: The political/economic context. In *Education reform: Making sense of it all,* ed. S. B. Bacharach. Toronto: Allyn & Bacon.

Barnard, C. I. 1938. *The functions of the executive.* Cambridge, MA: Harvard University Press.

Campbell-Evans, G. H. 1991. Nature and influence of values in principal decision-making. *The Alberta Journal of Educational Research* 37, 2: 167–78.

Cuban, L. 1986. Principaling. *Peabody Journal of Education* 63,1: 107–19.

Gilligan, C. 1982. *In a different voice: Psychological theory and women's development.* Cambridge, MA: Harvard University Press.

Gordon, David. 1984. *The myths of school self-renewal.* New York: Teachers College Press.

Gousha, R. P. 1986. *The Indiana school principalship: The role of the Indiana principal as defined by the principal.* Bloomington: Indiana University School of Education.

Guba, E. G., and Lincoln, Y. S. 1994. Competing paradigms in qualitative research. In *Handbook of qualitative research,* ed. N. K. Denzin and Y. S. Lincoln, 105–17. Thousand Oaks, CA: Sage.

Hall, G., Rutherford, W. L., Hord, S. M., and Huling, L. L. 1986. Effects of three principal styles on school improvement. *Educational Leadership* 41, 5: 22–31.

Hodgkinson, C. 1978. *Towards a philosophy of administration.* Oxford: Basil Blackwell.

———. 1991. *Educational leadership: The moral art.* Albany: State University of New York Press.

Kingdon, H. D. 1985. The role of the teaching elementary school principal. *Principal Issues* 4:20–23.

Lang, D. 1986. Values and commitment. Unpublished doctoral thesis, University of Victoria, BC.

Larsen, T. J. April,1987. Identification of instructional leadership behaviours and the impact of their implementation on academic achievement. Paper presented at the Annual Meeting of the American Educational Research Association, Washington, DC.

Leithwood, K. A., and Montgomery, D. G. 1986. *Improving principal effectiveness: The principal profile.* Toronto: OISE Press.

Rokeach, M. 1973. *The nature of human values.* New York: Free Press.

Sergiovanni, T. J. 1984. Leadership and excellence in schooling, *Educational Leadership* 41, 5: 4–13.

Shakeshaft, C. 1987. *Women in educational administration.* Beverly Hills: Sage Publications.

CHAPTER ELEVEN

Examining Educational Purposes and Underlying Value Orientations in Schools

Pauline E. Leonard

Research into the influence of personal and professional values of teachers' and administrators' decision making (Begley 1988; Begley and Leithwood 1990; Campbell 1994; Campbell-Evans 1991; Ashbaugh and Kasten 1984) is ongoing. However, there is still concern for the lack of "clarity, coherence, and relevance" (Begley 1996, 404) between value theory and educational practice. This is, at least in part, because investigating educational values in school settings poses a notable challenge, which is rooted in elusive abstraction and ontological and epistemological ambiguity. For, despite the pedestrian familiarity of the term *value,* its everyday usage contributes more to obfuscate the task of defining and understanding value than it does to clarify its meaning. Furthermore, deliberations on issues related to values are often obscured by the synonymous usage of terms such as *morals, ethics,* and *values.* Even where meanings are differentiated, a situation often develops where "the murky domains of moral and ethical philosophy and value inquiry . . . [have] innumerable varying and often competing definitions" (Campbell 1992, 3). The situation then becomes a methodological challenge as well, inasmuch as a lack of clarity and consensus about what values are makes it difficult for researchers to know not only *what* to look for, but also *how* to look for it. Notwithstanding this challenge, or perhaps because of it, research into values and education is essential for increasing our understandings and "wisdom" (Hodgkinson 1991, 11) in the field of education. The assumption that is embedded in this position is that knowledge and wisdom are champions of educational growth and excellence.

A Multiperspective Conceptual Framework

This chapter is part of a larger study related to educational values and school culture. The investigative approach was influenced by Hodgkinson's (1991) discussion of organizational theory, of the layers of values that comprise organizations, and of the importance for educational leaders to have knowledge members' values at various levels of the organization. While these layers of values and their variations may be conceptualized in distinct ways, in actuality, they interact in a "systemic way" (Hodgkinson 1991, 68). Therefore, to accommodate the systemic notion of value interaction, the conceptual design in this study was based on the understanding that school organizations may be studied by examining them from various *perspectives,* that is, from the perspective of an individual, of a subgroup, or of the group as a whole.

Though this research was not solely concerned with administrator leadership, Hodgkinson's conception of how the leader is immersed in a field of values reflecting multiple choices, whereby decisions must be made, is a useful one for it underscores the potential for variations in values and value conflicts within a school system. In order to better understand this complex phenomenon, the framework for this study focuses on the examination not only of the value orientations of individual members and groups within an organization, but on the *variations in value orientations* and the *value conflicts* that individuals may have experienced in their daily interactions with others within the school. Applying the multiperspective approach, the larger study comprised four major themes: 91) educational purpose; (2) curriculum metaorientation, (3) leadership, and (4) educator professionalism. This chapter will report and discuss the findings related to educational purpose.

The following questions guided this aspect of the research:

1. What are the value orientations pertaining to educational purpose from the perspective of the district, the school, the Primary Team and the Junior Team?
2. What variations in orientations exist between perspectives?
3. What types of value conflicts arise from variations in orientations?

Purposes of Education and Values

Kluckhohn (in Hodgkinson 1997, 111) defines value as "a conception, explicit or implicit, distinctive of an individual or characteristic of a group, of the desirable which influences the selection from available modes, means, and ends of action." Kluckhohn's conception of values as either distinctive of an individual or characteristic of a group implies that the road to understanding teachers' value orientations, variations in value orientations, and value conflicts is more accessible through the examination of *both* values held collectively (i.e., by a group or subgroup) and values held individually (i.e., by a member of the group or subgroup). The aim of this values inquiry was to examine and better understand values pertaining to the purpose of education from various perspectives of the organization—the district, the school, the subgroup, and the individual teacher.

Purposes of education and values are inextricably related inasmuch as the former are the value imperatives (Hodgkinson 1991, 23), or the "end" values, of a society that educators consider necessary to emphasize at a given time (Peters 1977), They give content and direction to educational aims (Garforth 1985, 67), shape and dictate the means (Hodgkinson 1991, 23) by which to achieve these aims, and are key elements to curriculum development (Miller and Seller 1990). Examining the values embedded in beliefs about the purpose of education helps us to better understand the connection between educators' philosophical beliefs and their practices. Further understanding should help narrow the aforementioned relevancy gap between theory and practice regarding educational values, particularly by shedding light on the varying degrees of "motivational force" (Hodgkinson 1997, 111) or commitment to espoused beliefs about educational purposes. Moreover, given that values may stem from "conscious or *unconscious* motivational dynamics" (Hodgkinson 1997, 111), an examination of educators' beliefs about the purpose of education may also reveal much about the level of value consciousness that educators bring to their educational decision making. The issue of value awareness is important, particularly as it relates to choice in educational decision making and whether or not value choices are consciously executed. Garforth (1985) reminds us that choice is implicit, not explicit, when decisions are made in habitual fashion. Unexamined educational values and the choices that are implicit in holding them make for unreflective action. Therefore, values require ongoing scrutiny and evaluation to avoid having them unconsciously accepted or perpetuated in an incognizant way.

Research Design

In that the paradigm "guides the investigation . . . in choices of method" (Guba and Lincoln 1994, 105), the research design needs to be compatible with the constructivist and interpretive nature of this study. Therefore, consistent with interpretive inquiry, and in keeping with the descriptive intent to understand and interpret basic assumptions, espoused values, and cultural artifacts, rather than to explain any causal relationship between variables, this study was a qualitative, instrumental case study (Stake 1994, 237). Further, it was an *instrumental* case study in the sense that a particular case (i.e., a multicultural elementary school) was examined to provide insight into an issue (i.e., value theory and educational practice). Pseudonyms are used for the school, the district, and all participants in this study.

Sample

A purposive sampling procedure was used to select one multicultural, urban elementary school as the focus of this study. Hillside Elementary School is one of approximately 130 other schools in a large Canadian metropolitan school district. This particular school is located in a residential area and is largely surrounded by apartment buildings and town houses. At the same time it had an enrollment of approximately six hundred students in grades junior kindergarten through sixth and there were approximately forty teaching staff, including twenty-five classroom teachers, the principal, the vice principal, and various specialist positions (i.e., computer, french, resource, reading recovery, music). Approximately 70 percent of the staff at hillside were white females, while approximately 19 percent were white males. nine percent of the staff were of various racial and ethnic background. Overall, 90 percent of the staff had been born in Canada. By contrast, the student population was highly diverse in that approximately 87 percent of either, or both, of the students and their parents had immigrated to Canada. There were forty-eight countries and thirty-three languages represented in the school.

In this research, attention was focused on eight individuals working as members of three teams: Primary Team (junior kindergarten to three), Junior Team (years four to six), and Administrative Team. The Primary Team consisted of three female teachers, Bernie, Gail, and Mavis, and one male teacher, Ted. These teachers had from seven to twenty years of teaching experience, with most or all of this having been in their current school district. However, each of these four teachers was new to Hillside Elementary School. The Junior Team was comprised of two female teachers, Ester and Louise. Ester had spent approximately seven years teaching, all at Hillside. However, she had held several different assignments during this time. Louise had spent three years at Hillside and four years elsewhere in the district. Both teachers had elected to work together as a team. The Administrative Team included one male principal and one female vice principal. Mark Butler was into his second year as principal at Hillside Elementary School. He had over twenty years experience both as a teacher and as an administrator in other multicultural schools in the district. The vice principal, Karen Brown, was also new to the school, having been in her current position only four months at the start of this research. She had experience both teaching in other schools in the district and also as a district program consultant.

Establishing Educational Purposes and
Underlying Value Orientations from Different Perspectives

Educational purposes are generally broad statements (Cohen 1982; Garforth 1985; Miller and Seller 1990) regarding beliefs about the overall purpose of schools. As already addressed, the purpose of this study was to examine both *espoused* values and *basic assumptions* pertaining to the purpose of education. Espoused values were determined primarily by analyzing both document statements and participants' oral statements as articulated in their responses to direct questioning about what they *believed* to be the purpose of education. Uncovering basic assumptions presented a greater challenge inasmuch as it was a more time-consuming process and it required time for participants to become involved in a self-examination of values. This process was undertaken during a five-week study at Hillside Elementary. During that time, the researcher spent two full weeks with each of the two teacher teams. This participative interaction and involvement in various classroom activities presented frequent opportunities to make observations and to pursue answers to questions pertaining to understanding teachers' underlying value orientations and their value conflicts. Also, in order to gain insight from a school perspective, the interactions of Hillside's teachers, students, visiting and volunteer parents, and administrators in the school were observed. Consequently, as the investigation unfolded, I interviewed five additional teachers, two parents, four specialists, and the two administrators. These interviews were semistructured in that they were characterized by both guiding and emergent questions. Unscheduled and informal discussions with varied members of the organization helped reveal how things "were done" at this school.

The participatory nature of this investigation contributed to a better understanding of both the relationship between espoused values and basic assumptions and the connection between educators' philosophical beliefs and practices, in two important ways: (1) it revealed information about the nature of the consistencies and inconsistencies between espoused educational purposes and those educational values that are tangibly manifested in rituals, artifacts, and behavior; and, (2) it provided for examination and analysis evidence of educators who were both consciously and unconsciously motivated in their commitment to educational values.

In the early stages of the data analysis, four main categories of educational purpose emerged: social development, personal development, career development, and intellectual development. Further analysis led to a bifurcation of two of these categories: social development was subdivided into social adaptation and social reconstruction, while intellectual development was subdivided into academic development and cognitive development. In the case of the former, initially, all statements pertaining to the social purpose of education were coded as social development. However, there emerged two distinct classifications of social development, which were comparable to what Eisner (1979) terms "social adaptation" and "social reconstruction." According to Eisner, these two educational purposes are similar in that they both require a look at society and the world to determine what schools should teach. They differ in that the first is to serve the interests of society, while the second is to "fix" it. Regarding intellectual development, this category first included all statements related to the development of the mind. As I continued to analyze the data, however, I came to see a distinction between statements that emphasized intellectual growth in terms of acquiring knowledge of subject matter and statements that centered around the development of intellectual processes; hence, the development of the categories "academic development" and "cognitive development." These two purposes of education also are similar to Eisner's classifications, development of "cognitive processes" and "academic rationalism."

Consequently, whereas the data shaped the emergent categories, the literature on educational purpose influenced the manner in which I labeled and defined the categories (see table 11.1). Put another way, the data analysis informed the content of the categories, the literature review influenced the labels for the categories. Table 11.1 outlines a sample of key elements from the data that characterize each educational purpose. Not all perspectives were oriented to all six educational purposes. For example, the district perspective did not include social reconstruction as an educational purpose, and Ted on the Primary Team made reference to only social adaptation. The data analysis is presented under each of the six orientations and includes, where applicable, each perspective in the following order: district, school, Primary Team by individuals, and Junior Team by individuals. Table 11.2 displays the educational purposes from each of these perspectives.

District Perspective

Document analysis revealed a strong and explicit emphasis on *social adaptation, academic development,* and *career development* as the overarching purposes of education at the district level. There were many policy statements regarding "empowering students to . . . participate responsibly in a pluralistic, global society," helping them to become "contributing citizens to Canada and the world," teaching them to make decisions and "accept their consequence according to societal standards." Data also showed that it was deemed highly important to prepare students to be "key contributors to our global economy" and to help them "meet the challenges and demands of our high-tech, multicultural workplace."

The best way to do this, the data suggested, would be through emphasizing the students' academic development. While it was espoused that programs should be personally "relevant" and that self-esteem and self-discipline were necessary for the development of cognitive skills and an interest in "life-long learning," there was a greater emphasis on literacy and mathematics being the "top two priorities." These were the areas that were

Table 11.1 Educational purposes

A. *Social Adaptation*
- Citizenship Skills (e.g., participation in a pluralistic, global society, celebrate Canadian heritage, acceptance of societal standards)
- Standards of Behavior (e.g., punctuality, rule compliance)
- Social Skills (e.g., co-operation, tolerance, compassion, caring, respect, participation)
- Respect for Cultural Differences (e.g., religion, race, ethnicity, gender)
- Moral Development
- Maintenance of Status Quo

B. *Social Reconstruction*
- Developing Critical Social Consciousness
- Alleviate Ills of Society
- Focus on Controversial Issues (e.g., religious values, sexual preferences, political corruption, race, gender, prejudices, etc.)

C. *Personal Development*
- Self-esteem
- Self-discipline
- Life-long Learning
- Emotional Well-being
- Personal Meaning

D. *Career Development*
- Career Education Skills
- Technology Skills (e.g., to meet demands of high-tech multicultural workplace)
- Specialization (e.g., specialized programming for future success)

E. *Academic Development*
- Literacy
- Numeracy
- Rationalism
- Arts and Sciences

F. *Cognitive Development*
- Developing Problem-Solving Skills
- Strengthening Intellectual Faculties

---

subjected to intense and continual evaluation, particularly in the form of district-level testing.

School Perspective

From the perspective of Hillside Elementary School, there was a strong emphasis on social adaptation as a fundamental purpose of education. Principal Butler placed great emphasis on the teaching of social values:

Table 11.2 Educational purposes

EDUCATIONAL PURPOSE	DIST	SCH	PRIMARY TEAM				JUNIOR TEAM	
			BERNIE	GAIL	MAVIS	TED	ESTER	LOUISE
Social Adaptation	X	X	X	X		X		X
Social Reconstruction			X		X			
Personal Development		X	X		X			X
Career Development	X	X						X
Academic Development	X	X	X					
Cognitive Development	X	X	X		X		X	

X = Orientation to educational purpose

> I guess the more I look at it the more I'm concerned that we must develop a set of values that we all agree upon, more than teaching them how to read and write, 'cause those are the skills that we need to get through life. I guess if I see any discouragement it is the number of children who can't get along. And I think it's increasing. . . . Our kids have been pushed into a multicultural society. They haven't grown up in it, and they don't know how to cope with that. I don't know where we go with that, but I think we do need to get back to accepting more responsibility for the teaching of values.

The principal's belief that the school must take responsibility for the teaching of values was borne out in tangible ways at Hillside Elementary School. For example, one weekly ritual was to introduce a "thought for the week" as part of the daily morning announcements. Some of these thoughts included: "Truth is still truth, even if it makes you angry," "If you think you're beaten you are, if you dare not, you won't, and if you think you can't win, you most certainly won't," "Knowledge without action is not knowledge," and "Don't complain if you have to struggle, that is when the work begins. There is no victory where there is no battle." The values implied in these statements are: 'truth,' 'competition,' and a 'work ethic.' Other adages, such as the following moral message, were relayed daily through the public address system: "When a bird sees a trap it stays away. Some of *you* seem to be attracted to trouble." The principal stated that the thought for the week "introduces some values into the system which are sadly needed."

Other methods of transmitting moral and social values were evident. Values such as 'peace' and 'respect' were manifested in the various bulletin board displays throughout the school. One such mural display was centered around the theme Keep Making the Road of Peace, and depicted a picture of the world divided into the following labeled sections: "Love," "World Peace," "Perfect Team," "Friendship," "One Human Family," and "Take Down Invisible Walls." A poster with the words, " A great school is built on a solid foundation: RESPECT" conveyed the idea that there would be more learning and less conflict if everyone respected one another.

Respect for cultural differences was encouraged at Hillside Elementary. Acknowledgement of the multicultural student population was implicit in the principal's recognition, through the morning announcements, of the various festivals and holidays such as Hanukkah, Christmas, and Kwantas. Bulletin board displays and posters also represented people of many races and ethnicities. Over thirty flags from around the world hung in the main foyer, and the word *peace* in four languages was clearly visible on its walls.

Students' *personal development* also revealed itself as an important aspect of education's purpose. School documents contained many statements pertaining to developing and maintaining each "student's sense of self-worth, self-discipline, and personal growth." There were also tangible manifestations of the importance of personal development as an educational purpose. For example, both the principal and the vice principal encouraged teachers to engage, with students, in activities geared to achieving stated goals. One teacher suggested that extra curricular clubs such as the Green Club and the Games Club, were set up to "give them things to do at lunch . . . and the more they're together the more they're involved, the more they like the school, the more they like the school the less trouble they get into." This also helped them to develop "pride" in their school. The principal considered these clubs to be "phenomenal." There were numerous bulletin board displays reflecting these goals as well, such as one that stressed the importance of "emotional" intelligence. Moreover, the youth care worker was in the process of working with the teachers to create and cultivate a "behavioral" program where the focus was on helping students to understand, and "feel better" about, themselves as ways to improving their behavior.

Document analysis revealed that academic, cognitive, and career development also fell under the rubric of educational purpose at Hillside Elementary School. Nevertheless, there seemed to be a tacit assumption that academic goals needed to be "suited to the needs" of the students at Hillside Elementary. According to Principal Butler, in the case where district expectations were "too high" for students, they were "modified." In contrast with the district perspective, the development of literacy and mathematical skills did not appear to take priority over the development of each student's social and personal well-being.

Primary Team Perspective

The members of the Primary Team varied somewhat in their espoused orientations to educational purpose. First of all, Bernie stated that education's "main purpose was to train people and prepare people for the outside world." Consequently, "it should be maintaining the status quo, teaching conformity [and] teaching people how to respect authority." By comparison, Mavis emphatically stated that the purpose of education was *not* to maintain the status quo, nor was it to help students adapt to current societal standards. The beliefs she espoused reflected more a social reconstructionist position, inasmuch as she thought that schools should be concerned with the interests of *all* society, not just those of the dominant class, stating that we should move "away from maintaining society the way it is [because] I think we are almost putting our cultures, our Canadian expectations onto these children."

A third member of the Primary Team, Gail, maintained a contrary position to Mavis's social reconstructionist view. Moreover, though Gail supported the social adaptation principle of preserving society, her view was somewhat different from Bernie's. Whereas Bernie's social adaptation position emphasized socio-economic reproduction, Gail's stressed the perpetuation of *moral* values. As she put it, "Education should provide students with a strong sense of core moral values, particularly values which helped to propagate Canadian culture while at the same time respected the diverse nature of its population." In her words, "Canada has to have a strong moral—*country* moral—and people coming into the country, while they may have different morals . . . they have to fit it into the Canadian society."

Another Primary Team teacher, Ted, expressed beliefs about the purpose of education that also reflected a social adaptation position. According to him, the manifestations of behavioral problems in schools today are more intense, and the focus of teachers's attention was generally not on something trivial like chewing gum "because you're concerned with kids fighting and kids hurting one another." To counter this growing violence, Ted believed it was necessary to "foster a caring attitude in kids." This would better serve the primary purpose of education, which he deemed "to fit into society."

Interestingly, whereas Bernie's discussion of the purpose of education strongly suggested a social adaptation position, she also believed that schools should address controversial issues such as homosexuality. She felt that it was "absolutely appalling" that homosexuality was not a part of the school curriculum. It was difficult for her to reconcile personal beliefs about diversity, understanding, and tolerance with the practice of "excluding homosexual discussion" from her curriculum. Bernie felt this "hugely contradictory" and believed that teachers would be likely to leave such controversial issues alone for fear of being "sold up the river." In this regard, Bernie's position was more in line with a social reconstruction perspective in that the emphasis was on alleviating some of the perceived ills of society stemming from discrimination on the basis of sexual orientation.

Mavis and Bernie displayed congruent views in terms of their emphasis on *personal development* as an educational purpose. Bernie suggested that the goal she had for her students was to "help them understand that they can enjoy their life through the arts and through physical fitness without necessarily being rich." She believed that in helping her students "accept their lot" in life and by "helping them to maximize what they're gonna face," she was providing, for those situated at the lower level of the social class, a way to compensate for their unfortunate place in society. Mavis also felt that the purpose of school included individual self-fulfilment, as "it's very important that the children feel that they can achieve and work towards individual self-fulfilment and feel positive about what they're doing." These two teachers also shared the belief that cognitive development is part of the purpose of education. However, the challenge in achieving this purpose is that schools end up taking on the responsibilities of the family, which make it difficult to attend to intellectual needs. As Bernie stated: "I think my commitment is supposed to be to their intellectual development for the most part. And I think that's one of the problems that come up, is that we're trying to do all of those things [social, emotional, moral, physical] and that's a parent's job, not a teacher's job." However, she conceded that while it may not be the teacher's job to do "all those things," intellectual development cannot be achieved until emotional, physical, and social needs are met. So there were few alternatives. Similarly, Mavis believed that it was important to develop cognitive skills as opposed to rote memorization, which she thought were geared toward nonreflective thinking processes. She felt it was more important that they "be able to solve problems, locate information, in that sense" than "to be able to tell me what a nebula is."

Last, Bernie believed *academic development* to be an integral part of the purpose of schooling but felt restricted by board-prescribed curricula. She felt that a lot of the academic curriculum was "wonderful, exciting stuff but there's stuff that I have to do because it has to be done right now and I can't do what the children are wanting to." In other words, mandated curriculum guidelines inhibited the natural process of academic development in the students.

Junior Team Perspective

Louise and Ester, the two Junior Team teachers, differed in espoused orientations to educational purpose. Louise believed that school's primary responsibility was to teach children how to behave in a society. She suggested that this purpose is becoming increasingly more difficult because of the cultural diversity in many schools today. Part of the reason it is so difficult is because "with the number of different cultures we have here in Canada, different cultures have different ideas of what's acceptable and what's not acceptable." Louise's discussion suggested that the cultural diversity in expectations for social behavior and the varied standards of behavior learned in the home creates a problem for many schools today. In her view, similar to Primary Team teacher Gail's social adaptation position, schools need to educate children about what is appropriate social behavior in Canada.

Louise also suggested that the *personal development* of students in terms of fostering their self-esteem and confidence is important. She described her job as one which was "to make sure that these children are feeling good about themselves and that they are capable." And, inasmuch as it was her job to help students make the link between particular subject areas and the types of careers that required knowledge in these areas, career development was a school purpose. She stated that "in the elementary and intermediate schools is when we can introduce the children to all the different possibilities that are out there" and show students the "different things that you can do with different areas of the curriculum." She believed it is important to help students understand the relevancy of what they were learning in school and how it can be applied in the workplace and that students should be taught to explore the variety of occupations that might stem from knowledge of the arts and sciences.

Ester, the second member of the Junior Team, suggested that the overarching purpose of education is to foster *intellectual development,* particularly in the sense of stimulating students' interest in learning. Academic disciplines such as mathematics, science, and literature could be the means to sparking this intellectual curiosity. However, the purpose of education is "not specifically teaching them math" but "to teach the children how they can gain information through technology." Whereas Ester spoke of fostering the whole child, she elaborated on the idea of learning *how* to learn. Her underlying belief was that literacy and numeracy are not in themselves ends, but the tools that students needed to learn. A corollary to students learning how to learn, according to Ester, is that they will be able to keep abreast of a fast-changing technological society. This is necessary, especially in light of the fact that schools cannot and should not, be expected to keep up with these technological changes. Consequently, the onus for learning is on the student. Nevertheless, the school's responsibility is to make sure that students are equipped intellectually to handle these new and ever-changing learning environments.

Discussion

What becomes apparent in the analysis of educational purposes from the various perspectives of the educational organization (i.e., district, school, teams) is that there were variations in orientations, both across perspectives and within perspectives (e.g., within teams). For example, Hillside Elementary School emphasized social and personal development, but the district stressed academic development, particularly related to literacy and numeracy skills. There were other differences between perspectives as well. Mavis' position on social reconstruction as an educational purpose differed from that of the school perspective, and she had expressed deep concern about the danger of imposing dominant societal values on diverse cultures. Mavis was emphatic in her belief that the purpose of school was not to help students "fit" into society as it was. Further, as table 11.2 indicates, three of Mavis's Primary Team colleagues were oriented to a social adaptation educational purpose. Bernie suggested that, although it may be unsavory in some respects, schools do and should serve to preserve class structure. Gail felt that more emphasis should be placed on preserving Canadian culture, and Ted felt that the purpose of school was to help individuals lead productive lives. In the case of the Junior Team, Ester espoused cognitive development as the primary purpose of schooling, whereas Louise felt that *one* of the purposes of schools was to teach students what is "acceptable" in Canada.

What is interesting in this aspect of the study is that there were few reports of value conflicts related to these variations in orientation to purpose of education. Despite seemingly diametrically opposed views about the purpose of education, particularly in the case of the Primary Team teachers, the teachers did not report value conflict related to, or even awareness of, their divergent views. This is arresting in light of the nature of the team relationships, which included daily collaboration, both in planning for instruction and in implementing co-operative teaching strategies. It is also in direct contrast to the findings in the larger study where teachers and administrators described numerous value conflicts related to variations in orientations to curriculum, educator professionalism, and leadership. With this finding, a fundamental question is delivered: Why did differences in beliefs about the purpose of education not generate value conflicts?

This salient finding may be better understood in light of the difference between *espoused* values and basic assumptions or *core* values. As earlier addressed, this participant observational study included not only making observations of cultural artifacts and examining espoused values, but also creating opportunities for teachers to examine their underlying values. Through an interactive approach, participants were encouraged to engage in self-analysis, which helped to uncover some of their basic assumptions about the purpose of education (Schein 1984; 1990). The findings in this study show that while espoused values varied, the core values, or underlying basic assumptions, were more congruent. That is, the core values pertaining to educational purposes from each perspective appeared to be grounded in some manner in what Miller and Seller (1990) describe as a *transmission* position. The following brief outline of the authors' framework supplies a context for this discussion of congruent basic assumptions.

Miller and Seller (1990) provide a three-dimensional framework for categorizing major curriculum positions or "meta-orientations" which they call "transmission", "transaction," and "transformation", each of which is grounded in particular educational philosophies and overall purposes. The authors state that the transmission meta-orientation, is characterized by an emphasis on the acquisition of basic skills and cultural values and mores. The overall educational goal embedded in this orientation is the mastery of content, skills, facts, and the perpetuation of moral and social values. While the transaction meta-orientation is also one where the development of rational intelligence is deemed important, the emphasis is not on learning through rote memorization but on inquiry learning. Knowledge acquisition is a *process* of creative problem solving, critical thinking, and investigative study. Learning occurs when there is interaction between the learner and the environment. To the extreme of the transmission position is the transformation orientation which focuses on "subjectivity," "intuition," and "shared decision-making." The primary emphasis of the transformation position is the development of the *whole* child—intellectual development is thought to be just one aspect of student learning and not to be isolated from the emotional, social, physical, and spiritual aspects of student growth. Moreover, knowledge is conceptualized as holistic, and students are to be provided with opportunities to discover the interdependency and interconnectiveness of subject matter and learning. In terms of the perspectives analyzed in this study, although there were differences in which aspects of the transmission orientation were emphasized, either the transmission of facts, skills, and knowledge, or the perpetuation of moral and social values, there was underlying consensus in basic assumptions about the purpose of education being one to help students "fit" into society.

As previously addressed, the school espoused an emphasis on transmitting and perpetuating moral and social values for the purpose of teaching the skills that, according to Principal Butler, the students needed "to get through life." This was borne out in various ways, such as in the principal's weekly ritual of announcing the moral thought for the week, in the numerous bulletin board displays, and in the adoption of the Canadian wolf as a mascot, all of which served to preserve and transmit moral and social values such as respect, trust, truth, honesty, a work ethic, cooperation, participation, and competition.

The social adaptation philosophy, reflected in the school's purpose, included a focus on respecting cultural differences. This was also made evident in bulletin board displays and posters and in the various cultural festivities that were recognized through public announcements, through organizing cultural events, and through the festival concert where presentations were inclusive of the various cultures represented in the school. However, there needs to be a distinction made here between a school's purpose being one that helps students to *recognize and respect* the cultural differences in which they find themselves in the larger society and a school's purpose being to *uncover and examine* prejudices related to cultural biases, racism, sexism, and so on. That is not to say that these issues would go unaddressed at Hillside. Nor does it suggest an assimilationist ideology where students are expected "to relinquish their own cultural heritages and embrace the dominant Euro-Western ways" (Ryan and Wignall 1994, 1). It does mean that "fixing" the ills of society as related to issues of diversity did not appear to be a primary purpose of this school. The emphasis at Hillside Elementary was on fostering a respect for cultural differences by learning about, and sharing this knowledge of, the various cultures and by encouraging students to love and respect each other and their differences. Implicit in these actions and beliefs is that it is one's moral and social responsibility to participate, cooperate, and be productive in the larger society in which one lives, be it multicultural or otherwise.

While there was an emphasis on social adaptation in terms of the social and moral development of students at Hillside Elementary, the Primary Team and Junior Team teachers were also very much involved in academic and cognitive development, despite advocating commitment to other aspects of the student development. Also, much of the evaluation focused on determining progress in literacy and mathematics, which proved congruent with the district-level emphasis on academic development. Consequently, Hillside Elementary as a whole, along with the Primary and Junior Teams, reflected a combination of district and school aims, so that the overall purpose of education became one that was to transmit the facts, skills, *and* values necessary to function in society. So, whereas there was an emphasis on the social and personal in terms of the overall goals of school, teachers worked to meet the goals of the district as related to teaching and evaluating academic skills. Consequently, both the school and the district reflected primarily a *transmission orientation* in relation to educational purpose. The difference was really in which skills deemed most necessary to function in existing society were emphasized.

In reality then, the district and the school perspectives were not that different. However, this does not address the issue of differences within teams. For example, were not Mavis's social reconstructionist position that the curriculum should be more inclusive of the multicultural values that were reflected in the student population at Hillside antithetical to Gail's position that there should be more emphasis on teaching "Canadian" morals and values and developing a country identity? At first glance, the answer is yes. However, upon re-evaluation of these teachers' beliefs, and through observations of their classroom practices and interactions with students, it became evident that these teachers agreed, more than they disagreed, when it came to some very basic assumptions about human nature and their expectations for student behavior in the classroom. Further, there was no evidence that they considered questions about whether these values were those of a dominant culture or those of a minority culture. In actual fact, it appeared to be the consensus that these were "universal" values. Yet even early theories of cultural relativity related to dominant and variant value orientations (Kluckhohn and Strodtbeck 1961) strongly suggest that there was great potential for variations in orientations among the highly multicultural student population at Hillside Elementary. Nonetheless, these teachers placed considerable import on the transmission and perpetuation of moral and social values related to time (e.g., punctuality, productive use of time), related to the nature of human relationships (e.g., collaboration, cooperation, sharing, respect for authority, truthfulness, compassion), related to the nature of human activity (e.g., strong work ethic), related to the nature of human nature (e.g., truthfulness), and related to the nature of authority (e.g., respect for authority, compliance to rules).

Whether or not these are desirable or appropriate values for students to learn is not the issue here. The point is that these teachers did not seem to know which values were considered to be characteristic of the dominant society and, consequently, which values were being imposed on students. Indeed, Mavis admitted to feelings of ambiguity and confusion about which values she was unconsciously transmitting to her students and which of them might be in conflict with their own values. So, whereas she espoused a belief that the purpose of education was not to impose the values of a dominant society on minority students, she reported no value conflict with her colleagues who espoused divergent views. Therefore, she experienced no difficulty in collaborating with these teachers to implement teaching strategies that would help students learn "acceptable" classroom behavior.

To summarize, there was more congruency between and among the various perspectives than was initially apparent in the examination of espoused values. Each perspective reflected, in varying degrees and emphasis, a basic assumption consistent with a *transmission* orientation to educational purpose. Essentially, all agreed that the overarching purpose of school is to educate students through the inculcation of facts, skills, and values necessary to function in society.

Conclusion

Although what has been discovered in one school cannot be generalized to all school settings, there are implications for theory, research, and practice that arise from this study of educators' value orientations. First of all, if we accept the Socratic view that we are wise to the extent that we are aware, not of how much we know, but of how little we know (Alexander 1989, 13), then it follows that this study contributes something to our wisdom in education. In particular, it has added to our knowledge of how little we may know about our underlying values and just how strongly they are implicated in what we are doing in our schools. This revelation suggests that educators need to better understand the connection between their deep-seated educational beliefs and their educational practices. When the link between theory and practice is examined in such a way, then "conscious reflective intentional action [occurs] as opposed to mere reflect or mechanical responses to stimuli" (Hodgkinson 1991, 43). This type of understanding, suggests Hodgkinson, brings us closer to the realm of praxis, or *enlightened* practice.

Praxis begins with engaging in the pursuit of clarifying philosophical beliefs and values. Educational leaders can play a significant role in creating a school culture of praxis, a culture that is conducive to continual examination and negotiation of educational values. This should serve to help align underlying basic assumptions about education with espoused values, ensuring that all stakeholders are working toward achieving what they truly believe to be the school's overarching purpose. However, the challenge for leaders is the "creation of democratic school cultures in which multiple voices and ways of being in schools . . . are legitimated" (Anderson 1996, 947). Considering that today's school leaders "have little or no training" (Duke 1996, 863) in how to build new cultures that require people to examine, negotiate, and perhaps change their values intensifies this challenge. This is an area that also warrants further examination.

The implication for value theory and research is also related to the connection between espoused values and underlying basic assumptions. Initially, given the apparent inconsistency between teachers' underlying basic assumptions and their espoused values in this study, there is the temptation to hastily (and erroneously) dismiss the latter as insincere claims, regarding beliefs about the purpose of education. No doubt, there is the possibility that educators may espouse what they perceive as currently "popular" or "acceptable" value orientations pertaining to the purpose of education, yet not be deeply committed. However, espoused values deserve more credit and attention than this. Examining them may reveal much about why advocated educational goals are seemingly unattainable in particular school cultures. Moreover, if espoused values eventually get "transformed" (Schein 1984) into underlying assumptions, then they are the precursor to understanding the process of how particular values become a part of our educational landscape. Examining, analyzing, and describing organizational members' value orientations, variations in value orientations, and value conflicts pertaining to educational purpose is a good first step to increasing our understandings of this phenomenon, thereby narrowing the gap between value theory and educational practice.

References

Alexander, H. A. 1989. Liberal education and open society: Absolutism and relativism in curriculum theory. *Curriculum Inquiry* 19, 1: 11–31.

Anderson, G. L. 1996. The cultural politics of schools: Implications for leadership. In *International Handbook of Educational Leadership and Administration*, ed. K. Leithwood, 947–63. Dordrecht: Kluwer Academic Publishers.

Ashbaugh, C. R., and Kasten, K. L. 1984. A typology of operant values in school administration. *Planning and Changing* 15, 4: 195–208.

Begley, P. T. 1988. The influence of personal beliefs and values on principals' adoption and use of computers. Unpublished doctoral thesis, University of Toronto, Toronto.

———. 1996. Cognitive perspectives on values in administration: A quest for coherence and relevance. *Educational Administration Quarterly* 32, 3: 403–26.

Begley, P. T., and Leithwood, K. A. 1990. The influence of values on school administrators. *Journal of Personnel Evaluation in Education* 3: 337–52.

Campbell, E. C. 1992. Personal morals and organizational ethics. Unpublished doctoral dissertation.

———. 1994. Personal morals and organizational ethics: A synopsis. *The Canadian Administrator* 34, 2: 1–10.

Campbell-Evans, G. H. 1991. Nature and influence of values in principal decision-making. *The Alberta Journal of Educational Research* 37, 2: 167–78.

Cohen, B. 1982. *Means and ends in education.* London: George Allen & Unwin Publishers Ltd. Duke, D. 1996. Perception, prescription, and the future of school leadership. In *International handbook of educational leadership and administration*, ed. K. Leithwood, 841–72. Dordrecht: Kluwer Academic Publishers.

Eisner, E. 1979. *The educational imagination.* New York: Macmillan.

Garforth, F. W. 1985. *Aims, values and education.* Hull: Christygate Press.

Guba, E. G., and Lincoln, Y. S. 1994. Comparing competing paradigms in qualitative research. In *Handbook of qualitative research*, 105–17. Thousand Oaks, CA: Sage.

Hodgkinson, Christopher. 1991. *Educational leadership: The moral art.* Albany: State University of New York Press.

———. 1997. *Administrative philosophy: Values and motivations in administrative life.* Tarrytown, NY: Pergamon.

Huberman, A. M., and Miles, M. B. 1994. Data management and analysis methods. In *Handbook of qualitative research*, ed. N. K. Denzin and Y. S. Lincoln, 428–44. Thousand Oaks, CA: Sage.

Kluckhohn, F., and Strodtbeck, F. L. 1961. *Variations in value orientations.* New York: Row Peterson.

Miller, J. P., and Seller, W. 1990. *Curriculum perspectives and practice.* Toronto: Longmans.

Peters, R. S. 1977. *Education and the education of teachers.* London: Routledge & Kegan Paul.

Ryan, J., and Wignall, R. 1994. Administering for differences: Dilemmas in multi-ethnic schools. Paper prepared for the Annual Meeting of the Canadian Society for the Study of Education.

Schein, E. H. 1984, Winter. Coming to a new awareness of organizational culture. *Sloan Management Review.*

———. 1990. Organizational culture. *American Psychologist* 45, 2: 109–19.

Stake, R. E. 1994. Case studies. In *Handbook of Qualitative Research,* ed. N. K. Denzin and Y. S. Lincoln, 236–47. Thousand Oaks, CA: Sage.

CHAPTER TWELVE

Value Preferences, Ethics, and Conflicts in School Administration*

Paul T. Begley

Values are those conceptions of the desirable which motivate individuals and collective groups to act in particular ways to achieve particular ends. They reflect an individual's basic motivations, shape attitudes, and reveal the intentions behind actions. For these reasons, values are considered important influences on administrative practice. The leadership literature, dating back to Barnard's *The Functions of the Executive* (1938), acknowledges the place of values in administration. Values have been variously portrayed as personal, professional, organizational or socio-cultural in nature. Until recently, despite their generally acknowledged importance, the influence of values on administrative action has remained largely unexamined and understated in most of the research literature on leadership and administration.

This chapter outlines a conceptual framework recently developed by the author to carry out research on the value orientations of school administrators, and reports the findings from two separate studies, one conducted in Umea (Sweden) during the latter part of 1996, the other in Toronto (Canada) early in 1997. Both studies are components of a long term research project being conducted by the OISE/UT Centre for the Study of Values and Leadership. They are also a continuation or extension of earlier work carried out during the late 1980s by Begley (1988) and Campbell-Evans (1991).

Why Study Values?

Traditionally, researchers have found values difficult to quantify in any objective sense, largely because they resist empirical verification. Accurate portrayals of the impact of personal or professional values on practices are difficult to develop from the usual third party research perspective. Perhaps this partially explains why not many choose to carry out research in this field. Practitioners, for their part, typically manifest little patience for the often obtuse vocabulary of philosophy and the paradigm-bound constructs

---

* Portions of this chapter were previously published in the July 1998 issue of *Journal of School Leadership*. Lancaster PA: 1997 Technomic Publishing Co., Inc.

common to most values theory. Their priorities naturally focus on solving the practical problems of the day, and much of the existing values literature simply lacks relevance for them.

When administrative values have been researched, the findings usually have been limited to descriptions or lists of value types, often correlated to certain administrative practices (e.g., Leithwood and Steinbach 1995). Not many have ventured to delve below the surface to discover the intentions that motivate the adoption of particular values under particular circumstances, which, in turn, generate attributable actions. Another limitation worth noting, concerning the extant research on administrative values, is that it tends to be organizational or collective in nature, rather than focused on the personal or professional arena.

Despite these difficulties, a significant resurgence of interest in values as an influence on administrative practice has occurred. Among practitioners, there has been an increased intellectual appetite for books and in-service courses dealing with subjects such as moral leadership and ethical decision making. Similarly, within the research community more researchers are selecting valuation and ethics as topics worthy of investigation, reclaiming a territory long dominated by the theorists. Why this sudden surge of interest? The answer, quite simply, is that administrators and researchers have become increasingly sensitive to values issues because of the increasingly pluralistic societies in which they live and work. Moreover, this trend clearly runs counter to the prevailing stereotype of administrative practice, which holds that administrators are more likely to be pragmatically and unreflectively focused on procedural matters.

As suggested earlier, administrative practitioners often manifest a low tolerance for abstract models and theoretical debate when it strays any distance from the practical problems of the day. Like most people, however, they intuitively know to rely on the clues provided by the actions and the attitudes of people around them to obtain predictive insights into the nature of values held by these individuals—a generally sound strategy perhaps, but with some limits to its reliability. Observable actions may or may not be accurate indicators of underlying values, particularly when individuals articulate or posture certain values while actually being committed to quite different values. Political leaders are usually a rich source of examples of such complex behavior. The attitudes and actions manifested by individuals may be usefully construed as observable ripples and splashes on the surface of a body of water. It is important to keep in mind that the true intentions behind these observable actions may be alternately transparently obvious, superficial, or running deep to the core. They can also remain fully obscured below the surface of the self, the organizational structure, or the society.

Personal Preferences and Transrational Ethics

Prior research conducted on the influence of values on administrative practices (Begley, and Leithwood 1990; Campbell-Evans 1991; Leithwood, Begley and Cousins 1992) suggests that the dominant value types, or more accurately the prevailing *motivational bases* (Hodgkinson 1991), associated with administration are the rational values of consequentialism and consensus. Evidence of nonrational motivational bases, such as *personal preference* and *transrational principles,* seems to occur much less frequently, or their relevance to a given administrative situation is relatively short-lived (Begley 1996). This has led some theorists and researchers (e.g., Evers and Lakomski 1991; Leithwood et al. 1992) to dismiss these value types as relatively unimportant influences on administrative practices. However, there are plausible explanations for the relatively infrequent occurrence of these nonrational value types in previous research studies, and recent research findings suggest that personal preference and transrational ethics can be important influences on administration even though they may be less frequently *articulated* by administrators. The supporting evidence for this assertion is presented later in this chapter. However, the basic premise is that the lower frequency for self-interest values and ethics is an outcome of a prevailing social bias in our Western societies toward the rational value types (this bias being an outcome of organizational socialization, cultural expectations, traditional administrative theory, and positivistic research methodologies).

Value Conflicts in School Administration

Prevailing notions of postmodernity suggest that the work of educational leaders has become much less predictable, less structured, and more conflict-laden. For example, few would challenge the observation that there is considerable social pressure for greater stakeholder involvement in significant decision making within school organizations. However, the achievement of consensus among even the traditional educational stakeholders has become more difficult than it was a decade ago. School administrators increasingly encounter situations where consensus cannot be achieved. In some respects, this renders obsolete the traditional rational notions of problem *solving* because even though administrators must respond to value-conflict situations that arise, there may be no solution possible that will satisfy all. These value-conflict situations can occur within the individual, for example, relatively unnegotiable personal core values of the individual may run counter to professional or organizational requirements. Value conflicts may also occur as outcomes of interactions among two or more individuals.

Finally, value conflicts may be outcomes of an incongruence or incompatibility among one or more of the value arenas identified by the literature; that is, conflicts occurring among the domains of personal values, professional values, and/or organizational values.

Constructing a Values Typology

A critical first step in conducting research in the values field is adopting a particular working definition of values. Kluckhohn proposes the following: "Values are a conception, explicit or implicit, distinctive of an individual or characteristic of a group, of the desirable which influences the selection from available modes, means, and ends of action (Parsons and Shils 1962, 395)." Conceptualizing values in this manner highlights their function in the making of choices. In administration, the making of choices is usually termed "decision making" and /or "problem solving," an activity familiar to most administrators. This definition also expands the scope of the term *value* beyond the relatively narrow philosophical domain of the metaphysical (the study of first principles) to allow consideration of several other value constructs relevant to educational administration. This broader scope includes social ethics (Frankena 1973; Cohen 1982; Beck 1993), transrational principles (Hodgkinson 1978), the rational moral values of administration (Willower 1994; Strike Haller & Sotis 1988), and the realm of self-interest and personal preference (Hodgkinson 1978; Evers and Lakomski 1991). It becomes possible, even necessary, to distinguish the values manifested by individuals from the more collective social values of a group. One important outcome is that the interactive relationship between personal values and social values becomes highlighted.

Hodgkinson's (1978) values typology serves as a foundation for the conceptual framework being proposed here (see figure 12.1). Stated briefly, this values typology incorporates four motivational bases, or value groundings, that constitute the source of values, beliefs, attitudes, and actions for individuals. These four bases are personal preference, consensus, consequences, and principles. Personal preference represents a conception of what is "good." Such values are grounded in the individual's affect or self-interest, constitute the individual's preference structure, and are self-justifying and primitive or subrational. The remaining three motivational bases more accurately represent a *philosophical* hierarchy of values, differentiated on a continuum of "rightness" or correctness of value. *Consensus,* a second motivational base in Hodgkinson's typology, is grounded in expert opinion, peer pressure, or the will of the majority in a given collectivity. Next is the motivational base of *consequences,* where intentional action is focused by a desirable future state of affairs or analysis of likely outcomes. The fourth and final motivational base, situated at the highest level of Hodgkinson's philosophical hierarchy, is *transrational principle*. These values are grounded in principle, the metaphysical, and take the form of ethical codes, injunctions, or commandments. They are not scientifically verifiable and cannot be justified by logical argument. They are based on will rather than on reason. According to Hodgkinson, the adoption of transrational values implies some act of faith, belief, or commitment (1978, 112). A critical distinction to keep in mind about the four motivational bases is that although two of the bases, consensus and consequences, may be arrived at rationally, the remaining two, personal preference and principles, are nonrational, more accurately *sub*rational and *trans*rational, respectively.

Criticisms of Hodgkinson's values typology usually focus on his portrayal of a hierarchy of values. With reasonable justification, some critics (e.g., Evers 1985; Evers and Lakomski 1993) identify epistemic difficulties distinguishing between transrational principles and subrational personal preferences. Others (e.g., Begley and Leithwood 1990) find that the values manifested by individuals in particular roles, for example, school administration, do not necessarily occur in patterns that reflect Hodgkinson's hierarchy. For instance, values of consequence or consensus may dominate. Rather than reconfigure the values model for particular social roles, it is useful to distinguish the philosophical and logical portrayal of value types from the more situational values patterns manifested by individuals operating within particular functional roles.

Values and Cognition: An Integrated Model

Figure 12.1 illustrates the hypothesized relationship between an empirically verified (see MacPhee 1983; Lang 1986; Begley 1988; Campbell-Evans 1991; Leithwood and Steinbach 1991) theory of values in administration proposed by Hodgkinson (1978) and an adaptation of the information processing theory employed by Leithwood and Montgomery (1986) to gain insights into the valuation processes employed by school administrators. Within this integrated framework, the familiar *executive* function of information-processing theory, which operates as the repository for the short-term or long-term goals and principles of the individual, functions as a screen for relevant inputs among those received by the brain. Aligning transrational principles and subrational personal preference values with the executive usefully reconciles the epistemic difficulty Evers (1985) associates with the separation of these two value types in Hodgkinson's typology. Thus, inputs identified by the executive as worthy of recognition by the mind may range from the relatively trivial perceptions of good, pleasure-seeking, or interest in personal gain, to the highest ethics of human enterprise includ-

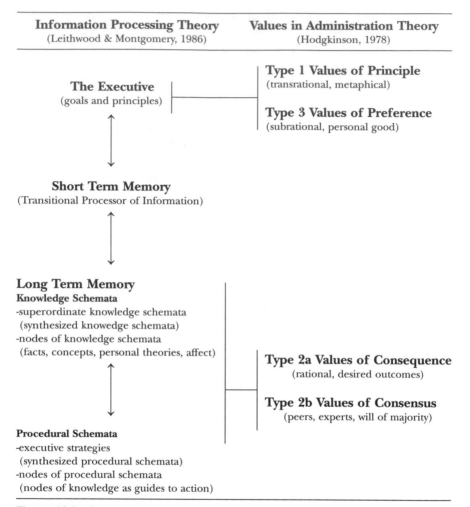

Information Processing Theory (Leithwood & Montgomery, 1986)	Values in Administration Theory (Hodgkinson, 1978)

The Executive
(goals and principles)

Type 1 Values of Principle
(transrational, metaphical)

Type 3 Values of Preference
(subrational, personal good)

Short Term Memory
(Transitional Processor of Information)

Long Term Memory
Knowledge Schemata
-superordinate knowledge schemata
 (synthesized knowedge schemata)
-nodes of knowledge schemata
 (facts, concepts, personal theories, affect)

Type 2a Values of Consequence
(rational, desired outcomes)

Type 2b Values of Consensus
(peers, experts, will of majority)

Procedural Schemata
-executive strategies
 (synthesized procedural schemata)
-nodes of procedural schemata
 (nodes of knowledge as guides to action)

Figure 12.1   Integrating cognitive information processing theory and values
theory (Begley, 1996)

ing spiritual faith, justice, and humanism. The common denominator for these two value types operating within the executive is that neither requires rational processing in the way values grounded in consensus or consequences do. They are the nonrational bases of thought and action.

Within information-processing theory, *short-term memory* performs the rational processing function between the executive and long-term memory. The third component of the model, *long-term memory*, in turn, is where existing schema of knowledge and procedure reside. These guide action and augment themselves as new schema develop in response to new information. The processes of long-term memory are rational, although they may become relatively automatic as an outcome of frequent use. This theorized function of long-term memory correlates well with Hodgkinson's rational motivational bases, consequence and consensus. Furthermore, the hypothesized development of *superordinate*, executive knowledge, and procedural schema, synthesized from the various existing and developing nodes, also begins to suggest how the goals and principles of the executive might evolve or formulate from more rational processing of inputs.

This generates an implication for values theory. Perhaps rational values grounded in consensus or consequences also evolve or became synthesized into transrational principles in a similar process. For example, this might explain how transrational dietary laws, recorded in the Bible and other sacred books, may have evolved from the hard consequences of experiences in the distant past. As a second example, consider how a transrational commitment to democratic forms of governance common to Canada, Sweden, and other countries may be the outcome of longstanding commitments to collective social action.

Methodological Challenges

As suggested earlier in this chapter and discussed in the introduction to this section of the book, conducting research on the nature and function of values in administration is fundamentally problematic. Values resist empirical verification. Like the wind, they are unseen forces. However, one may discern easily the impact of values on the empirical world, just as one can observe the movement of waves on the sea or the swaying of trees, all manifestations of the wind. Nevertheless, the presence or influence of values cannot be reliably or explicitly tracked by scientific methods alone.

The key to understanding the nature and function of values is to focus on the motivating force dimension. Hodgkinson argues (1991) that motivational bases are at the core of the being of individuals and that values held by an individual reflect these motivational bases. However, caution must be exercised when one is tempted to establish links between a motivational base and a particular value because a given value may be held at any of several levels of motivation ranging from preferences, the rational values of consequence and consensus, to the level of transrational principles. Furthermore, it is common for individuals to deliberately or unwittingly manifest or articulate one value while being actually committed to another, usually one associated with self-interest or preference but also occasionally with a transrational motivational base. A final complication that can arise in the thorny context of research methodology is potential divergence among several potential research perspectives; the value intended by the acting first person (e.g., the administrator), the value perceived by a recipient or participant second person (e.g., a teacher), and the value interpretation assigned by some third-party observer, such as the researcher.

There are a number of obvious implications. First, qualitative research methods are those most appropriate to this type of inquiry; such as collecting data in face-to-face situations, using stimulated recall activities and case problem analysis. One way to counter the liabilities of relying on the accuracy of third-party/researcher value attributions of observed actions or speech is to develop a partnership with the participants/respondents in the study. Action research strategies (see Hossack 1997 for a concise description) seem most appropriate to these circumstances, where the ideal partnership would be characterized by mutual trust, good faith, and a commitment to deliberative dialogue about the value situations being examined.

Collecting and Analyzing Values Data

Recent efforts to apply the action-research principles described above to values research generated a set of procedures that graduate students quickly dubbed the "Three P's" approach (i.e., personal, peer, and professor) because of its three-perspective approach to data analysis. These procedures have been employed successfully as a values-auditing activity within graduate courses as well as for collecting research data with samples of principals in Canada, Sweden, and Australia. Findings reported here will be limited to the Canadian and Swedish research studies.

One study was conducted in the Canadian province of Ontario and a second in Umea, Sweden. At both of these sites, a sample of experienced (two years or more in the role) school principals was identified. The Ontario sample was composed of seventeen currently practicing elementary and secondary school principals, all but one of whom were also regular instructors in local university-sponsored principal preservice courses. For the most part, these individuals knew each other well as a result of extensive professional contact and had an established culture of interaction as small-group instructors within preservice principals courses. The Swedish sample was composed of eighteen experienced and currently appointed school administrators from eight school districts in northern Sweden. They too had an established pattern of regular interaction and shared experiences accumulated as a result of their participation as a group in state-sponsored in-service sessions (National Head Teachers Training Program) run by Umea University over several years. Efforts were made to ensure representation by gender, school panel (elementary and secondary), and school size with both samples.

Data was collected as part of a two-day action-research conference focused on values and educational leadership. As preparation for the two-day session, each participant was asked to develop a one- to three-page narrative of a "critical incident" that he or she had experienced in his or her work as a school administrator. It was deemed important that these be produced before the individuals interacted as a group and participated in the workshop sessions. A set of nine-paragraph case situations was also developed in advance of the two-day sessions. These were used to generate a second category of data. The nine cases were arranged in sets of three, each set of cases addressing school situations corresponding with one of the three key dimensions of school leadership identified by Begley (1995) as the common core of school administration practices in Canada and Australia. The dimensions of practice highlighted by the case situations are: Management, Instructional Leadership, and School/Community/Culture Facilitation.

The analysis of the case-situation responses and critical incidents prepared in advance was conducted by the participants and researcher in three steps. The first step was *self-analysis*. Each person analyzed, using motivational bases as classifying criteria, their own written responses to three case situations selected for interpretation from among nine available cases. They coded their responses according to the motivational bases manifested (preference, consensus, consequences, and principles) by their actions, recorded thoughts and speech. The second step was to have the same case-situation responses analyzed a second time by a peer or colleague in the group. Once this peer analysis was conducted, the individuals met in pairs to compare and discuss their analyses of the cases. There were a few situations where changes were made to value attribution as outcomes of this deliberation, but this did not occur often and there was virtually no evidence of disagreement among the research partners on final coding. The third analysis of the case-situation responses occurred several weeks later when the researcher reviewed the value analyses a third time. Once again, it was found that little disagreement occurred (for example, in the case of the Ontario sample, only two value attributions were questioned by the third-party researcher analysis).

Research Findings

Before discussing the outcomes of the two studies described above, it is important to be clear about the generalizability of findings. Generalizing the value orientations of the individuals in this study to those of other persons working in additional settings is obviously not possible. Although the findings of this research may allow the identification of the *potential* for particular responses within an individual or among individuals who share similar professional or personal circumstances, the possible variations in response are too great to permit anything like the *prediction* or *prescription* common to the findings of traditional positivistic research.

Are Personal Preferences and Principles Important Influences?

The answer to this first research question for Canadian administrators is, relatively frequently for transrational principles and relatively infrequently for subrational personal preferences. Transrational principles were evident in responses to seven of nine of the case situations. The two excluded situations are (6) Teacher in Tears (an instructional leadership situation), and (9) School Council (a school/community facilitation situation). They are very particularly evident in responses to four case situations: (3) Outward Bound (a management situation), (5) Unacceptable Reports (an instructional leadership situation), (7) Gym Use (a school/community facilitation situation) and (8) Racial Slurs (another school/community facilitation situation). Transrational principles seemed to be employed by the Canadian administrators in response to situations that involved matters such as student safety and interpersonal communications and facilitation. They are less strongly associated with instructional leadership and management functions.

In contrast, subrational values of personal preference occur only in five of the nine cases (identified by only four of the seventeen individuals) within the Canadian sample. Personal preference values simply do not figure prominently in the professional practices of these principals.

There are strong parallels evident in the Swedish data findings, but also some contrasts. Transrational values or principles were articulated relatively infrequently by the Swedish administrators. They were weakly represented in four case situations only: (3) Outward Bound (a managerial situation); (5) Unacceptable Reports, (7) Gym Use (an instructional leadership situation); and (8) Racial Slurs (a community facilitation). However, these are the same cases where the Ontario principals tended to frequently manifest type-one principles. We can only speculate on why this contrast with the Canadian group occurs. One potential explanation is the social turmoil of recent years in the Ontario setting, brought on by persistent fiscal problems and the social plurality of the southern Ontario context. Social diversity and a lack of consensus among educational stakeholders may be driving administrators there to augment the more usual rational value arguments with ethical arguments. Alternatively, it may be connected to the Canadian group's longtime association with the university-based principal preparation programs. However, it is not clear how this latter characteristic of the sample would produce a higher incidence in transrational value orientations.

As was the case for the Ontario sample, subrational personal preferences were quite infrequently cited by the Swedes. They were weakly represented in only four case situations: (3) Outward Bound, (4) P.D. Days, (7) Gym Use, and (9) Parent Councils. Personal preference values apparently have limited influence in Swedish educational administration, or perhaps more accurately, they are seldom articulated in public responses to educational situations.

Implications. Evidence of the nonrational motivational bases of *personal preference* and *transrational principles* seems to occur much less frequently than does evidence of the rational value types. The relevance of principles or ethics to a given administrative situation seems to be prompted by particular circumstances where an ethical posture is socially appropriate (e.g., the role of the arts), where consensus is perceived as difficult to achieve (e.g., racism), or when urgency requires quick action (e.g., student safety). Furthermore, it may be that the weak influence of personal preferences on administrative practice could be viewed as a good thing. After all, principals are in the end "agents of society" and accountable to society for their actions. While values of personal preference are definitely evident as influences on some administrative processes, in this research they were less frequently *articulated* by administrators, probably because of a prevailing social bias toward the rational value types, this rational bias being perhaps an outcome of organizational socialization and cultural expectations.

These findings are consistent with the outcomes of prior research by Begley (1988) and Campbell-Evans (1991). For example, Begley examined the function of values as influences on the decisions of fifteen elementary school principals who formed the sample. That study found that values were significant influences on the initial decision of principals to adopt computers. Most principals based such decisions on rational values of consensus and consequences. This pattern perhaps reflects the tangible and technical nature of the particular educational innovation, computers in schools. Had that study focused on messy interpersonal conflicts, as was the case with Ashbaugh and Kasten (1984) and the critical incidents of our study, the personalistic and transrational value types might have been in greater evidence. Furthermore, in Begley's study the few principals whose decisions were initially guided more by principles or personal preferences seemed to be increasingly influenced by rational concerns for consequences as time went by—probably as a result of acquiring more relevant knowledge about computers and their use.

The relative infrequency of the nonrational value types suggests that ethics and personal preferences play a limited role in the administrative practices of the principals participating in this research. However, it does not necessarily lead to the conclusion drawn by some researchers and theorists that these value types are therefore not important influences on administrative practices. My data suggests that in some instances they are clearly very powerful influences. These findings are also consistent with those of Leithwood and Stager (1989) who found that principles or ethics served to provide structure for problem solving when principals lacked problem-relevant information or the problem was considered unique. Leithwood and Stager also found that such values were rarely acknowledged by principals in response to problems about which much was known; problems where knowledge, and procedural schemata were well established.

The Impact of Value Conflicts

As previously asserted, value-conflict situations have become much more common to the experiences of school administrators. One could go so far as to say they are becoming a defining characteristic of the role for most school principals.

The data collected in Umea and Toronto provide some insights into the nature of value conflicts encountered by school principals. Data relating to value conflicts were drawn primarily from an analysis of the "critical incidents" prepared by the school principals participating in the study. The large-group process and relatively small amount of time set aside for considering the "critical incidents" (approximately two hours in the group setting) limited the kind and amount of data that could be collected and displayed. However, from an action-research perspective and that of the participants in the two-day gatherings, the analysis of the critical incidents within the group setting was a worthwhile final application activity that consolidated their new learning about administrative valuation processes.

For the purposes of this study, analysis was limited to the critical incident narratives developed by the principals in the Toronto and Umea samples. The types of evidence sought were.the value types manifested in response to the situations described, and whether the conflicts were interpersonal (involving more than one person) or intrapersonal (occurring within the individual). Table 12.1 illustrates the data display that resulted from the analysis of the Canadian data only. Note that in four cases participants chose not to release their critical-incident narratives for inclusion in this research report, something that was clearly an option for them.

Value Types Associated with the Critical Incidents

After examining the critical incidents developed at both research sites, it was apparent that the principals interpreted "critical incident" as a situation that cannot be solved in such a way that everyone is pleased. This perhaps explains the very low representation of values of consensus in table 12.1. In the Swedish sample, there were even fewer occurrences of consensus values; in fact, there was only one such coding across eighteen narratives. In contrast, the other rational value type, values of consequence, was as strongly represented in the critical incidents as it was in the responses to the prepared case situations, for both the Canadian and Swedish responses. The data suggest that values of consequence remain the primary currency of educational administration for these individuals, even for the most awkward of conflict situations in schools.

Another striking contrast to the data in table 12.1 and also replicated in the Swedish data is the increased frequency of principles and values of personal preference with the critical incidents. This was especially striking with the Swedish data because transrational principles were relatively infrequent in their responses to the prepared case situations. This, perhaps, echoes once again Leithwood and Stager's (1989) findings: Principles or ethics serve to provide structure for problem solving when principals lack problem-relevant information or the problem is considered unique. The critical incidents that principals identified in this study were often unstructured or messy interpersonal problems. These nonrational value types are rarely acknowledged by principals in response to problems about which much is known, that is, problems where knowledge schema and/or procedural schema are well established.

Table 12.1   Data from the Canadian sample

CASE #	NUMBER OF PRINCIPALS SELECTING THIS CASE	ANALYSIS OF VALUE TYPES			
		TYPE 1 PRINCIPLES	TYPE 2A CONSEQUENCES	TYPE 2B CONSENSUS	TYPE 3 PREFERENCE
Management					
Case #1.	5	1	5	-	-
Case #2.	4	1	2	3	1
Case #3.	8	4	8	2	1
Instructional					
Case #4.	10	2	8	8	-
Case #5.	1	1	1	-	1
Case #6.	6	-	4	5	1
Facilitation					
Case #7.	4	2	3	4	-
Case #8.	5	4	3	3	1
Case #9.	8	-	8	5	-

Nature of the Conflicts Reported by Swedish and Canadian Principals

An examination of the critical incident data reveals that the conflicts reported by the Canadian principals were almost exclusively interpersonal in nature. The situation was identical for the Swedish data. All the critical incidents prepared by the Swedish administrators involved an interpersonal conflict; between teachers and principal, pupil and principal, parents and principal, and other variations. There was only one exception, Ralph, who reported on the personal struggle he experienced early in his career in trying to reconcile the death of a student from his school who was babysitter to his children and also a family friend. Ralph, the research partner, and the researcher all agreed that this was clearly an intrapersonal value conflict between Ralph's professional and personal roles.

These findings are consistent, once again, with Leithwood and Stager's (1989) findings on the kinds of problems that principals find most difficult to resolve, those involving interpersonal conflict. They are also consistent with the findings of another study, this one focusing specifically on values. Ashbaugh and Kasten (1984) employed a values model derived from Hodgkinson (1978). Their findings suggest that personalistic (Type 3) and organizational (Type 2) values dominate administrative decisions. However, the decision processes they examined related predominantly to personnel and community relations problems. This may explain the higher number of values of preference reported in their study. Ashbaugh and Kasten's findings regarding problem difficulty are consistent with Leithwood and Stager's (1989) findings. In both studies, principals perceived personnel problems as the most difficult to solve. The findings presented here are similar in that incidents the principals tended to identify as critical usually involved interpersonal situations.

Implications. Hodgkinson advises those interested in analyzing and resolving value conflicts to consider whether the conflict occurs between levels or at the same level of the values hierarchy (1991, 145). Any parent who has debated, from a consequences level, the purchase of expensive running shoes for an adolescent operating from the consensus (peer pressure) level will understand the significance of this advice. The knowledge schema, if not the procedural schema, of the two parties (parent and adolescent offspring) are in high contrast and subsequently produce orientations implying quite different choices. Hodgkinson also indicates that the most profound of value conflicts occur when two or more principles are in conflict (1991, 150). Because they and personal preferences are nonrational (either transrational or subrational), conflicts occurring at those levels are extremely difficult to resolve. In the case of personal preferences, the conflict may resist resolution, but the consequences of this failure are likely relatively trivial, or at least nonlethal, as in the selection of new wallpaper for the dining room or choosing television channels in a family setting (1991, 49). On the other hand, principles involve deeply held beliefs, fundamental values, and/or spiritual matters of faith. Conversely, they can also address the darker side of transrational principles: for example, the negative kinds of blind faith associated with Nazi Germany decades ago, or the charismatic cults in Jonestown (Central America) or Waco, Texas, encountered more recently. Fortunately for educational administrators, value conflicts occurring at the level of personal ethics are relatively infrequent, and researchers do not often choose to explore this class of values conflict. This is not to say that such profound conflicts do not occur. Social controversies over race, language, religion, abortion, family life studies, or AIDS prevention strategies spill over fairly regularly into school settings. However, such conflicts may be essentially private battles, hotly contested, mercifully short in duration, fought by individuals within themselves, and sometimes not even formally acknowledged.

Conclusion: The Values of School Administration

The rational values of consequence and consensus appear to be the primary currency of the administrators from Canada and Sweden who participated in these two studies. These findings are consistent with at least three other studies that utilized Hodgkinson's values model (MacPhee 1983; Ashbaugh and Kasten 1984; Lang 1986). This is so, to the extent that personal values were found to be significant influences on decision making, the rational value types predominate in the valuation processes of school principals, personal preferences are infrequently articulated, and transrational principles are employed under particular circumstances.

Several implications for theory and research are apparent. The traditional functionalist perspective on organizational decision making, perhaps best articulated by Simon (1965), proposes the notion of a value-neutral administrator. According to such a perspective, effective administrators should pursue organizational goals without reference to their personal values—a separation of personal and organizational goals. The findings reported here suggest that administrators are indeed most responsive to value types such as consensus or consequences, even in those situations when decisions appear to be also influenced by preference values or ethics. Furthermore, in a manner that appears consistent with Simon's conception of the proper role for values in administration, principals do not appear to rely often on personal preference as a guide to professional action.

With respect to subrational and transrational values and their hypothesized relationship to the executive of information-processing theory, it may be that there is a set of core values that individuals employ when knowledge schema is unavailable, ambiguity thrives, or urgency requires. When such values are extensively developed, or when situations of alienation, displacement, or social chaos present a fertile environment for their manifestation, these core values may be one source of a leadership phenomenon sometimes termed "charismatic leadership" (Yukl 1994), in its positive as well as its darker manifestations. Within the realm of the rational values types (consequences and consensus), the motivational bases of individual, collective social, and organizational values can all be well illustrated by the data. The sophisticated knowledge schema of expert problem solvers is accommodated, as is the procedural schemata of management. As well, important insights are provided into the causes and nature of value conflicts when personal, professional, and organizational values are incompatible.

This chapter began with the belief that theory and research on leadership values are highly relevant to the field of educational administration. However, what has often been missing in values theories and models is the degree of relevance that would allow practitioners to usefully apply theory as guides to practice. Just as staff developers are increasingly making use of situated learning strategies such as cognitive apprenticeships (Prestine and LeGrand 1991), problem-based learning (Bridges 1992), and leadership profiles (Begley 1995) to increase the relevancy of preservice and in-service leadership development programs, the path to greater relevance in research may be to the adoption of action research methods as a way of clarifying the nature and function of values in administration.

References

Ashbaugh, C. R., and Kasten, K. L. 1984. A typology of operant values in school administration. *Planning and Changing* 15, 4: 195–208.

Barnard, C. I. (1938). *The functions of the executive.* Cambridge, MA: Harvard University Press.

Beck, C. 1993. *Learning to live the good life.* Toronto: OISE Press.

Begley, P. T. 1988. The influence of personal beliefs and values on principals' adoption and use of computers in schools. Unpublished doctoral dissertation, University of Toronto.

———. 1995. Using profiles of school leadership as supports to cognitive apprenticeship. *Educational Administration Quarterly* 31, 2: 176–202.

——— 1996. Cognitive perspectives on values in administration: A quest for coherence and relevance. *Educational Administration Quarterly* 32, 3: 403–26.

Begley, P. T., and Leithwood, K. A. 1990. The influence of values on school administrator practices. *Journal of Personnel Evaluation in Education* 3: 337–52.

Bridges, E. M. 1992. *Problem based learning*. Eugene, OR: ERIC.

Campbell, E. 1994. Personal morals and organizational ethics: A synopsis. *The Canadian Administrator* 34, 2:1–10. Edmonton, Alberta: University of Alberta.

Campbell-Evans, G. H. 1991. Nature and influence of values in principal decision-making. *The Alberta Journal of Educational Research* 37, 2: 167–78.

Cohen, B. 1982. *Means and ends in education*. London: George Allen & Unwin.

Evers, C. W. 1985. Hodgkinson on ethics and the philosophy of administration. *Educational Administration Quarterly* 21, 1: 27–50.

Evers, C. W., and Lakomski, G. 1991. *Knowing educational administration*. Toronto: Pergamon.

Evers, C. W., and Lakomski, G. 1993. Cognition, values, and organizational structure: Hodgkinson in perspective. *Journal of Educational Administration and Foundations* 8, 1: 45–57.

Frankena, W. K. 1973. *Ethics*. Englewood Cliffs, NJ: Prentice Hall.

Hodgkinson, C. 1978. *Towards a philosophy of administration*. Oxford: Basil Blackwell.

———. 1991. *Educational leadership: The moral art*. Albany: State University of New York Press.

Hossack, L. A. January, 1997. An action research primer for principals. *The Canadian School Executive* 9–13.

Lang, D. 1986. Values and commitment. Unpublished doctoral thesis, University of Victoria, BC.

Leithwood, K. A., Begley, P. T., and Cousins, J. B. 1992. *Developing expert leadership for future schools*. London: Falmer Press.

Leithwood, K. A., and Montgomery, D. G. 1986. *Improving principal effectiveness: The principal profile*. Toronto: OISE Press.

Leithwood, K. A., and Stager, M. 1989. Components of expertise in principals' problem solving. *Educational Administration Quarterly* 25, 1: 126–61.

Leithwood, K. A and Steinbach, R. 1991. Components of chief education officers' problem solving strategies. *Understanding school system administration: Studies of the contemporary chief education officer*, ed. K. A. Leithwood, and D. Musella, New York: Falmer Press.

——— 1995. *Expert problem solving*. Albany: State University of New York Press.

MacPhee, P. 1983. *Administrators and human comprehension: The intrusion of values*. Unpublished M.A. thesis, University of Toronto.

Parsons, T., and Shils, E. A. eds. 1962. *Towards a general theory of action*. New York: Harper.

Prestine, N. A., and LeGrand, B. F. 1991. Cognitive learning theory and the preparation of educational administrators: Implications for practice and policy. *Educational Administration Quarterly* 27, 1: 61–89.

Roche, K. 1997. Catholic principals' responses to moral and ethical dilemmas. Unpublished doctoral dissertation, University of Toronto.

Simon, H. 1965. *Administrative behaviour,* 2nd ed. New York: Free Press.

Strike, K. A., Haller, E. J., Soltis, J. F. (1988). The ethics of administration. New York: Teachers College Press.

Willower, D. 1994. *Educational administration: Inquiry, values, practice.* Lancaster, PA: Technomic Publishing.

Yukl, G. 1994. *Leadership in organizations.* Englewood Cliffs, NJ: Prentice Hall.

CHAPTER THIRTEEN

Moral and Ethical Dilemmas in Catholic School Settings

Kevin Roche

The vagaries of the postmodern world present a complex dilemma for school administrators acting in the face of increasing moral confusion and ambiguity. Frequently, a plethora of confusing and conflicting values preclude the determination of any clear choice, action, or decision. Daily, school administrators confront moral and ethical dilemmas that demand a response. To date, empirical research relating to administrative values has focused on three central issues: identifying the values employed by educational administrators, whether administrators give more credence to particular values than to others, and the extent to which values influence administrative decision making. The study reported herein moves beyond this preoccupation with the nature and influence of values to an investigation of how school administrators actually respond to moral and ethical dilemmas, the most difficult value conflicts they encounter.

Over the last decade, social theorists have begun to describe the increasing social impact of phenomena such as pluralism, technological innovation, societal fragmentation, the decentering of the traditional majority population, and the disconnectedness of particular individuals and groups. During this time, school administrators have also confronted these practical realities of postmodernism on a daily basis, often in the restructured environment of decentralization and school-based management. Despite the onset of postmodernity, or because of it, the principals' unenviable task becomes the determination of which and whose values, beliefs, knowledge, and understandings are to prevail. Greenfield's (1991) argument that, in these times of uncertainty, teachers, students, and parents demand that school administrators be conscientious moral actors poses a new dilemma for school principals in the necessity to choose between: "a confusing plurality of values, some particularist, some claiming a universal validity, but each rooted in different traditions, histories and theoretical and political trajectories, and many of them in stark contradiction, one to the other" (Weeks, in Squires 1993, 189).

No less than other administrators, Catholic school principals are faced with taking action in a context characterized by moral and ethical ambiguity. Changes within the church and society in recent decades have served to destabilize the once-definitive Catholic values, beliefs, and teachings. For school principals charged with the responsibility of developing and maintaining a distinctive Catholic culture, moral contradiction, conflict, and uncertainty have become commonplace. Ironically, despite the widespread cultural, social, and economic diversity that challenge, confront, and complicate the leadership task, the church and society have rising expectations of the moral authenticity of school leaders. Yet, the once-single voice of a worldwide church no longer clearly articulates a universal ideology. Somewhat paradoxically, the disposition of all principals to action incurs an inherent moral dilemma: it is not merely a question of whether they are ethical administrators or not, it is that they must choose one value or set of values over another. Often it is not obvious what or who is right or wrong, or what is the truly moral or ethical response among many. Even at times when principals are confident of the appropriateness of a particular response, their morally preferred course of action is often precluded by contextual factors.

The studies of Begley (1988), Campbell-Evans (1988), Leithwood and Stager (1989), and Leithwood and Steinbach (1995) suggest that when dealing with value conflicts, principals usually select from a range of essentially rational responses. In a study of value conflicts that confront school principals, Ashbaugh and Kasten (1984) found that when the metavalues of the organization conflicted with principals' transcendent values, there were three possible responses: principals complied with the values of the organization (even if they personally believed them to be unjust), they compromised their own integrity in order to improve their career prospects, or they chose to leave the role. Campbell's (1992) study of how teachers and principals cope with conflicting moral and ethical values identified three general responses made by teachers in response to transrational value conflicts they encountered: (1) taking a moral stand, (2) suspending morality, and (3) conforming or complying. Campbell concluded that, in contrast to teachers, principals adopted a rationalist, technocratic, and bureaucratic approach in order to avoid or resolve transrational value conflicts in a consequential, utilitarian, and morally neutral manner.

The central purpose of the research reported in this chapter was to determine how five principals in Catholic school settings actually respond to moral and ethical dilemmas within their professional role. Among other concerns (which lie outside the scope of this chapter), the study also sought to identify some of the moral and ethical dilemmas experienced by Catholic school principals and to determine how regularly the principals perceived themselves as dealing with such dilemmas.

Theoretical Framework

Hodgkinson's (1978; 1991) hierarchical conception of three categories of values was used to differentiate transrational values (based on personal principles or beliefs) from those held at the rational (grounded in the determination of consequences and/or consensus) and subrational (based on preference) value levels. This differentiation forms the basis of the consideration of value conflicts occurring at the transrational level (i.e., moral and ethical dilemmas) that invoke responses that may be motivated by values held by principals at any of the three levels.

A synthesis of related literature identified four possible responses that formed the basis of a response classification framework developed specifically for the purposes of the study: (1) avoidance, (2) suspending morality, (3) creative insubordination, and (4) personal morality.

Avoidance

Avoidance can be of two types: cognizant and noncognizant. Cognizant avoidance typically occurs when principals are fully aware that the conflict they are dealing with is of a transrational nature and knowingly choose to reduce the conflict to a rational or subrational level in order to achieve resolution. Noncognizant avoidance occurs when principals fail to grasp that particular moral and ethical issues are in contention, preferring to deal with the issue at arm's length through a reliance on formal and/or established procedures. Both cognizant and noncognizant avoidance allow consequentialist and nonconsequentialist solutions (Strike, Haller, and Soltis 1988). The consequentialist approach is based primarily on calculating the good in terms of consequences, where the ends justify the means. The nonconsequentialist approach is concerned with some clear intrinsic view of the right or one's duty, in which a sense of duty or principle prescribes the ethical decision (Preston 1996, 40).

Suspending Morality

Drawing on work of Milgram (1974) and Hodgkinson (1978), Campbell (1992) describes, at considerable length, the actions of those who compromise or suspend their own moral judgments in order to accommodate organizational ethics and imperatives. Many principals argue that it is their professional obligation and responsibility to adhere to the official directives of school board personnel (e.g., superintendent, director), the formal policies, rules, and regulations that exist (perhaps especially for these occasions), and/or the needs or wishes of the school community (e.g., teachers, parents, students).

Creative Insubordination

Creative insubordination usually involves adapting system policies, procedures, and programs in a way that fits the principal's values, philosophy, goals, and situation (Haynes and Licata 1995, 21). Creatively insubordinate responses are usually harmless, perhaps mischievous, and at times (although rarely) destructive (Crowson 1989). Creative insubordination has two main purposes: to ensure that system directives do not impinge unfairly or inappropriately on teachers and students and to avoid the possible backlash that outright defiance might incur. Crowson (1989) and Haynes and Licata (1995) argue that when principals use creative insubordination, the counterbureaucratic behaviors they adopt often contain a moral element designed to balance antieducational consequences.

Personal Morality

Nelson's (1984, 111) description of stands and stances as patterns of relationships parallels administrative responses based on personal morality. Stands and stances include patterns of action in the world: ways of expressing and effecting theories, moralities, principles, visions, emotions, and the like. Thus, they are more than simple techniques for action; they extend to the choice and ordering of ends as well as means.

Nelson's distinction between the political stand and the political stance is crucial to understanding responses motivated by personal morality. The political stand offers a way of taking responsibility for the world as well as oneself, without eroding principles; the political stance fits the give and take of ordinary politics, when principle is created by and for compromise (Nelson 1984, 106). Taking a moral stand involves an undaunted, unmoving, enduring commitment to a personal moral principle in the face of all consequences. Alternatively, moral stances or postures are more common in the cut and parry of everyday life. As a strategy, perhaps best described as holding out for a better deal, taking a moral stance has the initial appearance of the moral stand. Taking the high moral ground is often foreshadowed by a rational assessment of probable outcomes, which gives reason to be confident about the likely success of the response.

Methodology

To better understand how Catholic school principals respond to moral and ethical dilemmas, a qualitative research design based on semistructured and unstructured interviews was developed. Since the accuracy of verbal reports depends on the procedures used to elicit them and the relationship between the requested information and the actual sequence of heeded information (Ericsson and Simon 1984, 27), the combination of the study's research methods, the overall structure, and the ordered sequencing of the interviews served to limit the concerns of validity usually attributed to verbal reports.

The sample consisted of five (two female and three male) Catholic elementary school principals, each with a minimum of one year's experience in his or her current position. The schools were all systemic parish schools in the same diocese within Australia. The selected principals came from schools within the same region in which they are grouped by the Catholic Education Office for administrative and organizational purposes. The selection was based on willingness to participate in the study.

The study focused on the principals' responses to four hypothetical case scenarios (vignettes) and their deliberated responses to recent moral and ethical dilemmas obtained through one retrospective and two semi-structured interviews with each. The structure and research strategies adopted for this study sought to address the considerable difficulties associated with the validity of verbal reports (e.g. Nisbett and Wilson 1977; Ericsson and Simon 1984). The responses provided in the first interview called upon the respondents' short-term memory and hence were high in validity, notwithstanding that these interviews involved hypothetical situations. By comparison, the retrospective (second) interview focused on actual events but relied on the respondents' long-term memory. Biderman (1967) in Ericsson and Simon (1984, 45) argues that if the experimenter specifies the relevant time period and the particular type of events to be recalled, recall increases considerably. Thus, in order to reduce concern about the validity of reports gleaned from long-term memory, the respondents were asked to report on specific dilemmas that had occurred in the previous twelve months.

As was the case in Campbell's study of personal morals and organizational ethics, the vignettes employed in this study served as memory triggers that, in many cases, reminded respondents of similar situations encountered in the past (Campbell 1992, 202). Hence, the particular types of events to be recalled were illustrated by example in the first interview, prior to the respondents recalling actual experiences in the retrospective interview. Further, the ordering of the interviews from specific situations in the first interview and retrospective interview to the general questioning of the third interview acknowledges that more valid information is attained by cuing subjects with specific items than by asking general questions (Ericsson and Simon 1984, xlix).

Summary of Results

Data from the interviews were initially reported in the first-person format. Rather than attempt to condense the extensive results, this section summarizes the findings in relation to the study's purposes, as outlined earlier within the context of the existing literature and research base.

Generally, it was found that respondents in this study were willing participants, speaking freely, openly, and at considerable length. They spoke with surprising candor, their ready responses clearly indicative of much experience and critical, personal reflection. Not only did the principals provide definitive responses, but they were able and eager to articulate the moral basis of their responses. The respondents appreciated the essence of each dilemma, openly acknowledging the central principles underlying the various perspectives that challenged or supported their position. They spoke willingly of the struggle that characterized the resolution process; the struggle itself evidenced by the apparent contradictions in many of their explanations.

Hypothetical scenarios readily gave way to vivid memories of similar experiences that the principals had previously encountered. At times, individual respondents exhibited signs of tension, worry, and some distress as they recalled the circumstances of recent dilemmas. Although some responses evidenced the quick reply that the ready exercise of formal authority affords, more commonly the principals pondered and agonized over achieving a fair, just, and moral solution. Critics might well point to the uses and abuses of the power of office, which undeniably were evident on occasion. For the most part, however, the burden of responsibility rested heavily on the principals' shoulders; loneliness and isolation frequently featured in their responses.

Although in no way meant to be judgmental, the study uncovered an obvious incongruence that at times lay between the respondents' articulated values and their actual behavior, idealistic intentions suffering greatly at the hands of practicality. Moral and ethical intent, though readily articulated, often proved elusive in application. On occasion, some respondents expressed lingering doubts long after resolution was achieved. Resolution itself was often problematic and incomplete, typically giving rise to a number of new, smaller dilemmas. Nonetheless, the principals were quite forthright, confident of their actions, and decisive in their responses to moral and ethical dilemmas. Aware of the complexity of the issues and the dearth of simple solutions, the respondents openly expressed feelings of self-doubt, optimism, and some disillusionment, but especially of genuine care for those within their school communities.

Types and Frequency of Moral and Ethical Dilemmas

The different types of dilemmas identified by the literature to date (see Crowson 1989; Greenfield 1991) were represented in the dilemmas reported by the principals. In simple terms, these dilemmas could be described as involving teachers, parents, children, and formal administrative authority (usually in the from of the church hierarchy or school system policy). The main focus, of all but two of the actual dilemmas recounted, involved interpersonal conflict, consistent with the findings of a number of preceding studies (e.g. Ashbaugh and Kasten 1984; Leithwood and Stager 1989; Begley and Johansson 1997) that these were the most difficult problems for administrators to resolve.

Although a number of dilemmas did involve personnel, issues of teacher competency did not dominate to the extent suggested by the Kirby, Paradise, and Prottis (1992) study. The range of dilemmas included the particular circumstances and behavior of children, the implementation of school and system policy, teacher lifestyle, and issues that were related to competency. Further, findings related to a hypothetical dilemma concerning a teacher suffering from ill health coupled with the principals' common agreement that they had encountered similar situations support Wignall's (1994) observation that principals are increasingly affected by dilemmas related to competency and the legitimate needs of teachers coping with illness. Finally, although the principals themselves nominated dilemmas involving teachers, parents, and/or children as frequently occurring, four of the five principals nominated dilemmas involving parents as the most frequently occurring dilemma type.

Four of the principals in the study perceived that they encountered moral and ethical dilemmas on a daily basis. The exception, Principal Elizabeth Wright (pseudonyms are used throughout the report), recounted two such dilemmas that were on her mind "at that moment," confirming that value conflicts of this nature were a frequently (daily) occurring phenomena for the principals in the study. Even though this finding concurs with the contention of those that argue that administrators increasingly encounter value conflicts (e.g., Leithwood, Begley, and Cousins 1994), it contrasts with those research studies to date that suggest that, for administrators, nonrational value conflicts occur infrequently (e.g., Campbell-Evans 1988; Campbell 1992). Further, this finding supports Begley and Johansson's (1997) reluctance to dismiss nonrational values as significant influences on administrative practice, despite the contention by those, such as Evers and Lakomski (1991) that believe nonrational value types ought not be important influences on administrative practice. Finally, while this finding agrees with Begley's (1996a, 574) observation that transrational value conflicts do occur, it also suggests that his contention that "fortunately for educational administrators, value conflicts occurring at that level are relatively infrequent" may be premature; their insignificance in the literature perhaps due in part to the fact acknowledged by Begley himself (1996a, 574) that few researchers have chosen to explore this class of values conflict. Similarly, although Leithwood's (1996, 2) skepticism about the practical utility of scholarship aimed at promoting more ethical administrative practice in schools partly because virtually all relevant evidence suggests that administrative practice is already highly ethical may reflect the lack of research attention given to transrational value conflict.

Principals' Responses to Moral and Ethical Dilemmas

All four of the responses incorporated in the response classification framework developed for this study were clearly evident in the principals' responses.

Avoidance. In championing his own value paradigm as a mechanism for value adjudication, Hodgkinson (1991, 145) claims that his analytical model of the value concept "can be applied to the most tortuous and vexing of complex controversial issues and conflicts." Yet, inexplicably, when it comes to moral and ethical dilemmas, the most difficult of value conflicts, Hodgkinson's (1991, 151) only advice to the would-be ethical principal is that it should be the administrative maxim to avoid for as long as possible, or at all, if possible, the emergence of this category of value conflict to the extent that it is within the leader's power to do so.

In this study, focused on transrational value conflicts which could not be avoided, there was enough evidence to suggest that total avoidance of moral and ethical dilemmas was a popular option when it was available as a choice. For example, Principal Brian Davis actively sought to avoid teacher lifestyle dilemmas by openly encouraging his teachers "not to get into the situation to begin with." Similarly, James Hegarty and Malcom Burnes avoided potential dilemmas in relation to the placement of children in particular classes by preselecting children of potentially difficult parents in their preferred classes. This strategy was consistent with other studies that clearly identified outright avoidance of transrational value conflicts as a preferred option of administrators (e.g., Ashbaugh and Kasten 1984; Campbell-Evans 1988).

At face value, the findings of this study that personal preference did not form a basis for dilemma resolution was hardly surprising given the gravity of the dilemmas discussed. Nevertheless, in line with Begley and Johansson's (1997, 26) conclusion, personal preference was identified as an influence on administrative processes, particularly evident in the principals' commonly held preference for the prevention or avoidance of moral dilemmas. At times, personal preferences contravened principles of equity and social justice (e.g., the practice of encouraging teachers not to commit themselves to certain "undesirable" lifestyle situations and the biased preselection of classes at the expense of those children whose parents chose not to interfere). Although such preferences could well be understood as a desire to promote organizational peace and harmony on one hand and to avoid trouble and hassles on the other, such practices obviously undermine a principal's claim to moral authenticity.

Total avoidance notwithstanding, this study found that a significant number of responses by principals to moral and ethical dilemmas could be described as avoidance, whereby transrational value conflicts were reduced to the rational value level. To a limited extent, this finding is consistent with the studies of Begley (1988), Campbell-Evans (1988), Leithwood and Stager (1989), and Leithwood and Steinbach (1995), which found that when dealing with value conflicts, principals select from essentially rational values. However, principals in this study, at times, chose from a number of responses, both rational and nonrational.

The findings of this study suggesting that principals' rational responses to moral and ethical dilemmas included both consequentialist and nonconsequentialist solutions contrast with Campbell's (1992, 416) findings that principals' responses to such dilemmas can be defined, for the most part, by consequentialist approaches to decision making and conflict resolution. Moreover, the principals' frequent employment of non-consequentialist strategies and, to a lesser extent, the attempt by some principals to achieve both consequentialist and nonconsequentialist solutions, where possible, also contrasts with those studies (e.g. Begley 1988, Campbell-Evans 1988) which found that consequentialist approaches dominated principals' decision-making processes.

Suspending Morality. On a number of occasions some of the respondents used a process described herein as "suspending morality" to resolve moral and ethical dilemmas where organizational ethics and imperatives conflicted with their own personal morality. The defining characteristic of these responses is a principal's deference to system or school-level imperatives despite personal misgivings. Seven out of eight principals in Campbell-Evans's (1988) study chose to suspend their morality when they implemented systemwide policies they disagreed with before working to change them. In similar circumstances within the context of this study, only one principal (James) indicated that he would take the same approach. Another principal (Malcom) would initially resist the policy before putting aside his own misgivings to implement the policy as directed. Despite the number of instances in which principals suspended their own morality, only on one occasion did a principal (Elizabeth) actually convert to the moral position expressed within an organizational imperative.

Principals in this study often suspended their own morality because of the inevitability and/or desirability of the outcome rather than the moral appeal of the alternative position. Professional duty, fear of reprisal, and a professional role ethic to "stick to policy" variously described important influences on the decision by principals to put aside their own misgivings. Often principals were caught in what Campbell (1992) calls "the false necessity trap," believing that they had no choice. Brian observed that "if the

Bishop speaks out, one must do what he says." Others felt obliged to honor organizational and professional role ethics such as doing "what's best for the kids," "supporting the teacher no matter what," and "sticking to policy." Given the possible consequences incurred by principals who disobey system imperatives, it seems that genuine necessity more aptly describes those instances where the choice is "to follow the directive, resign or get sacked" (James).

Creative Insubordination. Although much of the literature relating to value conflicts (e.g., Ashbaugh and Kasten 1984; Campbell-Evans 1988; Leithwood and Steinbach 1995) ignores principals' recourse to creative insubordination, this response was clearly evident in the study. On various occasions, principals sought to modify, adapt, or overturn system policies (e.g., sick leave, non-Catholic enrollment) that they believed impinged unfairly on teachers, children, and families in their school community.

The problem with all forms of creative insubordination is that to employ the strategy some form of dishonesty is necessary. When principals sought to achieve or protect a moral or ethical principle by pretending to implement the policy as directed, they often felt guilty or uncomfortable about the pretense. Thus, Malcom's creatively insubordinate strategies, in relation to the school system's sick leave policy, appeared to achieve his desired objectives, yet he continued to feel uneasy and unhappy about the deception. Even though it is possible that principals use creatively insubordinate strategies for dubious personal reasons or inappropriate intentions, in this study this response was employed for the perceived benefit of school communities rather than any personal gain.

From this perspective, creative insubordination appears to be a genuine moral response that may well avoid subsequent criticism on the basis of what Haynes and Licata (1995) call "the legitimacy of the justifiable," illustrated by Malcom's lack of concern that school system authorities may discover his insubordination "because they know the (sick leave) policy doesn't stand on solid ground anyway." The three principals who employed creative insubordination had clear moral intentions and a firm belief that not only were the school system's demands, as expressed in particular policies, detrimental to their community, but they were neither legitimate nor morally justifiable.

Personal Morality. The many responses given by principals that were based on the personal morality of individual principals in the study further challenges the traditional perspective of the school administrators as rational, technocratic bureaucrats.

MORAL STANCES. Detailed analysis of the study's findings highlight the close resemblance of creative insubordination responses to those described in this study as moral stances or postures. In the first instance, the response is covert, designed to ensure that system policies do not impinge unfairly or inappropriately on a particular school community. Taking a moral stance is overt, chosen as a calculated strategy by principals who initially claim the high moral ground but realize that any subsequent advantage is likely to be short-lived. A crucial distinction between the two responses is that creative insubordination is more genuinely concerned with achieving certain desired ends, one way or another; moral stances involve holding out for a better deal than that originally offered within the terms of the policy or directive.

Data collected in this study suggest that principals (such as Elizabeth and Brian) turned to creative insubordination as a last resort, after their initial moral stance had unsuccessfully run its course. In all, moral stances, while perhaps very common in the cut and parry of everyday administrative practice, were a far less frequent response to the moral and ethical dilemmas that were the focus of this study. On one occasion Maria chose to adopt a moral stance against a teacher rather than her preferred option of the moral stand because of a perceived lack of support for her position from formal administrative authority. At other times, a moral stance was taken by principals who believed that the comparative morality of their position justified their open disapproval of a particular policy or decision, if only for a short time. Whenever principals in the study did adopt a moral stance, they were resigned to the fact that the achievement of their preferred outcome was unlikely, if not unrealistic. For example, after writing to his parish priest to no avail, James informed the Catholic Education Office of his school's inability to meet workplace, health, and safety regulations with regard to the provision of fire extinguishers, because his parish priest refused to authorize the expenditure.

MORAL STANDS. At first glance, the findings of this study that three principals would take the supposedly rare moral stand in five instances (Maria and Malcom on two occasions each) are surprising. Though the stand has its appeal in the preservation of personal integrity regardless of the consequences, the severity of the possible consequences is such to discourage its common usage. James explained the difficulty: "I mean you can buck the system. . . . but how long will you last?" Closer analysis reveals that on only one occasion did a principal (Maria) indicate that she would take a moral stand against her employer. All other stands were taken against teachers or parents, indicative perhaps of the difference in degree that possible repercussions could incur when moral stands are taken against one's employer as opposed to members of the school community.

Campbell does not unconditionally advocate that principals should take moral stands since an individual's "own sense of right and wrong may represent little more than personal subjective preference, emotivism or self-interest" (1992, 441). This observation appears to underlie her conclusion that "in many cases one may indeed question their lack of moral courage" (442). Contrarily, findings reported here identify personal morality as a significant basis of principals' responses to moral and ethical dilemmas. Typically, these responses embraced a strong moral component where principals not only were aware of the moral precepts at risk, but they took active (if not always overt) measures to protect and preserve the integrity of the principles in question.

Discussion

Understanding Rational Responses

Schein's (1984, 3) conception of "espoused" and "assumed," or "unconscious," values recognizes a cyclical relationship among values, behavior, and assumptions: as a value leads to a behavior, and as that behavior begins to solve the problem that prompted it in the first place, the value gradually is transformed into an underlying assumption.

If applied to individuals, this conception suggests that unconscious or assumed values were once espoused values that over time and through experience became taken for granted. On one level, Catholic school principals, as agents of the church and society, might well be legitimately expected and morally bound to follow established policy. At another level, it seems likely that, with experience, principals hold or develop a host of personal and professional values consistent with those on which particular policies or procedures are based. Similarly, an experienced principal may employ a number of organizational and professional role ethics (such as supporting the teacher "no matter what") as a matter of standard practice. With repeated applications over time these explicit values and ethics become unconscious or assumed, added to those other nonconfrontable, nondebatable implicit assumptions held by the principal and/or the school. Over time, related principals' behavior becomes automatic as the regular, unquestioned application of policies and procedures becomes a matter of mere routine.

Such a possibility may in part explain the findings of Leithwood and Stager (1989), Campbell-Evans (1991), and Begley and Johansson (1997), indicating that where principals know a lot about a problem they rarely acknowledge the influence of values. Conversely, this possibility is also consistent with the finding of Begley (1988), Leithwood and Steinbach (1991), and Begley and Johansson (1997), indicating that when domain-specific knowledge is absent or unavailable, transrational values are employed because high ambiguity and/or urgency make rational processes (such as the application of existing policy) impossible or inappropriate. When principals knowingly or unknowingly choose to resolve moral and ethical value conflicts by rational processes that seemingly ignore the inherent transrational values, they rely on policies and procedures based in part on unconscious or assumed values. Arguably, these assumptions form part of the domain-specific knowledge available to principals in the more common instances where they do know a lot about a problem. When unique and/or urgent moral dilemmas occur which escape the ready application of existing policy and practice (and their inherent assumptions), principals look to (transrational) espoused values to effect resolution.

From this perspective, the principals' common concern in this study that they be consistent in the application of policy is more than an expressed concern that they appear to be fair, just, and equitable in their dealings and/or decisive in their decision making. Persistent adherence to established policy, rules, and procedures such as a school's discipline policy or a principal's professional role ethic to do "what's best for the kids" exemplifies the rational application of policies and procedures once based on espoused values but now subsumed into the realm of unconscious assumptions. Perhaps the apparent reluctance on the part of some administrators to reflect on the appropriateness of the basic assumptions underlying established policy and practice in specific instances and current circumstances lies at the heart of those noncognizant responses where principals were unaware, failed, or refused to acknowledge important moral considerations. Although arguably indicative of a lack of a clear moral framework, this study suggests that the problem is as much a result of uncritical, nonreflective practice indicative perhaps of poor administrative expertise.

These findings stand in stark contrast to the claims of those (e.g., Campbell 1992) who infer that the predisposition of administrators toward the rational resolution of transrational value conflicts is somehow inherently amoral. Given that principals do frequently employ rational processes that include consequentialist and nonconsequentialist perspectives, this study contends that subsequent responses may be moral, amoral, or (rarely) immoral. Campbell (1992, 430) asserts that principals often based their responses to moral and ethical dilemmas on consequentialist rather than ethical arguments designed to "avoid trouble as much as possible rather than doing the right thing . . . right and wrong in the larger sense were usually ignored."

Alternatively, this study argues that principals often base their responses to moral and ethical dilemmas on consequentialist and nonconsequentialist arguments that reflect the espoused (explicit) and assumed (implicit) values on which their policies and practice are based. Moreover, this study contends that principals are not necessarily unconcerned with issues of right or wrong simply because they employ consequentialist solutions. As the findings clearly indicate, consequentialist and nonconsequentialist solutions employed by principals typically were justified on moral and ethical grounds, which is not to say that all responses were, in fact, moral or ethical (as evidenced by the practice of "getting rid" of troublesome children and "attacking teachers in their time of weakness").

Articulated versus Actual Commitment to Values

Critics of administrators and administrative practice might well point to the numerous examples within this study's data where articulated values stand as an obvious contradiction to the lack of demonstrated commitment to those same values. When a school community perceives a significant degree of dissonance between what school leaders say and what they do, the apparent hypocrisy often results in a credibility or authenticity crisis for the principal concerned. When school principals espouse Christian values but display inconsistent or little apparent commitment to those same values, the resultant perception of double standards can demoralize teachers, parents, and children. Such a situation has enormous implications for the development and maintenance of Catholic school cultures.

From the outset, this study is clearly intended not to judge or criticize the actions of the respondents. The very nature of the topic at hand involves the resolution of moral and ethical dilemmas that by definition, occur when two principles of right and wrong conflict at the same time. That the respondents' responses were, at times, contradictory, is to be expected as to honor one principle is to deny the other. The principal may, in fact, value both precepts. Any suggestion that principals purposely espouse one value while being committed to another is not supported by the findings of this study. On those occasions when the problem of dissonance was evident in their responses, the principals seemed to be genuinely unaware of the disparity.

The dissonance that did occur was often evident in those instances when the rights of the individual had to be weighed against the best interests of the majority, such as putting the rights of a teacher over what was best for the students in his class (Elizabeth); falsifying sick leave records to burden the system rather than his own school with the teacher replacement costs (Malcom); respecting the perspectives of others but discounting the life world of a teacher suffering from chronic health problems (Maria); deciding "to get rid of" a persistently misbehaving child by threatening expulsion when such a decision lay outside of the principal's jurisdiction (James); and publicly announcing a systemwide policy while working to undermine it (Brian).

Begley (1996c) posits that the problem of administrators articulating one value while being committed to another raises the possibility that one cognitive knowledge schema might reflect a commitment to one set of values while a selected procedural schema might articulate a response to another set of values. Certainly, when principals resolve that the "focus of any decision you make is what is best for the children" and yet preselect children into a class with a less than competent teacher because "some parents couldn't care less what class their child was in" (Malcom), Begley contention seems well illustrated. Similarly, Begley's and Johansson's (1997) contention that dissonance usually occurs between articulated values and actual commitment to values lower down the hierarchy is aptly illustrated by the same example.

Other findings in this study suggest that these issues may be compounded by the problem of articulated (explicit) and assumed (implicit) values. Begley and Johansson (1997, 4) raise the difficulty caused by articulation when they suggest that the less frequent articulation of nonrational values by principals might be related to "prevailing social bias towards the rational value types." At face value, Schein's (1985) contention that over time, and with experience, espoused (articulated) values become unconscious assumptions as policy and practice become routine is consistent with Begley's (1996a) assertion that values move away from the nonrational value types toward the rational. However, there was no evidence in this study to suggest that articulated values that transform into assumptions over time become more or less rational merely because they are articulated less often. This study challenges the view that rational values are restricted to values "analogous to consensus and consequences" (Begley, 1996a, 581). Rather, findings in this study extend the current understanding of rational values to include nonconsequentialist values that may have become implicit or unstated but are nonetheless held at the rational level as a result of experience over time.

Compounding the problem of articulation is the apparent assumption in the literature and particularly in Hodgkinson's (1978, 1991) values theory that nonconsequentialist principles are, by definition, nonrational and that consequentialist are rational. There were many examples in this study where nonconsequentialist values were articulated at the rational level and where values articulated at the rational level were held at the transrational level. In stark contrast to the accepted view (e.g. Hodgkinson 1991; Campbell 1992), this study contends that consequentialist and nonconsequentialist values may be held at the rational and transrational levels in both implicit and explicit forms.

In order to resolve moral and ethical dilemmas that occur at the transrational level, principals may draw from a number of implicit and explicit values, which span the three levels of Hodgkinson's typology. These implicit and explicit values guide the decisions and actions of principals. The fact that these values may be rational or nonrational, consequentialist or nonconsequentialist, explicit or implicit further adds to the difficulty of understanding the subsequent responses of principals. In times of moral crisis, they present a confusing plethora of possible motivations, the interplay of which may well be described in predominantly rational terms.

Conclusion

The complex reality of the administrators' postmodern work-world includes moral and ethical dilemmas that are "inevitable, endemic, and perpetual" (Handy 1994, 48). The administrator's task of resolution is fraught with difficulties and challenges, the complexity of which escapes many of those outside the role. Increasingly, administrators are called to act morally as they respond to the turbulent demands of the growing numbers of those "yearning to reclaim the moral-ethical-spiritual domain of leadership" (Duignan 1997, 3).

Through the use of hypothetical case scenarios and a consideration of actual situations, this study investigated how five Australian Catholic school principals respond to moral and ethical dilemmas. Principals were found to use a variety of responses, including avoidance, suspending morality, creative insubordination, and their own personal morality. Subsequently, this chapter has presented a number of the study findings that challenge some prevailing notions of administrators and administrative practice. These findings remind researchers and theorists alike of the tentative nature of the existing knowledge base in the values domain within educational administration. Thus, extravagant claims are not made for the importance of this study's findings or their implications. Perhaps the worth of this study may best be judged by the extent to which it inspires others to consider and reconsider the nature and influence of values, value orientations, and value conflicts on administrative practice.

References

Ashbaugh, C. R., and Kasten, K. L. 1984. A typology of operant values in school administration. *Planning and Changing* 15, 4: 195–208.

Begley, P. T. 1988. The influence of personal beliefs and values on principals' adoption and use of computers in schools. Unpublished doctoral dissertation, University of Toronto.

———. 1996a. Cognitive perspectives on the nature and function of values in educational administration. *International handbook of educational leadership and administration Part I,* ed. K. Leithwood et al. Dordrecht/Boston/London: Kluwer Academic Publishers.

————. 1996b. Cognitive perspectives on values in administration: A quest for coherence and relevance. *Educational Administration Quarterly* 32, 3: 403–26.

————. 1996c. Academic and administrative perspectives on values. Paper presented at the conference Values and Educational Leadership, OISE, Toronto.

Begley, P. T., and Johansson, O. 1997. Values and school administration. Paper delivered at the Annual Meeting of the American Educational Research Association, Chicago, Illinois.

Campbell, E. C. 1992. Personal morals and organizational ethics. Unpublished doctoral dissertation, University of Toronto.

Campbell-Evans, G. H. 1988. Nature and influence of values in principal decision-making. Unpublished doctoral dissertation, University of Toronto.

————. 1991. Nature and influence of values in principal decision making. *The Alberta Journal of Educational Research* 37, 2: 167–78.

Crowson, R. L. 1989. Managerial ethics in educational administration. The rational choice approach. *Urban Education* 23 4: 412–35.

Duignan, P. A. 1997. The dance of leadership: At the still point of the turning world. Victoria: ACEA Monograph Series.

Ericsson, K. A., and Simon, H. A. 1984. *Protocol analysis: Verbal reports as data.* Cambridge, MA: The MIT Press.

Evers, C. W., and Lakomski, G. 1991. *Knowing educational administration.* Toronto: Pergamon.

Greenfield, W. 1991. Rationale and methods to articulate ethics in administrator training. Paper presented at the Annual Meeting of the American Educational Research Association, Chicago, IL, April 3–7.

Handy, C. 1994. *The empty raincoat: Making sense of the future.* London: Random House.

Haynes, F. A., and Licata, J. W. 1995. Creative insubordination of school principals and the legitimacy of the justifiable. *Journal of Educational Administration* 33, 4: 21–35.

————. 1978. *Towards a philosophy of administration.* Oxford: Basil Blackwell.

————. 1983. *The philosophy of leadership.* Oxford: Basis Blackwell.

Hodgkinson, C. 1991. *Educational leadership: The moral art.* Albany: State of New York Press.

Kirby, P. C., Paradise, L. V. and Protti, R. 1992. Ethical reasoning of educational administrators. *Journal of Educational Administration* 30, 4: 25–32.

Leithwood, K. 1996. An organizational perspective on values for leaders of future schools. Paper presented at the conference Values and Educational Leadership, OISE, Toronto.

Leithwood, K. A., Begley, P. T. and Cousins, J. B. 1994. *Developing expert leadership for future schools.* London: The Falmer Press.

Leithwood, K. A., and Stager, M. 1989. Components of expertise in principals' problem-solving. *Educational Administration Quarterly* 25, 1:126–61.

Leithwood, K. A., and Steinbach, R. 1991. Components of chief education officers' problem solving strategies. In *Understanding school administration,* ed. K. A. Leithwood and D. Musella. New York: The Falmer Press.

———. 1995. *Expert problem solving.* New York: State University of New York Press.

Milgram, S. 1974. *Obedience to authority: An experimental view.* New York: Harper and Row.

Nelson, J. S. (1984). Stands in Politics. *The Journal of Politics* 46, 1: 106–31.

Nisbett, R. E., and Wilson, T. D. 1977. Telling more than we know: Verbal reports on mental processes. *Psychological Review* 84: 231–59.

Preston, N. 1996. *Understanding ethics.* Leichhardt, NSW: The Federation Press.

Schein, E. H. 1984. Coming to a new awareness of organizational culture. *Sloan Management Review,* Winter: 3–16.

———. 1985. *Organizational culture and leadership.* San Francisco: Jossey Bass.

Squires, J., ed. 1993. *Principled positions: Postmodernism and the rediscovery of value.* London: Lawerence and Wishout.

Strike, K. A., Haller, E. J., and Soltis, J. F. 1988. *The Ethics of school administration.* New York: Teachers College Press.

Wignall, R. 1994. Persistent dilemmas of life-threatening illness and work. Revised paper presented to International Inter-visitation Program of the Commonwealth Council for Educational Administration, Toronto and Buffalo.

CHAPTER FOURTEEN

A Feminist Perspective of Women Superintendents' Approaches to Moral Dilemma

Margaret Grogan and Francie Smith

Superintendents of kindergarten through twelfth grade public schools must respond daily to a wide variety of issues, some of which can become serious moral dilemmas. By the time superintendents become involved, the situations are usually extremely complex and any course of action proposed is likely to have far-reaching consequences for members of the greater school community. What influences the identification and the resolution of those dilemmas? Is there *one right way? a bottom line?* a decision rule? Are there established practices in the field of educational administration that guide the superintendent?

This chapter draws on data gathered in the 1995 through 1996 school year in the initial stage of a study done with eleven women public school superintendents in two U.S. States (see Grogan and Smith, 1996). Sixty-minute interviews were conducted with each superintendent to learn about her approaches to resolving some of the moral dilemmas she faced in the course of her work. We discussed, from the feminist perspective, the moral dimension of leadership in the superintendency based on the lived experiences of those in the study. The first section of the chapter provides some information about the context of the study that is used to ground our comments. The second section discusses the feminist framework used to analyze the data, and the third and fourth sections illustrate the discussion by focusing on some actual experiences. The final section considers the relevance of a feminist moral perspective for the superintendency.

The study investigated the extent to which superintendents are influenced by the organizational imperative. Interview questions were designed to find out how superintendents defined dilemmas in their professional lives and what kinds of options they considered in resolving them. As researchers, we took a feminist approach to moral inquiry, relying on actual experience rather than on hypothetical prompts (Held 1993). Superintendents were asked whether they perceived any of the dilemmas they talked about to be moral or ethical ones or whether they thought of them as

* Originally published as Grogan and Smith, "A Feminist Perspective of Women Superintendents' Approaches to Moral Dilemmas." *Journal for a Just and Caring Education*, 4, 2, April 1998.

technical issues and therefore to be resolved merely by following district policy and procedures. The data centered on the various kinds of dilemmas faced by superintendents in the daily execution of their duties. While the study examined the broader question—the extent to which superintendents are influenced by organizational ethics, the portion of the study that is of most interest to us in this chapter is the discussion of what constitutes a moral dilemma for the superintendents and how they approached resolving such dilemmas.

It is important to understand the deliberate choices of superintendents as the group participating in the study. The focus on superintendents was influenced first by a belief that all human beings, no matter what their status or what position they hold, should be able consider their choices and actions from a moral and ethical perspective. Second, superintendents were chosen because a moral and ethical perspective is "especially important when individuals have power and influence over the lives of others" (Strike, Haller, and Soltis 1988, 6).

A Feminist Framework

To focus on certain aspects of the superintendency, a feminist framework was used. This framework is based on the feminist view that women and others similarly situated on the fringes of power have been less well served than the middle- to upper-class white male who traditionally has wielded the most power. A feminist approach motivates us to seek ways to disrupt the social structures that have reproduced the patterns of domination and subordination in our everyday lives. One way to do this is to conduct research that adds the previously unheard voices of women to the traditional conversation about what is "known" in any particular field. Since the superintendency in the United States has always been, and is still, overwhelmingly male,[1] it is imperative that the lived experiences of women in the superintendency be added to the picture. Thus, a feminist framework can be seen in the first instance to be a methodological one.

In the second instance, however, a feminist framework means that data from the study are analyzed from a feminist perspective, which, for the purposes of this chapter, is a feminist perspective of morality and ethics. Often suggested as alternatives to traditional moral theory, concepts of feminist morality are explored in a growing body of literature (Baier 1991; 1995; Belenky et al. 1986; Card 1991, 1995; Collins 1991; Hekman 1995; Held 1993, 1995; Jagger 1989; 1991; 1995; French 1985; Friedman 1991; 1995; Gilligan, 1982 / 1993; Gilligan, Ward, and Taylor 1988; Lyons 1990; Noddings 1984; Ruddick 1980; Tronto 1993; 1995; Walker 1995). While there is not always agreement about what "feminist morality" means, there are several underlying themes in this literature.

One thread is an ongoing discussion of an ethic of care. It is often argued that because women have traditionally been most responsible for child care and other service activities, many women's moral reasoning stems from a capacity or a duty to care. However, no claim is made that all women reason thus, nor that all men reason otherwise. Much of the current literature is inspired and sometimes provoked by the work of Carol Gilligan (1982, revised 1993). Although her initial work was limited by its attention to white, middle-class women, Gilligan argues that women's moral development is framed by the private sphere, which places an emphasis on creating and maintaining relationships as well as on connected knowledge. Her college student and abortion studies provide particularly rich examples to support this theory.

A focus on care also comes out of close attention to women's mothering experiences (Noddings 1984; Ruddick 1980). Noddings, for instance, writes of caring as a respect for "the welfare, protection or enhancement of the cared for" (1984, 23). Tronto argues that care is both a practice and a disposition. She believes that "we can recognize care when a practice is aimed at maintaining, continuing, or repairing the world" (1993, 104). However, many feminists, want to distance themselves both from the exclusive realm of mothering and from the subordinate connotations of valuing activities that have kept women oppressed (Card 1995). What seems to us to be most important in advocating an ethic of care is that it provides a foundation of respect upon which to build relationships, thus promoting a sense of interdependence. Care, as Beck defines it, is community. "Caring proceeds in the context of interdependent relationships in networks that might be labeled communities" (1994, 20). Still, care often has been disregarded in traditional moral theory precisely because it is associated with the private sphere and with the particular. Therefore, another point of discussion among feminist moral theorists is a call for the reconstruction of moral theory to include the moral voices of women and others who have been marginalized by traditional theories (Hekman 1995).

In contrast to the traditional moral theorists, many feminists "consider the realm of what has been misconstrued as the 'private,' as offering guidance to what human beings and their relationships should be like in regions beyond those of family and friendship" (Held 1993, 56). Because many women's moral reasoning is "contextual and narrative" (Gilligan, 1982 / 1993, 19), it is argued that such experience can offer not only substantive guidance to moral issues but also a methodological one as well. That is, by paying attention to how moral reasoning can be based on the concrete and local as well as on the abstract and "universal," we can better understand the complete realm of morality.

Another issue for many is that a moral orientation of care is often *contrasted* with a moral orientation of justice. Gilligan (1982 / 1993) saw the need to combine the two, but in situating care in women's experiences as different from men's experiences, she suggested opposition between the two orientations. There is certainly no such opposition reflected in the superintendents' comments in this particular study, nor would it be desirable (Held 1995; Starratt 1994). However, there is an argument for reasoning, informed by care, as generating actions that are morally preferable to those based solely on justice. This argument proceeds from the recognition that care prompts individuals to perceive particular situations directly. In other words, this orientation does not rely on universalizing principles or on abstractions. "This direct perception is said to facilitate action that is more context-sensitive than actions guided by moral rules that, because of their generality, are necessarily indeterminate" (Jagger 1995, 188).

For us, it is this last point that holds most promise for application to individuals in the superintendency. Despite the fact that superintendents of Kindergarten through twelfth grade schools must be fully aware of the larger social, political, and economic context of their "fiefdoms," their decision making must be grounded in the local. Far removed from the luxury of philosophical conjecture, superintendents' everyday experiences mire them in concrete struggles that by their very nature are shaped by contextual concerns. We develop this point in the final section. It is important beforehand, though, to look closely at what the women superintendents in the study had to say about their dilemmas.

The Substance of Superintendents' Dilemmas

The study found that even though the school budget and other financial concerns were mentioned by most of the participants, all superintendents indicated that among the most difficult situations for them to resolve were decisions involving staff and students. For instance, decisions of whether or not to recommend termination of employees, expulsion of students, school closings, and the like, formed the basis of most dilemmas. Though not always first on the list, termination and suspension of employees was mentioned by all the women as the situation that caused them most concern. In their own words, the superintendents rank the difficulties of their decisions, "A much more difficult decision was firing the food service director who was a personal friend of one of the board members. . . . Any effort to dismiss long-term employees is the hardest" (Gavinson[2]).

> The two areas that are the most difficult, of course, have to do with personnel, whether it's pupil personnel or actual employees. Number one would be to make the decision to expel a student . . . and the second one would be to fire

an employee and/or put the employee on leave without pay or probation. (Eliot).

Oh, we had a bus driver who assaulted someone in the neighborhood, and that person incurred five or six thousand dollars in medical bills. I mean it was a bad assault. And [the bus driver] was convicted of this assault. But we had issued her a contract because it hadn't been decided and we felt that she deserved the benefit of the doubt. . . . This is one of the hardest ones—you talk about difficult. (Brady)

Personnel is the first [on the list]. I'd say that's the area that causes the most denigration, the most pain. The ones I had to deal with. (Rose)

Almost equally difficult for these superintendents were decisions involving student-related matters. As Patricia Eliot suggests above, it was either first or second on their list for potential dilemmas. Others echoed this sentiment.

The second most difficult decisions I make are probably related to student discipline. When it gets to my level it is usually pretty bad. (Shaw)

The most recent decision, really a hard decision I had to make was what to do with two girls after school when no one came to pick them up. . . . I called numbers that they had told me not to call. (Merchant)

In our small high school we had a seventeen-year-old student who was driving an automobile that killed a lady in his neighborhood. Her son was his classmate at the small school. I was asked by members of the staff, and by a number of community members to not allow that young man to return to the school. But of course, he has not gone to trial . . . he has broken no school rules. (Peterson)

These comments notwithstanding, a few participants also described dilemmas in areas other than employee or student personnel. Situations revolving around the construction, provision, or demolition of facilities created dilemmas for Betty Talbot, Margaret Mansfeld, and Cara Gavinson, for example. Stephanie Rose also had difficult decisions to make regarding transportation and pay for extracurricular activities. Nevertheless, from the data, it is clear that the most common source of dilemmas are those conflicts that arise out of situations related to personnel. Bonnie Shaw argues that this is largely due to the complexity of such issues. She defines the different parties that she must consider. "Whenever I deal with difficult situations with people, reprimands, probation, dismissal, reduction-in-force, . . . I have a difficult time balancing what I know is right for the system, what I know is right for youngsters, and how this will impact the individual" (Shaw).

And although most of the participants sought "win-win" solutions to their dilemmas, they recognized that many times it was impossible. At least one of the many parties involved in the situation would not do as well from a decision as others would. For example, in the case of an employee suspended without pay, Patricia Eliot acknowledges, "He lost money. He lost his well-being." Similarly, the seventeen-year-old driver in Mabel Peterson's story would not be able to return to his high school to finish his schooling. "[We tried] to make it as much of a winning situation for him as possible. We did add something to the normal policy, to the normal home schooling, you know" (Peterson).

In another predicament, Catherine Brady talks of how to discipline two students who fight on the bus. When one is a regular student and one is a special education student, she points out that the latter is going to be better served than the former. "The nonspecial education student is kicked off the bus for three days, but the special education student is not." However, beyond the justice issue of treating similar students fairly, she identifies that the main source of her concern in such cases is that the special education student in the end, is not well served: "I think the law is messed up. I think the law has gone to such an extreme that we take away the sense of responsibility that a lot of special education kids need to make it in life. You know, by the time they get out of school they think anything they do is OK because the law protects them, and I think that is a tremendous disservice that the federal law has wrought" (Brady).

Yet another dimension is acknowledged by Betty Talbot in discussing the case of a bus driver who was fired for punching a student. She felt strongly that the bus driver was not as well served as the student because in her estimation, "The good guy lost in this case." She said, "He has been a good and loyal worker all these years and has done everything that I could ever have asked of him. But the law says you can't punch kids. We cannot keep somebody who does that to a kid, no matter how much the kid might deserve it" (Talbot).

Looking at these dilemmas from a feminist point of view, one source of conflict is certainly the strong sense of concern the superintendents had for each of the individuals in the cases. None of the superintendents talks of the individuals involved in the situations dispassionately. It is very suggestive of what Patricia Hill Collins (1991) calls "talking with the heart" (1991, 215). In Collins's definition of the ethic of care, personal expressiveness and emotion are fundamental elements. These elements also emerged in the discussions about the various courses of action the superintendents identified as ways to solve the dilemmas.

Options and Actions

Not surprisingly, the superintendents summarized their options as child centered. They stated repeatedly that the children they serve were at the very core of every consideration. Whenever the dilemma pitted children's concerns against adult ones, there was no doubt in the participants' minds as to where their priorities lay. According to the participants, most of their options were dictated by a strong sense of student priority. But this perspective is not one that simply places a disembodied notion of "children" in the foreground. It is a very particular one.

For instance, in Samantha Merchant's dilemma mentioned earlier, what should she do for two girls who were still at school when she was about to leave at five o'clock? The difficulty was compounded by stresses in the children's family and the fact that the mother did not have a telephone. Additionally, the mother had requested that her family, the children's grandparents, not be called even in an emergency. Caught up in the tensions between justice and care, Merchant considered her options: leave the children at the school, call the county sheriff, call the grandparents, call the Department of Human Services (DHS), or send them home with another district employee. Choosing the last option, she went home and then made some phone calls.

> One of the people who I called got the mother, went and picked her up, and she came here and it was a rather hysterical moment because she thought something had happened to her children. . . . That was a situation where I did a lot of talking, counseling . . . with the mother and . . . her brother. . . . [I did not call DHS] because I had not had too much contact with DHS about this family. . . . I hesitated to do it. But I did go the next day because again what's best for the children. (Merchant)

In one of her dilemmas, Catherine Brady maintains that her options were fundamentally dictated by a concern for the welfare of the students. Recently, she had to deal with a situation created when a convict escaped from the local maximum security prison. "This was a bad person, you know, eight life sentences." Very quickly Brady became aware that she could either close the schools or keep them open. "We could have closed the schools, which would have been the easy thing, but then in my mind I thought that will put all those kids at home, and that convict is out there, and what if one of these kids is home and he is in the house. You know. And so I felt that my responsibility was a larger responsibility than just the schools. I felt that it had to do with kids' safety" (Brady).

Describing it as "a larger responsibility," Brady's course of action was really dictated by a very localized concern for the children in her district who faced an immediate threat. "We chose the option of having school but having some special safety precautions here at school. . . . It was so out of the norm, and you don't know how people are going to react, and I had to say to myself, I'm going to do what I think is right. The heck with what people think" (Brady).

Mabel Peterson, too, grounds her decision of what to do about a coach firmly in her perceptions of what is best for children. "On the coaching incident we had three [options]. We could have probation, which I guess in effect is what we did. We could have terminated, or we could have said, 'sorry, we're going to keep him forever; we don't think you have any valid concerns'" (Peterson). She talks of how she considers all the parties involved but acknowledges that the students' interests are uppermost in her mind: "In the case of the employee are we being fair to the employee who has a career invested in this job? As well as a livelihood and all that. And yet again trying to remember that all of us—it sounds so trite when you put it into words—but [I] try to make that more than just a trite expression, [we're] here to serve children" (Peterson).

Situations become especially hard when the course of action involves choosing between different groups of students. Ann Boyd considers a difficult decision the district had to make over whether to hire an extra teacher for the first grade or serve the growing numbers in that grade with two teacher assistants. She expresses her dismay at having to choose among first graders, sixth graders, and high school students: "I had a tough time saying, 'Well if we hire a teacher there, I know we can't afford to hire a teacher everywhere.' Are our first graders worth more than our sixth graders? . . . [And] there have been some instructional needs at the high school. . . . We have not been able to purchase materials because of this" (Boyd).

In another scenario, Betty Talbot's ability to localize a situation prompted a course of action that was very difficult. When she recognized that the children were at actual physical risk, she gained the necessary impetus to reorganize the district. Unfortunately, she had little community support for change. When she arrived at the district, she took stock of a situation in dire need of attention.

> Our schools were nearing one hundred years old. They were decaying around the children, and there was no interest in replacing them, since the general notion was that either they were good enough fifty years ago and they still would be good for another fifty years, or they only serve a population that is going nowhere anyway, so why bother educating them. I came with the expectation by the school board that I would build schools. I had their support from the beginning on that. But, when I looked around and I saw the shocking abuse, it was something I had never seen before and hope to never see again. I

spent a year attempting to get people to realize the problem, until I was called to one of the schools to discover that twenty minutes before the children arrived the ceiling had fallen down on the desks. When I looked at the rubble all over the room and realized that children could have been under it, I came right back to my office and called the State Department of Education and asked for their help. (Talbot)

Faced with community indifference and outright opposition from powerful figures both inside the district and outside, Talbot had to test the extent of her convictions. Ultimately, in partnership with the State Department of Education, the State Board of Education, the governor's office, the Secretary of Education, to some degree the general assembly, and the school board, she closed five elementary schools and replaced them with two new ones. She doubled the size of the middle school and refurbished the high school. In the process, Talbot made the decision to eliminate fifty-two positions. New to the state and the region, she did not feel she had the same options an insider might have had.

The options that were available to me were less than they were to other people. The options for most people here would have been to have done things the [traditional] way, which is [in] a nice quiet back room—let's talk together kind of thing. I know you, you know me, I know your family, I know your ancestors, so therefore we can come to an agreement. Men do that. I didn't have entree to the back room. There wasn't any opening for me to have any kind of discussion with anybody. Those options were not available to me, and I realized that after a year. So I called in the media, and I primed the media, and we did a TV/media/newspaper blitz. In four months the job was done. (Talbot)

Talbot acknowledges outright that as a woman superintendent she did not have all the options available to others. Approaching the situation in the traditional way frustrated her. While it is possible that another approach may have yielded the same result in the end, Talbot's energy to mobilize key resources stemmed from her vivid visualization of the potential fate of those elementary children under the rubble.

From a feminist moral perspective, one cannot help but notice that many of the superintendents situate their reasoning in the "local, contextual and concrete" (Hekman 1995, 160). Catherine Brady and Bonnie Shaw both provide further excellent examples of perceiving particular situations directly. In the first instance, their reasoning is based on considering what they would want for their own children.

I decide what is right based upon having a nine year old myself—what I would want someone to do to protect her. You know, if there is a teacher in the classroom I don't think should be there, I say to myself if [my daughter] was in that classroom, how would I feel. And I don't think anybody deserves less than I would have for her. And it makes the job more difficult because you think so much, you think so deeply about things. (Brady)

If this were my child . . . I would not want the severity of the punishment to be what it was. I would want counseling. I would want, well, I would want for my child what every parent wants for their child. (Shaw)

Clearly, Shaw and Brady like other superintendents in the study respond from an empathetic position, from a position that considers what it is like for the other. From the point of view of feminist morality, this response is described as morally desirable because it emphasizes that others are "actual others in a particular case at hand, and not repeatable instances or replacement occupants of a general status" (Walker 1995, 142).

We got $6 million to renovate that building, and it is a beautiful building today. They gutted the inside and fixed that building—because I said to myself, what kind of learning can take place in a building where the paint is peeling off the walls? It used to be a primary building, and so all the boards were like down here and the kids were up here. It smelled. The heat didn't work half the time. And I just couldn't tolerate it. (Brady)

We have gotten into some weapons decisions with very young children. A second grader who brought a knife, and of course state and federal policy now is very clear about dangerous weapons in that we're supposed to recommend a 360-day expulsion from school and yet with an eight-year-old kid who obviously did not take the knife to school for any reason other than he had it in his book bag because he was fighting imaginary dragons out in the backyard and then got afraid to try to get it back in the house. And so took it on to school and it was discovered. So, you know, age of the student, all those kinds of things. (Peterson)

In talking of what makes many decisions so difficult, Stephanie Rose mentions pain, again echoing Collins's (1991) notion of legitimate feeling. Rose argues that the pain is caused by her "recognition that they're human beings and they're going to hurt from some of those decisions. . . . It's going to impact them personally, economically, mentally." Like the superintendents above, she puts herself in the shoes of those with whom she has to deal. She says, "I have had some experience base to the point that I know what it feels like to lose a job, to have a family that is unemployed, to have a sense of no control, a sense of futility at times." In a similar frame of mind, Patricia Eliot chooses a course of action that is modified by a keen sense of how her employee would feel. Despite her abhorrence of his wrongdoing, she found a way for him to take early retirement: "I think that I was able to uphold my principles, but not in a harsh way with him. I could simply have fired him. I had the justification. I could have fired him, nothing said. But I didn't approach it in that manner. I tried to give him some dignity even though he had been wrong for a number of years. I tried to let him keep his dignity in the situation. . . . I didn't want to destroy him in the community, with the people that he had known for years and years" (Eliot).

Overall, many of the superintendents' responses were guided by this sense of care and empathy. The ability to understand the position of the other is clearly demonstrated in these examples, and a sense of relationship pertaining to the interdependence of all the members of the organization is present. When we take the whole picture into account, it is clear that an ethic of care is one of many principles these superintendents used to guide their thinking. It appears to be an important feature of their reasoning, but is certainly neither the only, nor, at times, the dominant, moral orientation. Many of the discussions also are shaped by a recognition of what is just. In an interesting comment about firing employees, Catherine Brady, for instance, distinguishes her reasoning in two different cases in this way:

> In one case I had a custodian that was drunk all the time, and I had to tell him that he wasn't going to have a job anymore. He basically had missed work and not called in sick, and I said, "Why didn't you call in sick?" I looked for every answer that could be a possible excuse, but when he looked at me and said, "Because I didn't feel like it," I said, "Well, then, you can't work here anymore." And I knew that it was taking away his livelihood. But, he had had this history of drinking and not doing what he was supposed to do. (Brady)

There is little doubt in Brady's mind that her action is just and fair both because the custodian had brought it upon himself and because employees as a general category must come to work and do what they are supposed to do. In the next case, though, Brady's reasoning takes a different turn.

> Another situation, I had a teacher, one time that was an LD teacher and I found out that he had showed an R rated movie to his LD class. I called him in, and I said, "Why did you do this?" "Didn't you know this was not a movie for special education kids to see or any kids to see?" And he said, "Well, I was so busy passing out the popcorn that I didn't notice." I said, "You go home, and you never come back in." And I knew that I could have faced all kinds of lawsuits on that, but it was such an irresponsible thing to do and one that had the potential of hurting children. and I really felt strongly about that one because I felt that the children that he had in the class were children whose parents would be the least likely to even know the difference or complain—

they would be intimidated by the system. Any system. And so they could very easily become victims if somebody wasn't looking out for them. That's why I felt so strongly. So those two decisions were hard. The first one not so much as the second one. They were both easy in terms of thinking of the welfare of the children, but not easy in terms of taking somebody's job away. (Brady)

Here, the issue for Brady crystallizes around the realization that the children in this particular case "could very easily become victims if somebody wasn't looking out for them." This suggests that she might not have fired the teacher if he had shown the same lack of judgment in a different situation, with a different set of students.

In summary, as the superintendents relate their experiences of resolving moral dilemmas in the course of their work, we are provided with a clear picture of thoughtful, seasoned educational administrators. Both the substance of the dilemmas and the way they were considered are indicative of the tensions and pressures of the contemporary superintendency. There was no suggestion that the issues identified as most troubling could be resolved only by attention to policy. To be sure, all participants expressed a healthy respect for following policy, but most of the dilemmas they identified fell outside the strict boundaries of administrative guidelines. Thus, the stories reveal other ways of reasoning. Most evident is the reliance on localized knowledge of the particular people involved in the incidents, on the capacity to imagine the other's situation based on prior personal experience and on the ethic of care, guiding choices of action.

Conclusions

So what does this exploration of women superintendents' moral dilemmas offer? To recall one of the basic tenets of the feminist project: it has provided us, first of all, with concrete examples of superintendents' moral experiences. Held defines moral experience as "the experience of consciously choosing to act, or to refrain from acting, on grounds by which we are trying conscientiously to be guided" (1995, 154). She argues that a feminist view of experience emphasizes the narrative account of what actually occurred in real situations. "It is experience as subjectively engaged in, not as studied by a scientific observer" (154). Therefore, these stories contribute to a better understanding of the context of moral choices to be made by superintendents as a group.

However, it is also important to ground our conclusions in the lived moral experiences of women superintendents for two other reasons: (1) to balance the research that suggests that male superintendents' experiences are synonymous with superintendents' experiences in general, and (2) to make available to all superintendents and potential superintendents such approaches to the superintendency that are offered by women superintendents who have been immersed in moral traditions that consciously or unconsciously have been shaped by the private sphere. The latter is consistent with another aspect of the feminist project—a restructuring of moral theory to include the multiple moral voices of those silenced by the traditional account of morality. Talking of this reconstructive effort, Hekman defends it as worthwhile so that we can "comprehend moral action in the contemporary world" (1995, 160). She asserts a poststructural or postmodern claim that "moral voices vary with race, class and gender even within a particular social situation" (160).

We argue that what most distinguishes the voices of the women in the study is their care or concern for the individuals who are at the center of any dilemma. It follows then that we believe that approaches to moral dilemmas that draw on an ethic of care or as Jagger (1995), phrases it "care thinking" must be accorded the same respect as those which draw on other principles such as justice, honesty, or equity. We do not argue that we can view the superintendency as a "private sphere." On the contrary, few are as aware of their public responsibilities as the women superintendents in the study. This does not mean that lessons learned in the private sphere cannot be very instructive in the public. It is significant that the women superintendents in the study refused to retreat to the abstract when explaining their reasoning. These are highly educated women, many with doctorates, who are very capable in the best Western moral traditions, of analyzing their thoughts along such lines. But they do not do it. Instead, they situate all of their decisions in the particular and recall all of the human details that prompted them to act or not to act in each case. As suggested earlier, this is promising because it suggests that a superintendent does not have to divorce herself from the kind of thinking she might use privately. These women's moral knowledge is informed by their feelings as well as by their thinking. Their capacity for empathy is derived from the connectedness that shapes most of their human relationships.

Patricia Hill Collins makes the important point that although "white women may have access to a women's tradition valuing emotion and expressiveness, few Eurocentric institutions except the family validate this way of knowing" (1991, 217). We would agree and would go further to say that women who wish to be successful within the discourses that have encouraged androcentric thought and practices, such as educational administration, have been forced to abandon care-thinking as inappropriate in that environment. However, the women's voices reported here suggest that an ethic of care is alive and well and that it underlies the resolution of many moral dilemmas faced by a superintendent. Indeed, in the absence of male superintendents' voices to the contrary, it is also perfectly possible that all superintendents reason thus. This would be particularly encouraging because it would allow us to associate the superintendency with a much more human, interpersonal image than we have in the past.

Finally, we suggest further scrutiny. We believe that an ethic of care, derived from the attention to the particular that characterizes much of the discussion reported, needs to be understood more fully. While it is beyond the parameters of this chapter, we would not like to leave the impression, here, that all action motivated by a concern for the other is necessarily in the best interests of the other.

As alluded to earlier, one important caution identified by many feminist moral theorists is that of the patriarchal dimension of care. As authors of this chapter, we advocate care as a desirable principle upon which to base decisions. We argue that it is one that complements and enhances a justice orientation (see also Starratt 1994). But we are aware that, most particularly in the private sphere, care is often associated with unequal relationships, say between father and son, parent and small child. Therefore, when talking of the superintendency, a position that for so long has been held almost exclusively by men, we are wary of reinforcing any image that echoes domination. Instead, we believe that care is predicated on respect for the other and on a humility that makes no assumptions about what it is truly like to be the other. As Noddings (1984) points out, our knowledge of caring is rooted in our good memories of being cared for as children. If that is so, as adults we will most likely associate care with support and opportunities for growth. The challenge seems to be how to tailor our actions to allow for others to experience care as positively as we remember it.

Notes

1. Glass's (1992) nationwide figures show 6.6 percent of superintendents are women, and Montenegro (1993) reports about 7.1 percent of U.S. superintendents are women.

2. In line with accepted procedures in reporting qualitative research, all names have been fictionalized and some of the details changed to protect the identity of the participants, although the integrity of the situation has been retained.

References

Baier, A. 1991. Whom can women trust? In *Feminist ethics*, ed. C. Card, 233–45. Lawrence: University Press of Kansas.

———. 1995. The need for more than justice. In *Justice and care*, ed. V. Held, 47–60. New York: Teachers College Press.

Beck, L. 1994. *Reclaiming educational administration as a caring profession.* New York: Teachers College Press.

Belenky, M., Clinchy, B., Goldberger, N., and Tarule, J. 1986. *Women's ways of knowing: The development of self, voice and mind.* New York: Basic Books Inc.

Card, C.1991. The feistiness of feminism. In *Feminist ethics,* ed. C. Card, 3–31. Lawrence: University Press of Kansas.

———. 1995. Gender and moral luck. In *Justice and care,* ed. V. Held, 79–100. New York: Teachers College Press.

Collins, P. 1991. *Black feminist thought.* New York: Routledge.

French, M. 1985. *Beyond power: On women, men and morals.* New York: Summit Books.

Friedman, M. 1991. The social self and the partiality debates. In *Feminist ethics,* ed. C. Card, 161–79. Lawrence: University Press of Kansas.

———. 1995. Beyond caring: The de-moralization of gender. In *Justice and care,* ed. V. Held, 61–78. New York: Teachers College Press

Gilligan, C. 1982/1993. *In a different voice,* new ed. Cambridge, MA: Harvard University Press.

Gilligan, C., Ward, J., and Taylor, J., eds. 1988. *Mapping the moral domain.* Cambridge, MA: Harvard University Press.

Glass, T. 1992. *The 1992 study of the American school superintendency.* Arlington, VA: American Association of School Administrators.

Grogan, M., and Smith, F. April, 1996. Exploring the perceptions of superintendents: Moral choices or procedural alternatives. Paper presented at the Annual Meeting of the American Educational Research Association, New York.

Hekman, S. 1995. *Moral voices, moral selves.* University Park: The Pennsylvania State University Press.

Held, V. 1993. *Feminist morality: Transforming culture, society, and politics.* Chicago: The University of Chicago Press.

Held, V., ed. 1995. *Justice and care.* Boulder CO: Westview Press.

Jagger, A. 1989. Feminist ethics: Some issues for the nineties. *Journal of Social Philosophy* 20: 91–107.

———. 1991. Feminist ethics: Projects, problems, prospects. In *Feminist ethics,* ed. C. Card, 78–104. Lawrence: University Press of Kansas.

———. 1995. Caring as a feminist practice of moral reason. In *Justice and care,* ed. V. Held, 179–202. New York: Teachers College Press.

Lyons, N. 1990. Visions and competencies: An educational agenda for exploring ethical and intellectual dimensions of decision and conflict negotiation. In *Changing education: Women as radicals and conservators,* ed. J. Antler and S. Biklen, 277–94. Albany: State University of New York Press.

Montenegro, X. 1993. *Women and racial minority representation in school administration.* Arlington, VA.: American Association of School Administrators.

Noddings, N. 1984. *Caring: A feminine approach to ethics and moral education.* Berkeley: University of California Press.

Ruddick, S. 1980. Maternal thinking. *Feminist Studies* 6: 342–67.

Starratt, R. 1994. *Building an ethical school.* Washington DC: Falmer Press.

Strike, K., Haller, E., and Soltis, J. 1988. *The ethics of educational administration.* New York: Teachers College Press.

Tronto, J. 1993. *Moral boundaries: A political argument for an ethic of care.* New York: Routledge.

———. 1995. Women and caring: What can feminists learn about morality from caring? In *Justice and care,* ed. V. Held, 101–16. New York: Teachers College Press.

Walker, M. 1995. Moral understandings: Alternative "epistemology" for a feminist ethics. In *Justice and care,* ed. V. Held, 139–52. New York: Teachers College Press.

CHAPTER FIFTEEN

The Canadian Superintendency:
Value-Based Challenges and Pressures

Keith Walker and Don Shakotko

He is a little man in a long green coat and a cocked hat, standing with one leg on a steep roof, playing the fiddle. He is all of us, trying to make some meaningful music out of our lives but lacking a level place on which to stand. "We are all fiddlers on the roof, trying to scratch out a pleasant little tune without falling down and breaking our necks. And how do we keep our balance? I'll tell you," sings Tevye in the opening song of the musical inspired by Chagall's painting, "in one word, I'll tell you, tradition! Because of our tradition, everybody knows who he is and what God expects him to do" (Smedes 1983, 1).

Tevye's song foreshadows a lament that tradition once provided the sense-making grounds for the delicate work of balancing life. The nineteenth-century Russian Jews in the community depicted in *Fiddler on the Roof*, had, for generations, grounded their lives on the values rooted in their theistic beliefs and religious rituals. Tevye was confronted with contesting values that challenged his fatherly duties and pressed against his decision making. Yes, he is all of us, but we want to suggest that he is especially the school system administrator. This contemporary public figure faces extreme value demands both from within school communities and beyond. School system leaders appreciate that it is exceedingly difficult to form consensus around what ought to constitute the driving values of their organizations and what should be the "grounds" or rationalities for their deliberate action. Fairholm said, "Leadership in this cultural environment is difficult at best, impossible at worst . . . there is little hope that acceptance of multiple and diverse internally competing values systems will produce stable, effective, responsive economic, social, or governmental organizations" (1994, 1). The sloped roof of an administrator's work is a given. In this chapter we consider the place of value-based pressures in the work of Canadian school superintendents, who, like the fiddler, work hard to play their "educational songs" and make a way for others to do the same. Put another way, we have brought some description to the nature of the sloped roof: the downward gravitational pulls, the unevenness, and the gusts of wind that superintendents say they experience in their work as ethical leaders and value mediators. These are expressed through the influences and forces at different cultural, subcultural, organizational, group, and individual levels (Hodgkinson 1991; 1983).

As Holmes has indicated "the beliefs and values of senior administrators have not been a major focus of educational research" (1991, 155). The field of educational administration has only rarely researched the ethical challenges and pressures of system-level educational leaders. In the last two decades many educational administration scholars have addressed the topic of ethics. Most of these efforts have been oriented to normative ethical analyses (e.g., Beck 1994; Starratt 1994; 1991; Sergiovanni 1994; 1992; 1990; Strike, Haller and Soltis 1988; and Kimbrough 1985) or meta-ethical analyses (e.g., Beck and Murphy 1994; Hodgkinson 1991; 1983; 1978; Evers 1987; and Rizvi 1985). Leithwood has suggested that researchers have focused on leader practices in relation to goals, culture, and roles, but much less attention has been given to the leaders' organizational processes, attitudes, values, and beliefs. "Obviously," he says, "what leaders do, the roles they practice, is a function of how they feel and think. It makes sense, then, that future research . . . ought to devote more energy to understanding the attitudes, values, beliefs, traits and dispositions of leaders" (1992, 179).

The longtime dean of values and valuation in school organizations, Donald Willower has said that school administrators typically deal with value problems on a daily basis. However, the bulk of the discussion and debate in the literature of educational administration appears to be irrelevant to the ongoing efforts of practitioners seeking to do the right thing. Much of what professors interested in values write about is highly abstract and often involves pregiven programs or solutions. In the end, ethical problems are concrete, touching the lives of real individuals in real social and organizational settings (1994, 482).

The obvious point of departure from these comments would suggest a need for a description of the concrete world of ethical challenges and pressures, as experienced by educational leaders. To use Duke's (in this volume) metaphor: one can understand leadership in the same way one can watch a parade. You can watch up close to "appreciate the movement, sounds and expressions of individual marchers" or stand back further to get a "panoramic perspective." We hope these descriptions provide some insight into "the day-to-day business of leading" expressed by Canadian school superintendents—a close-up view. We provide a preliminary perspective on the value-based challenges and pressures that actually touch superintendents and move more abstract discussions of values to the day-to-day kind of descriptions. Toffler (1986), Bird and Waters (1987), Jackall (1988), and others have led the way in seeking to develop firsthand descriptive reports of the nature of ethical decision making among administrators rather than asking them to measure up to a priori ethical templates.

In this case, the normative challenges of school superintendents were determined through the use of forced-choice descriptions, open-ended questions, and semistructured interviews. The guiding question was—What are the ethical challenges and pressures that impinge on the work of super-intendents of education? A survey entitled "Ethics and the Canadian School Superintendency" was sent to a random sample of eight hundred Canadian superintendents to solicit information concerning these aspects of their ethical decision-making in the late spring of 1995. The twenty most impor-tant value-based pressures facing those leaders responding to our survey were as follows (in order of importance):

1. provincial/state-level financ-ing of schools;
2. declining provincial/state government support;
3. accountability;
4. system-level financing of schools;
5. parent involvement in educa-tional decision making;
6. parent participation in edu-cational processes;
7. administrative/board relations;
8. personal time management;
9. strategic planning;
10. caliber of board members;
11. special education/main-streaming;
12. site-based management;
13. new teaching demands;
14. staff recruiting and selection;
15. changing priorities in curriculum;
16. community involvement;
17. staff and administrator evaluation
18. deterioration of the family;
19. assessment and testing; and
20. teacher empowerment.

In the winter of 1996 a cross-Canada set of interviews was conducted with superintendents of education. In Canada, superintendents (or "direc-tors of education" as they are called in two provinces) are typically locally employed chief educational officers. Here we offer a brief overview of those who participated in this study. Fifty-two superintendents agreed to be inter-viewed in their own offices in all but one province (Newfoundland) and the two territories. The last of these were interviewed in the spring of 1996. These CEO's were responsible for delivery of educational services in a range of school jurisdictions (from the largest to some of the smallest—in terms of number of students and staff). Some superintendents were in large urban centers, others were in rural centers, and still others were in remote parts of Canada. With respect to the survey, three-quarters of the 197 respondents held the senior-most professional position in their organization and the majority (74 percent) were between forty-six and fifty-five years of age. Ninety percent held Masters degrees and/or doctorates, and 87 percent percent were males. In terms of differences, half described their work set-tings as rural or small town based, with others evenly representing those in both "moderate-sized city" and "large-city" school systems. Half the respon-dents had twenty or fewer schools in their system, and just under 20 percent had more than fifty schools to superintend. Three-quarters worked in public (typically nonsectarian or secular) school systems, and another one-fifth worked in Catholic school systems. Half were from the western provinces, and two-fifths were from Ontario and Quebec. We noted that almost two-thirds of respondents had been superintendents for fewer than ten years. The findings described here focus on the common, rather than diverse, experiences and perceptions of leaders.

Our analysis of challenges and pressures on the work of educational leaders is reported under six categories: economic pressures, conflicting interest pressures, political dynamics, organizational pressures, ethical constraints, and personal pressures. The arbitrary categorization of pressures and challenges should not be understood to suggest that pressures are distinct and unrelated. On the contrary, the pressures and challenges were typically over-lapping, ill-defined, and complex. However, without question the most common pressures and challenges described by CEOs were related to economic pressures.

Economic Pressures and Challenges

While economic conditions, priorities, and the ultimate supply of resources were most often beyond the direct control of these leaders, they were forced to consider it an increasingly important professional function "to utilize all the resources" at their disposal and to effectively and ethically cope with the consequences of ever-shrinking finances. One leader, for example, said the "economic squeeze is going to force people into some very difficult decisions" and "There is nothing that really causes angst or conflict within me, but if there is anything it would be related to economics." Another leader speculated that in "the 1990s our work is more money-oriented. . . . I am Scrooge where I don't want to be."

One leader said, "I firmly believe that if we continue to go the way we are going, the system will become bankrupt—it will be crushed under its own weight. The costs are exponential . . . as long as the teacher keeps getting 4 percent a year as in the last one hundred [years] we are broke and no society will be able to sustain this kind of an institution. We are the inheritors of an overly ambitious social experiment."

Another leader thoughtfully reflected, "I am concerned about the future, and I had one of the more difficult winters, so far as choices and options for damage control, that I have ever had. There is a shift of emphasis for me from development and moving forward to an improved defense mode that believes that right now we will suffer inevitable damage and the decisions made will be decisions to minimize the damage rather than think that something good will happen. That's my mental environment these days." The strain of these economic pressures was evident in many interview conversations. For example, "We are into some very, very difficult times, that is for sure. I mean hopefully we will be able to maintain an ethical approach when dealing with school closures and dismissals, but they are going to be strained—we are all going to be strained. When we look at having to close schools in the future, and it seems to me that is going to be fairly likely . . . for economic reasons, not for kids, not for programming, not for what is good for communities but for purely economic reasons. Its pretty tough sometimes to be ethical under those circumstances."

Economic pressures were described by some leaders as increasing the odds for poor decisions because of fewer options, forcing more unilateral kinds of decisions and, literally, over-taxing the good will of rate payers. They attributed the need to take more personal and professional risks and to spend more energy fighting for money to provide services. One said, "When you are short of resources there is a political program . . . people like me need to fight to preserve some of the educational programs by crossing over into the political area, and we do so at some personal risk. I have alienated or threatened trustees more this winter than I have in a long time—it has been a calculated risk, but I believed it was necessary."

Educational leaders reported encountering a multitude of problems, illustrated by the following questions:

"Should we close the school for economic reasons?"

"Should we bow to the political pressure to save the town by keeping the school open?"

"Should we close the school and give the kids a real education—how can you get a kindergarten education with just two students in the class?"

"Do we close a relatively new development center because funding such a limited number of students is difficult to defend in times of economic crunch?"

"Should we be eliminating programs like industrial arts, home economics, and maybe band because of their high cost?"

"Is it right for us to have a band program when we know that only the well-off families can afford to rent the instruments?"

"Who should be declared redundant? What decision-making process should be used? How open can the process be?"

"How can we go on reducing the budget through cost-cutting measures, including teacher cuts, while trying to maintain soundness of educational program?" and

"Do you make staff cuts right across the system, or do you avoid cuts in the areas that can afford them the least?"

The obvious shortage of funds from "reluctant-to-pay-more-taxes" local people and the off-loading provincial governments (hoping to reduce state debt) had caused many leaders to begin investigating alternative sources of funds. Related to this relatively new or renewed thinking about fund raising were a myriad of questions and concerns such as, "Do we get into corporate or alternate funding plans . . . if so, to what extent and what are the down sides to this?" "To what extent do we need to avoid commercialism?" and "Do we hire a staff person to look after fund-raising for us?" How "in times of scarce resources do you decide between allocations of human and financial resources to the academic needs of pupils and/or their personal, social, and cultural needs?" "How do we, as school leaders, do our part to deal with the poverty cycle?" and "How are we to juggle the different sensitivities and priorities when the social support networks are not being picked up by other agencies?" The economic needs of their jurisdictions were very evident as agenda items and influences in the work of CEOs, but the increased demand for their attention to such factors was commonly perceived to be at odds with conventional notions of schools. Economic pressures were often expressed as conflicts of interests.

Conflicting Interests Pressures and Challenges

A related set of pressures and challenges identified by district leaders were the commonly expressed difficulties connected with stewardship of the public trust. Many interviewees described their work as mediating value conflicts. The leaders felt they were responsible for transforming educational aspirations into realities for some mutually exclusive public interests. The leaders described the pressures they had experienced as people in their constituency demanded more for their money from the education system. An associated pressure impinging on leaders was identified as the service-orientation of public education. This view, that students and parents are to be considered as clients, provided a great deal of pressure on leaders.

Leaders also referred to the challenges and dynamics that occur with parents. One leader said, "Some parents will find it comfortable complaining to me about a teacher but be unwilling to talk directly with the teacher. . . . They won't go to the teacher, but they will go everywhere else in the world and tell people about the problem."

Another administrator reported on his ambition for parental participation together with the pros and cons inherent in this initiative. He said, "We want to allow parents to express themselves more fully in the schools. This will bring on more direct, and daily, dealings and involvement with administration. [But] once you start paying more directly for something—you start wanting to have more say into what's going on. That can be good, and that can be bad. This is going to bring out where the trust level is and enhance trust between the educators, home and the school, or it is not."

Perhaps one of the most emotional and energy-draining kinds of problems experienced by leaders were those relating to the appropriate distribution of goods and services to students. Leaders felt it was their responsibility to ensure the provision of resources and services to all who are entitled. The superintendent often assumed the position of arbitrator of these goods and, in some cases, corrector of past inequities. In this area of challenge, the CEOs sought to mediate demands on limited resources. This genre of value pressures encountered by CEOs was also expressed by questions such as the following: How do we establish an approach wherein there is an "equality of benefit for kids and a fairness of working conditions for teachers?" How am I to "handle the political pressures I get from high socio-economic areas [in my system] for special treatment?" and "Our community has two areas which are characterized by their socio-economic levels. Over the years, favoring one side of the community over the other has amounted to a subtle but severe form of racism. How do I avoid this?"

The leaders also expressed a feeling of stress with respect to the expectations placed on the leader as a mediator between superordinate (the board of education) and subordinates (principals and teachers). This middle person position provided its own set of decisions on the leaders. They said, "The stress, the expectations from all quarters place expectations on me that I know what the needs are. As the one who has the most contact with the board—[the principals] expect me to reflect their reality. On the other hand, the superintendent needs to reflect the board's tacit and official values."

Another major set of value pressures concerned employee and employer welfare issues. Some of the respondents and interviewees expressed the sense that they had been dealing with much more complicated and more frequent incidences of employee-related problems than they had five or ten years earlier. These problems related both to employee benefit abuse and hard evaluation questions. The following questions illustrate the everyday mediatory pressures facing CEOs in this connection:

"How should we decide on requests for sick leaves when there is little evidence of illness?"

"Another gray area is with larger benefits such as sick leaves, mutual terminations, and severance. You used to get one of these every five years, now it's every two or three months."

"We have teachers who want to superannuate in December [of this year]. This will result in their being able to maximize their pension. It is good for them but provides a problem for our system. . . . I either [find] suitable replacements for those who superannuate or will have to let the superannuates continue to teach and draw both salary and their pension. Do I recommend the dismissal of a younger teacher who is in need of work to accommodate double-dipping on the part of a senior retiring staff? How will this be perceived by the public, and what decision is in the best interests of our system?"

One CEO said, "While all decisions made by CEOs can be considered difficult and have ethical overtones, the most difficult are those associated with the dismissal of tenured staff after their classroom effectiveness has diminished and they are no longer perceived as contributing to education."

Later in the chapter, we will describe some personal pressures, but organizational conflicts of interest often took the form of personal pressure as well. This was exemplified by one administrator who defined values mediation as "doing an unpleasant duty well and professionally, in spite of personal feelings." He recalled trying to reverse his Board's decision to lay off a particular staff person, but having failed to convince them of his perspective felt that he owed them his loyalty despite his contrary personal beliefs. He reasoned that they had erred to the serious detriment of a staff person. At the time, he held that he must carry out the board's decision and that he should do so in a manner that completely expressed their wishes. He indicated to the interviewer that this incident had given him occasion to seriously assess the ethics of the board members and his own future with the school system. Upon reflection, he felt that he had made a poor decision and that he should have threatened his resignation to encourage their reconsideration.

A range of value questions related to the evaluation of employees such as sexual orientation and gender issues, equity-plan adoption, and consideration of the ethical impact of personnel decisions on students, staff, and their families were sobering sets of concerns with few secure responses in hand. Several examples will suffice to illustrate the pressures accompanying these value quandaries: How do you "balance the need that teachers have for independence and the need to hold them accountable?" and "I am still wrestling with whether or not to develop an education equity plan for the school system . . . more specifically, I wonder whether or not I should develop hiring targets?" and What do we do about "gender equity in our school system?"

The leaders' professional obligations to ensure that the greatest bene-fits of the education enterprise were directed to the students were ex-pressed in certain terms by most of the leaders. The rights of students and the rights of others had to be upheld. These worries were attended by many value problematics, as illustrated by the following: "When dealing with stu-dent suspensions and expulsions from school, how should I integrate the student and parent rights with the needs for social interest and social order in the school?" Sometimes we are confronted with "situations where I have to weight the rights of the group versus the rights of an individual. I am still not sure—how do you work this through?"

There were more specific "laws of mediation" formulated by the CEOs that related to the concepts of a mandated duty or public trust, which required more of an educational leader than mere legal compliance. These notions were generally centered around the leader's responsibility to be child-focused in their professional attentions. It was common for CEOs to see themselves as the guardians of the educative mandate and to view other professionals as "ethical failures" when this mandate was ignored or poorly carried out. One interviewee said, "Anytime one's own private behavior impinges negatively on the welfare of children then the person should be responsible enough to censure themselves." In such instances, to fail eth-ically had two aspects: getting into the position of not being able to do work for kids properly and, second, to fail to recognize and correct the disadvan-tageous situations for children and youth.

Further sources of pressure that were said to challenge educational leaders' work were identified as "high-need dumpings" and special inter-ests. To elaborate on the so-called high need dumping phenomenon, the leaders said that increasing social needs and accelerated institutional divest ment were the major sources of school systems taking on more responsibil-ity and pressure. The all-too-rarely-articulated social pressures, community-level dysfunctions and pathologies were well described by one rural superin-tendent who said,

> There are just a ton of, what I call secondary, pressures that nobody wants to talk about—things like increased alcohol abuse—we have had more cases of family violence, sexual abuse. Yet everybody still wants to operate on the basic assumption that our towns are still the fine, warm, little, wonderful, pure places they were historically—that everything is fine. Damn it all, everything isn't fine!! There is sort of a group and community denial of what is happen-ing . . . [and] this has made the job more complicated, and it has put a lot more pressure on the CEO to keep it all hanging together.

Another leader provided an example of the pressure of more con-sciously articulated social demands, "The expectations on schools is the most crucial problem today. What is society expecting of us? Right now the mandate of schooling is just everything. We are mom—picking up everybody's clothing. Everybody thinks we are an assembly line—just have to make a correction in the education system and it will clean up the problems." The load and weight of increasing social expectations is expressed by two other leaders, as follows:

> It seems like there are more and more problems coming all the time. There is just a tremendous number of social kinds of issues coming—from hungry children to abuse—you name it. And that takes up a lot of your time just dealing with the people—your own people within the structure who are responsible for those things

> Almost any problem that society identifies—the [supposed] solution is education. So the schools have accepted this wider mandate. This increases the pressure—the one time you can capture the kids—a universal program when the child is available is when they are in school.

Sometimes social needs could be legitimately incorporated into the school system purposes, while sometimes they could not be met, and the need to expend political energy to safeguard the school system resources drew on the attentions of leaders and, subsequently, on the mediatory nature of their work.

Political Pressures and Challenges

Almost all of the interviewees drew attention to the tension between political and professional dynamics within their organization. For many leaders, the professional view was synonymous with "the educational view," and this was commonly accepted to be antithetical to the political perspective. A CEO commented that the weight of political pressures was particularly onerous on him. He said, "I'd say the weight of the more political aspect of the job has increased substantially over the years. The financial management end of it has increased tremendously, but that still comes under the umbrella of a political liaison type role. I have found that if anything weighs me down it is the political liaison type role that we have to play." Another leader said, "Who do you believe and what do you follow? Are you being swayed to politics or the administrative side of things? In a sense the pressures come from being a person in the middle. You have to be a person of principle as opposed to being a person who is swayed by the social context of the dealing with people daily or political context under your political masters."

Leaders characteristically responded to the politics within their organizations in one of three ways. The sense of the first response may be captured with the words *fear* and *avoidance*. One interviewee provided comment on this response: "There is always . . . the fear of politics. It is part of what I do . . . the one dilemma that is always on the CEO's mind is having to make an educational sacrifice for a political gain. It is the biggest fear, and sometimes we are so overwhelmed by forces out of control and the politics of the situation that it is really hard to keep a focus on the educational decisions that have to be made."

Second, there were other leaders who believed that political activity was never intended to be a part of their administrative office. Still others believed that as one climbed the hierarchical ladder in educational leadership, one would accrue ever more political involvement. Some leaders spoke disparagingly of fellow leaders who were perceived to be over-political in their practice. One such leader said, "My board knows, when they are dealing with me, that I am leaving the popularity—the acceptability to the public—o them. The difference between a professional and a nonprofessional is that a professional knows the correct thing to do and has a scientific basis and does not care what the pressure or circumstances might try to dictate."

A third, and conjunctive, position appreciated the inherent presence of the political realities but combined these with the pressure-filled occupation of maintaining one's professional integrity throughout all the tensions and demands.

A common theme of discussion centered on the concept and pressures of political favors. Leaders who were interviewed provided warning signals for those who would be tempted to engage in these politically oriented exchanges:

> Daniel Webster said, "The devil appears on a Friday afternoon when you are really tired; he comes in the form of a friend and asks you for a favor you know you shouldn't give." You give that first favor and you know you have to give the second, third, fourth, and fifth, and pretty soon you don't have a professional model or code to follow—you give your job away—decision by decision You do sell your soul a little bit . . . I think most CEO's end up selling their souls a wee bit. [For example] we have a fantastic bus route—fattest part of system is buses, but it is a sacred cow. To what degree do I shoot down the sacred cow so kids can benefit . . . don't think we need the [extra] buses [but] I gave in quickly because it was politically wise to do so.

Organizational politics appeared to relate to three main sets of adult stakeholders: the governing board; the professional staff; and the parents. Each of these was said to bring unique pressures to bear on their value mediation work. In some instances, the pressures were not consciously applied but were, rather, inherent in the mere presence of the stakeholder(s). Boards of education and parents were the most frequently identified sets of adult stakeholders who had influence on the work of these educational leaders.

Some leaders felt the pressure to ensure that the educational agenda of the professionals was given priority consideration. They saw themselves as being under pressure guiding the boards to make the right educational decisions. One CEO said, "Our board puts a lot of faith in the recommendations of their superintendent. That puts on a lot of pressure in the sense that once you put a recommendation—that is likely the way it will go." Several leaders commented on times when they had come head-to-head with their boards. While these were rare occasions, the circumstances tested leaders' typical unwillingness to surrender their ethical integrity.

One leader said, "Sometimes you are going to lose no matter which way you go." He indicated that this was a significant source of pressure and that he coped with it by working hard on his communication with stakeholders. One other superintendent elaborated on this issue of zero-sum decision making and his mediatory logic in response to the influence of dissatisfied stakeholders when he said,

> I think you will always meet people who are not satisfied with what you are doing—it doesn't matter how good you are at what you do. You are always going to have that—so you may as well do what is right. You've got to pay the price—you are going to have to pay a lot more if you don't do the right thing. If you do the right thing you are going to get the largest percentage of people who do support you and do appreciate what you are trying to do. . . . The same number of people are going to dislike you anyway—you might as well be happy and live with what is right . . . it is this that helps me to sleep well at night.

Another said, "Stakeholder analysis is not always an easy thing to do" because while "kids are first," the "teachers are the most important resource in the organization." He had to take many important stakeholders into account in his decision making. This a prime example of the current reality that situates leaders with multiple constituencies. Similar pressures were often expressed in organizational terms.

Organizational Pressures and Challenges

The organizational pressures were related to the leaders' understandings of their organizational responsibilities, together with their perceptions of the political interplay with people inside the organization. When we asked superintendents to rate the most essential performance areas (using American Association of School Administrators' standards for superintendents), they indicated their strongest support for value literacy, dialogical competence, and value-based performance. For these leaders "understanding, articulating, and modeling appropriate values, ethics, and moral educational leadership" were the most essential features of their work. Performing the executive roles of developing a collective vision, based on needs, developing priorities, formulating solutions, planning and scheduling personal and organizational work, securing and allocating human and material resources, and managing and developing procedures for working with the Board of Education were also considered essential features of their work (though to a lesser extent). What makes these views interesting is the observation that the above performance areas are much more value-driven than are some of the more technical and managerial functions that comprise the typical superintendent work life. Of course, there are many variables one might imagine that would intervene in these responses (e.g., jurisdictional size, specific work descriptions, social system pressures and demands).

Leaders were asked to describe their experience of the "weight of responsibility" as educational leaders. They described their perceptions of the demands placed upon them by the organization to fulfill particular mandates, to react and negotiate, to sustain, to manage as well as to provide visionary educational leadership. One CEO recounted his specific mandate from the board of education as "marching orders" and commented as follows: "When I came in here the trustees required me to put the budget in order. . . . they wanted their people to be happier and to be more accountable. . . . They wanted me to get the public relations of the school system together and to gain more revenues for the system." Another superintendent expressed his view that the educational leader was the key team leader responsible for the vitality and relevance of the organization. Another response was typified by the superintendent who said, "I see my role as anticipating and envisioning: first of all to anticipate the snags and warding them off, second, I think your goal is to have a vision." Others indicated their roles as reactors and negotiators. The constraint of avoiding duplicity was foremost in the minds of leaders as the one example below indicates: "As CEO, while we aren't Godlike, but you have to stay credible. You don't want to be in the board's back pocket or the reverse."

With respect to other organizational constraints, one administrator made reference to the expectation of his immediate response to crises from those within the organization. He said, "There is a heavy expectation from the people that you have worked through concerns in your own mind. So if you speak to an issue the public will expect that you have thought it through. You have to be responsive. People expect you to act immediately if this is warranted. You lose the confidence of people if your timing is off."

One of the younger superintendents commented on how he screened choices through his perceptions of his roles and responsibilities. He said,

> You get inoculated over time to the pressures and the responsibilities. Partly, I think it is the career ladder that you go through before you get the director-ship. You learn how to handle the jobs—it is what you do and what you enjoy. You have parents, board members, teachers relying on you to expedite things, and I take that responsibility very seriously . . . [because] for me the job needs to be done well because kids are important. The pressures of the day-to-day thing—well I tend to get off on it. I would have made a good missionary because my work is important to me and I believe in what I do.

Such words indicate the external and internal (ethical and personal) pressures of the superintendency. Among this array of pressures were the ethical constraints and purposes impinging on leaders' work lives.

Ethical Pressures and Challenges

When asked if they had a personal set of rules or principles by which they made most of their ethical choices, nine out of ten said yes. Some of these described their rules or principles of choice as related to "good-bad," "moral," "right vs. wrong." Many more mentioned the consequences of their decisions or specific values such as honesty, respect and concern for others, justice, and efficiency. Honesty was the most commonly mentioned principle or rule. The word *honesty* appeared most frequently in survey responses. The second most frequently mentioned rule or principle theme was "treating people with dignity and respect." A smaller number of respondents said their choices were concerned with compliance with written rules, community standards, personal values, religious ideals, the golden rule, knowledge or experience, and professionalism. Interestingly, those who claimed not to have a personal set of rules or principles or who were uncertain did not differ from those who did.

Superintendents were asked to cite a piece of advice, the principle, or perspective that they had found most helpful in making ethical decisions. We hoped to discover more about the tacit constraints and value-based pressures through this line of questioning. Their responses were categorized as follows: the best interests of students (e.g., "benefit to kids" "students come before everyone"); personal integrity or authenticity ("you have to be able to look at yourself in the mirror each morning" and "to thyself be true"); general advice (e.g., "keep on the high road," "trust others," "seek the greatest good for the greatest number of people," and "do the right thing"); the golden rule; honesty and openness (e.g., "be up-front," "Keep trustees informed," and "give information to parents and teachers as available"); consult or get advice; be fair and just; show respect or concern for others; document and get the facts. We would impute these pieces of advice back to the advisors with the suggestion that these may, with further study, turn out to be value constraints held by the advisors themselves.

From the survey data, six factors were thought to be important pressures on superintendents that promoted unethical action: the behavior of superiors, personal greed, society's moral climate, lack of formal organizational policy, behavior of peers in the organization, and the unethical practices of the profession. During the interviews, leaders provided the following examples of unethical practices that frequently occur within their profession: giving false references, posturing, rumor-mongering, personnel abuses, exploiting children, and financial wrongdoings. To get a more empirical sense of systemic ethical pressures and challenges, we asked if there were generally accepted practices within the profession that they regarded as unethical: half responded yes, one-third, no, and the remainder were not sure. Those who responded with a yes or not sure were asked to describe an unethical practice or possible unethical practice that they would like to see eliminated. The most frequently mentioned practices included general dishonesty or lack of forthrightness, excluding dishonesty pertaining to references, politics or the promotion of a personal or private agenda at the expense of the common good, dishonesty or lack of forthrightness concerning references on a candidate for a position, hiring practices involving favoritism, unions' protection of job security, improper personal gain, inappropriate or unethical criticism of colleagues, and sick leave or overtime misuse.

Responding to our survey, the superintendents rated the following systemwide pressures or challenges as problems they most had to deal with using a values-based approach: appropriate use of scarce and shrinking resources, board member politics, special needs students educational cost versus the general needs of the majority, deciding which staff position(s) to reduce, dealing with incompetent personal, conflict between rate payers' interests and educational needs, conflict between the rights and needs of one versus the rights and needs of many, pressure from special interest groups, criticizing fellow professionals, and deciding which program(s) to eliminate. Pressure points that had been dealt with to a lesser extent included withholding purposeful information, abuse of personnel, general mistreatment of staff, infringements on the rights of others, infringing on the privacy of others, infringing on autonomy of individuals, reports of sexual misconduct and assaults, maintaining safe and secure places for students and staff, dealing in a fair manner with staff, businesses-school relationships, a general lack of diligence and preparedness, maintenance of personal integrity, maintenance of organizational integrity, maintenance of central office integrity, multiple and conflicting loyalties, lying or misrepresenting the facts, insincerity, misinforming, deceit in communication, breaking confidences, multicultural conflicts and politics, conflict arising from telling the truth and being honest, disrespect for democracy, sabotaging collaborative decision-making processes, school closures, pressure from high socio-economic areas for special treatment, dismissal of tenured staff, discerning between the rights of students and the rights of others, and role conflicts as the chief executive office, the educational leader of the professional staff, and a member of the community.

We asked superintendents to provide examples of a relatively difficult type of ethical problems that they had to deal with. The eight most frequently mentioned were release of confidential information or criticism of colleagues; professional incompetence of a teacher or administrator; problems with hiring and staffing; problems in relation to facilities or finances; conduct in relation to money (e.g., expense claims, misappropriation of funds, giving contracts to friends); inappropriate sexual conduct (e.g., sexual harassment or abuse of peers or students, unsanctioned or inappropriate sexual relations); problems with program, curriculum, or student-teacher ratio; and personality conflicts and communication problems.

To get a more elaborate sense of their pressures, we were interested to know what each superintendent thought would differentiate the easy from the more difficult ethical decisions. They provided written responses which we have categorized according to six discernible themes: the seriousness of the consequences for the "object" of the decision; the extent of ambiguity as to the proper or best decision; the extent of involvement of personalities or emotions; the seriousness of the consequences for the maker of the decision; the presence or absence of rules, law, code, or precedent to follow; and extent of ambiguity as to facts.

The most important factors or forces related to superintendents' work-related ethical decision making were (in order of importance) personal principles, personal rules, personal convictions, professional expectations, organizational expectations, and personal upbringing. It is interesting to note that religious constraints and special interest group pressure were indicated to be the least effectual forces or factors in the minds of respondents. Perhaps the most notable aspect of this ranking of the factors is that the top three are all personal factors, even the fourth ("professional experience") is a personal factor in that each person's professional experience is unique to him or her as a person. It was quite clear from interviews and surveys that the pressures and challenges of the superintendency were often faced at a personal level.

Personal Pressures and Influences

The work of the educational leader was portrayed by interviewees as challenging, diverse, lonely, exciting, serious, costly, and satisfying. In the surveys, superintendents typically distinguished their work lives as highly demanding (vs. easy), worthwhile (vs. futile), exciting (vs. calm), hectic (vs. serene), and fulfilling (vs. unfulfilling). For example, one superintendent said that the "pace of change [in this system] is very quick and fast. This is related to your philosophy. If you see yourself as a change agent, and if you want to create positive change and you want to invent the future that your mission statement calls for—then life is hectic because you want to stay out in front of change and you want to create the kind of change that is beneficial." When CEOs were asked if the pace of work life put constraints on their ability to make value-based decisions, leaders suggested that sometimes the events of time "overtake" the decision-making process and that a post hoc or retrospective rationality often comes into play. In some instances leaders seemed "driven" in their pursuit of goals and dealing with the demands of their work. This positive and consuming drive was reflected in the common practices of leaders to prioritize values and their willingness to sacrifice less important goods. For example, interviewees indicated their willingness to sacrifice positive perceptions, friendships, family, and even personal security for the attainment of educational or professional goals. One superintendent, when asked how the people he worked with most closely would describe his motivations related to value-based pressures, responded:

> I think if other people were asked about me, they'd probably say that I am motivated by ambition, energy, and arrogance. The basic inaccuracy in their perception is that the professional style that they see is after I have decided on the goal or after I have been given the goal. I can be fairly ruthless in getting to the goal. I don't think they sense the sensitivity and the problem I have trading off the sensitivity and the things you do to certain individuals to get them oriented to the team goal. I believe I am more sensitive and caring and that I understand them better than they realize. But my dedication to the goal, and to getting to what it is that we need to do, leads me to deal with them in, sometimes, ruthless ways.

This leader was conscious of what he perceived to be the inaccurate views, held by others, of his motivations. He believed that those he worked with had generally misjudged his attitudes and actions.

Another administrator, when asked what motivated or constrained him to be an ethical educational leader, responded:

> Professional pride—I think I do a good job, and I know that many people don't like me. I am not that popular in some areas, but I think that people do

respect and accept me. I do the job—in the way that I think it needs to be done. I like this business; I like the job; I like trustees; I like kids; I like schools; I like rural areas. Some of the things I have to do I don't enjoy, but I think I am making a difference. It may be arrogant, but I believe if I don't get up in the morning and don't come into work that I've probably missed an opportunity somewhere in the day to do something that will make the system or students or teachers or somebody better.

This leader conveyed his own sense of assurance that his motives were pure and his personal role was significant. He made professional decisions that gained him respect but not popularity. He felt his positive affections for education, people, and schools together with his essential service to his system made him ethically upright. He was confident in his sense that his decisions were professionally motivated as he operated in his assumed role as an agent of betterment.

The vulnerability of the senior administrator was raised as is the tension sometimes experienced when support from significant others declines or when one's survival is pitted against one's value sensibilities. One CEO stated,

You can talk ethics, and you can talk everything, but when you are in that situation and you are being attacked personally, your family—you have threatening calls coming to your home, you know . . . your credibility, your salary, everything being attacked publicly. It is pretty easy to sit here in this period of calm and talk about values, but when you are in that situation, it is survival. If your board starts to fold on you when the heat comes then sometimes you may have to decide between doing the ethical thing and the sane thing.

The most important influences that motivated the surveyed superintendents to act ethically were their conscience or respect for themselves; specific values such as fairness, justice, honesty, caring, religious beliefs, church, or spirituality; thinking about consequences, impact, or effects of actions; their parents or upbringing; and mentors, colleagues, or other persons that they admired. Educational leaders said they were influenced by both familial and professional role models as well as by educative relationships. One-third of survey responses suggested that familial role models had been the most important influences on their abilities and inclinations to mediate values in their leadership work. Parents were the most commonly cited influences on educational leaders. Professional role models accounted for another third of the responses. For many leaders, another CEO had been the most important influence on their leadership values.

In terms of possible sources of information used to make value judgments, the superintendents gave greatest weight to (in order) other school-based administrators, central office professional staff; professional association/other superintendents, teachers, educational leaders from other jurisdictions; school board members, support staff, parents, consultants, and provincial/state department of education.

"Virtually all the superintendents will tell you they like their jobs—why, because they are energizing, dynamic, and prestigious and you make a decent salary" said one CEO. One leader said, "If you watch our [CEOs] retire, they in one way, shape, or form just about everyone of them will make some reference to the family. They say to the people in the audience who are not at retirement—don't forget your family, don't forget your personal life, don't forget—but I think everybody does—the good superintendents do because this job can be almost all consuming." For some of these educators, the definition of good leadership was inseparably linked to the psychological phenomenon of being "engrossed" and "consumed" by one's job.

The work of a chief educational officer was considered by some to be exciting and unbounded, yet directed and demanding. These characteristics are well expressed by one superintendent of education who said he had taken the job and stuck with it for many years: "To me it is the sense of direction and seeing things happen that keeps me going. I like the variety—I am standing on roofs, talking to people, hammering through a collective agreement, looking at cracked tiles, talking to bus drivers, going to meetings . . . you know that is great—I can't think of other jobs that have the variety and the freedom. You report to the board who meet once per month. I can go wherever I want when I want."

Several leaders expressed their motivations for working as superintendents by their preferences related to having the power to change things, working through ambiguities, being close to the action, always dealing with new challenges, working in a job that is never quite done, and dealing with difficult people situations. They said, "I like change and I have the ability to change things. The challenges—there is always something happening. Going through the ambiguities and getting through to the knowns. I like being close to the action."

We were interested in the sense of professional efficacy experienced by these leaders and so provided each with negative and positive statements concerning their sense of self-efficacy as educational administrators. We found high agreement amongst respondents to the notions that they were "making a difference in the lives of the staff in our organization" and had been "successful in efforts to initiate, implement, and institutionalize system changes." Such responses indicate that superintendents believe in their individual capacity to effect change, in their personal ability to improve situations, and in the responsibility of the individual for the results of their work.

Leaders seemed to have been motivated in their work by both positive and negative considerations. One of the clearest expressions of a fear-oriented motivation was provide by a CEO who had been in contact with educational leaders who had been caught in their moral wrongdoings. He said, "I've been involved on a professional discipline committee. I've seen how members have been cornered and there is no place else to go . . . [they've] put in a lifetime building something that they believed in . . . that's a factor in my own case. . . . I have been exposed to several instances where there has been unethical conduct." It is interesting to observe the humility and, in some instances, the insecurity and loneliness of CEOs. For example, one said, "Your strength is your weakness—I like the job 'cause I can make a difference, but I fear making some of the decisions that I make because you have to play God in peoples' lives."

This paradox of having the power to make a difference for good and having the same power to cause harm was indicative of the admission by leaders of the inherent mediatory nature of their leadership. This particular leader recognized his power as a constraint that he had to ameliorate with the constant self-reminder of his own finitude. With respect to the insecurity issue, one CEO, for example, shared his personal feelings as follows: "The only other thing about the job that is personal . . . maybe the other CEOs are fairly good at hiding it . . . my security needs tend to be pretty high. In this job you are always just one bad decision away from a lot of bad problems. . . . Sometimes they do some pretty astute political jobs . . . [but] so long as you keep looking over your shoulder and using your wits [you'll be okay]." A number of leaders expressed a sense of loneliness and the threat that this psychologically problematic condition had been exacerbated by some tough ethical decisions. They said, "It sure is lonely when you're going through the tough kinds of personnel problems that I faced my first years in the system—you are all by yourself—its a really lonely job 'cause you have a board that has expectations for you and teaching staff who perceive you a certain way (a hatchet man basically), and there is a lot of pressure."

What most worries the typical superintendent? Our respondents said they were concern about undone tasks or unresolved problems. In our interviews we often heard them describe taking work and worries home with them. There was a sense that there was an endless number of unfinished tasks, that time too often overtook their deliberate decision making. As one might expect, there was a high sense of self-concern over whether they had made the right decision. Often these feelings were accompanied by too few facts, too hurried decision time-lines, ambiguous situations, or situations where they knew there were completing interests and arguments but had to take a position. There was concern over how to deal with nonproductive staff. Whether by motivation, training or removal processes, this concern weighed heavily on superintendents. Some were frustrated by their own impotence, legal or contractual barriers, human empathy, the feeling that children were caught up in the middle of these problems, and the occasional sense that some of the low productivity was the result of systemic inflexibility or rigidity. Superintendents confessed concern over their lack of control over events that affect schools. The concerns seem to contradict the high sense of efficacy expressed by superintendents, but in this case, after taking into account interview data, we found that leaders struggled with transitioning into trust culture from a control and command type of structure. The fact that they often had to take the heat or added burden for negative events that were beyond their control certainly seemed to complicate their work.

Personnel concerns weighed heavily on CEOs. An administrator commented that he did not enjoy being in "a God-like spot where I have to make decisions . . . which assumes I am omniscient. This takes real moral courage." Some leaders struggled with the realization that they did not have the access nor the capacity to make their judgments on the basis of adequate factual information. One said,

> A couple of things that have always weighed on me. It has always had the profound effect on me that those decisions have profound effects on people's lives. If we are dealing with situations where teachers are transferred and are very emotionally upset about it—these have a real influence in what happens. I have to deal with people in a very important part of their lives without knowing them any better than they know me, without maybe having all of the information, without being able to get it, not being able to understand all the information even if I had it.

Perhaps the description above of the inadequacy of factual information gives an insight into why some leaders had assumed the role of organizational knowledge and value brokers and why some placed such considerable pressure on themselves.

Concluding Remarks

We have indicated that superintendents do their work in diverse settings and circumstances but that they typically conceive of their work-life as highly demanding and pressure-filled. Providing value-based, visionary, and strategic leadership is thought to be the most essential function in the performance of leaders' duties. Most of these leaders have an articulated set of rules or principles by which they make their choices in the midst of challenging circumstances. They concern themselves with the magnitude of undone tasks, making the "right decision," dealing with unproductive staff and financial matters and shrinking resources, and coping with the conflicts entailed responding to increasing needs with disproportionate budgets.

Superintendents' work is constituted by complex tensions and conflicts that bear enormous weight. We have reported on survey findings and with the use of interviewee words described pressures and challenges related to economic pressures and challenges, conflicting interests, political pressures organizational pressures, and ethical and personal factors. Many of their pressures come from competing group values and interests. Leaders were commonly concerned about the dynamics and tensions related to political and professional conjunctions. They found great challenge in dealing with issues of competence, confidences, personnel, unethical behavior of others, and programming problems. One would have predicted that educational leaders' value-based work would be tempted by and, perhaps, tempered by influences beyond the concrete, sequential, and rational pathways of tightly coupled and closed systems.

The educational enterprise is going through some major redefinition with respect to the role of public schooling and the contraction or expansion of conventional roles of school systems in the delivery of various services (see Begley in this volume). The surfacing of pressures provides the possibility of using these commonsense expressions to form a substantial basis for understanding their work. The insights garnered from these leaders not only gives voice to the subjects but also provides invaluable material for those who would seek to prepare future leaders. Such descriptions facilitate higher-level consideration of and reflection on issues and dilemmas facing educational leaders with deference to their particular situations.

These findings provide several specific sets of rather obvious implications for superintendents, researchers, and those involved in the delivery of professional development or executive preparation programs. Of course we know that leaders in virtually every public and private sector now recognize that they have the task of managing and influencing multiple constituencies (Gardner 1990) who have wide-ranging sets of values. These values and consequent interests both confuse the leader's constituents and contend for predominance. Educational executives clearly find themselves in the middle of increasingly complex webs of values. These values come from such social system sources as religion, philosophy, culture, the law, and the professions. In addition, organizational forces in an organization affect the superintendent's values, ethical decisions, and actions. This chapter has presumed that the work of superintendents is fundamentally values-oriented and that a subset of values is ethics. The chapter provides preliminary descriptions of ethical challenges and pressures that bear on educational leaders. As Hodgkinson has indicated,

> Educational administration is a special case within the general profession of administration. Its leaders find themselves in what might be called an arena of ethical excitement—often politicized but always humane, always intimately

connected to the evaluation of society. . . . It embodies a heritage of value, on the one hand, and is a massive industry on the other, in which social, economic, and political forces are locked together in a complex equilibrium of power. All of this calls for extraordinary value sensitivity on the part of educational leaders. (1991, 164)

Educational leaders have the distinct and "interesting" challenge of a public trust that instructs them to preserve and communicate the values of society (now so very diverse) and yet, at the same time, to be on the forefront of educational, social, and technological change (Foster 1986, 68). Many years ago, Sergiovanni and Carver described the presence of a "web of tension" in the work lives of educational managers (1980, 19). The leaders who provided the data for this chapter told us that educational administration requires managing complexity and that much of their training had not provided them with the support for wrestling with conflicting values or making difficult ethical decisions.

The work of superintendents has been considered from many vantage points, but only rarely, and recently, have researchers given explicit attention to their administrative subjects through the lenses of descriptive ethics. The content of individual educational leaders' ethical, personal, organizational, and social system value sets and their mediating frameworks have been largely ignored.

As more eyes seem to be drawn in hope and expectation toward the superintendency to lead the educational enterprise through the transitions and tests of the next years, it is important that we gain clearer appreciations for the nature of this work. These preliminary data provide an introductory account of the value-based content, pressures, and challenges of Canadian superintendents' decisional wrestlings. It is hoped that such descriptions will facilitate higher levels of consideration, focus, and reflection on the value issues and dilemmas faced by educational leaders.

References

Author. 1993. *Professional standards for the superintendency*. Virginia: American Association of School Administrators.

Beck, L. 1994. Reclaiming educational administration as a caring profession. New York: Teachers College Press.

Beck, L. G., and Murphy, J. 1994. *The role of ethics in educational leadership preparation programs: An expanding focus*. Newbury Park, CA, and University Park, PA: Corwin Press.

Bird, F., and Waters, J. 1987. The nature of managerial moral standards. *Journal of Business Ethics* 6: 1–13.

————. 1989. The moral muteness of managers. *California Management Review* 8: 73–88.

Chapman, C. H., ed. 1997. *Becoming a superintendent: Challenges of school district leadership*. Inglewood Cliffs, NJ: Prentice-Hall.

Enns, F. 1981. Some ethical-moral concerns in administration. *The Canadian Administrator* 20, 8:1–8.

Evers, C., ed. 1987. *Moral theory for educative leadership*. Victoria: Ministry of Education.

Fairholm, G. W. 1994. *Leadership and the culture of trust*. Westport, CT: Praeger.

Foster, W. 1986. *Paradigms and promises*. Buffalo: Prometheus Books.

Frankena, W. K. 1973. *Ethics*, 2nd ed. Englewood Cliffs, NJ: Prentice-Hall.

Gardner, J. 1990. *On leadership*. New York: The Free Press.

Gronn, P. 1987. Notes on leader watching. In *Ways and meanings of research in educational administration*, ed. R. J. S. Macpherson. Armidale: The University of New England.

Hampshire, S. 1983. *Morality and conflict*. Cambridge, MA: Harvard University Press.

Hodgkinson, C. 1978. *Toward a philosophy of administration*. Oxford: Basil Blackwell.

————. 1983. *The philosophy of leadership*. Oxford: Basil Blackwell.

————. 1991. *Educational leadership: The moral art*. New York: State University of New York Press.

Holmes, M. 1991. In The values and beliefs of Ontario's chief education officers. *Understanding school system administration*, ed. K. Leithwood and D. Musella. London: The Falmer Press. p. 154–174.

Jackall, R. 1988. *Moral mazes: The world of corporate managers*. New York: Oxford University Press.

Kimbrough, R. 1985. *Ethics: A course of study for educational leaders*. Arlington, VA: The American Association of School Administration.

Konnert, M. W., and Augenstein, J. J. 1995. *The school superintendency: Leading education into the 21st century*. Lancaster: Technomic Publishing.

Kowalski, T. 1995. *Keepers of the flame: Contemporary urban superintendents*. Thousand Oaks, CA: Corwin Press. Inc.

Leithwood, K., and Musella, D., ed. 1991. *Understanding school system administration*. London: The Falmer Press.

Macpherson, R. J. S. 1984. On being and becoming an educational administrator: Some methodological issues. *Educational Administration Quarterly* 20: 58–75.

———— 1987. *Ways and meanings of research in educational administration*. Armidale: The University of New England.

Madson, P., and Shafritz, J. M., eds. 1990. *Essentials of business ethics*. New York: Penguin Books.

Maxy, S. 1991. *Educational leadership*. New York: Bergin and Garvey.

Norton, M. S., Webb, L. D., Dlugosh, L. L., and Sybouts, W. 1996. *The school superintendency: New responsibilities new leadership*. Boston MA: Allyn & Bacon.

Rizvi, F., ed. 1985. *Working papers in ethics and educational administration 1985*. Australia: School of Education, Deakin University.

Sergiovanni, T. 1990. *Value-added leadership.* San Diego: Harcourt Brace Jovanovich.

———. 1992. *Moral leadership.* San Francisco: Jossey-Bass.

———. 1994. *Building community in schools.* San Francisco: Jossey Bass.

Sergiovanni, T. J., and Carver, F. D. 1980. *The new school executive: A theory of administration,* 2nd edition. New York: Harper and Row.

Smedes, L. B. 1983. *Mere morality.* Michigan: W. B. Eerdmans Publishing Company.

Starratt, R. 1994. *Building an ethical school.* London: The Falmer Press.

Starratt, R. J. 1991. Building an ethical school: A theory for practice in educational leadership. *Educational Administration Quarterly* 27, 2:185–202.

Strike, K., Haller, E., and Soltis, J. 1988. *The ethics of educational administration.* New York: Teachers College Press.

Toffler, B. L. 1986. *Tough choices: Managers talk ethics.* New York: John Wiley and Sons.

Willower, D. J. 1994. Educational administration: Inquiry, values, practice. In *Leadership and Diversity in Education,* ed. J. Burdin, 241–80. Pennsylvania: Technomic Publishing Company.

CHAPTER SIXTEEN

Values and Educational Leadership: An Agenda for the Future

Paul T. Begley

The incentive for preparing this book can be stated quite simply: both the timing and the circumstances were exactly right. During 1996 two research centers were established, both devoted to the study of values. One is the OISE (University of Toronto) Centre for the Study of Values and Leadership. The other is its University Council for Educational Administration (UCEA) affiliate based at the University of Virginia (Charlottesville), the Center for the Study of Leadership and Ethics. Later that year an important gathering of the minds occurred at the inaugural Values and Educational Leadership Conference in Toronto. Philosophers, theorists, and researchers in the values field assembled for three days at *the Toronto Conference* to initiate what has since become a sustained dialogue and an annual conference. Many outstanding papers were delivered at this first conference, the best of which have been edited, updated, and brought together in this volume.

Since 1996, when the two values research centers were established, a considerable amount of momentum has developed. International linkages have been established with other university-based research centers in Sweden, Australia, and Hong Kong. At OISE of the University of Toronto the number of thesis research projects addressing values and ethics inquiry is steadily increasing. Papers are now also regularly delivered in the name of the UCEA values center at the annual meetings of the American Educational Research Association and other international conferences such as the New Horizons in School Leadership Conference (March 1998) held in Umea, Sweden. Finally, conference papers delivered in 1996 are now appearing as journal articles, several in the *Journal of School Leadership*. The progress made in two short years has been remarkable, and our perception is that the academic community is beginning to take notice.

Yet, one could still ask, why study values, or why connect values and educational leadership at all? The contributors to this book provide compelling answers to such questions. Donald Willower's answer to the values question is, "Because a significant portion of the practice in educational administration requires rejecting some courses of action in favor of a preferred one, values are generally acknowledged to be central to the field" (1992, 369). Similarly, Christopher Hodgkinson, as cited by Walker and Shakotko in the conclusion to chapter 15, tells us,

> Educational administration is a special case within the general profession of administration. Its leaders find themselves in what might be called an arena of ethical excitement—often politicized but always humane, always intimately connected to the evaluation of society. . . . It embodies a heritage of value on the one hand, and is a massive industry on the other, in which social, economic, and political forces are locked together in a complex equilibrium of power. All this calls for extra-ordinary value sensitivity on the part of educational leaders. (1991, 164)

Other voices have since joined these pioneers of the field, and although it would be safe to say that all the contributors to this book agree on the importance of values as a topic for inquiry, beyond that some quickly part company. Leithwood is not convinced that values inquiry is properly focused if it strays from the future needs of organizations. Evers and Lakomski propose coherentist perspectives as a comprehensive and epistemologically justifiable foundation for a philosophy of educational administration. Willower is more in favor of Deweyan pragmatism. Hodgkinson believes scholars should be studying the problems of emotions, ethics, and ego. Ryan and Foster remind us that it is a postmodern world, while Campbell is critical of moral relativism. Finally, those with practitioner orientations (i.e., Begley, Grogan, Walker and Shakotko, Roche, Leonard) prefer a situated problem-based approach or to focus on the resolution of value conflicts in specific contexts. The overall effect is to illustrate that theory and research about values and leadership are still very much works in progress. The field remains fragmented at this time, and although this book demonstrates that many academics are actively engaged in dialogue with each other, there is still no strong consensus on the nature and function of values as influences on administration.

What questions does this book answer? We believe several: What are the historical roots of the field, and who are key players? What perspectives and approaches appear most promising at this time? What are the problems and challenges associated with inquiry? Finally, what are the next steps? The remainder of this chapter is devoted to addressing these questions.

Key Players and Promising Approaches

The most important and highly recommended scholarly work that focuses on values and leadership inquiry is that by Christopher Hodgkinson (1978; 1983; 1991; 1996) and Donald Willower (1992; 1994). These two individuals have probably done more to promote and advance inquiry into the moral aspects of administration than any other academics in North America.

Willower's intuitively practical Deweyan tradition of reflective inquiry still holds considerable appeal for those attracted to the more rational modes of pragmatic inquiry. Hodgkinson's values typology, and the derivative models generated by his disciples, is still perhaps the most comprehensive of frameworks for examining values in administration, in that it incorporates the rational values of consequences and consensus as well as subrational emotions and transrational ethics. Thomas B. Greenfield (Greenfield and Ribbins 1993), another giant of the field, is also deserving of mention, although his direct commentary on values is quite limited.

More recently, Evers and Lakomski entered the arena with their two important books (1991; 1996). Their commitment to developing a philosophy of educational administration based on holism and coherentist perspectives has promoted significant debate and will continue to shape the direction of inquiry in educational administration for some time. Research by Leithwood (Leithwood and Steinbach 1995), Begley (Begley and Leithwood 1990; Begley 1996), Leonard (1997) and Roche (1997) makes useful contributions to our understanding of the nature and influence of values on problem solving. In particular, this research begins to confront the limitations of ethics as guides to practice. A final, encouraging trend pertains to situated learning approaches. These include problem-based learning (Bridges and Hallinger 1995), context-specific inquiry through action research (Begley and Johansson 1998), and cognitive apprenticeships (Hallinger, Leithwood, and Murphy 1993; Prestine and LeGrand 1991; Begley 1995). These are all perspectives that readily embrace the consideration of values as influences on leadership and administration. Indeed, as an outcome of organizing three annual conferences focusing on values and leadership, it is apparent that there is room to accommodate a broad range of perspectives within the values and leadership sphere, including those focused on personal experience, professional practices, social-cultural studies, and the organizational.

The Problems and Challenges

Some would still dismiss values as a concept too abstract for practical inquiry. These include those scholars who adhere to the notion that scientific inquiry requires the separation of fact from value. However, there are other more moderate dissenting postures. Leithwood, for example, urges caution and a tempering of enthusiasm for a wholesale commitment to the study of values. This orientation is common to those academics who consider values from an organizational perspective, as well as those whose work is representative of mainstream or dominant social perspectives. The need to clarify values becomes important when one needs to be clear about intent and purposes. If one's view of society is that "it ain't broke," then there is little need to "fix it." Those scholars whose work reflects the interests of socially marginalized or minority groups of any sort are clearly attracted to the adoption, or critiquing of, particular values postures, for example, the ethic of care familiar to feminist perspectives (see Grogan, chapter 14). Others, such as Robinson (1996) treat values as one of many potential contextual influences, or "constraints" on problem solving. This is in sharp contrast to other scholars such as Begley (chapter 12), who proposes values as antecedent influences acquired through formative experiences. The latter is more characteristic of postures emphasizing individual perception, constructivism, or existentialist orientations.

Other persistent sources of difficulty or challenge for values inquiry derive from the traditional paradigmatic boundaries that Evers and Lakomski have discredited. Yet even their holistic perspectives on coherentism may be viewed by critics (e.g., Hodgkinson and Maddock, in Evers and Lakomski 1996) as just another set of paradigmatic boundaries that, for example, may exclude the consideration of certain value types, usually the nonrational ones.

The introduction to part 3 of this book addresses another challenge— the difficulty associated with conducting research on values. Methodology remains a difficult topic, yet several (e.g., Leonard 1997 and Roche 1997) have begun to experiment with promising new approaches and hybrid theoretical frameworks. Action research techniques (see Begley chapter 12), in particular, show good promise.

Finally, there is the challenge to values inquiry presented by prevailing pluralistic circumstances of our social communities. The persistent climate of upheaval characteristic of our schools and communities, and the increasing diversity of our societies are having a profound impact on schools and leadership practices. Increasingly, value conflicts have become a defining characteristic of school administration, thereby promoting interest in the study of values and ethical decision making. However, at the same time administrators are discovering that some of our most cherished ethical foundations, especially those derived from a Western Judeo-Christian tradition, must be carefully re-examined in terms of their appropriateness to changing social circumstances.

Next Steps: Mapping the Field

One useful first step toward developing an agenda to guide the future of values inquiry is mapping out the field in such a way as to reveal the patterns and gaps in existing knowledge. This is no easy task given the variety of theoretical and research traditions represented even within the confines of this book. One attempt at developing such a framework is presented here as a concluding statement in the hope that it will stimulate further reflection, dialogue, theory-building, and research on values and educational leadership.

Begley's (1996b) efforts to map existing theory and research led to his adoption of a linguistic metaphor in three parts (semantics, phonetics, and syntactics). Using a linguistic metaphor seems appropriate because anthropologists and sociolinguists regularly analyze language to derive insights into a culture's roles, norms, taboos, values, and world views. It is on this naturalistic basis that a metaphor based on language was proposed as a way of bringing additional coherence to the subject of values in educational administration.

Using a linguistic metaphor for sorting out the theories and research frameworks associated with existing values inquiry allows their classification under three categories: theories and frameworks that are *defining* and metaphysical (semantic), those that are *descriptive* (phonetic), and those that are context specific or *applied* (syntactic). Table 16.1 illustrates this classification scheme. A second dimension of the displayed matrix portrays three value categories; subrational and transrational values, the rational value types manifested by individuals; and third, the rational values characteristic of groups, collectives, and organizations.

To elaborate further on the categories, consider that the word *semantic* pertains to meaning. In the present context, the term is used to cluster together values theories and applications of values models that emphasize the motivational bases and philosophical or first principles aspects of values, literally the meanings associated with a particular value that may be manifested in multiple ways. An obvious example of a theory meriting placement in this category is Hodgkinson's value theory because of its focus on motivational bases and philosophical grounding.

A second cluster of theories and models is grouped around the word *phonetics*. This word is applied conventionally in reference to distinct symbols such as letters and other phonetic symbols used to represent the sounds of speech or to describe how a word is vocalized. In the context of mapping values theory, the term *phonetic* is used as an organizer for theories and models that are descriptive of particular values as they become manifest in the actions of individuals or collectives, as opposed to providing insights into their meaning or motivational bases. Clive Beck's (1993) values model and several derivative models (e.g. Leithwood's in Leithwood, Begley, and Cousins 1992) are examples of frameworks properly placed in this category.

The third and final category in the linguistic metaphor is *syntax*, generally used to denote espoused or appropriate patterns of language usage.

Table 16.1 Mapping theories and conceptions of values using a linguistic metaphor

VALUE TYPE (Hodgkinson 1979)	LINGUISTIC METAPHOR		
	SEMANTIC (meaning)	PHONETIC (descriptive)	SYNTACTIC (application)
Sub/ Transrational (Type 1 & 3)	Hodgkinson (1978) MacPhee (1983) Ashbaugh & Kasten (1984) Lang (1986) Begley (1988)	Beck (1993)	Lang (1986) Begley (1988) Ashbaugh & Kasten (1984)
Rational Values: Individual/Personal (Type 2)	Simon (1965) Hodgkinson (1978) MacPhee (1983) Ashbaugh & Kasten (1984) Begley (1988) Campbell (1994)	Beck (1993) Campbell-Evans (1991) Leithwood & Steinbach (1991)	Begley (1988) Campbell-Evans (1991) Leithwood & Steinbach (1991) Barth (1990) Strike (1990) Sergiovanni (1992) Willower (1994)
Rational Values: Collective/Objective (Type 2 Meta-Values)	Hodgkinson (1978) Evers & Lakomski (1991)	Beck (1993) Leithwood & Steinbach (1991)	Hambrick & Brandon (1988) Leithwood & Steinbach (1991) Willower (1994)

In the context of theories and models of administrative values, the term is used to cluster the literature and research on values that describe values in particular applied settings or used to attain specific ends. Examples of this are Leithwood's administrative problem-solving model (Leithwood and Steinbach 1995) and Sergiovanni's (1992) promotion of collaborative cultures.

A number of theories and frameworks have been clustered within the dimensions of figure 16.1 to illustrate this mapping strategy. However, it must be noted they are an illustrative sampling, not an exhaustive listing of all the available literature on administrative values. The patterns that emerge highlight the key differences among the frameworks and illustrate much of the preceding discussion about inquiry in the values field. It becomes apparent that the bulk of the available findings of applied research on the subject clusters in the domain of rational values, the administrative mainstream of consensus and consequential decision making. Relatively few research studies address the nonrational value types. The exceptions listed in figure 16.1 are Ashbaugh and Kasten (1984), Lang (1986), and Begley (1988), all studies that relied on the Hodgkinson model to distinguish nonrational value types. It is also apparent that theorists and philosophers such as Hodgkinson, Evers, and Lakomski restrict their intellectual activity to the semantics of value meanings, seldom venturing into the realms of application, which are more comfortably the domain of practitioners. Conversely, those operating primarily in the syntax category of practical applied administration do not necessarily operate from established theory. Examples of such work, based on expert opinion rather than theory, include Barth (1990) and Sergiovanni (1992). The concept of 'values' is an essential component of their argument, but the theoretical underpinnings are relatively unexamined. A few researchers, notably Ashbaugh and Kasten (1984), Begley (1988), and Campbell-Evans (1991), do appear in all three categories of the linguistic metaphor map. This perhaps illustrates the virtue of research that is grounded in theory, descriptive of the nature and function of values in administration, and situated in administrative contexts specific enough to have practitioner relevance.

As a closing comment, it is worth re-emphasizing the nascent quality of the field of values inquiry. Understandings about the values and ethics of leadership are still evolving, and it remains a contested field of inquiry. Yet the contributors to this book remain highly dedicated to the task and continue to actively promote theory building and research on values and valuation processes. They do this through their own work and through the various research centers with which they affiliate. Willower, Hodgkinson, Evers, and Lakomski are perhaps the current leaders in the field. However, a new generation of scholars is now making its presence known. The momentum is building, and we look forward with keen anticipation to the significant developments yet to come.

References

Ashbaugh, C. R., and Kasten, K. L. 1984. A typology of operant values in school administration. *Planning and Changing* 15, 4: 195–208.

Barth, R. S. 1990. *Improving schools from within.* San Francisco: Jossey-Bass.

Beck, C. 1993. *Learning to live the good life.* Toronto: OISE Press.

Begley, P. T. 1988. The influence of personal beliefs and values on principals' adoption and use of computers in schools. Unpublished doctoral dissertation, Toronto: University of Toronto.

———. 1995. Using profiles of school leadership as supports to cognitive apprenticeship. *Educational Administration Quarterly* 31, 2:176–202.

———. 1996a. Cognitive perspectives on values in administration: A quest for coherence and relevance. *Educational Administration Quarterly* 32, 3: 403–26.

———. 1996b. Cognitive perspectives on the nature and function of values in educational administration. In *International Handbook on Educational Leadership and Administration,* ed. K. A. Leithwood. The Netherlands: Kluwer Academic Press.

Begley, P. T., and Johansson, O. 1998. The values of school administration. Paper delivered at the Annual Meeting of the American Educational Research Association, San Diego.

Begley, P. T., and Leithwood, K. A. 1990. The influence of values on school administrator practices. *Journal of Personnel Evaluation in Education* 3: 337–52.

Bridges, E. M., and Hallinger, P. 1995. *Problem based learning in leadership development.* Eugene, OR: ERIC.

Campbell-Evans, G. H. 1991. Nature and influence of values in principal decision-making. *The Alberta Journal of Educational Research* 37, 2:167–78.

Evers, C. W., and Lakomski, G. 1991. *Knowing educational administration.* Toronto: Pergamon.

———. 1996. *Exploring educational administration.* Toronto: Pergamon.

Greenfield, T. B., and Ribbins, P. 1993. *Greenfield on educational administration.* New York: Routledge.

Hallinger, P., Leithwood, K., and Murphy, J. 1993. *Cognitive perspectives on educational leadership.* New York: Teachers College Press.

Hodgkinson, C. 1978. *Towards a philosophy of administration.* Oxford: Basil Blackwell.

———. 1983. *The philosophy of leadership.* Oxford: Basil Blackwell.

———. 1991. *Educational leadership: The moral art.* Albany: State University of New York Press.

———. 1996. *Administrative philosophy: Values and motivations in administrative life.* Oxford: Elsevier.

Lang, D. 1986. Values and commitment. Unpublished doctoral thesis, University of Victoria. Victoria, BC.

Leithwood, K. A., Begley, P. T., and Cousins, J. B. 1992. *Developing expert leadership for future schools*. London: Falmer Press.

Leithwood, K. A., and Steinbach, R. 1995. *Expert problem solving*. Albany: State University of New York Press.

Leonard, P. 1997. Understanding the dimensions of school culture. Unpublished doctoral dissertation, University of Toronto.

MacPhee, P. 1983. Administrators and human comprehension: The intrusion of values. Unpublished M.A. thesis, University of Toronto.

Prestine, N. A., and LeGrand, B. F. 1991. Cognitive learning theory and the preparation of educational administrators. *Educational Administration Quarterly* 27, 1: 61–89.

Robinson, V. 1996. Problem-based methodology and administrative practice. *Educational Administration Quarterly* 32, 3: 427–51.

Roche, K. 1997. Catholic principals' responses to moral and ethical dilemmas. Unpublished doctoral dissertation, University of Toronto.

Sergiovanni, T. J. 1992. *Moral leadership*. San Francisco: Jossey-Bass.

Willower, D. 1992. Educational administration: Intellectual trends. In *Encyclopedia of educational research*, 6th ed., 364–75. Toronto: Macmillan Publishing.

Willower, D. 1994. *Educational administration: Inquiry, values, practice*. Lancaster, PA: Technomic Publishing.

CONTRIBUTORS

Derek J. Allison is associate professor in the Department of Educational Policy Studies at the University of Western Ontario, London, Ontario, Canada.

Paul T. Begley is associate professor and head of the Center for the Study of Values and Leadership in the Department of Theory and Policy Studies at the Ontario Institute for Studies in Education of the University of Toronto, Ontario, Canada.

Paul V. Bredeson is Professor of Educational Administration at the University of Wisconsin—Madison, Wisconsin.

Elizabeth Campbell is associate professor in the Department of Theory and Policy Studies at the Ontario Institute for Studies in Education at the University of Toronto, Ontario, Canada.

Daniel L. Duke is professor in the Department of Educational Leadership and Policy Studies at the Curry School of Education, University of Virginia—Charlottesville, Virginia.

Frederick S. Ellett, Jr. is associate professor of philosophy at the University of Western Ontario, London, Ontario, Canada.

Colin Evers is associate professor in the Department of Education at the University of Hong Kong.

William Foster is professor in the Department of Education at Indiana University, Bloomington, Indiana.

Margaret Grogan is associate professor and co-director of the UCEA Centre for the Study of Leadership and Ethics in the Department of Education Leadership and Policy Studies at the Curry School of Education, University of Virginia—Charlottesville, Virginia.

Christopher Hodgkinson is Professor Emeritus at the Faculty of Education, University of Victoria, British Columbia, Canada.

Olof Johansson is associate professor and head of the Center for Principal Development at Umeå University, Sweden.

Gabriele Lakomski is associate professor and reader in the Department of Educational Policy and Management, Faculty of Educational Policy and Management, Faculty of Education at the University of Melbourne, Parkville, Victoria, Australia.

Kenneth Leithwood is professor and head of the Centre for Leadership Development in the Department of Theory and Policy Studies at the Ontario Institute for Studies in Education at the University of Toronto, Ontario, Canada.

Pauline E. Leonard is assistant professor in the Department of Educational Administration at the University of Saskatchewan, Saskatoon, Saskatchewan, Canada.

Kevin Roche is a research associate of the Centre for the Study of Values and Leadership at the Ontario Institute for Studies in Education of the University of Toronto, Ontario, Canada.

James Ryan is associate professor in the Department of Theory and Policy Studies at the Ontario Institute for Studies in Education at the University of Toronto, Ontario, Canada.

Don Shakotko is a doctoral student in the Department of Educational Administration at the University of Saskatchewan, Saskatoon, Saskatchewan, Canada.

Francie Smith is assistant professor in the Faculty of Education at the University of Oklahoma.

Keith Walker is professor in the Department of Educational Administration at the University of Saskatchewan, Saskatoon, Saskatchewan, Canada.

Donald J. Willower is professor in the Department of Educational Policy and Theory at Pennsylvania State University, University Park, Pennsylvania.

INDEX